# THE CLOSING

## OF THE

# AMERICAN

# BORDER

Terrorism, Immigration, and
Security Since 9/11 WITHDRAWN

# EDWARD
# ALDEN

HARPER

www.harpercollins.com

Published in cooperation with the Council on Foreign Relations.

The Council on Foreign Relations is an independent, nonpartisan membership organization, think tank, and publisher dedicated to being a resource for its members, government officials, business executives, journalists, educators and students, civic and religious leaders, and other interested citizens in order to help them better understand the world and the foreign policy choices facing the United States and other countries. Founded in 1921, the Council carries out its mission by maintaining a diverse membership, with special programs to promote interest and develop expertise in the next generation of foreign policy leaders; convening meetings at its headquarters in New York and in Washington, DC, and other cities where senior government officials, members of Congress, global leaders, and prominent thinkers come together with Council members to discuss and debate major international issues; supporting a Studies Program that fosters independent research, enabling Council scholars to produce articles, reports, and books and hold roundtables that analyze foreign policy issues and make concrete policy recommendations; publishing *Foreign Affairs*, the preeminent journal on international affairs and U.S. foreign policy; sponsoring Independent Task Forces that produce reports with both findings and policy prescriptions on the most important foreign policy topics; and providing up-to-date information and analysis about world events and American foreign policy on its website, CFR.org.

FIRST EDITION

*Designed by William Ruoto*

Library of Congress Cataloging-in-Publication Data is available upon request.

ISBN: 978-0-06-155839-9

08  09  10  11  12      ID/RRD      10  9  8  7  6  5  4  3  2  1

*To Franz Schurmann and Jutta Hennig,*
*for their guidance and inspiration*

# Contents

Acknowledgments      ix

Introduction      1

1    The Borders      25

2    The President      53

3    The Cops      80

4    The Technocrats      117

5    The Scapegoat      147

6    The Consequences      182

7    The Triage      215

8    The Fence      255

Conclusion      288

Sources      305

Index      333

# Acknowledgments

ALTHOUGH I DIDN'T KNOW IT at the time, this book began in a way most reporters would be slightly embarrassed to acknowledge—with a call from a public-relations firm. Ninety-nine percent of the time, I would have ignored such a call amid the crush of my daily deadlines, but this one was especially intriguing. It came in early 2003 from Josh Shuman, who now runs his own PR shop in Jerusalem. He was calling on behalf of Liam Schwartz, a prominent Israeli immigration attorney who was suddenly seeing a surge in cases in which Israelis could not obtain visas to travel to the United States. I was working in Washington for the *Financial Times*, and I saw immediately that the story had the sort of ironic twist that made it compelling—the United States' closest ally in the Middle East, and one that had itself been the target of so many terrorist attacks, had unexpectedly found itself in the crosshairs of the Bush administration's war on terrorism. Schwartz quickly made me recognize that the Israeli angle was only a tiny part of a broader global story. In its effort to keep terrorists out of the country, the U.S. government was making it far more difficult for almost everyone to get into the United States. Outside of certain institutions such as the universities, however, the issue had received almost no media attention because no one wanted to raise complaints and look soft on the terrorist threat. Shuman's call led me to write a full-page story on the issue (one he tells me he still has framed in his office). That story, in turn, led me to another immigration attorney, Bernard Wolfsdorff of Los Angeles, who told me about a young Pakistani client of his—an outstanding doctor who had been unable to return from Karachi to his job as a cardiothoracic surgeon at UCLA Medical Center. A few days later, I was speaking by telephone with Faiz Bhora, who had been waiting nearly eight months for the visa that would allow him to come back to the United States.

While I would write many other newspaper stories on visas and other post-9/11 border security issues, the idea of writing a book on the subject did not occur to me until I left the *FT* in October 2006 and joined the Council on Foreign Relations (thanks to a tip from my friend Greg Ip, formerly of the *Wall Street Journal* and now of *The Economist*). Doug Holtz-Eakin brought me on to work primarily on trade and international economic issues, but he was also enthusiastic about my interest in the economic and political impact of the post-9/11 border security measures. Sadly for me, though happily for John McCain, Doug left the council to join the eventual Republican nominee's presidential campaign before I arrived for my first day on the job. The colleagues he left behind, particularly Gary Samore, the director of studies, and Janine Hill, the deputy director, immediately encouraged me to turn what was still a vague set of ideas into a book proposal. I got tremendous support and guidance as well from Sebastian Mallaby, who replaced Doug as the director of the council's Maurice Greenberg Center for Geoeconomic Studies, and who has created an energetic and congenial environment in which to explore big questions about the intersection of economics and foreign policy.

I could not have landed in a better place to pursue this project. The council's president, Richard Haass, fosters an atmosphere in which fellows are not only encouraged to do important work but also able to draw on the immense resources and prestige of the council. For a journalist who's usually happy just to get his phone calls returned, it has been a luxurious place to work. The council's greatest single asset is its research assistants, who are far brighter, better read, better traveled, and more accomplished than most people twice their age. I had the good fortune of having two supremely talented research assistants to help with the book. Divya Reddy, who is now with the Eurasia Group, carried out copious research on nearly every issue, produced detailed backgrounders on individuals and events, and conducted a number of interviews. Andrew Rottas provided superb research for some of the later chapters and was instrumental in nursing the book from early drafts to final publication. This book would not have happened without them. I also received valuable research help from Swetha Sridharan, Heather Rehm, and Leigh Gusts.

Many others at the council contributed directly. Aimee Carter invited me to speak about early drafts of the book to a meeting of corporate members, and Irina Faskianos did the same for a meeting of younger council members known as term members. Both those sessions produced valuable feedback and important contacts. The council also puts tremendous emphasis on making the work of its fellows available to the widest possible audience. I want to thank in particular Lisa Shields, Anya Schmemann, Patricia Dorff, and Leigh-Ann Krapf for their efforts on that front.

This book would not have been possible without the generous support for the council provided by Bernard Schwartz. The fellowship that he created, and which I inherited, was set up to focus on issues of American competitiveness and the relationship between business and foreign policy. For Bernard, many of the crucial questions about the future of the American economy center on domestic policy, particularly investment in infrastructure and education. But he has been enthusiastic about my work on the foreign dimensions of competitiveness, especially trade and immigration. The U.S. economy will not thrive if we do not educate and train Americans and give them the most advanced tools to work with, but it also depends on attracting and retaining the best that the rest of the world has to offer. I also want to thank Jeanette Clonan of BLS Investments, who has been similarly supportive of my work throughout.

One of the things that have repeatedly amazed me during my years covering government in Washington and elsewhere is the willingness of many government officials to talk candidly about their work. While I suspect this puts me in a small minority, I do not share the prevailing journalistic view that the actions of government have been wholly debased by partisan maneuvering and self-interested corporate lobbyists. This may be because most of my experience has been covering the agencies in Washington that are responsible for implementing policy rather than watching the high-level political machinations of the White House or Congress. In the agencies I have found, with only rare exceptions, decent people struggling with extremely hard problems. They are buffeted by the political winds, and sometimes led astray by lobbyists or by their own desires to join the lucrative lobbying ranks, but for the most part they are smart and dedicated people serving their country under trying circumstances. And few circumstances in recent history have been more trying than those brought about by the 9/11 attacks.

I received help from too many individuals to acknowledge every one by name, and some, particularly those still serving in government, preferred to remain anonymous. Steve Fischel, who spent three decades in the State Department writing many of the rules and regulations for implementing U.S. visa policies, was the first to put me on to the tragic story of the late Mary Ryan, the State Department assistant secretary who was the only government official fired as a result of the 9/11 attacks. Sadly, Steve's own life ended tragically in June 2008 after he was stricken by an aortic aneurysm in Vancouver, my hometown, where he was attending a meeting of immigration lawyers. He had would have been sixty in July, and he is greatly missed. Dennis Murphy, who spent three decades in the Customs Service and the Department of Homeland Security, was tremendously helpful throughout the project, as were Randy Beardsworth and Stewart Verdery, two other former senior DHS officials.

I am also immensely grateful to Faiz Bhora, Dia Elnaiem, Imad Daou, Benamar Benatta, and others for sharing what were often quite painful personal stories. Some of their cases remain unresolved. I know they all hope that by sharing their experiences, they have played some small role in sparing others similar ordeals. I hope I have done justice to their sagas.

Outside the government, Ed Rice of the Coalition for Employment Through Exports generously shared a large packet of information he assembled in 2002 and 2003, when American businesses first faced visa problems and began quietly, and mostly unsuccessfully, to lobby for changes.

One of the requirements for council fellows producing a book is that they assemble a study group composed of council members and others to review chapter drafts and offer suggestions on research and writing. I want to thank in particular Susan Ginsburg of the Migration Policy Institute, who served as a senior counsel to the 9/11 Commission and was the commission's team leader on the portion of the report investigating how the nineteen hijackers entered the United States. The commission's monograph, *9/11 and Terrorist Travel*, which was published shortly after the main report, remains the most important single source on terrorism and border security, and it was invaluable for this book. I was honored that Susan agreed to chair my study group, and her knowledge, wisdom, and insight throughout the project were invaluable. Other members of the study group who sharpened my work immensely were Cris Arcos, Steve Flynn, Clark Kent Ervin, Peter Andreas, Kevin Nealer, Jess Ford, Theo Gemelas, Elisa Massimino, Tom Pickering, Susan Martin, Alan Platt, Bill Sweeney, Shaarik Zafar, Rose Mary Valencia, Steve Clemons, Kristin Roesser, and Paul Blustein,

Outside of the study group, several other colleagues read part or all of the manuscript and provided valuable feedback, suggestions, and correctives. These included Richard Haass, Peter Spiegel, Randy Beardsworth, Scott Moyers, Dennis Murphy, Sebastian Mallaby, Ben Bain, Divya Reddy, Louise Alden, and Tom Sandborn.

Some of the reporting for the book was done during my six years in Washington working for the *Financial Times*, from 2000 to 2006. The *FT* is the world's paper of record on globalization and its discontents, and in many ways this book is just a smaller part of that larger story. While in Washington, I worked with many remarkable journalists, including James Harding, Gerry Baker, Patti Waldmeir, Stephen Fidler, Peter Spiegel, Richard Wolffe, Deborah McGregor, Alan Beattie, Guy Dinmore, Demetri Sevastopulo, Andrew Balls, Chris Swann, Holly Yeager, Stephanie Kirchgaessner, Perry Despeignes, Josh Chaffin, Jeremy Grant, Caroline Daniel, and Ed Luce. Ed also generously shared with me some of the lessons he had learned in writing his superb book on India, *In Spite of the Gods*. I want to thank Philipp Dermann and Nancy McCord as well for all their work in making a hectic bureau function a little more smoothly. My editors and others in London were also unfailingly encouraging of my reporting on the impact of the post-9/11 U.S. border measures, a story that often had more resonance for overseas readers than for American ones. I'd like to thank in particular Ed Carr, John Thornhill, James Montgomery, James Lamont, Pat Ferguson, Hal Weitzman, Annie Counsel, Leyla Boulton, Guy de Jonquieres, Quentin Peel, Chrystia Freeland, Andrew Gowers, and Lionel Barber.

I owe James Harding another debt of gratitude for introducing me to his book agent, Andrew Wylie. Although Andrew has handled many of the best nonfiction writers in the world, he patiently walked a novice book writer through the process of refining his often vague ideas into a workable book proposal. I am immensely grateful for his counsel. Tim Duggan at HarperCollins was a superb editor, always offering exactly the right mix of encouragement, criticism, and prodding. He improved and sharpened the book in immeasurable ways. I also want to thank Allison Lorentzen and Campbell Wharton at HarperCollins.

I can trace at least some of my interest in borders to the decision by my parents, Tom and Louise Alden, to move with their four small children from Schenectady, New York, to Vancouver, British Columbia. Vancouver is a long way from anywhere else in Canada, but it is very close to the United States, and I remember many childhood car trips traveling back and forth across the border at Blaine, Washington, while my father admonished me to stay quiet and look serious while he answered the border inspector's questions. Even between such close neighbors as the United States and Canada, those crossings were an early and powerful lesson to me that we do not live, and never have lived, in a world of open borders.

Finally, this book has been just one small chapter in my journey with the love of my life, my wife, Fiona James, and our beautiful children, Callum and Charlotte, who have already written many books between them. They would often greet me when I arrived home with the puzzled question, "Daddy, aren't you finished with your book yet?" I thank them for everything that truly matters.

THE **CLOSING** OF THE **AMERICAN BORDER**

# Introduction

DR. FAIZ BHORA SHOULD HAVE been operating on babies' hearts. Instead, in the spring of 2003 he had been waiting almost nine months for some word from the American consulate in Karachi, Pakistan, that he would be allowed to return to the United States. Since coming to the States nearly a decade before on a training program for foreign doctors, the diminutive Pakistani had climbed to a stature reserved for the most talented of American surgeons. He had studied for five years in general surgery at George Washington University Hospital in Washington, D.C., finishing his term as chief resident. In 2000, he had become one of just 120 surgeons in the United States selected each year to train in cardiothoracic surgery, which involves the most delicate and life-threatening operations on the heart and lungs. He was one of only two chosen for residencies at the prestigious UCLA Medical Center in Los Angeles, one of the country's top programs.

It was no accidental appointment. Years earlier, Bhora had identified the man he wanted to be his mentor—Hillel Laks, a globally renowned pediatric heart surgeon who had saved, among countless others, the life of actor Sylvester Stallone's baby daughter Sophia Rose by performing open-heart surgery to repair a hole in her heart. Only half a dozen hospitals in North America were doing such surgeries, and UCLA's was widely regarded as the best. Laks, a South African–born Orthodox Jew who first came to the United States to train at Harvard, had pioneered a host of new surgical techniques, from transplants with artificial hearts to delicate procedures for operating on infants. He was the first to experiment with repairing damaged hearts for transplants in elderly patients who were not eligible to receive healthier hearts. In more than two decades as the chief of cardiothoracic surgery, he had built UCLA's transplant program into the world's largest, working fifteen hours a day, six days a week, save only Saturday, the Jewish Sabbath, when his religion forbade him to drive or work. For Laks, medicine was not just a profession but a religious calling. "According to the Jewish religion, a doctor is a messenger," he said in a speech in 2002. "It's a God-given gift that human beings are able to treat disease and therefore one has to be the best messenger that one can."

Bhora himself seemed to be on a similar path. A Muslim born to two doctors in Karachi, Pakistan, he was seized from a very early age with the conviction that following his parents into medicine was a moral obligation. He was sent to England for his high school studies, and by the age of twenty-one had graduated from Pakistan's best medical school, the Aga Khan University in Karachi. Like most ambitious young Pakistani doctors, he had come to the United States to do medical research, hoping to gain a residency position in a U.S. hospital. Six months as a researcher at the University of Michigan were followed by a year at Johns Hopkins in Baltimore. By 1995, he had been offered a surgical residency at George Washington, a challenging urban hospital just a five-minute walk from the U.S. State Department. In early 2000, by which time he had become the hospital's chief resident, he invited Laks to come and speak at the hospital, hoping to increase his chances of winning one of the coveted residencies at UCLA. Before Laks's arrival, Bhora called the surgeon's secretary in Los Angeles to try to find something memorable he could offer during his visit to Washington. She told him that Laks, who is an avid amateur photographer, was a fan of Annie Leibovitz's portraits. Following the talk, Bhora took Laks to an exhibition of her photographs that had just opened at the Corcoran Gallery of Art near the White House. "I really buttered him up," Bhora admits.

His two years under Laks at UCLA were the final steps in an exhausting fifteen-year training. When he finished his surgical residency, he was offered the opportunity to join the faculty at the UCLA hospital. Before he could take up his new post, however, Bhora needed to return home to Pakistan to apply to the State Department for a new work visa to remain in the United States. Under U.S. immigration law, most foreign doctors arrive on a special training visa, and they must leave the country after their studies are finished. To hire Bhora as a member of the hospital faculty, UCLA had to persuade the U.S. government to allow him to remain on an O visa reserved for individuals of "extraordinary ability" who had "risen to the very top of the field of endeavor." It would have been hard to write a resume that better fit the criterion.

In July 2002, Bhora flew back to Karachi, expecting it would take him no more than thirty days to receive a new visa and return to Los Angeles to take up his position. One of Los Angeles's top immigration lawyers, who had been hired by the university to ensure it would not be without the services of such a valuable surgeon, had assured him the process would take a month, perhaps two at the outside. Seven months later, he was still at his parents' home in Pakistan, waiting to hear back from the U.S. embassy. "Since August, I've been waiting for the phone to ring," he said by telephone from Karachi in February 2003. "My life is on hold."

Dr. Bhora's brilliant career was an unlikely casualty of the September 11 terrorist attacks. In January 2002, at the instigation of Attorney General John Ashcroft and with the acquiescence of the State Department, the United States had created a new security review mechanism under the code name Condor. Fearing that another wave of terrorists might be planning additional attacks, Ashcroft's Justice Department had forced an end to the pre-9/11 process for reviewing visa applications from citizens of Muslim countries. Normally, like any visa application, Dr. Bhora's request would have gone to a State Department consular official at the U.S. embassy in Islamabad, and the decision would have been made by that official after a personal interview and a brief review. But following 9/11, the Justice Department had asserted its power to scrutinize visa applications back in Washington on national security grounds. State Department officials feared the move would cause international repercussions, alienating countries like Pakistan that were seen as critical U.S. allies in the war that was raging in neighboring Afghanistan against Al Qaeda and the Taliban. But after a bitter interagency struggle, the State Department acquiesced to the new procedures. As a result, every visa application for men between the ages of sixteen and forty-five from Muslim nations—regardless of their past history—would be sent back to Washington to be scrutinized by the FBI and the CIA. The visa could not be approved until those security scrubs were completed.

Though he had lived most of his adult life in the United States, and had gone from one prestigious job to another, Bhora fell into the Condor net. He met with a U.S. consular officer at the embassy in Islamabad in August who was prepared to approve his visa on the spot. But under the new regulations, the officer had no choice but to send the application to Washington for a security review. And there—along with tens of thousands of other visa applications from around the world—it sat, and sat, and sat.

ON SEPTEMBER 10, 2001, THE United States was the most open, and some might have said most naïve, country in the world. When nineteen hijackers flew commercial jets into the World Trade Center skyscrapers and the Pentagon, there were millions of foreigners in the country whom the U.S. government knew almost nothing about. Many had arrived legally—including the hijackers themselves—but there was no way to know what they had done since they had set foot on U.S. soil. Others were here illegally, either by overstaying tourist visas—as had five of the hijackers—or by crossing the thousands of miles of lightly defended land borders with Mexico and Canada. Government scrutiny for the more than 7 million visas granted each year to foreign visitors was cursory, while another 11 million travelers from Europe and nearly 25 million visitors from Canada and Mexico crossed with virtually no scrutiny at all. U.S. policy was explicitly to facilitate and promote travel, believing it could only bring economic, social, and cultural benefits to the country. In a strong economy where openness had ushered in a golden age of globalization—the kind that had brought together an Orthodox Jew from South Africa and a Muslim from Pakistan to repair the hearts of American babies in a hospital in Los Angeles—such casualness had seemed inconsequential. But in the aftermath of the worst terrorist attack on U.S. soil, which had left nearly three thousand people dead and their grieving families behind, the risks suddenly appeared vastly to outweigh the benefits.

This book tells the story of how, since the trauma of 9/11, the United States has been turning its back on that openness. The nineteen men who had inflicted such catastrophic damage all came from outside the country and had turned America's welcome mat into a weapon that could be used against the United States. At every level of the administration and Congress in Washington, there was a desperate desire to do everything that could be done to prevent another attack. The immediate reaction was swift—a virtual closing of the borders right after the attacks, followed by a series of harsh measures targeted primarily at immigrants from Arab or Muslim countries. Even as some of those controls have been eased, however, the United States has been making it harder and harder for people from across the world to travel to, study, or work in the United States. And the enormous economic benefits and global goodwill that once flowed from the country's openness are now gradually being choked off.

DIA ELNAIEM WAS BORN AND raised in rural Sudan, the youngest boy of eleven children, three of whom died early in childhood. His father had been wounded twice in World War II, including in the epic battle of El Alamein, fighting alongside the British against the Nazis in North Africa. A brilliant student, he was able to attend the University of Khartoum in the Sudanese capital on a full scholarship, and he graduated at the top of his class with an

honors degree in zoology and a mission to rid his country of leishmaniasis, a disease that had tormented its people for centuries.

Leishmaniasis is one of the most insidious diseases of the developing world, afflicting about 12 million people in some ninety
countries, but nowhere more so than in Sudan. Spread by the bite of
a common sand fly, which is smaller than a mosquito, it creates painful skin lesions on a victim's face, hands, and arms that take months
to heal, often leaving behind ugly scars. In more serious cases, which
are common in countries like Sudan where many suffer from mal-
nutrition, the disease can lead to infections that enlarge the liver and
spleen, and to anemia. Some ten thousand people in Sudan, most
of them children, die each year from complications related to the
disease.

Following his graduation, Elnaiem went to work as a teaching
assistant at the University of Khartoum, and then won a fellowship
in molecular entomology at the University of Liverpool School
of Tropical Disease, specializing in vector-borne diseases, particularly leishmaniasis. After completing his doctorate, he was offered
a research position at the University of Texas Medical Branch in
Galveston, working with Gregory Lanzaro, one of the world's leading experts on insect-borne tropical diseases. Soon after his arrival,
Lanzaro moved his Texas lab to the University of California in Davis, just outside Sacramento, and Elnaiem followed, bringing his
wife and two children over at the end of July 2002.

Just before his family was set to arrive in California, however,
his supervisor urged him to attend an academic conference in Brazil
as a representative of the UC Davis lab. Most of Lanzaro's research
involved sand flies from South and Central America, and Elnaiem
believed research on these insects held the key to developing a vac-
cine for leishmaniasis. But Elnaiem was wary—he had seen reports
in the news about visa problems facing foreign researchers and students. So he contacted the U.S. embassy in Rio de Janeiro and
explained his situation. Officials there assured him that he would
need only a stamp on his visa, a straightforward and quick process.
He sent a second e-mail to be sure and received the same answer.
With those responses in hand, in August 2002 he left his family

for the five-day conference in Brazil. They had arrived in California just three days before, coming to an empty apartment he had rented. But he had no time to add his wife to the bank account or introduce her to any of his colleagues. He left her cash for ten days, which seemed more than sufficient since the Brazilian conference was scheduled to last less than a week.

When the conference concluded in Salvador Bahia in northern Brazil, he flew back to Rio and went to the U.S. consulate first thing the next morning to get the stamp on his visa that would allow him to return to the United States. As Elnaiem still vividly recalls, the consular officer saw his Sudanese passport, "picked it up with two fingers and his face changed." Before he could return to the United States, the officer informed him, he would have to undergo a security review in Washington. The assurances he had received in advance were worthless.

For the next six months his home would be a student hostel in Rio, sleeping on a cot in a room with eight other beds and sharing a common bathroom down the hall. It was two months before he heard anything from the embassy; they asked him to provide his full curriculum vitae and to fill out an additional form with questions such as "Do you know how to fly a plane?" and "Do you have knowledge of nuclear technology?" He often considered returning to Sudan but kept talking himself out of it, hopeful that the next day would bring a response from the embassy and fearful that if he abandoned the security review it would be like an admission of guilt and would bar him from ever returning to the United States. By January 2003, his Brazilian visa had expired as well, and he had decided there was no choice but to return to Sudan. He wrote to the University of California telling them he would be forced to leave his research position.

As a final gesture, he sent a letter to Senator Dianne Feinstein of California, who had been one of the most aggressive members of Congress in pushing for tighter rules on visas for students and researchers after 9/11. Surely, he wrote, his ordeal could not have been an intended consequence of the measures she supported. Just before he was set to return to Sudan, he received a response from her office promising to investigate. The next day he got a call from the U.S. consular officer in Rio telling him that his approval had finally arrived from Washington. On February 11, more than six months after coming to Brazil, he was on a flight back to California.

Apart from the personal ordeal for Elnaiem and his family, the actions of the U.S. government are likely to prolong the suffering for millions of victims of leishmaniasis. His research was unique, and he had spent an entire year collecting samples of sand flies that needed to be stored under controlled temperatures and monitored regularly. They could be left alone for a week, but not for months. There was no one at his lab in California who knew how to care for the breeding colonies, and when he returned to Davis all of them, including new samples he had collected and shipped from Brazil, had died. He estimates that the six months he was stuck in Brazil set back his research by at least two to three years.

THE CLAMPDOWN AT THE U.S. borders after 9/11 was never intended to have the effects it did on people like Faiz Bhora and Dia Elnaiem. Top American officials, the most important of them President George W. Bush, insisted they wanted to avoid shutting out people the country needed in the name of security. Bush came to the White House from the governor's mansion in Texas caring deeply about encouraging immigration. One of his first major policy initiatives was to launch talks with Mexico on a migration pact to permit new legal ways for Mexicans to live and work in the United States. Among his last was a failed attempt in 2007 to push a bill through a divided Congress that would have granted legal status to many illegal immigrants in the United States and offered new legal channels for future immigrants. He brought in Tom Ridge, another border governor, as his first homeland security adviser, and later made him the first secretary of Homeland Security. Like the president, Ridge believed strongly in open borders and constantly talked about balancing the new security requirements with openness.

Yet the way Bush defined the post-9/11 war on terrorism—as a global struggle for survival with a foe he deemed as menacing as

Nazi Germany or the nuclear-armed Soviet Union—made a nuanced and proportionate response all but impossible. When he came to office, Bush wanted to leave a legacy as the president who had built new bridges across the Rio Grande and shored up those to the rest of the world; instead, he will leave behind nearly seven hundred miles of steel fence on the Mexican border and a world that has grown much warier about coming to the United States. His administration's response to the terrorist attacks did not mesh easily with the president's pro-migration convictions, and indeed there is no evidence in any of his public statements that he has ever grappled with the contradiction. Within hours of the 9/11 attacks, he had made prevention of another terrorist attack the single, unequivocal, overriding priority of his presidency. For the officials charged with carrying out that task, immigration and visa laws were the most powerful tools they had. It gave them the unquestioned authority to carry out exhaustive screenings of travelers or immigrants who fit any profile that caused concern and to bar from the country anyone who raised the smallest of red flags. It allowed them to arrest and detain on minor transgressions those already in the United States who came under suspicion. The result was that, while the administration talked about balancing security and openness, almost all of its resources and effort went into time-consuming background checks on foreigners, new controls at the borders, and aggressive enforcement against anyone caught committing even the most minor infraction of the labyrinthine immigration regulations.

"It's always a question of how much security is enough," said General Bruce Lawlor, a highly decorated Vietnam veteran who was in charge of the U.S. Army's civil defense preparations against a major terrorist attack on U.S. soil when he was plucked to help lead the White House response after 9/11. "You had to make a risk-based assessment. Everybody said that, but when you asked them to do it, their tolerance for risk was zero."

The conception of risk changed completely after the attacks. Over and over again, as I talked with government officials about the post-9/11 world, I heard the same refrain: no one wanted to be hauled before Congress or another national commission after the next attack and be forced to explain why he hadn't done absolutely everything in his power to prevent it from happening. No one was going to get punished for saying no to a foreigner, but the penalties for saying yes could be enormous.

In increments, and with many setbacks, the U.S. government has tried to develop what experts call a "risk management approach" to border security, in which the benefits of new security measures—reducing the likelihood of another terrorist attack, keeping out criminals, or slowing the flow of illegal migrants—are balanced against the economic and diplomatic costs that such measures have for the country. But it has taken hold very slowly even within the professional bureaucracy, and in the political debate it is utterly drowned out by the constant drumbeat of demands to enforce immigration law and seal the border against illegal entry. Admiral James Loy, a U.S. Coast Guard veteran who became one of the first and closest advisers to Ridge, thinks the government is gradually developing the skills needed to manage risk in its efforts to improve homeland security, what he called "the post-9/11 skill set and competency to cope with the world." But he acknowledged it has been a difficult concept to sell. "We as a nation had always sort of insisted on 100 percent solutions," said Loy. "We even named it things like 'unconditional surrender' and 'zero tolerance.'"

THIS IS THE NEW REALITY that zero tolerance has brought us.

- If you live outside of Canada, western Europe, Japan, and a handful of other countries, you now need a personal interview with a U.S. embassy official to get your visa to come to the United States, whether it's for four years of study or a week's vacation to Disneyland. Before 9/11, the State Department had broad discretion to grant visas to travelers without interviews, on the reasonable assumption that most people traveling to the United States posed no risk and that it was better to spend more time interviewing those who raised some concerns. But following the firing of the State Department's top consular official in 2002 over the issuing of visas to the hijackers, and the passage of a new law by Congress in 2004, virtually all visa applicants must now come in person to be fingerprinted and interviewed. If you live in Brazil, it will take you three to four months just to schedule the interview and, since there are only three U.S. consulates in the country, you may have to take a plane to appear for your two minutes of questioning. In 2006 in India, the maximum wait time for interviews was five months or more; delays have been reduced only through a massive redeployment of consular officers by the State Department that is probably not sustainable. In China, it takes more than a month just to get through that first stage; in Dubai, it takes two months.

• If you are a young male from a predominantly Muslim country—whether you yourself are a Muslim or not—in addition to being interviewed, fingerprinted, and photographed, you will be required to fill out a detailed questionnaire before coming to the United States, including information on relatives, bank accounts, and contacts in the United States. Every time you travel back to the United States—even if you are already living here with a green card or a work visa and are returning from a trip abroad—you will be pulled aside for "secondary" screening, where you could face a lengthy delay. The officer will probably rifle through your wallet or purse, writing down calling card numbers or any other scraps of information. You will also be required to "check out" from specific airports or land border crossings when leaving the country by informing U.S. border inspectors of your departure; failure to do so could result in your being barred from returning to the United States for five years or more.

For sixteen months, between September 2002 and January 2004, most men from predominantly Muslim countries were also required to re-register thirty days after they arrived in the country. Imad Daou, a Christian from Lebanon, came to the United States in July 2003 to begin postgraduate studies in computer science at Texas A&M International University (TAMIU), which is near the Mexican border in Laredo. He checked carefully with the university's international office to make sure he had met all the requirements of his student visa, and was assured he had. During his first weekend at the school, he was standing at a bus stop when he met Maria Guadalupe Garcia, a Mexican American who was studying for her master's in international business at TAMIU and teaching at a Laredo high school. He seemed, as she later put it, "lost and in great need of help"; the bus he was waiting for did not run on the weekends. She later invited him to attend Catholic mass with her and other students from the university dorms. They fell in love and got engaged, with plans to marry when the academic term ended in the spring of 2004.

In November 2003, she decided to make it official with her family. First, she introduced him to her parents in Del Rio, Texas, and then, with the easy informality that had long connected both sides of the border, they crossed the Rio Grande into Acuna, Mexico, to meet her sister and invite her to a Thanksgiving dinner in Texas the next day. The two had already crossed into Mexico several times together and had faced no problems coming back. But when they returned to the border after a two-hour visit, the U.S. inspector looked at Daou's Lebanese passport, checked in his computer system, and determined that Daou had failed to re-register after thirty days, as required. He was handcuffed and spent the next two months in jail in Laredo. In January 2004 the two were married in the jail right before Daou was deported back to Lebanon and barred from returning for five years. With his wife's help, after a year of e-mails and long-distance telephone calls, he was able to get permission to live in Mexico. They settled in Nuevo Laredo, a crime-ridden city largely controlled by the Mexican drug cartels that sits across the river from Laredo. They are both scared; the husband of his wife's best friend was shot and killed in front of his house. It is worse than the intermittent civil war in Lebanon, he says. Maria has continued to teach high school in Laredo, crossing the border early each morning and returning at the end of the day. In November 2008, Daou's five-year ban from the country will end, and the two are hoping that they and their two-year-old daughter will be allowed to move together back to Laredo. "They put the rules in place to catch bad people, and the good people fall into the trap because the bad people know how to get around them," he said.

- Regardless of where you are from, if you overstay your welcome by even a few days and get caught, the consequences will be grave. Valeria Vinnikova, a twenty-one-year-old German who did not require a visa to come to the United States, went to Hanover, New Hampshire, in July 2007 to spend time with her fiancé, Hansi Wiens, the squash coach at Dartmouth College. She had been given a ninety-day visitor's permit, which she thought expired on October 13. The two of them went to the U.S. Customs and Border Protection station on the Canadian border October 12 to seek a ninety-day renewal to allow her to stay with him in Hanover. But she had misread the scrawled handwriting on the permit, which actually expired on October 3. She was immediately slapped in handcuffs and taken to prison in Portland, Maine; she would spend nearly a month in three different jails, sharing cells with convicted criminals. Vinnikova was ordered deported, which meant that she would have been barred from returning to the United States for ten years, forcing her fiancé to choose between his marriage and his career. After the local community raised a massive outcry, the Department of Homeland Security agreed to release her and allow her to return to Germany "voluntarily," which means she will likely be permitted to return to the United States in the future.

- If you are crossing the land borders from Canada or Mexico to work or visit or shop, which millions do every year, you will face longer delays to enter the United States. Canadian and Mexican officials both say that the problems were severe for several years after 9/11, and then began to improve by 2005 and 2006, before worsening again in 2007. Stan Korosec, vice president of operations for the Blue Water Bridge, one of the key bridges that connect Michigan with Ontario, called 2007 "the summer of hell." Delays have grown even though the volume of traffic has fallen at the major U.S.-Canada border crossings since 9/11. On both borders, new requirements that travelers must show a passport or other secure identification when crossing—which are common sense from a security perspective—nonetheless were already causing delays in tests in 2007, and are soon to be enforced more rigorously.

- If you are living in the United States on a work or other temporary visa and are utterly fed up with the hassle, you can try to apply for a green card, and eventually citizenship. But don't hold your breath. Security background checks for green card and citizenship applications are now frequently measured in years rather than months. After returning to the United States, Dia Elnaiem said he had been unable to travel abroad again to do any fieldwork on his research because he feared that he would face the same long security delays when he tried to return. In 2005, he applied for a green card (permanent resident status) as an "outstanding" scientist. It took the FBI more than two and a half years to complete the security review; he finally got his green card in September 2007.

Given this array of obstacles, pitfalls, and even serious dangers, the results of a 2006 travel industry survey are not surprising: foreign travelers now consider the United States the most unwelcoming destination in the world, by more than a 2-to-1 margin over the next worst destination, the Middle East. Two-thirds of travelers said they were scared that the smallest mistake could cause them to be detained for hours or even turned back. Forty percent said that stories they had read or heard about people ill-treated at the U.S. borders had hurt their perceptions of the United States.

The statistics are telling. Between 2001 and 2003, the number of U.S. visas issued to foreigners fell by a third, from over 7.5 million per year to fewer than 5 million. Overall, 10 million fewer people traveled to the United States in 2003 than had come here in the year prior to the attacks. By 2007 that number had recovered to about 6.5 million. Yet even with a falling dollar, which has made the United States a bargain destination, overseas visits in 2007 were still down some 2 million people from pre-9/11 levels, despite a boom in international travel that should have brought millions more to the country. After nearly forty years of rapid growth, foreign student enrollment in U.S. universities fell after 9/11; it did not register its first increase again until 2006, at a time when foreign enrollments at universities in Europe, Australia, and Canada are increasing at double-digit rates.

Visa delays have also made it harder to attract foreign investors to the United States, which has long been one of the most investment-friendly countries in the world. State government officials charged with enticing foreign investors to their locales say that the difficulty of obtaining visas for foreign businesspeople is one of their biggest obstacles. Governor Mark Sanford of South Carolina, whose state has been among the most successful in attracting foreign investment in recent years, said: "When you go to Europe, the whole first half of every meeting is about how they've been traveling to the United States for twenty years and now they're treated like criminals by the immigration system."

But more than the statistics, it was the personal experiences of Faiz Bhora, Dia Elnaim, and others like them that first led me to question what was happening to the country that had long been the most open and welcoming in the world.

After 9/11 it was evident that the government faced enormous problems in securing the United States against another terrorist attack. It couldn't answer even the most basic question: who was in the country? In 1996 Congress had mandated an entry-exit system that was supposed to monitor the arrival and departure of foreign travelers, but the system had never been funded. It wasn't even in the pilot stage, in part because of strong opposition from U.S.

border states that feared such a system would create huge impediments to cross-border business. After the 1993 terrorist attack on the World Trade Center, Congress ordered the administration to track the whereabouts of all foreign students, but the effort was stillborn owing to strong opposition from universities and their many allies in Congress. As a result, one of the 9/11 hijackers entered the country on a student visa, but no one noticed when he failed to show up at school; another came on a tourist visa and attended flight school without authorization. Advanced information on passengers flying to the United States from overseas was clearly critical to preventing an attack involving airplanes. The foiled 1995 Bojinka plot, in which Ramzi Yousef and Khalid Shaikh Mohammed plotted to bring down as many as eleven trans-Pacific commercial jets, had already highlighted the vulnerability. But foreign airlines only provided such information on a voluntary basis, and many, including the ones that mattered most, like Saudi Airlines, still refused to do so. The creation of a comprehensive terrorist watch list to ensure that known terrorists were never granted a visa to come to the United States was a crucial and obvious tool, but before 9/11 the FBI and the intelligence agencies had refused to share much of what they knew with the State Department officials responsible for issuing visas.

In the absence of such tools, the government's response was necessarily improvised. "We were trying to do triage," General Lawlor admitted. Terrified by what they didn't know in the days and months after the attacks, Bush administration officials cast their nets as widely as possible. "Everyone knew it was an imperfect response," said a former senior official in the Justice Department, "but we didn't have the system that could possibly deal with anything complicated, and there was an imperative to act."

But while acting aggressively, the government was mostly missing its intended target—the handful of terrorists who might be planning serious harm to the United States—and the collateral damage was massive. In early 2003, I talked with a thirty-nine-year-old Israeli businessman who was in charge of development for a computer security company listed on the Nasdaq stock exchange.

For more than a year after the attacks he had been unable to renew his visa to travel to the company's U.S. headquarters. His family had fled from Iraq in 1970 when he was just seven years old, but in the eyes of post-9/11 America, that made him a citizen of a "terrorist-sponsoring state," and his visa renewal was tied up indefinitely in security reviews. In another case, a sixty-five-year-old Israeli grandmother was barred from attending her granddaughter's wedding in Los Angeles because she also had been born in Baghdad.

I went to a homeless shelter in Buffalo, where hundreds of Pakistanis had gathered to seek political asylum across the border in Canada. On September 11, 2002, a year after the attacks, the Justice Department launched the National Security Entry-Exit Registration System (NSEERS), a program that required all men aged sixteen to forty-five from Muslim countries to be fingerprinted and photographed; the men were forced to re-register with the government thirty days after coming to the United States, and then again after a year. Beginning in December 2002, those already living in the United States were also required to register; anyone in the country illegally would be detained and deported, and those who failed to register would be guilty of a criminal offense that could result in imprisonment. It was this scheme that had caught Imad Daou when he crossed the border to Mexico to visit his future sister-in-law.

As a consequence, families from as far away as Texas, Florida, and California had packed up their lives and headed north, hoping for a new start in Canada. Nasir, a young Pakistani who had just earned a master's degree in computer science and was afraid to give his full name, was bitter at being forced to leave. "They are looking at us as terrorists, troublemakers, and extremists," he said. Qaiser Syed, a forty-five-year-old Shia Muslim with a master's degree in finance and four children, was in the country on a legal work visa, but it was about to expire and he didn't see any hope of its being renewed. "I don't know what happened to this government," he said. "We Pakistanis are very hard-working. They say that the guy driving a taxi twelve or fourteen hours a day is a threat to the United States. He doesn't have *time* to be a threat to the United

States." Zahid Hussein, who worked for an electronics company in Houston, was there with his wife and two children. He was not bitter, but his response was poignant. "It is a great country. We call it a place of opportunity. We respect and understand their problems after September 11, so we are leaving." Out of the 140,000 people who came forward and registered under the program, more than 13,000 were arrested and deported.

And the deportees were the lucky ones. In early 2003 the Justice Department's inspector general—the department's internal watchdog—published the results of its investigation into the arrests and prolonged detention after 9/11 of more than 750 Arab and Muslim immigrants living in the United States. None was ever charged with a terrorist-related offense. Most were just victims of bad luck and were detained for minor immigration violations. Yet many were jailed for months or even years, while some were placed in high-security federal prisons where they were locked down twenty-three hours a day, kept from their families and from attorneys, and in some cases subjected to beatings and verbal abuse by prison staff.

Benamar Benatta, who was arrested the day after the attacks, would spend nearly five years of his life in prison without ever being charged with any connection to terrorism. A lieutenant in the Algerian Air Force and an avionics expert, he had come to the United States to attend a month of training seminars at Northrop Grumman, which was selling radar-equipped aircraft to Algeria. Over the previous several years, Benatta had fought with his military superiors over his refusal to participate in counterterrorism missions inside Algeria, which he believed were aimed mostly at innocent civilians. He had bribed his way on to the trip to the United States, intending to stay in the country. At 4:00 a.m. on the last day of his trip, he walked away from a Baltimore hotel and caught a bus to New York City. After working odd jobs for half a year, he feared that he might be arrested for overstaying his visa and decided to leave for Canada. On September 5, 2001, he arrived at the Canadian border at Niagara Falls and asked for political asylum, claiming he would be tortured or killed for deserting the military if he returned to Algeria.

Benatta had hoped to find sympathy in Canada, which had long been welcoming to political refugees. Instead, he was held in custody for a week after admitting to the Canadian border inspector that he was carrying false U.S. identification. On September 12, knowing nothing of the attacks in New York and Washington, he was put in the back of a police van, driven across the border and handed over to U.S. border agents. It was there, under interrogation by FBI agents, that he said he first learned of what had happened on 9/11. Four days later, he was handcuffed and chained and flown to Brooklyn's Metropolitan Detention Center.

As the Justice inspector general's report would document, many of the detainees imprisoned there were subjected to brutal treatment. Benatta was held in isolation for seven months in a tiny prison cell on the ninth floor, under two bright lights that burned twenty-four hours a day. When he fell asleep, the guards would bang on the door to wake him. He was subjected to strip searches two or three times each day, and when he was removed from the cell, prison guards twisted his arms and beat his head against the wall. In the winter, the cell was air-conditioned to near freezing, and on several occasions he said he was chained outside in the cold for two or three hours. In the summer, the cell was heated to sweltering temperatures. He was not permitted to shave or to cut his hair or nails.

Finally, at the end of April 2002, he was taken back to Buffalo to appear, for the first time, before a judge. There he was charged with possessing a false document—a phony Social Security card he had purchased to help him find work in New York. For the next four years, until July 2006 when the U.S. and Canadian governments worked out a deal to return him to Canada, he was held in a maximum-security prison for having violated U.S. immigration laws by overstaying his visa. A federal judge who investigated the case called his imprisonment a "charade" that "bordered on ridiculousness."

I met Benatta in Toronto in April 2008. The Canadian government had finally granted him asylum status, and after more than a year of searching he had found work, though at a job he loathed. He could not risk going to see his family in Algeria, and he had made few friends in Toronto. At thirty-three, he carries the weariness of a man twice his age and is haunted by nightmares and depression diagnosed as post-traumatic stress syndrome. "We are not talking about five years," he said. "They ruined my whole life."

Such stories are only glimpses of the changes that took place after September 11 in a nation built on the backs, and increasingly the brains, of immigrants. The reaction has been more subtle than during some of the more notorious anti-immigrant backlashes in U.S. history, which were similarly triggered by new threats to American security. The great immigration wave that began in the late 1890s ended after World War I largely as a result of rising fears that foreigners would bring in communist or other radical political ideas. In the 1920s, Congress imposed a series of draconian national origin quotas that contributed to an eightfold drop in immigration in the 1930s. Despite the appalling treatment of many legal and illegal immigrants after 9/11, none of the abuses compare with the years-long internment of legal Japanese immigrants and American citizens of Japanese descent during World War II. And while the politics of immigration have become increasingly strident since 9/11, there are strong voices on both sides of the debate. But the change has been profound nonetheless. A country that, before September 11, had been supremely confident and open to the world has become wary, protective, and scared. As Richard Armitage, the former deputy secretary of state, put it, "this export of fear and anger has hurt us in the world." In an effort to keep out anyone who might again inflict such grievous harm, the United States is building a system of border controls that could rob it of much of what has made it such an impressive and successful country.

Richard Florida, author of *The Rise of the Creative Class*, argues that the United States' biggest economic competitive advantage has been "its status over the last century as the world's most open country." That openness has attracted to the United States far more than its share of the most talented, brilliant, and creative minds from around the world, and this has been a key part of building the world's most dynamic and innovative economy. "What made America the world's greatest power was not just our technology, market size, or natural resources," he writes. "The fundamental cause lies in one thing: our amazing ability to attract the world's greatest scientists, engineers, and cultural entrepreneurs."

Amy Chua, in her recent book *Day of Empire*, argues that all of the most successful world powers in history have shared a common attribute—they brought in, developed, and encouraged the most talented people in the world. "At any given historical moment, the most valuable human capital the world has to offer—whether in the form of intelligence, physical strength, skill, knowledge, creativity, networks, commercial innovation or technological invention—is never to be found in any one locale or within any one ethnic or religious group. To pull away from its rivals on a global scale, a society must pull into itself and motivate the world's best and brightest, regardless of ethnicity, religion, or background."

To give only two small examples of how important such foreign talent is to the United States, more than one-quarter of U.S. scientists and engineers are foreign-born, and nearly one-quarter of all patent applications in the United States are filed by immigrants. Yet six years after the attacks—enough time for the government to find that elusive balance between security and openness—one of the country's leading corporate immigration lawyers told Congress: "At no time in our nation's history has access to talent been as limited as it is today."

Other impacts of discouraging foreigners from traveling or emigrating to the United States are harder to measure, but no less significant. Dozens of foreign leaders, and hundreds of top officials, were educated at American universities, and the vast majority of those countries are friendly to the United States. What are the consequences for U.S. foreign policy if future generations of foreign leaders, particularly in the Muslim world, go elsewhere for their education? Yet since 9/11, enrollment in U.S. universities from Pakistan and Indonesia, the world's largest Muslim-majority countries, has fallen by more than one-third. Even the Bush administration has come to recognize that the war against Islamic extremism—which began well before 9/11 and will continue long after—is not one that can be won through arms alone. It will be won, instead, by showing the Muslim world the possibilities of modernity and persuading their young that religious extremism offers no future. Yet, since 2001, the number of temporary visas granted each year to residents of Saudi Arabia has fallen by half, from 60,000 to fewer than 30,000. The United States admits fewer than half as many Pakistanis as it did in 2000, 40 percent fewer Egyptians, and 50 percent fewer Iranians. For all of Africa, the number of visas has fallen from 350,000 annually to 275,000.

A United States that cuts itself off from the Islamic world by making it harder and harder for Muslims to travel here has deprived itself of the most persuasive thing it can offer—the example of what it has achieved at home. The 2006 travel industry survey mentioned earlier found that nearly three-quarters of those who have traveled to the United States have a favorable or extremely favorable view of the country, compared with just half of those who have never been here. How much of the largely futile effort that falls under the name of "public diplomacy" could be scrapped if the government simply did more to encourage foreign travel to the United States?

THERE HAVE BEEN IMPORTANT ACCOMPLISHMENTS in improving border security since September 11, and this book tells the story of many of those, and of the officials who have dedicated themselves to building a system that will help prevent future terrorist attacks. Without question, it is much harder for a terrorist to get into the United States than it was before 9/11, and the country is safer because of it. The United States now gets advanced information on all foreign passengers, a requirement that allows for more thorough screening before they ever touch down in the country. The use of fingerprints to identify travelers, as well as closer cooperation with U.S. allies, has helped to reduce the use of fraudulent passports, which were formerly a serious security vulnerability. The watch lists of known terrorists—wh... and too indiscriminate—are much better than they were prior to the attacks, and the United States and its allies are sharing that information. Before 9/11, two of the hijackers were known to the CIA as Al Qaeda operatives, but that information was never passed to the State Department so that consular officers would refuse to issue them a visa. At the time, there were a dozen different terrorist watch lists, each controlled by different U.S. government agencies that did little or nothing to coordinate their efforts with other agencies. Today, the FBI maintains the Terrorist Screening Center, a central unit that lists the names of more than four hundred thousand people from all over the world believed to have some links to terrorism, with thousands of names added very month. Those names are at the fingertips of every visa officer in every U.S. embassy in the world.

But we are at a point at which tougher choices need to be made. The added security has come with a very high price tag: keeping out people that the United States badly needs and wants if it is to maintain its preeminent position in the world. Serious efforts have been made to improve the efficiency of the new security schemes. Yet few of the American politicians and the senior bureaucrats who run the new homeland security apparatus are asking whether the incremental added security that comes from layering on more and more new border measures is worth the cost. Instead of institutionalizing a balanced approach, we have created a massive Department of Homeland Security that is dedicated solely to making us safer. As Norman Neureiter, the former science and technology adviser to Secretary of State Colin Powell, put it: "We've built a huge 186,000-person bureaucracy. And what is its job? Homeland security. It's not a projection of freedom; it's not the Statue of Liberty. It's not all those things which are written—'Give us your huddled masses, give us your poor, your starving.' No. It's to build walls around America to keep us safe from anything—disease, nuclear, radioactive, or humans—that might cross our borders. And every day they need to go to work and do something."

Since I first began working on this story five years ago, there was one comment that has really stuck with me. It was made by Bill Reinsch, who has worked many years for both Republicans and Democrats, in Congress and in the executive branch, on issues that lie at the intersection of the global economy and national security. He now works for large U.S. companies that have seen their talent pool shrink with the imposition of new border controls, but his concerns are much broader than just the impact on corporate America.

"One of our secret weapons has always been bringing people here to see what America is like," he said. "The ones that stay enrich our society and the ones that go back enrich their societies because they take our values with them. We're throwing all that away. The long-term consequences of this are horrible."

# Chapter 1

# THE BORDERS

> *To shield America from the world out of fear of terrorism is,*
> *in large part, to do the terrorists' work for them. To continue*
> *business as usual, however, is irresponsible.*
> —The U.S. Commission on National Security/21st Century
> (Hart-Rudman Commission), February 2001

ON THE MORNING OF SEPTEMBER 11, Robert Bonner was set for a crash course on the inner workings of the U.S. Customs Service. Established in July 1789 by the Fifth Act of Congress, Customs was created to collect the taxes on imported goods that were the only, desperately needed source of revenue for the new American government. More than two centuries later, Bonner's concerns were rather different than those of the founding fathers. The income tax had largely replaced tariffs for financing the government, free-trade agreements had eliminated most duties on imports, and Customs, part of the U.S. Treasury Department, had become just another one of the dozens of obscure government agencies in Washington whose job it was to facilitate the orderly workings of the free market.

Bonner, who had been nominated by President Bush to be the next Customs commissioner, was scheduled to meet first that morning with Dennis Murphy, a twenty-seven-year veteran of the agency. As head of public affairs, Murphy was looking for Bonner's support in his efforts to get some favorable attention for the more than 19,000 employees in the U.S. Customs Service whose thankless job it was to keep out criminals and contraband. That required monitoring the $1 trillion in goods and 493 million vehicles and people that were to cross over the 7,500 miles of United States land borders and through its nearly 130 international airports and seaports that year.

In August 2001, almost all the news had been about modest drug seizures. Ninety-four pounds of cocaine, worth more than $2 million, was found stashed under the backseat of a car coming by ferry from the Dominican Republic to Puerto Rico, a U.S. territory where Customs inspectors are deployed. In another bust, 271.1 pounds of marijuana had been seized on the Bridge of the Americas that spans the Rio Grande from Juárez, Mexico, to El Paso, Texas. The driver, thirty-nine-year-old Bobbi Knisley from Denver, had concealed the dope in the auxiliary gas tank of her 1981 Ford 3500 and had then hidden the tank under a large toolbox. Customs inspectors at the border were suspicious about her answers to routine questions and ordered the vehicle pulled aside for a more thorough investigation. When Tyler, a drug-sniffing dog, started yelping, agents unbolted the tank from the flatbed and found a trapdoor that led to a secret compartment holding ninety bundles of marijuana.

Such busts made no headlines and had little effect in curbing the enormous flow of drugs into the United States. The Drug Enforcement Administration (DEA) reported that cocaine prices that year "remained low and stable, which suggests a steady supply to the United States." Marijuana was similarly a buyer's market.

That didn't discourage the irrepressibly optimistic Murphy. Unlike most government flacks, who are nervous political operatives whose jobs rest on their political loyalty to one party or the other, Murphy was a career U.S. Customs official who relished the opportunity to tell his agency's story to whoever might be paying attention. His most recent project had been the creation of an in-house television series, *America's Frontline*, in which he gave his best John Walsh imitation in telling what he called the "exciting real-life stories" of the agents and inspectors guarding the U.S. border. That month's show was to feature Customs agents on a training mission to Uzbekistan, one of the dysfunctional former Soviet republics that was a conduit for drugs and other contraband into the United States. The series had just won a Telly Award for video production quality.

But Murphy never got to make his pitch. At 9:35 a.m. on September 11, less than half an hour after the second plane crashed into the twin towers, Bonner was jolted by the shriek of sirens ordering an evacuation of the Treasury building, which sits across from the White House on Pennsylvania Avenue. From a window of his temporary office on the fourth floor, he could see black smoke rising from across the Potomac River, where American Airlines Flight 77 had just slammed into the side of the Pentagon. As he rushed outside the building, he ran into Kenneth Dam, the silver-haired patrician who was acting Treasury secretary. Dam hustled Bonner into his black limousine to drive to the secure Secret Service Command Center a few blocks away. Murphy and other senior U.S. Customs officials went the other direction, gathering around the corner in the Customs Situation Room at the Ronald Reagan Building and International Trade Center, a sprawling structure intended by Congress to "create a national forum for the advancement of trade." The New York attacks had already destroyed the Customs building adjacent to the World Trade Center, which had been the center for all northeast operations, so any decisions on what to do next had to come out of Washington.

Bonner was new to the Customs Service, but he was no novice. Highly ambitious even by Washington standards, he had been a federal judge and had headed the U.S. Attorney's office in central California. While there he led the prosecution of the killers of Enrique Camarena, an undercover American operative in the war on drugs who was kidnapped, tortured, and murdered by Mexican drug lords in a gruesome killing that had soured U.S. relations with

Mexico in the mid-1980s. As a defense lawyer, he had achieved
some small notoriety by defending Heidi Fleiss, the Hollywood
madam who was convicted on charges arising from running a pros-
titution ring for famous clients. Bonner had led the DEA from 1990
to 1993 in the administration of the first George Bush, stepping
in at a time when the use of crack cocaine had spread throughout
the major American cities, driving up the murder rate and sending middle-class Americans fleeing to the suburbs and beyond. He
had declared war on Colombia's Medellín and Cali cartels and the
network of distributors they had built in the United States and pre-
sided over a sharp, but temporary, drop in cocaine and marijuana
use. He was later to blast the Clinton administration over rising
drug use in the 1990s, saying that its drug strategy "had failed
miserably."

The war on drugs, which required a patient struggle against a
shadowy enemy, had given the Customs Service a reservoir of experience and knowledge for fighting the new war on terror that began
that morning. That advantage showed immediately: within two
hours of the attacks, the Customs Service had positively identified
all nineteen of the hijackers, a phenomenal investigative achieve-
ment that was strangely overlooked by the National Commission
on Terrorist Attacks on the United States, the 9/11 Commission,
which would later do an exhaustive investigation of the day's
events. For almost fifteen years, Customs had quietly been gathering and analyzing data on passengers on all incoming international
flights. The Advanced Passenger Information System, known by
the acronym APIS, had been set up on a pilot basis in 1988, just
before Bonner came to the DEA, largely as a tool to fight the drug
war. Under the scheme, U.S. airlines had agreed voluntarily to allow Customs and the INS to have full, immediate access to data
on the passengers on all incoming international flights. The data
were examined by specialized passenger analysis units set up by
Customs at each of the country's international airports, with input
from Customs' Office of Intelligence.

The information included basic biographical data such as

name, date and place of birth, citizenship, and passport numbers. But more importantly for investigators, many airlines had also agreed to give Customs access to their reservation data, setting out where, when, how, and by whom the airline ticket had been purchased. U.S. airlines would permit Customs and the Immigration and Naturalization Service to access this data after an inbound international flight had taken off, allowing inspectors to make some early judgments about who should be pulled aside for more thorough inspection upon arrival at a U.S. airport. Even though participation by the airlines was voluntary, by 2000 the United States was getting APIS data from sixty-seven carriers, covering about two-thirds of all incoming passengers.

For the airlines, the incentive was this: in exchange for a mild invasion of their passengers' privacy, the vast majority of travelers sped through INS and Customs inspection after they arrived in the United States. That kept the airlines happy and also appeased members of Congress, who got fewer complaints from angry passengers who were delayed at U.S. airports after returning from trips abroad. Passengers on international flights were screened while their flights were en route, cutting down on the time shuffling most passengers past the inspection kiosks. For Customs and the INS, the data was used to run checks against known criminals or those who had previously been deported from the United States or were otherwise ineligible for entry, data that was contained in a woefully incomplete form in government databases known as IBIS, for Interagency Border Inspection System, and NAILS, for National Automated Immigration Lookout System. Finding a way to make such distinctions among passengers had become increasingly urgent with the huge growth in international airline traffic into the United States in the 1980s and 1990s.

The agency wanted to be more proactive than simply checking names and passport numbers against databases, though. In particular, Customs was hoping to identify so-called swallowers—couriers who were used by the big drug cartels to smuggle cocaine or heroin into the country by ingesting rubber-encased pellets and defecating the valuable packages after they arrived. That was where the reservation data, known as Passenger Name Records (PNR), were so useful. If Customs agents knew, for instance, that a particular credit card had been used by the drug cartels in the past to purchase tickets for couriers, another use of that card for an airline ticket was a red flag that the passenger might be a swallower. Similarly, common addresses or telephone numbers could help reveal what Bonner called "relationships" between known smugglers or cartel members and those who were still unknown to Customs. Cash purchases or the purchase of one-way tickets would similarly trigger suspicion. The access to such data, as opposed to random searches of incoming passengers, greatly increased the odds that a drug courier could be singled out and stopped without needlessly inconveniencing the vast majority of lawful travelers. "You start to create a trail," said Chuck Winwood, a career U.S. Customs official who was the acting head of the agency on 9/11 while Bonner was awaiting Senate confirmation. While it was far from perfect, there was strong evidence that such targeting worked. In the two years prior to 9/11, under an initiative launched by Bonner's highly lauded predecessor Ray Kelly, the number of personal searches conducted by Customs officials on incoming passengers had fallen dramatically, from over 43,000 in 1998 to just 9,000 in 2000. Yet that smaller number of searches had actually resulted in more drug seizures.

Customs had kept fairly quiet about the program largely to avoid tipping off drug smugglers, but there was another reason for the secrecy. The way airline passenger databases were structured, it was impossible to segregate incoming international flights from thousands of domestic flights. That meant every day Customs had unrestricted access to personal data on every passenger on every flight in the United States. As later controversies over various Bush administration efforts to gather data on domestic airline passengers would demonstrate, had civil liberties groups been aware of the full nature of the pre-9/11 program, they almost certainly would have fought to shut it down. Data for passengers on incoming international routes were examined routinely, but Customs would also access the same reservation and passenger data for domestic flights in certain rare and urgent circumstances: for instance, if Customs believed that a drug courier might have stashed contraband on an incoming international flight that was continuing on to other U.S. airports. Such a scheme would allow another courier to board that same flight, recover the drugs, and evade Customs searches. Customs officials said domestic passenger lists would also be examined "judiciously" for undercover investigations where Customs agents might want to tail a drug courier or other suspect after he or she had already arrived in the United States.

On the morning of September 11, there was no question in the minds of the officials in charge that the circumstances were both rare and urgent. But Winwood, the acting Customs commissioner, was out of the country, spending a long weekend in Toronto, the first vacation he had taken in nearly two years, and the last he was to take until he left the agency the following April. Bonner was not yet confirmed by Congress and therefore without any legal authority to run the agency. So John Varrone, a veteran agent who had worked most of the senior jobs in the agency, was in charge in Washington and was meeting with his senior staff when the planes hit in New York. Less than an hour after the second tower was hit, the agency's chief of intelligence, Roy Surrett, came in and told Varrone that his agents had already pulled up the passenger manifests for the four flights. He brought Varrone a list of nineteen names that he thought were the hijackers.

Bonner, who was confirmed by the Senate eight days later, asked his staff to reconstruct the sequence that had allowed Customs to zero in so quickly on a list of names that turned out to be entirely accurate. When the passenger records were retrieved, two names had immediately jumped out from the manifests: Khalid al-Mihdhar and Nawaf al-Hazmi. Both had been known to the CIA since January 2000 as Al Qaeda operatives, but in the biggest single foul-up in the months leading up to the attacks, the CIA had failed to inform any other government agency, and the names of the two men were not put on watch lists until August 2001, months after they had already entered the United States. But when Customs ran the names of the passengers on the four planes, they popped up immediately as hits against Customs' own IBIS watch list, which included the names of suspected terrorists.

With those two names in hand, Customs began checking the other Arab names on the passenger lists. Common credit card numbers linked the two with nearly half of the other seventeen hijackers; common addresses or adjacent seat locations on the flights helped to link the remainder. The agency was quickly able to isolate nineteen men out of the 232 passengers on the four planes as the likely hijackers. Bonner would later tell the 9/11 Commission, though it never made the final report, that Customs was able to forward that information to the FBI and the intelligence agencies within forty-five minutes of the last plane crashing in Pennsylvania. He would later complain that "the FBI hasn't given Customs a single bit of credit for this."

It was a success that held a clear lesson for those in the government who cared to understand it as they began to build the architecture of homeland security. Information was the key: if the government had access to the right bits, could analyze them in the right way, and could get them to the right agencies, it increased the likelihood that it could keep not only known terrorists out of the country, but unknown ones as well. By the beginning of November, at Bonner's urging, Congress had included provisions in a new transportation security bill that would end the voluntary status of the advanced passenger information program, requiring not only U.S. airlines but all foreign airlines to provide such information on all incoming flights to the United States. The legislation would also give Customs access to the more detailed PNR reservation data.

With proper data that was easily accessible, Bonner later argued, "if you could identify one person who is a potential terrorist operative trying to enter the United States, you have a much higher likelihood of being able to identify [through relationships] other people you don't know about who are terrorists.

"You're not going to know all the terrorist operatives that Al

Qaeda has recruited and is sending to the United States," Bonner said. "You're just not going to know it. Maybe you know one out of ten. If you know two out of nineteen, you'll be able to identify the other seventeen—that's the point of the 9/11 story."

Bonner's insight—that the intelligent use of information and selective targeting was likely to be the most effective way to keep terrorists out of the United States—had first been articulated in 1998 by a congressional panel of blue-ribbon experts: the Hart-Rudman Commission, named for its cochairs, former Democratic senator Gary Hart and former Republican senator Warren Rudman. The group was tasked with examining the strategic challenges the United States would face in the next century and making recommendations for institutional and policy changes. The cold war was over, the Soviet Union had disappeared, and there was no longer a single threat that the U.S. defense establishment could organize around. The panel was asked to look ahead over the next twenty-five years and judge which of the panoply of possible threats—a rising China, the proliferation of nuclear weapons, rogue states, environmental degradation, or a myriad other possibilities—was the most urgent.

The group of fourteen commissioners was A-list enough to be taken seriously, but unlike many similar commissions, it was not so top-heavy with former administration officials as to make a radical critique impossible. Hart had been a respected member of the Senate, serving on the Armed Services and Intelligence committees in the 1980s. He had been the front-runner in the 1988 Democratic presidential nomination until the revelation of his extramarital affair with the much younger Donna Rice forced him out of the race. Since then he had quietly been rebuilding his reputation as a serious policy player. Rudman's career had been less eventful, highlighted by his role in the Gramm-Rudman-Hollings legislation that helped bring the U.S. budget back into balance after the Reagan deficits. But he was a political centrist, respected and trusted by the leaders of both parties. Among the best known of the other commissioners were the recently ousted Republican House speaker, Newt Gingrich; former Democratic congressman Lee Hamilton, the model of a sober, responsible politician on national security matters; and former Nixon and Ford defense secretary James Schlesinger.

The Hart-Rudman Commission had a strong cast, but nonetheless their report was completely ignored. It had the misfortune of landing in three phases that straddled the end of the Clinton administration and the beginning of the Bush administration—a period of enormous political turmoil in the United States spanning Bill Clinton's impeachment and the contested 2000 presidential election. The commission tried hard to turn the nation's attention away from Monica Lewinsky's dress and Florida's hanging chads. It warned that the United States was living in a fool's paradise of post–cold war bliss and that, despite a soaring economy and military might that dwarfed all of its potential adversaries combined, the dangers to the country had rarely been greater. It made an ominous and, as it turned out, accurate prediction: that within the next quarter century, the United States would face a deadly attack at home, most likely from a terrorist group. "America will become increasingly vulnerable to hostile attack on our homeland, and our military superiority will not entirely protect us," the commissioners wrote nearly two years before 9/11. "Americans will likely die on American soil, possibly in large numbers." The failure of U.S. national leaders to agree on a clear strategy for homeland security designed to thwart such an attack was, it said, "dangerous and intolerable." Given the broad range of its mandate—which was to examine the most severe emerging threats to U.S. security and make recommendations for confronting them—it was an unlikely and unexpected prediction, and it was greeted as such. The Bush administration thought rogue states like North Korea, Iraq, or Iran armed with ballistic missiles posed the biggest threat, not a band of religious fanatics hiding out in the mountains of Afghanistan.

Despite its stark language, the report may also have been a victim of its own nuance. It was not a call to arms. Instead, it demanded that Americans confront a paradox: that the very source of U.S. prosperity and success was also the source of its vulnerability to a catastrophic terrorist attack. The report pointed to two dominant trends shaping the post–cold war world. The first was globalization—"a tide of economic, technological and intellectual forces that is integrating a global community." The second was its antithesis—the rise of powerful forces of social and political fragmentation that was generating ethnic, tribal, and criminal violence around the world. The challenge for the United States, it argued, was to contain the instability caused by these forces of disintegration in order to continue reaping the economic and political benefits of a more integrated world. The problem was that the very thing that made globalization possible—a low-friction world in which goods, people, and ideas moved freely across national borders—also made countries far more vulnerable to attacks from those disaffected with the new order. As the most powerful and open country in the world, the United States was both an attractive target and an easy one. The commission wrote: "Terrorists and criminals are finding that the difficulty of policing the rising daily volume and velocities of people and goods that cross U.S. borders make it easier for them to smuggle weapons and contraband, and to move their operatives in and out of the United States."

Prior to the 9/11 attacks, the country had been lucky. There had been some very close calls. On December 14, 1999, a thirty-two-year-old Algerian carrying a fraudulent Canadian passport had driven a rented green Chrysler sedan onto the Black Ball ferry in Victoria, British Columbia. Since fleeing the civil war in his native Algeria and coming to Canada in 1994 on a forged French passport, Ahmed Ressam had claimed political asylum, and then remained in the country illegally after he failed to show for a hearing and his claim was rejected. While hiding out in Montreal, he fell into a life of petty crime and eventually became enthralled with a circle of radical Islamists preaching jihad against the United States. After traveling to Afghanistan to train at a terrorist camp, he committed himself to carrying out a spectacular attack on the eve of the millennium. His target was the Los Angeles International Airport, where he intended to set off 130 pounds of explosives in a suitcase bomb at the crowded security check-in.

In the summer, the Black Ball ferry is crowded with tourists traveling across the Juan de Fuca Strait between the quaint B.C. capital on Vancouver Island and Port Angeles, Washington, which is framed by the snowcapped Olympic Mountains. That December evening, however, only a few cars boarded; Ressam's was the last car to come off the last ferry of the day. The Customs inspector at the terminal, Diana Dean, became suspicious with his answers to routine questions. He said he was visiting friends in Seattle but then claimed he was staying at a hotel; he was sweating and fidgety. Suspecting that Ressam was a drug smuggler, she ordered him to open the trunk. While she and another inspector searched the car, Ressam was taken inside for questioning. In the spare tire compartment, the agents found several green bags filled with a white powder, as well as black boxes, pill bottles, and two jars of brown liquid. Their first thought was drugs, not bombs. As soon as the trunk was opened, Ressam broke free of the inspectors and fled through the streets of Port Angeles. He made it six blocks before they tackled and handcuffed him.

Ressam was unlucky, but also not very bright. The lack of border traffic that evening made it easy for Customs officials to act on their suspicions and subject his car to a thorough search without delaying other travelers. At nearby Blaine, Washington, where more than 9,000 cars and 2,000 trucks crossed each day, his odds of passing through undetected would have been much better. And Port Angeles is among the whitest places in the country, with a minority population of less than 9 percent. Customs officials have conceded that if Ressam had tried to cross in Michigan, for instance, where more than 100,000 Arab Americans live, he would likely have been waved through without a second look. Had he made it across the border, he would not have been the first. Some two dozen foreign terrorists had already managed to enter the United States before Ressam's arrest, including those who carried out the 1993 bombing of the World Trade Center, which killed six people and injured a thousand more.

The obvious solution to the threat of terrorists crossing U.S. borders was simply to beef up enforcement through tougher scrutiny of border crossers; greater inspection of vehicles; and the use of Border Patrol agents, physical barriers, and remote sensing devices to safeguard the barren regions between the official border crossings. But the Hart-Rudman Commission had a different analysis. It argued that there was simply no way to strengthen enforcement sufficiently without seriously inhibiting the free flow of goods and travelers, thereby damaging the U.S. economy. Stephen Flynn, a former Coast Guard commander who served as lead consultant to the Hart-Rudman Commission on homeland security issues, fleshed out that argument in a November 2000 article in *Foreign Affairs*. Flynn called for a "paradigm shift" in how the United States managed its borders. "The global economy's movement towards more open societies and liberalized economies does not just facilitate the movement of products and workers—it also expedites passage for terrorists, small arms, drugs, illegal immigrants and disease," he wrote. Yet the standard U.S. response to such threats had been to bolster border controls, increasing regulation and scrutiny of all goods and people coming into the United States. At the border with Mexico, in particular, where the rise in illegal immigration and drug smuggling had produced a political backlash in California and the Southwest, the U.S. government had already greatly increased its enforcement efforts in the 1990s even as it was implementing the North American Free Trade Agreement to remove barriers to trade between the two countries. Between 1993 and 2000, the INS had added more than 5,000 agents to the southwest border, tripling their numbers. Flynn argued that clamping down further in order to keep out terrorists would do more harm than good:

> Efforts to bolster regulatory, enforcement, and security operations at busy borders may result in a cure worse than the disease. Such endeavors place governments on a collision course with easy trade, which is the key to the sustained expansion and integration

of the global economy. Most successful enterprises need to move workers and products quickly, reliably and affordably around the planet. Delays associated with intensified inspections along borders undermine the competitiveness of exports by raising transaction costs. Overseas buyers are likely to avoid ports where there is a heightened risk that products will arrive damaged, spoiled or late. And rapid, hassle-free immigration controls are essential to both global business and tourism.

In place of traditional enforcement efforts, the Hart-Rudman Commission called for an approach that "balances prudence, on the one hand, with American values of openness and free trade on the other." Achieving such a balance would require an information and organizational revolution at the U.S. borders. The traditional approach was to subject everyone crossing the borders to a similar level of scrutiny. The driver approaching the inspection kiosk at Blaine, Washington, or San Ysidro, California, or the air traveler waiting in line at JFK Airport in New York, was usually utterly unknown to U.S. officials. At the airport, the name of an arriving passenger might produce a hit on government watch lists of known terrorists or terrorist-related criminals, which by 2001 contained some 60,000 to 80,000 names. But border officials had no training in detecting the sorts of fraudulent documents or travel patterns that might be used by terrorists; indeed, most did not even know that the computer searches they were using were intended to screen out terrorists. The closest thing the United States had to an advance screening procedure was the requirement that citizens of many countries obtain a visa before coming to the United States. But even these applications were subject to relatively cursory checks intended mostly to ensure that travelers would not overstay their visa or attempt to work while they were in the United States. And more than half of all air travelers came from countries where a visa was not required to enter the United States, mostly from Europe. Identifying a potential terrorist from that unknown mass of humanity required a lot of luck and the sort of instinct and experience that Diana Dean had shown in Port Angeles. It was a weak reed on which to rest the country's security.

The commission called for replacing this minimal inspection of every traveler with a more targeted approach. Confronting the terrorist threat without disrupting the growth of global business and travel required the sort of advance information—though much more and in greater detail—that Customs had tried to develop for identifying likely drug smugglers on incoming international flights. The theory was the same: better information would create better security with less disruption to ordinary travel. "Border agencies need faster and stronger capabilities to gather intelligence and manage data," Flynn wrote. "A well-informed customs and immigration agent can identify and target high-risk goods and people for inspection while quickly and confidently processing those that pose less of a danger." In particular, such information needed to be made available soon enough that border officials were not constantly required to make snap judgments based on a handful of routine questions.

The Hart-Rudman Commission called for three innovations. First, the United States needed to push its borders outward, developing what it called a "layered defense." For border security, that meant that rather than relying only on U.S. inspectors stationed at U.S. borders to identify and detain suspicious individuals or suspect cargo, the United States needed to work with foreign countries to analyze potential threats before they arrived at American shores. The actual border would serve as a last line of defense rather than as the first and only line. Second, the U.S. government had to work closely with private companies that shipped goods around the world to ensure that they did not become "unwitting conduits for criminal or terrorist activities." Cooperation with the private sector—rather than a purely regulatory process of heavy-handed government scrutiny—could improve security without disrupting commerce significantly. Third, and most important, the commission called for large new investments in intelligence gathering, data handling, and information sharing among government agencies in order to improve the ability of border agencies to target high-risk goods and people.

Such an approach, it argued, would avoid the need to choose between security and trade, between greater safety and greater openness. These innovations "would pay for themselves in short order." Americans would be safer because the government would be proactively targeting the travel of terrorists or the shipments of dangerous weapons rather than hoping to snag them crossing the border. And the improvements in data and management could also streamline the border, resulting in fewer disruptive inspections for legitimate businesses and travelers.

The commission did not ask all the hard questions. Getting the sort of data that would be needed would require cooperation from foreign governments and foreign-based companies. Would they agree? Many countries, particularly those that were the most likely sources of terrorist activity, were reluctant to cooperate with the United States for fear of arousing internal anti-American opposition. And even close allies in Europe had generally more stringent privacy standards that made information sharing difficult. Foreign companies were no better. While U.S.-owned airlines had been participating voluntarily in sharing passenger information before 9/11, most foreign airlines had refused, and there seemed no way to compel them to cooperate. The problem at home was, in some respects, worse. The U.S. government's information technology was a mess, and the relevant data needed to improve border security was scattered across half a dozen agencies with incompatible computer systems that had no interest in sharing what they knew. Civil libertarians were certain to object to intensive data gathering on millions of innocent people just to help identify a handful of potential terrorists or criminals. And how effective could such a system be, anyway? Customs' drug-targeting scheme assumed and accepted a high rate of failure; when combating terrorism a tiny number of failures could be disastrous. Even those who agreed with the commission's underlying analysis could plausibly argue that the risks of such a system were too great in the face of the terrorist threat.

But however flawed, the commission had at least provided a framework for thinking about the problem of border security in the era of globalization. As the immediate aftermath of 9/11 would demonstrate, the other options were not particularly attractive.

WHILE CUSTOMS OFFICIALS WERE BUSY combing passenger records from the four hijacked airplanes, Winwood, the acting commissioner, made another call from his interrupted vacation in Toronto, this one to Jim Ziglar. Ziglar had been confirmed just a month before as President Bush's choice to head the INS. He had been brought in to turn around what one former Justice official called a "hopelessly dysfunctional agency" that satisfied neither those who wanted more immigrants nor those who wanted to keep them out. He was something of a turnaround specialist, having rescued the failing Interior Department Bureau of Mines during the Reagan administration. He also had extensive Wall Street experience, having held senior posts at Paine Webber and UBS. When the White House sought him out, he was just finishing up a stint as sergeant at arms and doorkeeper, an antiquated title for the official in charge of managing the day-to-day operations of the U.S. Senate. But Ziglar, by his own admission, knew nothing about immigration and had no law enforcement background. Yet the INS, part of the Justice Department, contained the U.S. Border Patrol, which at the time was the second largest law enforcement agency in the country, after the FBI. The Border Patrol was responsible for keeping illegal migrants out of the United States, by apprehending them at the border, while the INS had additional agents who were responsible for tracking them down inside the country, usually through raids on employers who hired undocumented workers.

Until the creation of the Department of Homeland Security in 2003, Customs and the INS were roughly an equal presence at the U.S. border. The INS had more than 15,000 agents whose job it was to admit legal travelers and immigrants and keep out illegal ones. Customs had about two-thirds as many inspectors and investigators to carry out its task of admitting legal goods and keeping out illegal ones. The two agencies were often rivals. But on the day of the attacks there was little thought of past turf wars. At 10:00 a.m., Winwood recommended moving to a level one threat status at all three hundred land, sea, and air ports of entry into the United States, and Ziglar quickly concurred. Five minutes later, the order was issued.

If the passenger information system that helped to identify the hijackers is the equivalent of a sieve, allowing most people to pass through unhindered and leaving behind only a few to be examined, a level one alert is like a sponge that traps everything and everyone. The highest alert level short of a complete closure of the borders, it requires Customs and INS officers to carry out intensive examinations of all cargo and people approaching the border, from the trucker who has plied the same route every day for the past twenty years to the nurse driving through the tunnel from Windsor, Ontario, to Detroit for work each day, to the nervous young man with a Saudi passport and a tourist visa. Everyone approaching the border is asked for a driver's license and several other pieces of identification. Cars and trucks are searched thoroughly by border agents, including in some cases unloading and reloading the cargo of huge commercial rigs. Before 9/11, dedicated commuter and commercial lanes had been created to speed those who crossed regularly and had already been vetted by the U.S. government, leaving officials more time to focus on the real smuggling threats. Within hours of the attacks, these were closed and would not be reopened for another three months. The trusted and the distrusted, the known and the unknown, were treated the same.

By 11:00 that morning, the order to move to level one had been issued for every airport, seaport, and land border crossing in the United States. The effects were almost immediate, and they were dramatic. Since 1989, when the U.S.-Canada Free Trade Agreement went into force, bilateral trade between the two countries had more than doubled, to $350 billion. That meant a huge increase in truck and rail traffic across the border to handle the growing trade in goods. Yet U.S. spending on border infrastructure and personnel had stagnated, leaving primitive facilities and a shortage of staff to handle an ever-growing stream of goods and people. At the northern border, just 334 INS agents were assigned to handle a flow of people that could sometimes exceed 300,000 crossings each day. The commercial traffic alone was staggering. At the Ambassador Bridge across the Detroit River, for instance, the busiest land crossing in the world, keeping the traffic flowing smoothly on the busiest days required clearing a truck through the border every twelve seconds.

It does not take much to bring that massive flow of traffic to a standstill. More than a year after the 9/11 attacks, Brian Goebel, who started work on September 12, 2001, as a senior policy adviser to Bonner, was leading a congressional delegation on a tour of the Peace Bridge, which connects Fort Erie, Ontario, with Buffalo, New York. It was two o'clock on a weekday afternoon in October, and the line at the border kiosks averaged just two or three cars or trucks each, a delay of only minutes. As a demonstration for some members of Congress, Goebel asked the U.S. border officials to implement a 100 percent ID check, which simply required border inspectors to get a driver's license, passport, or some other government identity from everyone crossing the border. Within half an hour, the lineup on the bridge had extended to half a mile.

On September 11, the impact was similarly swift and devastating. Within two days, the queue of trucks and cars at the Ambassador Bridge had swelled, by different accounts, to anywhere between ten and twenty miles long. Trucks spilled onto the city streets of Windsor, and truckers abandoned their rigs and went to look for food and coffee. "I've been doing this for seventeen years and I've never seen anything like this," Mike Lagnos, a trucker heading to Michigan to pick up a shipment of auto parts, told the local paper. The trip across the border, which had taken minutes the previous week, now entailed a wait of anywhere between twelve and eighteen hours. The Ontario Provincial Police brought in portable toilets, while the Red Cross and the Salvation Army provided food and water to stranded truckers and car drivers. The fire department hooked up hoses to spray cooling water on a shipment of live cattle baking in the afternoon sun.

The delays were far more than an inconvenience. Since 1965, when the U.S.-Canada Auto Pact freed up trade in cars and car parts for vehicles manufactured in the two countries, the North American auto industry had become an integrated operation working across the northern border. The auto industry alone accounted for a quarter of the $1.3 billion in goods crossing the border each day. Ford, Chrysler, and General Motors had been among the first American companies to experiment with just-in-time delivery systems, which allowed companies to reduce the need to store costly inventory by carefully timing the arrival of parts. In the face of competition from Japan, where Toyota had pioneered the system, the practice had spread throughout the entire U.S. auto industry in the 1980s and 1990s. With the U.S-Canada Free Trade Agreement in 1989 and NAFTA in 1994 further deepening economic ties between the two countries, American automakers became bolder and bolder in shutting down warehouses to shave costs and better compete with their Japanese and Korean rivals. By 2001, the system was so finely tuned that a Canadian maker of auto parts in Ontario was expected to deliver shipments in as little as six hours after receiving an order from an assembly plant in Michigan. Ben Anderson, the chief inspector on the Detroit side of the Ambassador Bridge, called the truck traffic across the border "a rolling inventory, just another part of the assembly line."

Such a system could not withstand the shock of 9/11. "Just-in-time is the lifeblood of the auto industry and it works brilliantly, but it can't compensate for catastrophic events such as what happened in New York and Washington," said John Arnone of Ford Canada. "There are buffers built into our system for traffic and border delays, but this was immense." By the next day Ford, which used operations in Windsor to supply parts for eight of its fifteen U.S. plants, had been forced to shut down five of its assembly lines when engine and drive-train components failed to arrive from Canada, and would be unable to reopen them for several days. The hearing in Washington, Senator Byron Dorgan of North Dakota held up an orange traffic cone. This cone, he mocked, "represents the security at a good number of our northern border ports of entry." At many of the rural border crossings, the cones were put across the road when the last border inspectors went home for the evening at 10:00 p.m. A sign would inform drivers that the border was closed and they should return in the morning. The situation was not much better at the bigger crossings. According to a Senate subcommittee report, the Detroit border station before 9/11 required 174 INS agents to give proper, round-the-clock scrutiny to travelers crossing into the United States; it had 23.

THE U.S. BORDER WITH MEXICO was even worse. NAFTA had accelerated an explosion of trade, and the border was already groaning as U.S. officials attempted to dust off a dilapidated infrastructure to handle the new traffic. As at the northern border, the new inspection requirements after 9/11 quickly brought traffic to a crawl. At the bridge crossings between Nuevo Laredo, Mexico, and Laredo, Texas, vehicle waiting time increased from half an hour to more than five hours. At San Ysidro, the border crossing between Tijuana and San Diego, drivers were idling for as long as eight hours, while even pedestrians faced a two-hour wait. The maquiladora assembly plants that line Mexico's border with the United States immediately started to feel the pinch as shipments from overseas faced delays at the big U.S. ports like Los Angeles. The maquiladoras accounted for nearly half of Mexico's exports in 2000, but on top of a weakening U.S. economy, a strong peso, and rising competition from low-cost producers in Asia, their sales plummeted after the attacks.

At the northern border, the delays began to recede, but only because of the collapse of cross-border traffic, heroic work by overstretched Customs and INS inspectors, and the emergency deployment of National Guard troops to help with the inspections. By early October, the number of cars and trucks crossing the Ambassador Bridge to Detroit had fallen by half. In early December, smallest disruption was enough to bring production to a sudden halt—Ford closed its plant in Wixom, Michigan, where the Lincoln LS, the Ford Thunderbird, and the Ford GT were assembled, because of a shortage of door hinges. General Motors reduced or canceled shifts at four of its North American plants. Chrysler avoided lengthy closures: it shut all its plants on the afternoon of 9/11, and after that it closed only one Windsor plant for a few hours on September 13 due to a parts shortage—but only because clever advance planning allowed many of its truck shipments from Canada to be diverted to rail. On the Canadian side, unplanned production losses from parts shortages were costing Canadian companies between $1 million and $1.5 million every hour. Even the Japanese were not spared. On September 13 and 14, Toyota canceled shifts at its Georgetown, Kentucky, plant when a shipment of parts from Canada failed to arrive.

A week after the attacks, when stock markets reopened, share prices for the Big Three automakers tumbled far more sharply than most other stocks. Overall, they lost nearly 15 percent of their planned North American production for the week of the 9/11 attacks as a result of slowdowns caused by border measures. Within a day of the attacks, lobbyists for the Big Three were already begging U.S. Customs officials in Washington to add more inspectors to speed the border crossings and had taken their complaints to Bush's top economic adviser, Larry Lindsey. There wasn't much sympathy. As Chuck Winwood recalls, he lost his cool when, just three days after the attacks, he got a call from a northern state congressman complaining about the delays. "I said, 'Goddammit, do you realize our building is still burning in New York? We're still missing two people.'"

The problems were exacerbated by chronic understaffing at the Canadian border crossings. Despite the doubling in cross-border trade, the number of Customs and INS inspectors at the northern border had fallen by one-quarter over the previous decade as a result of tight government budgets and a redeployment of agents to shore up the southern border with Mexico. At an October 3 Senate

Governor Gary Locke of Washington State and other governors from the states bordering Canada pleaded with President Bush to authorize the deployment of still more National Guard troops to speed processing at the border. The number of Canadian shoppers, Locke said, had fallen more than 50 percent, costing retailers in northern Washington state more than $100 million in lost sales.

At the southern border, the consequences were even more severe, as the post-9/11 traffic jams continued throughout that fall. At the Tijuana–San Diego crossing, the number of Mexicans crossing each day into the United States fell from 130,000 to 80,000. The decline was similar on the Bridge of the Americas to El Paso. Many Mexicans who worked in jobs across the border in the United States abandoned their cars and took to walking across the border, leading to a tripling of pedestrian traffic. But on October 9, INS officials began checking the name of every pedestrian against the IBIS watch lists, looking for known terrorists or criminals. Before the attacks, less than 5 percent of all crossers at the southern border had been run against IBIS. Quickly, the pedestrian delays became as long as the vehicle delays.

Mexico's president, Vicente Fox, called the economic aftermath of 9/11 "cataclysmic" for Mexico. The border slowdowns rippled throughout the country, leading to layoffs in agriculture and manufacturing. The drop in tourist travel from Canada and the United States was similarly devastating. Mexico's economy, which had grown by more than 6 percent in 2000 and was forecast by the International Monetary Fund to keep growing at more than 4 percent annually, instead shrunk in 2001 and barely recovered in 2002.

If the land borders were congested, at least they remained open. For three days after the attacks, the Federal Aviation Administration ordered a complete closure of U.S. airspace, and then allowed only air cargo shipments to resume on September 14. Air freight accounts for about 40 percent of U.S. trade by value, with about half of that arriving on dedicated cargo planes and the rest coming in the holds of passenger planes. For U.S. computer makers, international cargo traffic between the United States and Asia was particularly critical. After flights were suspended the day of the attacks, computers being assembled in Taiwan, Singapore, and South Korea were already piling up in warehouses waiting for shipment to the United States.

The falloff in passenger traffic was similar. In August 2001, the U.S. airline industry had a record month, with 65.4 million travelers. It wouldn't see that number again for nearly three years. International and cross-border travel plummeted. Between August and October of 2001, the number of inspections at U.S. land, sea, and air borders fell by 24 percent. And there would be no quick reversal. Two years after the attacks, the number of international arrivals to the United States, including Canada and Mexico, had fallen from just over 51 million visits annually to just over 41 million.

IN THE TWO DECADES BEFORE the 9/11 attacks, globalization had produced substantial economic benefits for the United States and for much of the world. As of early 2001, the U.S. economy had enjoyed nearly two decades of robust growth, interrupted only by the brief and shallow recession of 1991, and the U.S. stock market had reached record highs. It seemed a virtuous circle. The lowering of trade and investment barriers through negotiated international agreements had allowed for a revolution in manufacturing processes in many industries, a revolution aided by enormous technological advances.

Prior to the late twentieth century, national boundaries had dictated production patterns. Most trade was in finished products made inside nations and then sold domestically or exported. Foreign direct investment largely took the form of multinational companies building smaller manufacturing plants in foreign countries in order to avoid tariffs and other import restrictions. Suppliers were located inside national borders, close to final assembly operations. During the 1980s and 1990s, the removal of trade and investment barriers, and the innovations in logistics and information technology that slashed costs for global transportation and communications created a different kind of capitalism. Vertically integrated companies were broken up into disaggregated global supply chains, with each part of the production process located in the most cost-efficient place. Capital and knowledge-intensive operations remained in the United States and other advanced countries, while increasing portions of labor-intensive assembly operations were outsourced to lower-wage countries from Mexico to China. Final production relied on the carefully timed and coordinated transport of components from across the world. The ability of U.S. companies to construct and coordinate the most efficient supply chains in the world became a big source of the country's competitive advantage.

It was not just the movement of goods that was integrating the world, but also the movement of people and ideas. Here, too, the United States enjoyed unmatched advantages. The country had become what Bill Gates, the founder of Microsoft, called an IQ magnet. "For generations, America has prospered largely by attracting the world's best and brightest to study, live and work in the United States," he told a congressional committee in March 2007. "Our success at attracting the greatest talent has helped us become a global innovation leader, enriched our culture, and created economic opportunities for all Americans." The United States has long beckoned to talented foreigners, those fleeing poverty and persecution or simply seeking opportunity. Enrico Fermi, who set off the first self-sustaining nuclear chain reaction, left Mussolini's Italy in 1938 and became a critical member of the Manhattan Project that allowed the United States to beat Nazi Germany in the atomic race. Edward Teller, the father of the hydrogen bomb, was a Hungarian Jew who had fled Germany in the 1930s. Andy Grove, one of the founders of the semiconductor giant Intel, was also a Hungarian who escaped to New York in 1956 after the Soviets crushed the Hungarian revolution. A similar list could go on many pages.

But the country had never seen a surge of foreign talent such as the one that took place in the last two decades of the twentieth century, when immigration to the United States rose to record levels. Sergey Brin, the cofounder of Google, was born in Moscow to Jewish parents, a mathematician and an economist, who fled from the Soviet Union in 1979 when Brin was just six years old. Vinod Khosla came from India to study engineering and business at Carnegie-Mellon and Stanford before going on to cofound Sun Microsystems and to set up one of Silicon Valley's first venture capital funds. Pierre Omidyar, the founder and chairman of eBay, was born in France to Iranian parents.

It was not just a few brilliant engineers and business leaders who came from abroad. As early as 1990, one-third of Silicon Valley's scientific and engineering workforce was made up of immigrants, primarily from China and India. By 1998, there were nearly 3,000 firms in the region led by a Chinese or an Indian chief executive, accounting for more than $16.8 billion in sales and 58,000 jobs. By the turn of the century, more than half of the Ph.D.-level engineers in the United States were foreign-born, as well as 45 percent of the Ph.D.-level life scientists, physical scientists, and computer scientists. Foreign-born scientists and engineers were also staffing research positions at many U.S. companies. Forty percent of the physical and life scientists in U.S. educational and health services and one-quarter of the physical scientists in manufacturing were from abroad.

In Washington, both the outgoing Clinton administration and the new Bush administration were avid supporters of that openness. Clinton had risked the wrath of the Democratic Party's trade union base by endorsing NAFTA, working closely with Republicans to help push the controversial trade pact through Congress in 1993 despite opposition from a majority of Democrats. Clinton went on to conclude negotiations and then win congressional approval of the massive Uruguay Round agreement that created the World Trade Organization. Then, in 1999, the Clinton administration negotiated China's entry into the WTO; this generated a surge of U.S. and other foreign investment in China, which helped to turn China into the world's second-largest exporting nation, after Germany but ahead of the United States, by the end of 2007. While both NAFTA and the Uruguay Round had been launched under

Republican administrations, the deals concluded by Clinton were responsible for tearing down more barriers to free global trade and investment than any other single administration had accomplished in U.S. history.

The story was similar on immigration. More new immigrants came to the United States in the 1990s than in any other single decade in the country's history. Only the first decade of the twentieth century had come close to matching those numbers. Most of the increase in the 1990s came through a generous system that encouraged the reunification of families, allowing immigrants who had already arrived in the United States to bring over not only spouses and children, but parents and siblings as well. The United States also opened its doors to more political refugees than ever before. And, despite efforts to tighten the border with Mexico, huge numbers of illegal migrants came as well, finding plentiful work on American farms, in hotels and restaurants, and in the booming construction industry. During the 1990s, both the administration and Congress were sympathetic to the pleas by U.S. high-tech companies to open the door to more foreign talent. Under pressure from U.S. computer, software, and semiconductor companies, Congress in 1998 raised the cap on H1-B visas—used by U.S. companies to hire skilled workers in short supply in the United States—from 65,000 to 115,000 annually; two years later Congress raised it to 195,000.

It was a record to please the most ardent globalist, yet when George W. Bush ran for president in 2000, he criticized the Clinton administration for not being liberal enough on either trade or immigration. On trade, he accused the Democrats of standing on the sidelines while Europe and Asia were pursuing new bilateral and regional agreements to reduce trade barriers further. The United States, he warned, would be left behind by its competitors if it did not become still more aggressive in pursuing trade opportunities around the world. On immigration, he promised to negotiate a new deal with Mexico that would provide a legal path for Mexicans to come and work in the United States. "Immigration is not a problem to be solved; it is the sign of a successful nation," he said in a February 2000 campaign speech. "New Americans are not to be feared as strangers; they are to be welcomed as neighbors." He called for making the INS "more immigrant friendly" by substantially reducing the amount of time needed to process applications. And he favored eliminating the caps that restricted U.S. companies from hiring foreign high-tech workers and similar limits on the hiring of temporary agricultural labor.

Bush came to office believing strongly that both open trade and a liberal immigration policy were crucial to the nation's future economic success. Even as 9/11 was transforming his presidency, there was no evidence that he was reconsidering either of those beliefs. Several days after the attacks, in fact, the president pulled Rob Bonner, his new Customs chief, aside. As Bonner recounts: "The president gave me a figurative thump on the chest and said: 'You've got to secure our borders against a terrorist threat. But you have to do it without shutting down the U.S. economy.'"

# Chapter 2

# THE PRESIDENT

OPENING THE U.S. BORDER WAS supposed to have been one of George W. Bush's presidential legacies. Along with education reform and tax cuts, it was one of only a handful of issues the former Texas governor felt passionately about when he came to the Oval Office in 2001.

Bush had staked out a clear position on immigration early in his career, especially on immigration from Mexico. In 1994, just weeks off his upset victory over incumbent Democrat Ann Richards in the Texas gubernatorial race, he put that on display during his first Republican Governors' Association meeting in Williamsburg, Virginia. The thirty Republican governors there were in a bullish mood, having taken a majority of the governors' chairs across the country. Nationally, voters had thrown the Democrats out of the House of Representatives for the first time in forty years in what Republican National Committee chairman Haley Barbour called "the greatest midterm sweep of this century." The governors were demanding that the new Republican majority in Washington begin dismantling federal programs and turning over more power to the states.

One of the new stars in the gubernatorial ranks was Pete Wilson of California, the most populous state in the United States. On the basis of his solid reelection, Wilson was already seen as a serious contender to be the 1996 Republican nominee for president. His signature issue had been support for a ballot question, Proposition 187, which would have denied public education, health benefits, and other social services to the state's illegal immigrants, most of them from Mexico. It further required local police for the first time to investigate the immigration status of anyone they detained, and to put into deportation proceedings those who were not in the country legally. Proposition 187 had been put on the ballot by local anti-immigration activists, with support from the Federation for American Immigration Reform (FAIR), a national lobby that favored reduced immigration, under the peculiar California rules that allow any issue to go to a popular vote if the signatures of at least 5 percent of voters can be gathered.

It quickly caught fire. California in the early 1990s was experiencing a rare and harsh recession that had hit the southern portion of the state particularly hard. Federal cutbacks in defense spending had led to the loss of thousands of jobs in aerospace and other military industries, while the state's high real estate and regulatory costs drove many companies to neighboring states. Yet from 1980 to 1990, illegal immigration had added 1 to 2 million people to the state's population, roughly a quarter of overall population growth. Legal and illegal immigration into the state had been running at more than 400,000 people a year, and the August 2000 Census would show that for the first time racial minorities outnumbered the state's white population.

The combination of high immigration, particularly of low-skilled Mexicans and other Latinos, and a grinding recession had worsened the gap between rich and poor. And California's local governments were handcuffed in their ability to provide services to the growing numbers of poor. Thanks to another plebiscite, Proposition 13 in 1978, municipal and county governments had been severely restricted in their ability to raise property taxes, denying them the resources to tackle the growing array of social and educational challenges brought by the new immigrants.

It was a combustible mixture and Wilson had stirred the coals, blaming immigration for California's rising budget deficits and demanding help from Washington. An August 1993 poll showed that 74 percent of Californians believed that illegal immigration was hurting the state. After a bitter and angry campaign, Proposition 187 had passed with nearly 59 percent support, while Wilson had easily defeated his Democratic opponent, Kathleen Brown, with 55 percent of the vote.

Despite his family name, Bush was virtually unknown, and certainly had none of the national stature that the immigration fight had brought to Wilson. At age forty-eight, he had never held public office before, having been defeated in a run for Congress in 1978. His 1994 victory in the governor's race over Richards, a strong incumbent, was attributed by the *New York Times* to "the national Republican surge and his own tightly focused conservative message." But on immigration, Bush's brand of conservatism was decidedly out of step with Wilson's. Within two days of his election victory, he was already distancing himself from Proposition 187, saying that "I am not opposed to educating or providing social services to people who are in our state."

Bush was not content to separate himself from Wilson in the press. At the governors' conference, he personally confronted the California governor and in front of other governors denounced Proposition 187 as a "catastrophic position." As the *Los Angeles Times* would later report on the exchange, Bush's bold challenge "left many political leaders stunned."

"He really minced no words," former Michigan governor John Engler, who had attended the meeting, said later. "He told Wilson 'You're wrong,' and that it was . . . a catastrophic position. He was very clear. He felt that Wilson had made the issue one where it had become an anti-Hispanic issue rather than a solution to illegal immigration."

Bush's beliefs about borders arose from a particular strain of western conservatism that was reinforced by his own life experiences. The Texas business community, from which Bush drew his greatest political and financial support, had long favored low-skilled immigration from Mexico. The steady supply of Mexican labor, whether through legal programs such as the bracero scheme—a large-scale temporary worker program from the 1940s to the 1960s—or through illegal immigration, had helped to keep wages down in agriculture, manufacturing, construction, domestic services, and the retail industry. For Bush, the free-market mantra of "matching willing workers with willing employers" was one he embraced as governor and would repeat throughout his presidency. And unlike California, which had relatively high taxes and generous social service programs, Texas had among the country's lowest taxes and stingiest public services. The Texas comptroller's office estimated in 2006 that the roughly 1.4 million illegal immigrants in the state paid out $500 million each year more in taxes than they received back in government services.

But the issue was personal for Bush as well. He was raised in Midland, Texas, where Hispanics number about a quarter of the population, by a Mexican housekeeper whom he later described as "a second mom." His own children were brought up by another Mexican nanny, Maria Galvan, who became a U.S. citizen at Bush's urging when he was Texas governor and later accompanied his family to the White House. His brother Jeb was married to a Latina. As governor and later as president, he promoted various Hispanics he saw as inspirational examples of the immigrant success story. The most prominent was his chief counsel and later attorney general, Alberto Gonzales, whose parents were migrant workers and whose grandparents had come to the United States from Mexico early in the twentieth century when there were no effective legal prohibitions against Mexicans who chose to move to the United States and stay permanently.

Immigration was a consistent theme in Bush's early forays onto the national stage. He repeatedly denounced efforts by Republicans in Washington to deny public education or welfare benefits to illegal immigrants. In the run-up to the Republican primaries for the 1996 presidential election, he penned a strongly worded *New York*

*Times* op-ed urging his party not to take "cheap shots" at Mexico. "The issues of the 1996 campaign will be emotional," he wrote. "There should be lively debate and discussion. But discussion about immigration and Mexico can turn ugly and destructive very quickly, severely damaging a positive and beneficial relationship." As he would throughout his presidency, and as Ronald Reagan had done for the Republican Party in the 1980s, he linked the issue of immigration closely to open trade. Freer trade, he wrote, "provides a much-needed boost for Mexico. As capitalism takes hold in that country, wages will begin to climb. As wages begin to climb, Mexico will strengthen its middle class. Then, and only then, will the problem of illegal immigration subside." On several occasions during the 1996 campaign, he picked a fight with Pat Buchanan, a former speechwriter for Richard Nixon who was running an independent campaign on the promise to dump NAFTA and build a wall along the U.S. border with Mexico. Bush denounced him as an isolationist and accused him of race-baiting. In the 2000 presidential campaign, he repeatedly personalized the issue, pleading with voters to consider what they would do if they faced the same dilemmas that confronted many illegal immigrants. "If people can't make a living at home, they have mouths to feed, and they are coming," he said in January 2000. "That's called family values, and they do not stop at the Rio Grande."

Nor was Mexico his only concern in the borders debate. In 1998, he was one of nine governors to sign a letter urging Washington to increase the number of highly skilled workers admitted to the United States, calling it crucial for the high-tech sector that was emerging in Texas.

If Bush's commitment to open borders was both ideological and personal, there was also a significant political dimension. His chief political adviser, Karl Rove, saw advantages in a liberal stance on immigration, even illegal immigration, believing that wooing the Hispanic vote away from the Democrats was central to making the Republicans a permanent majority in Washington. While American-born Hispanics were, like African Americans, an overwhelmingly Democratic constituency, foreign-born Hispanics were more open to the Republican message of faith and family values. With white voters in decline as a percentage of the population, and black voters unswervingly loyal to the Democrats, Hispanic, and to a lesser extent Asian, immigrants appeared to be the key Republican political constituencies of the future. To Bush, Hispanics seemed like a natural fit for the GOP. "As a Texan, I have known many immigrant families, mainly from Mexico, and I have seen what they add to our country," he said in a January 2004 speech on immigration reform. "They bring to America the values of faith in God, love of family, hard work and self-reliance, the values that made us a great nation to begin with."

Unlike Reagan, who had at times mused that the United States should just open its border entirely to Mexican workers, Bush was not in favor of dismantling all border controls. He had supported most of the efforts in the 1990s to beef up the Border Patrol and reduce the flow of illegal immigrants, though he had spoken out forcefully against building any sort of fence along the border. But for a Republican in the 1990s, he had gone extraordinarily far, not only in tolerating illegal immigrants, but in embracing them. As his nephew George P. Bush, the son of Jeb Bush and his wife Columba Garnica Gallo, had put it during the 2000 presidential primary campaign, when it came to Hispanics "our biggest challenge will be to separate my uncle from the rest of the Republican Party." Bush showed that such an effort could pay political dividends by increasing support among immigrant Hispanics in the country legally, who were taking out U.S. citizenship and registering to vote in growing numbers. In the 1994 governor's campaign he had learned some rudimentary Spanish, hoping to cut into Governor Richards's lock on the Hispanic vote. It was only moderately successful that year, when Bush took just a quarter of the Hispanic vote, but in his 1998 reelection he doubled that number. Then in the 2000 presidential election he won 35 percent of the Hispanic vote across the country and increased that to 40 percent in his 2004 reelection. Both elections were extremely close, and Bush would not have won either election without this strong showing among Spanish-speaking Americans.

GEORGE BUSH REPRESENTED ONE EXTREME of a national debate that stretches back to the end of the nineteenth century when the United States first began to impose curbs on unrestricted immigration. During this nation's first hundred years, its borders were truly open. A free person with the wherewithal to make the ocean journey to the New World was likely to find land to farm or a job for wages waiting for him when he arrived. Yet while America has mythologized its immigrant history, it has long been, as Daniel Tichenor writes, "profoundly ambivalent about the immigrant." It has welcomed them as hardworking contributors to the building of a nation but then turned around and barred them as threats to the country's security, its native-born workers, or even its identity as a nation.

From the first efforts at immigration and border control, the goal of U.S. policy was never to bar immigrants entirely, or to turn back all those who wanted to travel to its shores. Even in its most isolationist period, between the two world wars, the United States never tried to seal off the country. Instead, the goal of American border and immigration policies has been to separate the desirable from the undesirable, to make and enforce a distinction between newcomers who were seen as building the country and those who, it was feared, would tear it down. The very first immigration enforcement law ever enacted by Congress, in 1798, permitted the deportation of anyone deemed by the president to be dangerous to the country.

Over its history, Americans who favored high levels of immigration and travel to the United States took a broad view of the benefits and a narrow view of the threats, while immigration opponents took the opposite stand. The country has swung from open-door to closed-door policies as that perception of benefits and threats has shifted. The dilemma that faced the country after 9/11—how to let in those visitors, students, and immigrants the country wanted and needed while keeping out those who might do it harm—was given new urgency by the terrorist attacks. But it was an old problem that had never found a satisfactory solution.

For most of American history, the tools used to enforce such distinctions were crude, carried out through immigration or border control policies that discriminated against certain ethnic groups or nationalities that were deemed to pose the greatest threats to the United States. The first national bill regulating immigration was rather bluntly named the Chinese Exclusion Act. Passed in 1882, it responded to popular anger that Chinese laborers were driving down wages, and was further justified by a then not wholly disrespectable sort of racism that feared Asian migration would threaten the purity of Anglo-Saxon culture. For roughly two decades, from the 1860s to the 1880s, the United States had actively encouraged migration from China to meet the surging demands for labor to build the railroads and work the mines of the opening West. From 1850 until the early 1880s, roughly 250,000 Chinese came to the United States, most remaining in California, where they were lauded by the state's governor as "one of our most worthy classes of newly adopted citizens." In 1868 the U.S. Congress signed a treaty with China opening trade and promising that Chinese who emigrated to the United States would enjoy the same rights and protections as American citizens.

The Chinese were a small fraction of the more than 7.5 million people, mostly British, Germans, and Irish, who came to the United States over that same period. But they aroused greater fear and resentment. A softening of the California economy in the late 1860s helped create widespread opposition to further Chinese immigration. The 1882 Chinese Exclusion Act passed in Washington barred all immigration from China and made it easier to deport those already in the country. Over the next three decades, the Chinese population in the United States would fall by more than 40,000.

The act would have little effect on overall levels of immigration, however. During the first decade of the twentieth century, the

United States would see the highest levels of immigration relative to its population of any time before or since. From 1901 to 1910, 8 million people, mostly from Italy, Russia, Hungary, and other countries in southern and eastern Europe, would make the journey to the United States. Those numbers would continue to swell, reaching a record 1.4 million people in 1914, on the eve of World War I.

But from that apogee, the United States would not see similar levels of immigration for another three-quarters of a century. The conflagration that engulfed Europe for the next four years decisively tilted the American debate on immigration. Chinese exclusion had been driven by a sense of economic threat, the fear that Chinese laborers were willing to work for lower wages, thus taking money out of the pockets of an earlier generation of immigrants. And it had come from cultural fears—often expressed in blatantly racist terms—that Asian immigrants could not easily be assimilated into a Christian, mostly English-speaking country. But the war added a new and potent element. Old World conflicts that had left millions of dead on the battlefields of France and Belgium, and a Communist revolution in Russia that seemed an existential threat to a country built on free markets and democratic governance, raised new fears that immigrants could endanger the country's security. It was that fear that was decisive in tipping the country against an open immigration policy.

In June 1919, followers of the Italian anarchist Luigi Galleani, who had been driven out of Europe and fled to the United States in 1901, detonated bombs in eight American cities. In Washington, D.C., the explosive was triggered prematurely, spewing the body of the bomber across several city blocks and damaging rather than destroying the home of its intended target, Attorney General A. Mitchell Palmer. It was the second time Galleanists had tried to kill Palmer; the first was with an unsuccessful mail bomb. Such terrorist violence, and the fear that more violence could be imported, finally turned the country against the open immigration regime of the prewar period. Most telling was the split it created in American business, which had been a powerful lobby in favor of unrestricted immigration before the war. After the war, many big companies began to fear that the new immigrants from southern and eastern Europe would spread radical ideas that could threaten the capitalist system. In 1919, Palmer ordered the summary arrest or deportation of hundreds of suspected communist or anarchist radicals, and by 1920 the raids had swept up thousands of union organizers, socialists, and Communist Party members, or those suspected of such affiliations. The terrorists responsible for the bombings, however, were never found.

The raids were quickly followed by much broader prohibitions. In 1920, the new Republican Congress ordered the expulsion of any foreigner who "advised, advocated, taught, or published any views promoting the overthrow of government, or were somehow affiliated with organizations which did so." In 1921, Congress passed what was then the most restrictive immigration law in the country's history, imposing tight quotas based on national origins. It capped the total number of immigrants at 355,000 per year and greatly reduced the numbers permitted from southern and eastern Europe, largely on the grounds that immigrants from those countries were more likely to embrace "Bolshevik revolution, anarchy and other forms of political radicalism." In 1924, the law was further tightened to permit fewer than 200,000 immigrants annually, with just 16 percent of those from southern and eastern Europe. Asians were excluded entirely, demonstrating the toxic mixture of racist and security concerns that propelled the new restrictions. In 1929 the overall immigration cap was reduced again, to fewer than 160,000. Those limits would survive for more than a generation.

Despite efforts by both the Democratic Truman and Republican Eisenhower administrations in the 1950s to end national origin quotas, the practice of trying to distinguish desirable from undesirable immigrants based on their nationality or ethnicity remained the overriding feature of U.S. immigration policy until the middle of the 1960s.

THE RESPONSIBILITY FOR LETTING IN the good migrants and keeping out the bad ones fell mostly on the Immigration and Naturalization Service. The INS came to life in 1864 as the Bureau of Immigration, created as part of "An Act to Encourage Immigration" that was passed by Congress at Abraham Lincoln's request to address the acute Civil War–era labor shortage. Its original mission was to spread the word in Europe that the United States was open and eager for new immigrants. Lacking any real authority over the states, the bureau disappeared four years later, but then was reborn following the passage of the first comprehensive national immigration law, the Immigration Act of 1891. It was initially housed in the Department of Labor because its primary purpose was to bring sufficient workers from abroad to meet the demands of the growing U.S. economy. It was renamed in 1933 and then moved from the Department of Labor to the Justice Department in 1940 to reflect its new World War II mission of keeping foreign enemy agents out of the country. The INS was charged, for instance, with implementing the Alien Registration Act of 1940, also known as the Smith Act, which required registering and fingerprinting all foreigners entering the country and any non-U.S. citizen over the age of fourteen who was already living in the United States.

From the start, the INS was an agency at odds with itself. On the one hand, it was supposed to be filled with helpful, courteous staff who made travelers and intended immigrants feel welcomed to the country. On the other hand, it was supposed to uphold the nation's immigration laws, which meant effectively, and sometimes harshly, enforcing the rules against illegal entry. Its most important law—the Immigration and Nationality Act of 1952—has been amended and tinkered with by Congress so many times that it is an incoherent jumble of conflicting mandates.

The agency faced enormous pressure and dissent from all sides of the immigration debate. The travel industry and its allies in Congress demanded that the INS do everything possible to streamline the entry of tourists and other temporary travelers into the country. In 1990, under pressure from the travel industry and the airlines, Congress passed a law requiring that all foreign travelers be cleared through primary inspection at airports in less than forty-five minutes. That gave license to any member of Congress who wanted to complain about one of his constituents waiting an hour in line before getting back into the country. Prior to 9/11, the administration had been determined to do even better than that, setting a goal of completing airport inspections in an average of thirty minutes and land border inspections in an average of twenty minutes. Universities wanted large numbers of foreign students; business wanted a steady supply of foreign workers. And activists representing a broad array of ethnic groups, whose numbers were strengthened by the high immigration levels of the 1980s and 1990s, demanded further measures to reunify families and speed up the cumbersome process for legal immigration. At the same time, public pressure was growing to crack down on the rising number of illegal migrants, who were burdening schools and hospitals in the southwestern states and disrupting U.S. border towns that faced the nightly dash across the border by those hoping to find work in the United States. "You're caught between the exclusionists and the expansionists, between the nativists and the internationalists," said Michael Cronin, who held a series of senior INS positions over a three-decade career with the agency. "There's almost never a winning position."

Not surprisingly, the INS was never very good at its job. Report after report would skewer it as dysfunctional and suggest radical overhauls that were never carried out. But that did not stop Congress and successive administrations from throwing more and more money at the agency to try to make it work better. From 1975 to 1990, the INS budget tripled and the number of employees more than doubled. But by every measure, the agency's ability to carry out its mandate continued to deteriorate. The 1990s would see an even more aggressive effort to do more of the same, however. Mike Becraft, a career army man who joined the INS in 1993 after heading up the global counterdrug effort for the Joint Chiefs of Staff, said that over his decade with the agency it grew from a budget of $1.2 billion and a staff of 17,000 to a budget of $6.2 billion and a staff of 37,000. "We were expected to do everything right, and we didn't. You were forcing all this change on what had been a backwater organization."

THE INS HAD PROBLEMS AT both ends of its mission: the right people did not get in and the wrong people were not kept out. In 1990 Congress created the U.S. Commission on Immigration Reform, also known as the Jordan Commission, to propose remedies. According to the commission, "Serious problems undermine present immigration policies, their implementation and their credibility: people who should get in find a cumbersome process that often impedes their entry; people who should not get in find it all too easy to enter; and people who are here without permission remain with impunity."

On what was known as the service side of the organization—which involved processing applications for immigrant visas and citizenship—the system was defined by its backlogs. As the number of applications grew in the late 1980s and 1990s, it became increasingly difficult for the INS to make decisions in any sort of timely fashion. A huge industry of immigration lawyers grew up to try to help individuals manage the complicated process for entering, working, and staying in the United States while dealing with a bureaucracy that was incapable of making prompt judgments. In 1994, the INS set an internal goal of processing within four months all green card applications by foreigners already living in the United States and all applications for U.S. citizenship. But by the end of 1995 the average wait time instead grew to between ten and seventeen months. Between 1994 and 2000, the backlog of applications increased fourfold to nearly 4 million. There was a flood of new citizenship applications after Congress—responding to public anger over illegal immigration—voted to outlaw welfare and other public benefits for legal permanent residents, many of whom decided to take out citizenship. As of September 2001, nearly three-quarters of a million citizen applications had been sitting with the INS for more than twenty-one months waiting for processing.

On the enforcement side, the INS faced problems in almost every part of its mandate to keep out unwanted migrants. While most of the political focus was on shoring up the southern border, nearly 40 percent of those living illegally had initially come to the United States legally, most on tourist visas, and simply failed to go home. The system for preventing overstays was laughably archaic. When foreign tourists arrived in the United States, they would fill out an I-94 form, which required basic information like a name, birth date, nationality, passport number, and the address or addresses they would be staying at in the United States. The INS agent waiting at the counter would stamp the form, tear it in half, and return the departure stub to the tourist. When travelers arrived back at the airport to return home, they were supposed to give that stub to the agent at the airline counter; the airline would then deliver the stub, and thousands of others, to the INS. Eventually, the INS would enter the data into its computer system in an effort to determine whether the individual had left the country as required. In practice, however, there was no enforcement; only a small percentage of the I-94s were ever returned to the airlines, and the INS had utterly no idea which travelers had left and which had remained illegally in the United States. As Jim Williams, the official who after 9/11 was tasked with creating a workable entry-exit system, put it sarcastically: "If you dropped off your I-94, if you filled it out correctly, if someone could read your handwriting, if they typed it into the system correctly, then we had a fully functioning exit system."

If foreign visitors were caught overstaying their visa, there was little chance they would be forced to leave. While the Border Patrol would immediately return any Mexican caught sneaking across the southern border, those from other countries could not be dealt with so easily. The United States had far too few detention beds in which to house illegal immigrants pending deportation from the country. The vast majority, therefore, were dealt with through what became known as "catch and release." When the Border Patrol apprehended an illegal immigrant, he or she was usually released and ordered to appear at a later hearing before a deportation judge. While there were no good statistics, it was estimated that between 40 and 90 percent of those released never showed up for their hearings, instead disappearing again into the country. A Palestinian terrorist convicted for his role in a 1997 plot to set off a pipe bomb in the Brooklyn subway had tried three times to sneak across the border from Canada. On his fourth try, Canada refused to take him back, and the United States placed him in deportation proceedings. He was released and ordered to appear in court, but was arrested in his apartment before any hearing was held.

The INS also relied on a procedure known as "voluntary departure," in which someone caught in the country illegally would be given the chance to leave voluntarily without a formal deportation order, thereby avoiding a ten-year ban on his returning to the United States. But the Justice Department's inspector general estimated that as many as half of those who agreed to leave voluntarily never did so. Finally, even after an individual was ordered deported, many simply failed to show up at the airport to leave the country, and the INS made scant effort to track down those "absconders," who were thought to number in the hundreds of thousands.

Most of those in the United States illegally worked and stayed out of trouble, but the agency's efforts to keep out the truly undesirable were no more effective. In 1989, Congress had provided funding for the INS to develop a fingerprinting system known as IDENT for illegal migrants. The goal was to help the agency accurately identify illegal immigrants with known criminal records, including terrorists, as well as those who had been ordered deported or repeatedly caught entering the country unlawfully. When the INS apprehended an illegal immigrant, inspectors or Border Patrol agents were required to take two fingerprints to check against an INS database that contained the names of 240,000 criminals or terrorists, 300,000 absconders who had been ordered deported, and another 4 million who had previously been apprehended as illegal aliens.

But in 1998, a Mexican citizen named Angel Maturino Reséndiz, who had spent most of two decades coming and going illegally across the southern border, raped, stabbed, and bludgeoned to death Claudia Benton, a Houston pediatrician and mother of twin daughters. He was later linked to as many as fifteen murders, and in June 1999 he was put on the list of the FBI's Ten Most Wanted Fugitives. Reséndiz was well known to U.S. law enforcement. Since his first reported entry into the United States in 1976, he had run afoul of the law some two dozen times and been arrested for trespassing, burglary, auto theft, and aggravated battery. He served six years of a twenty-year prison sentence from 1980 to 1985, as well as numerous shorter jail terms in the United States. If anyone should have been a red flag in the IDENT system, it was Reséndiz. Yet in 1998 alone, prior to the Benton murder, Reséndiz had been apprehended by the Border Patrol seven times in Texas and New Mexico; each time he had been fingerprinted in the IDENT system and then released into Mexico. According to a Justice Department investigation, none of Reséndiz's extensive criminal history had been entered into IDENT. Incredibly, in June 1999, when the FBI was on a manhunt for Reséndiz, he was again apprehended by the Border Patrol, which instead of holding him took his fingerprints and returned him to Mexico. By that time, his record of illegal entries in 1998 had been entered into the computer system, but the agents did not deem that sufficient grounds for detaining him. He snuck back into the United States and committed four more murders that month before finally being arrested in July 1999. He was sentenced to death by a Texas jury in 2000 for the Benton murder and executed in 2006.

Overall, according to the Justice Department's inspector general, the IDENT system was so full of holes that such a mistake was utterly predictable. In 1998, the INS was only taking fingerprints from 40 percent of those deported, and including photos of less than a quarter—even though photographs were critical to confirming identity. And most INS agents were only dimly aware of the existence of the database, having received a pamphlet from headquarters but no training on the new system.

IN POLITICAL TERMS, HOWEVER, THE INS's biggest failing was not with visa overstayers or criminal aliens but with its inability to stop the growing numbers of illegal migrants from Mexico and Central America who were coming to the United States to seek jobs and a better life for themselves and their families. The aggregate numbers of Mexicans seeking work in the United States was remarkably stable for most of the twentieth century, averaging between 200,000 and 350,000 each year. What changed was the legal regime in the United States. Up until the 1930s, Mexicans were allowed into the country with virtually no controls, and during World War II and in the decade after, the United States established large guest worker schemes. But after 1965, when Congress passed a major immigration law that reopened the doors to most of the world, it shut down many of the Mexican guest worker programs. Mexicans began to enter the United States illegally in roughly the same numbers they had been entering under the legal guest worker programs. While it did not much change the economics, the result was a growing political problem.

In 1986, after more than a decade of difficult political debate and failed initiatives, Congress passed the Immigration Reform and Control Act (IRCA) in an effort to get control over the growing numbers of illegal migrants. Based on the recommendations of a congressional commission, the bill was a grand bargain. President Ronald Reagan, despite coming from the same California that would later spawn Pete Wilson and Proposition 187, was if anything more laissez-faire on immigration than George W. Bush. He had once told voters in Texas that the answer to the illegal immigration problem was to welcome in Mexican workers "for whatever length of time they want to stay." Despite his overall popularity, that view was deeply out of touch with public sentiment, which wanted the government to curb illegal immigration. The bargain called for a one-time amnesty for the nearly 3 million foreigners who had been living illegally in the United States for at least four years, in exchange for future measures to tighten controls at the border and enforce new penalties on employers who hired undocumented workers. When he signed the bill, Reagan called the employer sanction provision the "keystone," saying it would "remove the incentive for illegal immigration by eliminating the job opportunities which draw illegal aliens here."

In practice, the only part of the bill that worked as anticipated was the amnesty; several million illegal immigrants came out from the shadows to seize the offer of legal permanent residence. But the critical employer sanction provisions, which were supposed to dry up the demand for illegal migrant labor, were stillborn. To the Reagan administration and its business allies, tough employer sanctions smacked of the intrusive government regulation that the Republicans had pledged to tear down. The bill contained watered-down language that prohibited companies only from "knowingly" hiring illegal workers, a standard that produced a cottage industry in forged Social Security cards. And the Reagan administration did little to enforce even that toothless sanction. The bill had authorized $100 million annually to enforce employer sanctions, but only $34 million was spent in 1987 and $59 million in 1988, dropping to less than $30 million each year after that.

Nor was the administration any warmer to the identification requirements that would have been needed to make such a scheme work. The Social Security card, which was and remains the chief form of federal identity used for work authorization purposes, was virtually useless in helping companies decide which workers were illegal immigrants. As a paper document with no photograph or other identifier, it was extremely easy to forge. In practice, most employees were never even asked for the card but simply had to write down a number. The Social Security Administration made little or no effort to weed out fraudulent numbers, happy to collect the additional billions of dollars that all employees, legal or otherwise, were charged in Social Security taxes.

The congressional commission that in 1981 made many of the recommendations that were incorporated in the 1986 legislation had called for the creation of a secure national identification card, saying it was the linchpin for ensuring that employers hired only legal residents. An internal task force of administration bureaucrats set up by President Reagan endorsed the commission's major finding and recommended that the president agree to a national ID card and to criminal penalties against any employer who hired a worker without one. But many in Reagan's cabinet loathed the idea, seeing it as a government threat to individual privacy, civil liberties, and religious freedom. When the recommendation was presented to a cabinet meeting in 1981, the president's domestic policy adviser suggested that, rather than a costly ID card, the government should simply "tattoo an identification number on the inside of everybody's arm."

Reagan, who shared his adviser's antipathy toward the initiative, smiled and joked: "Maybe we should just brand all the babies." Not surprisingly, by the time the administration and Congress had finally negotiated the details of the 1986 bill, there was no provision for a secure identification scheme.

THAT LEFT BORDER ENFORCEMENT AS the government's only tool for staunching illegal migration. Following the 1986 law, the INS estimated that the number of illegal migrants in the United States continued to increase by about 300,000 each year. On September 19, 1993, the chief of the Border Patrol in the El Paso sector, Silvestre Reyes, decided he was fed up with playing cat-and-mouse with illegal immigrants, chasing them down after they had crossed the border into Texas. Instead, he took 400 of his 650 agents and deployed them on round-the-clock duty along the twenty-mile stretch of the border where most of the crossings were occurring. The results were almost immediate. In July of that year, his agents apprehended nearly 1,200 illegal migrants every day; by November that number had fallen to 75. Crime in El Paso began to fall and local approval of the initiative was nearly 100 percent. Operation Blockade, which was later toned down to the more politically acceptable Operation Hold the Line, was emulated across the southern border states. With the 1994 midterm congressional and state elections looming, politicians from across the country flew to El Paso to see the results for themselves and lend their support to Reyes, who would go on to became the first Hispanic elected to Congress from his Texas district. Nowhere was there more interest than in Pete Wilson's California.

President Bill Clinton had already been facing an outcry from California over illegal immigration. During the 1994 gubernatorial election, the Wilson campaign had flashed the White House telephone number on its campaign advertisements and encouraged voters to call Clinton and "ask him to control our border." With public sentiment in California mostly behind the Republican Wilson on the issue, Clinton did not want to give the impression that Democrats were weak on illegal immigration. In September 1994 his attorney general, Janet Reno, unveiled Operation Gatekeeper, an enforcement initiative aimed primarily at stopping the thousands of Mexicans who were running across the border near Tijuana and disappearing into the suburban communities south of San Diego. The Border Patrol immediately sent another 200 agents to the San Diego border with Tijuana and requested funding from Congress for an additional 700 in 1995. The operation doubled the 1993 level of deportations, increased efforts to prosecute immigrant smugglers, and authorized the construction of steel border fences, along with powerful stadium lights and motion sensors.

The first phase went into effect on October 1, 1994, with the new agents deployed along the fourteen-mile stretch of border from the Pacific Ocean inland. It was hoped that this show of force would discourage illegal immigrants from entering the United States, or at least force them to cross farther east in less populated mountainous regions where they were vulnerable to apprehension. Apprehensions went up threefold to 825 on the first day of the operation compared to the same time a year earlier. It was not an easy battle; at some places along the new steel barricades, Mexicans tried to dig tunnels underneath the border, which led the Border Patrol to anchor the fence in concrete and extend it as much as ten feet underground. But it had the desired effect of pushing the problem out of the urban San Diego region.

The INS judged the enforcement operations of the 1990s a success. In its first year, Operation Gatekeeper was estimated to have reduced illegal crossings by about 65 percent along the first five miles from the Pacific Ocean inland. By 2000, illegal border crossings in the San Diego region, which had once been the highest in the country, had dropped to a twenty-four-year low. Similar declines were seen in other populated areas, like El Paso, where the INS had concentrated its enforcement resources and where a majority of illegal immigrants had once crossed. But tough enforcement had the paradoxical effect of exacerbating the very problem it had been designed to solve.

FOR GENERATIONS, MANY MEXICANS HAD crossed with the seasons to work in the United States. Jeff Flake, a Republican congressman from Arizona who was one of the leading figures in the failed congressional effort at immigration reform that was launched in 2005, grew up on a huge ranch in Snowflake, Arizona. The town was named after his Mormon ancestors who had been sent by Brigham Young in the late nineteenth century to find new lands to settle. In the 1970s, when Flake's father ran an enterprise where a thousand cattle roamed over some 200,000 acres of high desert, the family would employ dozens of Mexican migrants to grow the corn and alfalfa that the cattle needed for the winter. Periodically the local Border Patrol would raid the ranch, round up any illegal workers, and send them back to Mexico. Most of them would return in a day or two and continue working. The record was held by a Mexican named Manuel Chidez, who was arrested nineteen times by the border agents but promptly came back to the ranch every time.

"There was virtually no control at the border," Flake said. "They would go back for birthdays, for Christmas, for holidays, because they could always come back across the border easily." But the increased border enforcement measures of the 1990s changed all that, ending what migration scholars have called the "circularity" of the labor flow between Mexico and the United States. As crossing the border became more difficult and dangerous, many illegal migrants felt they had no choice but to stay in the United States. Not wanting to be alone, they would smuggle their families across the border as well, settling into American communities and sending their kids to local schools. The new enforcement, coupled with a demographic bulge and a series of economic crises in Mexico, resulted in an explosion of illegal migrants putting down roots in the United States. With the road back to Mexico blocked, many began to move farther and farther from the border states of California, Arizona, New Mexico, and Texas. From 1920 through 1970, the number of Mexicans living in the United States had been remarkably stable, rising and falling from about 500,000 in 1920 to as low as 375,000 in 1940 and back up to 700,000 by 1970. But from then the numbers grew rapidly, reaching 2.2 million in 1980 and doubling to 4.3 million in 1990 following the 1986 amnesty. By 2000, that figure would double again, to more than 9 million.

"What was a circular pattern of migration became a settled pattern," Flake said. "In the 1970s and 1980s, the average time here for migrant labor was about two years; now it's over ten years. What we've managed to do so far at the border is to keep people from going back. I don't know that we've stopped anyone who really wants to get in from getting in. We've made it far more expensive and far more dangerous to come across, so those who are coming for work are going to come and stay."

What was happening on the Flake ranch was happening in the rest of the country as well. Prior to 1986, about 45 percent of Mexican migrants had returned home; by 2002 that number had fallen to 25 percent. It was not hard to see why. Crossing the border illegally had become a life-threatening undertaking. Over the decade, the number of Border Patrol agents grew from just over 3,000 to more than 9,000, with almost all of those deployed along the border with Mexico. But instead of reducing the number of illegal migrants coming across the border, enforcement drove them farther into remote and inhospitable deserts and created a thriving business for immigrant smugglers. According to Border Patrol officials, when Operation Gatekeeper went into effect the rates that immigrant smugglers, or coyotes, were charging quickly shot up from $300 to $700; by 1999 it had risen to $1,200, a figure large enough to attract the interest of Mexican organized crime, turning human smuggling into an operation almost as profitable as drug smuggling. But, financed by relatives already in the United States, the high cost for the coyotes did little to deter new border crossers. According to Peter Andreas, one of the leading academic experts on border enforcement, "By disrupting the traditional routes and methods of clandestine entry, law enforcement has transformed the once relatively simple illegal act of crossing the border into a more complex system of illegal practices."

The price was not the only thing that went up. The death rate among illegal border crossers soared; by the year 2000 more than five hundred people a year were dying in the deserts from dehydration, sunstroke, hypothermia, or snakebite, a fivefold increase in just five years. In May 2001, fourteen illegal Mexican immigrants were found dead of heat exhaustion and dehydration in the Arizona desert more than thirty miles from the nearest road or building. More than two dozen were abandoned with little water in 115-degree temperatures.

The deaths outraged officials on both sides of the border, even though they were the inevitable consequences of the enforcement policies the United States was enacting. "It is one of the most horrible deaths that can occur for a human being," said Johnny Williams, the INS regional director. "It is a grisly, terrible, terrible death."

GEORGE W. BUSH CAME TO the presidency in 2001 wanting to fix the illegal immigration problem, and he appeared to have an opportunity. Unlike in the 1996 Republican primary where Bush had battled his party's restrictionist wing, the 2000 election was not marked by any significant divisions over immigration or border security. His chief rival for the Republican nomination, Senator

John McCain, held similarly liberal views on immigration, and the booming economy, a record-high stock market, and low unemployment helped to keep the issue off the table in the general election campaign. Bush had made a few campaign promises aimed at appealing to Hispanic voters, including better service from the INS, but he had largely avoided the issue.

On entering the White House, however, he wanted to do something dramatic to solve the Mexican border problems. Within his first week in office, he had named one of his top aides, Josh Bolten, to lead an internal task force study on the issue.

He also had an eager partner on the Mexican side. President Vicente Fox was, like Bush, a border state politician, having been governor of the northern Mexican state of Guanajuato when Bush was governor of Texas. He was also, like Bush, a businessman, who had worked his way up to become the youngest chief executive of Mexico's Coca-Cola subsidiary. The two had first met in 1996 and got along immediately. While Fox later described his first impression of Bush as "quite simply the cockiest man I have ever met in my life," he took an immediate liking to him. Bush "reminded me of the brash Coca-Cola execs from Atlanta or the friendly, boisterous Texans who used to buy our carrots and onions on the streets of McAllen," the Texas border town just north of where Fox grew up in Mexico. He was flattered by Bush's effort to use his "grade-school Spanish" and surprised to find "this cultural sensitivity, together with a depth of knowledge about Mexican immigrants and a real compassion for the Latino citizens who lived, worked, prayed and voted in his state."

In 2000, Fox had been elected Mexico's president in one of the first truly free elections in the country's history, ending the century-long monopoly by the PRI. Since being elected, he had put the migration issue at the top of his agenda, even arguing that the two countries would eventually need to embrace a "NAFTA for people" in which labor would move across the two borders as freely as goods and capital. It was a controversial stance that aroused suspicion in the United States, but it had helped to put the subject on the table for negotiation. Fox had also expressed his admiration for the European Union model, in which trade liberalization was accompanied by cash transfers aimed at improving the economies of its poorest members as quickly as possible. Bush had already panned the idea as politically impossible when the two met in 1996, but Fox continued to push it.

Despite their differing visions, the men shared a common desire to end the tragic and dysfunctional status quo on immigration. In a pointed gesture, Bush did not take the traditional first presidential trip to Canada, but went instead to meet Fox on his ranch in San Cristobel, Mexico, in February 2001. In a joint statement, the two presidents agreed on the need for "an orderly framework for migration that ensures humane treatment [and] legal security, and dignifies labor conditions. For this purpose, we are directing our Governments to engage, at the earliest opportunity, in formal high-level negotiations aimed at achieving short- and long-term agreements that will allow us to constructively address migration and labor issues between our two countries." They agreed to set up a cabinet-level commission chaired on the U.S. side by Secretary of State Colin Powell and Attorney General John Ashcroft, and by their counterparts on the Mexican side, Foreign Minister Jorge Castañeda and Interior Minister Santiago Creel.

There remains much disagreement over what the two presidents meant by their joint declaration. Castañeda and the Mexican negotiators insist that the language clearly shows that the two sides had agreed to a comprehensive negotiation on all aspects of the immigration issue, which included, most importantly, the treatment of illegal Mexican migrants already in the United States and a scheme for orderly, legal migration in the future. The joint communiqué issued after the first meeting of the high-level working group, which was held in Washington on April 4, 2001, seemed to reinforce that impression. It said the two governments "recognized that the components of the agenda form a single undertaking" and that they were "seeking an in-depth solution on migration."

Many of the Americans disagree. John Maisto, who was the

top White House official in charge of Western Hemisphere affairs, said the United States never saw the talks as a formal negotiation. "The idea was to do it piece by piece, not something broad and overarching, because [Bush] didn't think it would sell politically." Jeffrey Davidow, who was the U.S. ambassador to Mexico at the time, said the United States always referred to the meetings as "conversations" or "discussions" rather than negotiations. He insisted, somewhat disingenuously, that the phrase "single undertaking" meant only that the United States had agreed to discuss the whole range of migration issues with Mexico, not that Washington favored a comprehensive deal.

The United States was also divided internally. Powell's State Department, which took the lead in the negotiations, was favorable to a broad deal that encompassed "regularization," or amnesty, for Mexicans already working illegally in the United States, a temporary worker program for the future, revisions to U.S. programs for seasonal agricultural workers, and cooperative efforts to reduce the number of deaths in the border region. But Ashcroft's Justice Department had a much narrower vision and was opposed to any amnesty plan that could be perceived as rewarding lawbreaking. It was pushing an alternative proposal, to which Powell strongly objected, that would have allowed only for a new temporary guest worker program.

In addition, despite Bush's political vision of bringing Hispanics into the Republican Party, there were many in the party who disagreed, including some members of the White House Domestic Policy Council, which was given the lead on the immigration portfolio.

George Lannon, who was one of the top State Department officials working on the deal, said that Ashcroft and officials in the DPC made it clear that they opposed amnesty, fearing that, like the 1986 amnesty, it would simply create another generation of Democratic voters. Other State Department officials say that Ashcroft was working to kill the negotiations well before 9/11, and President Fox would later write that Ashcroft had opposed the effort "with every legalistic argument the Justice Department could dredge up."

Even if the administration had been united, there was plenty of political opposition. Davidow describes a January 2001 meeting in Mexico City with Senator Phil Gramm, a conservative Texas Republican with enough clout to have blocked any deal. Asked whether there was any chance of Congress agreeing to an amnesty for illegal Mexican immigrants, he replied, "No way. The Democrats just want to get more of these people into the country so they will become citizens and vote for them. That's not going to happen." Later, Gramm would say that amnesty would only be approved over his "cold, dead body."

Despite the obstacles, and they were serious and perhaps insurmountable ones, the negotiations continued throughout the summer of 2001. Cabinet officials met again in August, setting the stage for a September 6 visit to Washington by President Fox. While the summit achieved no negotiating breakthroughs, and in diplomatic code both sides acknowledged the difficult issues they faced on the migration issue, the visit was an enormous political success. Fox was treated to a White House dinner and was given a standing ovation after a speech to Congress. He flew to Ohio for a campaign-style event with President Bush, where the two leaders competed to find new synonyms for friendship. The joint communiqué from the meetings said "the deliberations reflected the most frank and productive dialogue that had ever taken place over such a relevant issue for both nations."

They ordered their officials to keep working on the details of an agreement. The two sides met in the White House on the morning of 9/11. It was the last meeting they would have.

# Chapter 3

# THE COPS

THE NINETEEN NAMES THAT THE Customs Service had provided to the FBI that morning set off what would become the biggest investigation in the bureau's history. Agents immediately began checking the credit card and telephone records of the suspected hijackers, attempting to identify anyone whose path had crossed any of the terrorists'. By the end of the day, they were chasing down dozens of leads across the country, propelled by the urgent fear that 9/11 might be only the beginning of an even more devastating series of attacks. Within three days, the FBI had deployed more than 4,000 special agents, while the INS had reassigned 1,000 of its agents to work with the bureau on the investigation. There was, as one senior Justice Department official put it, "a real, not an imagined, threat that we had more coming."

But as Attorney General John Ashcroft would later acknowledge, there was not much for the FBI to go on. "The U.S. government and its elaborate net of security and intelligence-gathering agencies had far too little real awareness of what the terrorist presence within the United States actually was in the days after 9/11," he later wrote. Nor was there any obvious way to begin gathering such intelligence, since the FBI had pitifully few contacts among Arab Americans or Muslims, who were the most likely sources to help the bureau in identifying anyone considering a follow-on attack.

So that night, Ashcroft gathered all of his senior officials in a conference room adjacent to the FBI's Strategic Information Operations Center (SIOC), an enormous, windowless expanse of computers and large video display screens. The officials in the meeting included Ashcroft; his deputy Larry Thompson; his chief of staff David Ayres; FBI director Robert Mueller; Michael Chertoff, who headed Justice's criminal division and would later go on to become secretary of Homeland Security; and Jim Ziglar, the commissioner of the INS. They began discussing strategies for disrupting any new terrorist plots. What they needed they did not have, which was a sophisticated intelligence network that might allow them to identify a small number of potentially threatening individuals who could be hiding anywhere among the 300 million people who lived in the United States, or among the millions more still coming to the country from abroad. They began instead to discuss a much cruder approach, one that would later be dubbed the "spit on the sidewalk" strategy. As Ashcroft put it: "If a terrorism suspect committed any legal infraction at all, regardless how minor, we would apprehend and charge him." By creating what he called "noise in the system," the attorney general and his top officials hoped to throw any would-be attackers off balance and buy time until a more robust defense could be built.

But who was a terrorism suspect? Just hours after the attacks, the FBI knew only one thing for certain—that all nineteen were young Muslim men of Middle Eastern descent. And what was a "legal infraction"? While the idea was to use any minor violation as a pretense for holding a suspect, in reality there was only one tool that gave the FBI the powers that Ashcroft wanted it to have, which was to sweep terrorist suspects off the streets and hold them until they were no longer deemed a risk. And that power was held by the stepchild of the Justice Department, the INS.

Under the Fourth Amendment, the FBI cannot arrest and hold American citizens—or foreigners charged with a criminal offense—

without a probable cause. Within forty-eight hours, it must bring any suspect before the courts, demonstrate lawful grounds for continued detention, and allow the suspect access to a lawyer. But the safeguards are much weaker for noncitizens thought to be violating immigration laws. Ordinary due process rights that Americans take for granted—the reading of Miranda rights, protection from unreasonable search and seizure, the right to a government-appointed lawyer if they cannot afford one—are not required for noncitizens if they are being charged only with immigration offenses. As one senior government official quipped: "Immigration law is the same as tax law—you're guilty until proven innocent."

The INS had long operated under a regulation that required it to charge anyone suspected of an immigration violation "without unnecessary delay," a standard that had been interpreted to mean within twenty-four hours of being detained. In virtually all cases, those who were charged would be released on bail and ordered to return for a decision. Those who were ordered deported were almost always freed on bail until their deportation. As for those who were held in custody because they were deemed a flight risk, the INS was under an obligation to send them back to their home country promptly, but in no case were they to be held longer than ninety days. But as far as the Justice Department was concerned, these were merely regulatory protections, not constitutional ones, and officials there decided they had the power to authorize much longer detentions. Within a week of the attacks, Ashcroft had bolstered those powers through an executive order giving INS officials clear authority to detain without charge anyone suspected of violating immigration laws for at least forty-eight hours or, in the event of an emergency, for "an additional reasonable period of time"—a phrase that in theory allowed for very lengthy detention without any charges being filed. There was no question when the order was written that the Justice Department considered that the aftermath of 9/11 constituted such an emergency.

What about the courts? The U.S. Supreme Court had ruled categorically that everyone in the country, whether citizen or non-citizen, whether they were living in the United States lawfully or not, was protected by the Fifth Amendment, which prevents detention without due process of law. But immigrants and visitors to the United States are one step removed from the regular court system, and in practice it is a very big step. The Justice Department houses its own system of special courts empowered to hear deportation cases, asylum claims, and other immigration-related matters involving non-U.S. citizens. Critics of the high level of illegal immigration had long complained that those courts were too lenient, providing too many opportunities for claims and appeals by foreigners who were in the country unlawfully and wanted to stay. Before 9/11, immigration judges normally released most suspected immigration violators on bail pending their hearings, and the vast majority did not show and simply disappeared into the country. But again Ashcroft changed the rules, implementing a "no bond" policy for certain immigration detainees that required them to remain locked up while the FBI ran checks to see if they posed any security threat, even if the judge found the government's case that they should be imprisoned less than persuasive. And ten days after the attacks, to avoid any scrutiny of the new practices, Ashcroft ordered that all immigration cases deemed by the department to be of "special interest" must be considered by the immigration courts in secret.

Before that morning, immigration law had been mostly a regulatory tool, a quasi-judicial system for determining who could stay in the country and who would be asked, and sometimes forced, to leave. As a law enforcement weapon, it had been a very small stick. But as the officials gathered around Ashcroft that night began to consider how to respond to the crisis, they realized, as one INS official later put it, that their existing immigration powers were "vast and underused."

"If you get someone on an immigration violation you can do a lot more than you can with probable cause. And the Justice Department was quick to seize on this," said Mike Becraft, who was kept on by Ziglar and became the acting deputy INS commissioner on 9/11.

Ashcroft and his officials began to sketch out a strategy to wield the enforcement club. They proposed an aggressive campaign to send FBI and INS agents together into Arab American communities across the country, the most likely places where a future terrorist might be hiding. It would start with cities with the biggest Arab populations, such as New York, Detroit, and Jersey City, New Jersey, and continue from there. FBI agents would start knocking on doors and asking questions, backed up by INS agents empowered to detain all those who could not prove they were living legally in the United States. The detentions would serve three purposes: first, on the slim chance that the suspects were actually Al Qaeda terrorists, it would help to prevent another attack; second, the detainees might be terrified into cooperating with the government and provide leads to actual terrorists; finally, and most plausibly, the disruption caused by the arrests and the presence of agents rooting around in Arab American communities would make it harder for Al Qaeda to plan and carry out any follow-up operations. "Delay was victory," a former senior Justice official said. "First you delay, then you disrupt."

Among the officials in the room there was only a single dissent, but it was a heated one. Jim Ziglar would admit later that he "probably overreacted." Close associates of Ashcroft say that he did not like to be challenged in open meetings. "I always felt the best way to deal with John was one-on-one, not in public, and not even in front of his staff," one of his most senior officials said. And that night was not the best time to cross Ashcroft. He had accomplished little in the Justice portfolio since his Senate confirmation in February. His main priorities at the department had been to reenergize the traditional law and order portfolio by cracking down on violent crime, drugs, and child pornography, and he had discouraged the FBI from emphasizing counterterrorism or counterintelligence missions. In May he had released a list of his agency's top ten priorities, and terrorism was not among them; he had also rejected FBI requests for an increased budget for counterterrorism. The acting FBI director at the time, Thomas Pickard, said that Ashcroft did not even want to be briefed about terrorist threats, at one point telling him: "I don't want to hear about al-Qaeda anymore."

But his aides would later say that the attacks transformed him. He had been on a government plane heading to Milwaukee that morning to deliver a speech when the Justice Department's command center called to tell him that the two towers had been hit in New York. After putting down the phone, he turned to his staff and said: "This has changed the world forever." He then ordered the plane to return to Washington, taking a serious chance that it might be misidentified and shot down before it could arrive.

Ashcroft was also driven by strong Christian convictions, and he would later write that the attacks had created "a moral imperative for toughness." His father had been a minister in the Assemblies of God, the world's largest Pentecostal denomination, and while he was a pragmatic politician rather than a dogmatic ideologue, he had what legal scholar Jeffrey Rosen called a "deeply rooted moralism" in which "he view[ed] himself as an instrument of some unchanging higher purpose." As a former Justice aide told Rosen: "I think he sees this as a civilizational clash. He sees these people as enemies of everything he believes in, as a sort of religiously based threat. It really touched him in a more profound way than a secular person might have experienced."

But Ziglar had his own convictions, the product of his unusual political path through Washington. He had grown up in a working-class family in Pascagoula, Mississippi, a small town on the Gulf of Mexico near the state's border with Alabama. He was boyhood friends with Trent Lott, who would go on to become the Senate Republican leader before his incautious public enthusiasm for the segregated South of his youth would bring him down. In 1964, just out of high school, Ziglar had left home to come to Washington as a young legislative aide for Democratic senator James O. Eastland, one of the most openly racist senators ever to sit in the Congress, and a notorious red-baiter. But after putting himself through college and law school at George Washington University, Ziglar had abandoned the southern Democrats for the Republican Party, inspired in particular by Barry Goldwater and the party's libertarian wing. He had gone to work as an aide in the Justice Department under Attorney General John Mitchell when Mitchell was forced to resign under the cloud of the Watergate investigation, and he says the experience further reinforced his libertarianism and strong conviction that the Constitution's main purpose was to restrain government power. After graduating from law school, he had clerked in the Supreme Court under Justice Harry Blackmun, a Nixon appointee who became a liberal voice on the court and a forceful advocate of civil rights. Ziglar later said that Blackmun had been one of the strongest influences in his political life.

As the strategy for using immigration powers to arrest and hold Arabs and Muslims began to take shape that night, Ziglar spoke up. "You're talking about doing something that's grossly unconstitutional, when you start knocking on doors and picking up people without probable cause," he told Ashcroft and the other top Justice men in the room. "You know, we've got something called the Constitution, and what you're talking about is basically exercising a general warrant to knock on people's door without probable cause. And that's what caused King George to get his butt kicked by the colonists."

By his own account, the exchange turned ugly, with Ziglar holding his ground but finding no support in the room. "What are you going to accomplish by doing this?" he pushed back. "You're not going to get the information you're looking for and you're not going to find any evidence. And even if you did, you couldn't use it because the courts would throw it out." While such arguments would eventually look prescient, they had no impact that night. Ashcroft was looking for ways to act aggressively to head off any further attacks, and immigration law gave him greater powers than anything else in his arsenal. The objections of his own top immigration official were merely a nuisance.

But Ziglar's strident opposition would, as he later put it, "set the stage for the rest of my tenure at the INS." From that point forward, the agency responsible for managing the entry of foreigners into the United States would be turned by the Justice Department into an arm of the FBI. Its primary mission would become the aggressive enforcement of U.S. immigration laws, in the name of fighting terrorism, against almost any foreigner the Justice Department chose to target.

Ziglar and others in the INS would fight a series of internal battles to try to prevent, discourage, or remedy the worst of the abuses, but he no longer had the ear of Ashcroft and his top aides. After the night of 9/11, "I was persona non grata from then on," he says, "because I was not tough enough in the crisis."

FROM THE ONSET OF THE crisis, an administration that appeared to the country and the world to be united in its response to the worst-ever attack on American soil was in fact deeply divided about what the attacks meant for the U.S. tradition of open and largely undefended borders. Beyond their shared horror, and agreement that the attacks had exposed serious vulnerabilities that needed to be addressed, there was little consensus inside the Bush administration on what the United States should do to tighten its borders against future attacks. The arguments would span almost every significant aspect of the government's response, including reorganization of the federal bureaucracy, visa policy, domestic registration of foreigners, student visas, and border relations with Canada and Mexico.

The disagreements were all about fundamentally the same issue: with the president having declared a global war on terrorism, how broadly and aggressively should the administration use immigration and border enforcement as weapons in the new war? The administration had virtually unfettered authority to arrest non-Americans for minor immigration violations, beef up security at the land borders, and restrict visas for overseas travelers. Proponents of the aggressive strategy were determined to use these powerful tools to the fullest. If aggressive enforcement hurt innocent people—and it inevitably would—it was considered unavoidable collateral damage that was an acceptable price if it disrupted potential terrorist activity. Further, in the eyes of some in government, many of the victims were not innocent. Some of them had deliberately violated U.S. immigration laws to sneak into the United States or remain here after their visas had expired. Others had inadvertently committed technical violations but had still broken the letter of the law. If one of the results of fighting the war on terrorism was to crack down on nonterrorists who had nonetheless broken immigration laws, that was seen as a benefit, not a problem.

To the opponents, the aggressive and often indiscriminate use of immigration laws and visa rules to keep out foreigners or punish others on technical violations was self-defeating. First, it was looking for the proverbial needle in a haystack. It would require registering, investigating, and screening hundreds of thousands, even millions, of foreigners in the hope of finding some shred of evidence that would indicate that someone was a terrorist or had connections to terrorism. That would be an enormous waste of resources for little or no benefit. Second, it would alienate those groups whose cooperation the U.S. government would need to improve its ability to investigate terrorism. Would foreigners living in the United States willingly come forward if they feared that they would be arrested, detained, and probably deported for violations of immigration rules? And finally, it would anger foreign governments whose citizens were targeted by the new measures, jeopardizing relations with the moderate Muslim nations that were the United States' most important allies in the war on terror.

In the months following the attacks, two broad approaches—both of which were evident immediately on the morning of 9/11—would crystallize in the administration. The first was exemplified by the tight screening that had produced huge lineups at the Canadian and Mexican border crossings immediately after the attacks. Since the United States knew almost nothing about who was coming to the country or why, the only way to bolster security was to subject as many foreigners as possible to the broadest possible scrutiny, in the hopes of keeping out those who intended to harm the United States further.

I call the advocates of this approach the "cops." For the cops, every post-9/11 problem had the same answer—tough enforcement of immigration laws. Nearly everyone who was a target of terrorism-related suspicion was either an immigrant or a temporary visitor to the United States. Immigration law is filled with hundreds of "spit on the sidewalk" violations, making it easy to prosecute virtually any suspect for violating one immigration regulation or another—and in the process "prevent" future attacks by keeping them in jail or sending them out of the country. The result was that detention for immigration law transgressions became the primary prevention tool in the cops' arsenal. The initial proposal for the USA Patriot Act submitted by the Justice Department to Congress right after the attacks called for suspending habeas corpus for any foreigner living in the United States whom the attorney general wanted to hold in a terrorism investigation, a radical proposal that was summarily rejected by both Republican and Democratic leaders. In its place they passed provisions that allowed terrorist suspects to be held for seven days without charge, but required either criminal or immigration charges to be laid after that time. In practice, however, the department ignored the timelines and behaved as if habeas corpus had been suspended. As Ashcroft put it, "Aggressive detention of lawbreakers and material witnesses is vital to preventing, disrupting, or delaying new attacks. It is difficult for a person in jail or under detention to murder innocent people or to aid or abet in terrorism."

On the country's borders, prevention had been part of the mission long before 9/11, but it had been overshadowed by the goal of facilitating legitimate travel to the United States. The result was that millions of people were allowed to enter the country with minimal scrutiny. For both sides in the debate, this represented an extraordinary missed opportunity. If a target of suspicion was already inside the United States, it was difficult or sometimes impossible to track him down; it was better to keep such people out of the country in the first place. The border powers of the Justice Department were virtually unlimited. Under the 1952 Immigration and

Nationality Act, the attorney general had the ultimate authority to decide whether any foreigner would be allowed to enter the United States. Used precisely, such powers were invaluable in preventing further attacks, but used indiscriminately they were a blunt instrument that caught up many whose only offense was the color of their passport.

In the cops' approach, the distinction between antiterrorism enforcement and immigration enforcement became hopelessly blurred, and would become even more so the further the country got from the 9/11 attacks. Occasionally immigration law was used in the way that Robert Kennedy had used the tax laws to go after organized crime; that is, individuals who were suspected of having ties to Al Qaeda or other terrorist groups would be held on minor immigration violations so that they could be questioned, investigated, and, if necessary, prosecuted or deported. But far more frequently there was no evidence linking those detained to any terrorist group, and immigration violations became the only grounds for holding them. As part of the post-9/11 enforcement efforts, the INS detained thousands of people, and in some cases imprisoned them for many months, in the complete absence of any evidence tying them to terrorism. Over time, the original goal of identifying and arresting terrorists would become inextricably muddled with a broader crackdown on illegal immigrants.

The rival approach was based on the same set of ideas that had led Customs to create the passenger information systems that had first identified the nineteen hijackers. I have called the advocates of this approach the "technocrats," because they shared an extraordinary faith in the ability of the government to use technology, especially information systems, to keep out the bad guys and let in the good ones. For the technocrats, the biggest problem with the cops' solution was that it caused huge and unnecessary disruption. It might by chance catch some potential terrorists or other undesirables, and would certainly identify illegal immigrants, but it would also snare many, many innocent people whom the country wanted and needed. Admiral Brian Peterman, a Coast Guard veteran who became the top White House official on border and transportation security issues after 9/11, said that immigration laws were based on the presumption "that people from a certain country were homogeneous enough in their thinking and beliefs that we could handle them in a certain way. But what became evident to us was we really needed to handle people individually because there are bad people coming from what we consider good countries. So we needed to beef up how we were going to handle and screen individuals." Further, focusing on individuals rather than on broad national groups was the only way to improve security without undermining cross-border commerce and travel. "It was from the beginning always our goal to improve national security post-9/11 while also facilitating the movement of goods and people," Peterman said. "I was always firmly of the belief that if we did security well and right and carefully, we could actually make the movement of goods and people better than it was pre-9/11."

There were a variety of problems with the technocrats' approach, but the most serious was that it depended on technologies and elaborate systems that were not in place when the hijackers struck. Identifying, deploying, and in some cases designing such new technologies and building the new systems was a long, arduous, and expensive undertaking, and in the interim, the country might be left more vulnerable to another attack. Given that problem, it was not surprising that at the outset of the response to 9/11, the cops carried the day.

OVER THE NEXT SEVERAL MONTHS, Ashcroft's Justice Department would demonstrate that it was seized by its leader's moral imperative for toughness. In the immediate aftermath of the attacks, the attorney general's office considered what one former official called "a massive program for registering all aliens in the United States"—something that had been done in the country only once before under the Alien Registration Act of 1940. In the end it settled for a more limited program that targeted mostly citizens of Muslim and Arab countries. It pushed successfully for new visa screening measures that required exhaustive vetting of most male travelers from the same Muslim and Arab countries. Domestically, it took steps to empower local police to identify and detain any immigrant who was in the country illegally, supplementing the FBI and INS forces with hundreds of thousands of local cops. And it used the substantial powers it already had to detain thousands of Muslim immigrants living in the United States, in the worst cases jailing some of them for months and even years on immigration violations. Such actions would leave the Bush administration and its pro-immigration president open to the charge, as liberal legal critic David Cole would put it, that "the war on terrorism has been waged largely through anti-immigrant measures."

The first priority for Ashcroft's Justice Department was to track down anyone with terrorist connections who was already inside the United States and might be planning or considering further attacks. Ziglar had lost the fight over detentions on the first night, and his concerns over the constitutionality of the tactics were swept aside. He agreed to reassign 1,000 INS agents immediately to the 9/11 investigation, where they would trail behind the FBI and arrest anyone who was found to have violated U.S. immigration laws. By early November, the FBI and INS had arrested more than 1,200 individuals, all but a handful of whom were foreign nationals, as part of the investigation into the attack, which had been code-named PENTTBOM. More than 750 were imprisoned for sustained periods on immigration violations while the FBI decided whether they had some connection to terrorism.

"Let the terrorists among us be warned," Ashcroft announced. "If you overstay your visa—even by one day—we will arrest you. If you violate a local law, you will be put in jail and kept in custody as long as possible. We will use every available statute."

While Ashcroft had targeted his warning at "terrorists," the arrests were aimed almost exclusively at illegal immigrants with little regard to any evidence involving their connection to terrorism. As a later internal investigation by the Justice Department's inspector general found, if the FBI teams "encountered an illegal alien in the course of pursuing a PENTTBOM lead—whether or not the alien was the subject of the lead—the INS agent on the team examined the alien's immigration and identity documents to determine whether the alien was lawfully in the United States." If an INS agent was not present at the time, one would be sent later. Anyone who was found to have overstayed a visa or otherwise have violated an immigration law was arrested.

In many cases, the arrests were random. If FBI agents were pursuing a lead involving a particular individual and stumbled across a dozen illegal immigrants nearby, each was arrested as part of the investigation. "No distinction generally was made between the subjects of the lead and any other individuals encountered at the scene 'incidentally,' because the FBI wanted to be certain that no terrorist was inadvertently set free," the report said.

Shakir Baloch was arrested on September 20, 2001, outside a New York City driving school where he was studying to renew his limousine driver's license. A Canadian citizen born in Pakistan, Baloch, age forty, had been living in New York since 1998. Trained as a doctor in Pakistan, he had graduated with a certificate in ultrasound technology from Columbia Presbyterian Hospital in New York and was hoping to pass exams to obtain a medical license. He was approached by two plainclothes officers, who took him back to his apartment, where a dozen others were already searching the apartment without a warrant. After three hours of questioning, he was taken to the local INS office, where he was told he would be deported back to Toronto, and signed a waiver of his right to inform the Canadian government that he had been arrested.

He was not deported. Instead, Baloch was taken, like Benamar Benatta, to the Metropolitan Detention Center in New York. As he later testified before the United Nations in 2003, he was surrounded by six or seven guards. "They hit my head against all four corners of the room and punched my back repeatedly. They were yelling, 'You did this to us. We will kill you.' They warned me not to make eye contact with any guard. They were hitting me against the wall in this manner for an hour. Then they strip-searched me and gave me an orange jumpsuit to wear. I was transferred to the ninth floor."

For the next five months, he was held in solitary confinement in the prison. Bright lights were left on twenty-four hours a day, and he was given no pillow or blanket to shield himself from the light. The guards who patrolled outside his cell were making noise constantly, waking him when he managed to fall asleep. Baloch repeatedly asked for the right to call a lawyer or his wife and daughter to let them know he was alive. For ten weeks, that request was refused. Finally, on December 20 the Center for Constitutional Rights, a New York public-interest legal organization, filed a habeas corpus petition on his behalf, and in early January the government charged him with having illegally entered the country from Canada, and with possessing a fraudulent Social Security card. He was transferred to the general prison population. Despite being surrounded by serious criminals, he described the transfer as a relief. "I had access to a phone so I was able to call my family. There was a TV, newspapers, a kitchen, and a gym. I was not locked in isolation for twenty-four hours. I realized that on the ninth floor I had been treated worse than the biggest criminals in the United States." After nearly seven months in jail, he was put on a plane and flown back to Toronto. No allegations were ever made that Baloch had any links to terrorists.

The violations that resulted in detention ranged from deliberately overstaying visas and remaining in the country illegally to a host of niggling technical violations. Tarek Mohamed Fayad, a thirty-five-year-old Egyptian who was in the United States studying to be a dentist, was arrested at gunpoint on September 13 at a gas station in San Bernardino, California. He was transferred to a prison in Los Angeles and then flown to the MDC in New York. While friends contacted the Egyptian embassy, which found him a lawyer shortly after his arrest, the lawyer was not informed of the transfer, and it took her more than a month and the intervention of the American Immigration Lawyers Association (AILA) to track Mohamed down in New York. Like Baloch, he was held in solitary confinement. On December 18, he was granted voluntary departure to leave the United States and return to Egypt. The grounds for his detention? Owing to medical problems, he had been taking less than the twelve credit hours required for full-time student status and was therefore in violation of his student visa.

Another detainee, a thirty-seven-year-old Indian who had just graduated with a Ph.D. in computer science from MIT and was in the process of moving to New York City, was arrested by FBI and INS officials at a hotel on November 14, apparently on a tip from the hotel staff. He had followed the appropriate procedures by filing for a green card after his graduation, seeking permanent residence on the basis of extraordinary ability. But his attorney had made a mistake, filing the application on the sixty-first day after he graduated rather than within the sixty days required. He would spend five weeks in jail while the matter was sorted out.

Nearly all of those detained were from predominantly Muslim countries, particularly Pakistan and Egypt, but many of them in no way fit the profile of a likely terrorist. An exhaustive 2003 investigation by the Migration Policy Institute found that nearly half had been in the United States for at least six years, and a similar number had wives, children, or other family ties in the country.

Once arrested many of the detainees fell into a black hole. The INS immediately enacted a no-bond policy to ensure that no one would be released until the FBI had deemed they had no connections to terrorism. While the arbitrary nature of most of the arrests would later become clear, in the atmosphere of fear that followed the 9/11 attacks there was no one arguing against the cautious approach of vetting the detainees thoroughly in order to avoid mistakenly releasing a terrorist.

But it quickly became evident that the Justice Department had no intention of devoting significant time or resources to checking the detainees. INS officials, who were forced to go before immigration judges to justify the continued detentions, could get nothing from the FBI to use as evidence. In many cases, the FBI had assigned no agents to handle the individual cases, so that detainees were awaiting a clearance process that was not actually taking place. Larry Thompson, the deputy attorney general, later told the department's inspector general that the bureau simply had other priorities in its efforts to prevent another terrorist attack. He explained that "an individual arrested and detained posed no ongoing threat to the United States, and therefore law enforcement officials could focus on arresting others still at large who did pose a potential threat."

Ziglar and the INS tried to push back, fighting an internal war against Ashcroft's inner circle. "They knew they couldn't control me," he said later. His successful business career had left him financially independent, and his friendships in Congress gave him political cover. Firing Ziglar would have been a serious embarrassment to the administration, shattering the façade of a united response to the 9/11 attacks. And so Ashcroft tolerated him, pressing ahead with the aggressive use of his immigration powers in the face of continued opposition from his top official in charge of immigration.

As the delays in processing the detainees continued, the internal disputes became more heated. Several cases, including some brought to his attention by senators he had befriended when he worked on Capitol Hill, were "pretty bloody appalling," Ziglar recalls. "They put people in detention and the FBI wouldn't do anything for weeks, or even know that they were there. And [the detainees] just sat there and stewed and were lost. Their families didn't know where they were. Hell, *we* didn't know where they were. That's pretty ugly. This is the United States of America. This is not the Soviet Union." In one case, he took his complaint directly to the deputy director of the FBI, threatening to release a particular detainee unless the FBI could provide evidence immediately. "I was told, 'You don't have the authority,' and I said 'Just watch me.'" The detainee, whom Ziglar would not identify, was released.

But Ziglar never took his complaints to Ashcroft, and the inspector general's report later criticized the INS for not pressing the issue at a higher level. Ziglar insists it would have made no difference. "I knew I was already perceived as not being tough enough, so any objection I had to this would have been written off." He added that Ashcroft and his close associates simply never trusted him. As a result of his many years in the Congress, he had close contacts on both sides of the aisle. He was a friend with Senator Chris Dodd, a liberal, having worked with Dodd's father who was a senator before him. He had a long friendship with Ted Kennedy, a staunch liberal on immigration issues. And he was close to Pat Leahy, the Vermont Democrat who had mercilessly grilled Ashcroft during his confirmation hearing and was the most powerful opponent of the Justice Department's efforts to expand policing and surveillance powers after 9/11. With Ashcroft, said Ziglar, such friendships automatically made him suspect. "In the Justice Department in that era, you were either with us 100 percent or you're against us 100 percent. If your friends are my enemies, you're my enemy. It really was a very poisoned sort of atmosphere."

Mike Becraft, his deputy, agreed that Ziglar's focus on the constitutional rights of the detainees hurt him badly with Ashcroft and his closest aides. "He was a young man in the Nixon administration and was very worried about the potential for abuse of power," Becraft said. "And I think that rubbed the guys at the Justice Department the wrong way. There were guys at the Justice Department who didn't want to hear this. Jim had a different opinion, and it hurt him."

Officials close to Ashcroft dispute that interpretation, arguing that Ziglar's cooperation with the detention policy made him fully complicit with the decisions after 9/11. "Ziglar wants to be viewed as opposing detentions, but he was still the commissioner of the INS and he was the one who had the legal authority to detain or not to detain these people," said a former senior Ashcroft aide. "He had the responsibility to act, or if something was going on that he didn't like, to raise it with his superiors."

Despite his concerns and his many powerful friends on the Hill, Ziglar never took his complaints public, allowing the administration to maintain an appearance of unity that masked its serious internal divisions. "I always thought about it," he said later, "but I also knew that, given the tenor of the times, it was not going to be productive."

Of the 762 people detained in the months after 9/11 on immigration violations, more than 200 would spend from 51 to 100 days in jail, while another 175 would spend up to 150 days in jail. More than 125 would be held longer, some for a year or more. And not a single one of the detainees was ever charged with terrorism or a terrorist-related offense.

The post-9/11 arrests marked the most aggressive use of the department's immigration powers, but they were only part of a larger effort to use immigration laws in the hope of rousting terrorists. In December Ziglar announced a new initiative to track down foreigners in the country who had been ordered deported but had failed to leave. The pressure to go after the so-called absconders had come from Ashcroft's office; shortly after 9/11, a whistleblower from the INS had gone directly to the Justice Department, telling one of Ashcroft's senior aides that there were hundreds of thousands of foreigners in the country who had ignored deportation orders, including some with violent criminal histories. INS records indicated that some 314,000 absconders were still living in the United States.

To Ashcroft's people, the absconder problem was symptomatic of the long-standing failure of the INS to enforce the country's immigration laws. "The INS wasn't making any effort to find overstayers, and state and local authorities couldn't enforce immigration laws," a senior Justice official said. "And if you were ordered deported, the appeal process could take years, and even if there was a final order, the INS never came to enforce it. Everyone was released on bond, and the removal rate was only 13 percent. And no one who did law enforcement in Justice was paying any attention to the immigration system."

Ashcroft ordered Ziglar to begin tracking down, arresting, and deporting absconders. It was initially intended not as an antiterrorism program but rather as an effort to plug one of the most serious holes in INS enforcement capabilities. Under the new initiative, 314,000 names were to be put on the Wanted Persons list of the

National Crime Information Center, a database accessible to every local and state police department in the country. The vast majority of the absconders were Mexicans or other Latin American immigrants, reflecting their preponderance within the illegal immigrant population.

But almost immediately, the program morphed into a counterterrorism initiative. Deputy Attorney General Larry Thompson sent a memo to Ziglar and to FBI director Robert Mueller directing that first priority be given to the "several thousand among that group who come from countries in which there has been Al Qaeda terrorist presence or activity." He ordered that any absconder taken into custody be questioned about his knowledge of terrorist activity, and that the FBI be involved in vetting each of those detained.

It was the Absconder Apprehension Initiative that brought the INS and the FBI to the door of Sharif Kesbeh's home in a Houston suburb. Kesbeh, a Palestinian, was born in the West Bank town of Ramallah. Following the Six-Day War in 1967 between Israel and its Arab neighbors, Israel took control of the West Bank and Kesbeh's parents fled to Baqaa, a refugee camp north of Amman in Jordan. He was able to leave Jordan to study agricultural engineering in Egypt, went to work for Jordan's Ministry of Planning, and in 1979 was sent by the Jordanian government for graduate studies at Texas Tech in Lubbock, Texas. He returned and married a Jordanian woman, but longed to return to the United States. In the mid-1980s, they moved to Saudi Arabia, and in several years he was able to launch his own transportation business, delivering fertilizer from across the Middle East to farms in Saudi Arabia. But again war intervened. As a result of the Iraqi invasion of Kuwait in 1991 and the Gulf War that followed, Saudi Arabia shut its borders, destroying his business. On August 16, 1992, with no business and no prospects for rebuilding it, he took a gamble and brought his wife, Asmaa, and their six children to Texas.

The family's story was not an uncommon one before 9/11. Kesbeh had joined his two brothers, who were legal U.S. residents running a flag-making business in Houston. While initially on a six-month tourist visa, he was able to get a one-year work permit from the INS and renew it several times. Kesbeh and his wife enrolled their children in public schools, where the kids thrived, and within several years he had taken over the business from his brothers. He embraced the apolitical culture of American business, making and selling American flags, Confederate flags, Israeli flags, and any other kind of flag they could sell. The family applied for permanent residency as Palestinian refugees, but the INS rejected the application. Their final appeal before an immigration judge was turned down in 1997; on June 15, 1998, the INS in Houston issued a warrant for the deportation of Sharif Kesbeh, his wife, and six of his seven children. The youngest had been born in Houston and was therefore an American citizen.

Only a small percentage of those ordered deported actually appear voluntarily to leave, and historically the INS had done little to enforce the orders. So Kesbeh made a decision that many before him had made. "After six or seven years working hard to stand on our feet, if we leave the United States, our family life will be destroyed," he said later. "To leave your only source of income, to take the kids from an American school to an Arabic system school, means the destruction of the family." Immigration lawyers had told them that if they kept out of legal trouble, there was little chance the INS would ever show up to enforce the deportation order. So they took a risk and stayed.

For the Kesbehs, like millions of other illegal immigrants in the United States, the lack of status was a relatively minor inconvenience. As Sharif told journalist Michelle Goldberg, legal residency "was something we needed, but it was not something we needed badly." It did not prevent him from running a thriving business and paying taxes; it did not prevent his children from attending public schools; it did not prevent him and his family from getting driver's licenses or Social Security cards, or receiving medical care. Only occasionally would the problem surface. One son was reluctantly turned down by the navy, which was desperately in need of

Arab-speaking recruits, because he had no legal status in the country; two of his daughters were ineligible for college scholarships and had to attend cheaper community colleges.

But in March 2002 their luck ran out. Asmaa's parents, her younger sister, and her three-year-old nephew were killed in a car accident along Jordan's Dead Sea Highway. As is the Muslim tradition, their local friends in Houston gathered at their house for several days to mourn. It was that gathering that apparently drew suspicion. Four weeks later, eight armed officers burst into the house. Sharif and his eighteen-year-old son Alaa were taken away in handcuffs and put in jail, where they would remain for more than six months; his wife and daughters were fingerprinted and released.

The Kesbehs tried to fight their impending deportation back to Jordan. Noor Kesbeh, the eldest daughter, contacted a local television station, which ran a story on the arrests, and within a week the *Houston Chronicle* had dubbed them "the Palestinian Cleavers," an embodiment of the American dream of hard work made good. Sheila Jackson, the local member of Congress, championed their cause and introduced a bill that would have allowed the family to stay as permanent residents. Ted Kennedy took up the issue in the Senate and persuaded his friend Jim Ziglar to allow a six-month extension before their deportation.

But in the end the fight proved futile. Jackson was unable to get her bill out of the House Judiciary Committee, where it was blocked by Republican chairman James Sensenbrenner, a strong advocate of using immigration laws aggressively to fight the war on terrorism. With the country about to head into war with Iraq, it was hard to generate much public sympathy for an Arab family— even an obviously wholesome and hard-working one—that had clearly broken U.S. immigration laws to remain in the country. *People* magazine had come to the house to do a story on the family but decided not to run it; *Nightline*, the television news show, also approached them but did not air anything. Michelle Malkin, the acid-tongued commentator on Fox News, wrote that the Kesbehs "demonstrated their contempt for our immigration system by illegally settling into the American mainstream, establishing a retail business (selling American flags, of all things), obtaining Social Security cards and driver's licenses, and enrolling their kids in local schools."

Still, as they were packing up their house to prepare for the flight back to Jordan, the family's supporters in Houston rallied on their front lawn, hoping for some last-minute miracle. It did not come. On March 28, 2003, they were put on a plane for Jordan via Amsterdam, to their new lives in a two-room apartment above the home of one of Sharif's brothers in a conservative Muslim neighborhood in East Amman.

None of the children had lived in Jordan before. Sharif was unable to find a job, and so the older sisters have supported the family, struggling to put their younger siblings through private, English-speaking schools because none of them speaks Arabic well enough to attend the public schools. Noor Kesbeh said that moving to Amman was a complete "culture shock" for her and her sisters. It is a traditional neighborhood where women are not allowed to be out alone after dark. The girls had grown up playing basketball with the boys in their suburban driveway; now they mostly stay indoors, where all five share a single bedroom. Noor is the only one who wears the hijab to cover her head, and her sisters draw stares and taunts when they are in public.

Under the conditions of their deportation, all the Kesbehs— except the youngest, American girl—are barred from returning to the United States for at least a decade. Noor's brother Mohamed was able to win a scholarship to go to university in Canada, and she is hoping to find some way to follow him there. But mostly the family despairs. "We feel destroyed," Sharif Kesbeh said. "We are just counting the days to find a way we can get home to America. It's like somebody climbing a mountain, with difficulties, with seven kids, and before I reached the top somebody threw me down again to the bottom. All of these fifty-eight years working hard ended with zero."

In all, the INS files identified nearly 6,000 absconders from

Arab and Muslim countries, who were declared priority cases under the Absconder Apprehension Initiative. That resulted in about
4,000 active investigations. Just trying to find those 4,000 showed
that the INS's record keeping was even more abysmal than its
worst critics imagined. Nearly half of these "absconders" could not
be found, and many may have already left the country. Some 40
percent were in fact living in the United States legally, including
nearly two hundred green card holders and another eighty who had
already taken out U.S. citizenship. Just over 1,000 people were,
like the Kesbehs, were deported or agreed to leave voluntarily. The
Justice Department made no claims to have apprehended any terrorists through the initiative.

Other operations followed a similar pattern: first justified
as antiterrorism initiatives, they ended up as purely immigration
enforcement. Operation Tarmac focused on employees at the
thousands of businesses that operate at U.S. airports. More than
224,000 employees were audited; 900 were arrested on violations
of immigration laws. Operation Game Day was launched ahead
of the 2003 Super Bowl in San Diego amid fears that terrorists
might try to stage an attack during the game. The INS checked the
employment records of 11,000 security guards and 3,500 licensed
taxi and limousine drivers; 70 were found to be in the country
illegally.

WHILE THE JUSTICE DEPARTMENT'S FIRST goal was to arrest any suspected terrorists already in the country, its second was
to keep out any who might be planning to come to the United
States. Shortly after the attacks, the senior White House official
responsible for counterterrorism, Richard Clarke, called several
top Justice and State Department officials to berate them about
what he considered the huge security threat posed by the government's lack of knowledge and control over who was coming to the
United States and why, and directed them to come up with solutions quickly.

Visa policy was a shared responsibility of Justice and State. In practice it had been run entirely by the State Department, but in law no visa could be issued without the approval of the attorney general. On the day of the attacks, George Lannon, the State Department's principal deputy assistant in the Bureau of Consular Affairs, which handles visa policy, had ordered his staff to track down the visa records of the nineteen suspected hijackers and then turned the information over to the FBI.

But the two agencies drew very different lessons from the records. For State Department veterans, the issuing of visas to the hijackers had been an unavoidable tragedy. As Steve Fischel, another senior Consular Affairs official, put it: "There's absolutely no way that any highly educated, experienced consular officer would have denied those visas in light of the known facts. They didn't break the pattern in any way. There is nothing that set them aside from legitimate, qualified travelers." Mary Ryan, the assistant secretary for Consular Affairs, had asked a retired Foreign Service officer to review the decisions that led to the issuing of visas to the hijackers, and he had concluded that the department's procedures had all been properly followed.

For the Justice Department, which was looking for every means to prevent another attack, the reluctance of the State Department to begin making drastic changes to its visa procedures was almost unthinkable. "At State, there was a lot of throwing up their hands and saying, 'How are we supposed to stop this?'" recalled a former senior Justice official.

Justice immediately began pressing for changes. State officials insist that Ashcroft wanted a full-blown moratorium that would have stopped the granting of visas entirely, shutting down the country to most foreign travel until the FBI could get a better handle on the scope of the terrorist threat. Lannon said he was at meetings where the Justice Department and the FBI were proposing a six-month moratorium on all visas. Justice officials said they never proposed a moratorium, but were simply insisting on much tougher screening of foreigners coming to the United States, especially from countries where Al Qaeda was known to be active.

That recollection is supported by Ziglar and by other former INS officials. "Justice's position was not a moratorium on all visas," a former senior official said. "I remember once some FBI agents saying, 'Can't we just stop the foreigners from coming here?' and everybody in the room laughed because the FBI was just so stressed at the time. That was never a Justice Department position."

The compromise reached by the two departments called for detailed background checks on visa applicants from countries considered to have active terrorist groups. The State Department and the FBI already had schemes in place to cooperate on screening certain visa applicants. There were special security reviews for foreigners coming to do research in military-related technologies, for instance, and another for foreign officials or diplomats who might be spies. Why not a similar procedure for terrorism? Justice backed the scheme, because it gave the FBI new screening powers that it could use to keep anyone of concern out of the country, while State considered it the "minimum buy-in" for addressing the concerns over visa policy.

Still, virtually every facet of the new system was fought over at length. One Justice participant recalled an intense dispute over whether visa applicants should be asked if they were members of a terrorist group. The State Department dismissed the idea condescendingly. " 'Oh yeah, someone's going to write down that he's a terrorist,' they would say, and kind of laugh at us," the Justice official recalled. To State, the idea was ridiculous, a hopelessly unsophisticated approach that would needlessly annoy legitimate travelers while doing nothing to identify or deter actual terrorists. From the Justice perspective, however, if someone swore on a visa application that he had no connections to terrorism, and he had lied, it would be one more weapon the FBI could use to detain or prosecute that person in the future.

The list of countries targeted by the new security reviews was also a huge point of contention. The State Department was especially worried that the United States not appear to be targeting only Muslim countries. Officials suggested the inclusion of India, and some East African countries like Tanzania and Kenya, and even argued that one or more Western Hemisphere countries should be added to give more balance. Justice opposed adding countries just for the sake of diplomatic appearances, arguing that the scheme should target countries where there was known to be some activity by Al Qaeda or other Islamic terrorist groups. They settled on a list of some two dozen countries, all of them with significant Muslim populations, including Pakistan, Egypt, Indonesia, Malaysia, Lebanon, and Saudi Arabia.

As a first step, the State Department in November instituted an automatic twenty-day hold on all visa applications from those countries to allow additional time for background checks. In January, State launched a new scheme known as Visas Condor, directing U.S. embassies to delay processing visa applications by most male applicants from those countries until they could be screened by the FBI and the CIA. The initial procedure allowed the visa to be issued if the security agencies failed to come up with any derogatory information in thirty days. But within a few months it had become clear that, much as with the security reviews for domestic detainees, the FBI lacked both the resources and the desire to carry out the screenings quickly. By April the backlog of Condor checks had grown to more than 8,000 names. In July 2002, fearing that a visa could inadvertently be issued to a terrorist before a security review was completed, the State Department and the FBI agreed to drop the thirty-day clock and hold all visa applications until FBI had finished its checks.

It was the misfortune of Faiz Bhora, Dia Elnaiem, and thousands of others like them that they were seeking visas just as the clock had been eliminated.

THE INTELLECTUAL ARCHITECT OF THE cop approach was a conservative young legal scholar with no expertise in immigration policy or immigration law. Kris Kobach was thirty-five when he came to the Justice Department in 2001. After he left the administration two years later, he would become one of the country's most vocal opponents of illegal immigration, and a fixture on talk radio and conservative television.

In early 2001, however, he was a young man in a hurry, yet to turn an impressive hat trick of academic credentials into any real political success. The son of a prosperous car dealer from Topeka, Kansas, Kobach was chosen as valedictorian of his high school class in 1984 after leading his school's debating team into the state championships. He was also one of just six Kansans that year accepted into Harvard University. Upon graduating from Harvard, he won a Marshall scholarship to Oxford, and after completing his doctorate he returned to the United States to earn a law degree from Yale. After taking up a law professorship at the University of Missouri at Kansas City, he won a seat on the city council for Overland Park, an upper-middle-class Kansas City suburb, in April 1999. "I think most people who worked with him on the council understood almost immediately that his real interest was not in being on the city council," said the town's mayor, Republican Ed Eilert. He ran in the Republican primary in 2000 for a seat in the Kansas State Senate, but was defeated.

So in 2001, Kobach applied for and won a White House fellowship. The fellowships are prestigious nonpartisan awards designed to give political experience to midcareer people seen as having government leadership potential. The impressive list of alumni includes Generals Colin Powell and Wesley Clark. Kobach arrived just ten days before the 9/11 attacks, and was detailed to the Justice Department where Ashcroft wanted someone to work on immigration issues. It was a serendipitous appointment. While he had never shown any particular interest in immigration law or policy, Kobach knew an opportunity when he saw one and threw himself at his new portfolio. "He was given a mission and he went at it like he was doing a science project," Mike Becraft, Ziglar's deputy at the INS, later said. When Ashcroft began several weeks after the attacks to reach outside his narrow circle of top officials to solicit new ideas for fighting the terrorists, Kobach was ready. After a brown-bag lunch in the attorney general's office, Kobach stayed behind and told Ashcroft he had been working on the outlines of a new program to register all foreigners living in the United States. Ashcroft was intrigued.

The United States had some history of registering foreigners in times of crisis. In 1940, Congress passed the Smith Act, which required nearly 5 million non-Americans to register and give their fingerprints at a local post office, and to carry with them at all times an alien registration card. In 1979, after Iranian students seized the U.S. embassy in Tehran and held Americans there hostage, President Jimmy Carter ordered all Iranian students in the United States to register to prove they were in the country legally. More than 50,000 students registered and more than 6,000 were found to have violated their student visas. And after Iraq's invasion of Kuwait in 1991, the Justice Department had ordered the registration of Iraqis visiting the United States, a practice that was later extended briefly to Sudanese, Iranians, and Libyans. The policy was upheld as constitutional by the U.S. Court of Appeals, which ruled that the government had the power to enforce registration selectively "so long as such distinctions are not wholly irrational."

What Kobach wanted was a broad scheme on the scale of the World War II effort, and it appealed to Ashcroft's desire to use every power at his disposal to prevent another terrorist attack. For Kobach, the goal was to extend the enforcement powers of immigration law beyond federal immigration agents and give it to the thousands of state and local police across the country who were out on patrol every day. While most of the analyses of what went wrong before 9/11 have focused on the lack of intelligence sharing and the government's failure to "connect the dots," Kobach had a different evaluation based on a different set of missed opportunities.

On September 9, 2001, shortly after midnight, a Maryland state trooper had pulled over a red Mitsubushi Gallant doing ninety miles an hour on a rural section of Interstate 95 near the Delaware border. The officer asked the driver for his license and registration, and returned to his patrol car to run a radio check for any outstanding warrants. Finding none, he walked back to the car and handed the driver a ticket with a $270 fine. The fine was never paid. Two days later, Ziad Jarrah was at the pilot controls on United Flight 93 when it crashed into a field near Shanksville, Pennsylvania, after passengers tried to retake control of the plane.

At the time he was pulled over, Jarrah had overstayed his tourist visa by more than a year, and was also in violation of his immigration status because he had enrolled in flight training in Florida without a student visa. Jarrah was not alone. Of the nineteen hijackers, five were in violation of some immigration law at the time they carried out the attacks, and four of them had been stopped by local police in the prior year. Nawaf al-Hazmi, who had been living illegally in the United States since January, was pulled over for speeding in Oklahoma on April 1, 2001, while driving in a car with fellow hijacker Hani Hanjour. Hanjour, who flew the plane that hit the Pentagon, was himself stopped for speeding in Virginia on August 1, 2001; he had entered the United States on a student visa but had never attended classes, putting him in violation of his immigration status. And Mohammed Atta, the plot's ringleader, who was pulled over for speeding twice in Florida in 2001, had previously overstayed a visa and should not even have been let back into the country in 2001.

To Kobach, each of these encounters with the police had been a chance to cut the plot off at its head, but instead each of the hijackers had been sent on his way with a small fine. "I had the sense that these were missed opportunities of tragic and colossal dimension," he said. Or, as he would write, "The abuse of U.S. immigration laws was instrumental in the deaths of nearly 3,000 people."

His idea was to use the new registration system to give local and state police the authority to detain illegal immigrants, multiplying the force of several thousand INS agents by deputizing some 650,000 local officials to carry out immigration arrests. What he envisioned was a new national program that would require every foreigner coming to the United States, or already living here, to register with the government and give fingerprints and detailed background information. Having such information could be valuable in itself, simply because it would give the INS something it did not have—a clearer picture of the foreign population in the United States. And he thought it would be relatively uncontroversial; during his time as a Marshall scholar in Britain, he recalls, he had been required to register periodically with local police to keep them up to date on his current address and student status.

Under the scheme devised by Kobach and a team at Justice and the INS, which became known as the National Security Entry-Exit Registration System (NSEERS), failure by an individual to register, or to leave the country before his visa expired, would be grounds for a criminal warrant for arrest. So would any other immigration transgression, such as attending school without a student visa. Once such a warrant was issued, it would be entered into the National Crime Information System (NCIC), a huge database that was accessible to every local police department in the country. If Ziad Jarrah's name had been in the NCIC on September 9, the traffic cop who pulled him over would have known that from his radio contact with his dispatcher, and perhaps Jarrah would not have been sent on his way with a mere fine. "If we had some way of keeping track of who had exceeded their period of stay and finding a way to get that information to local police," Kobach said, "we might have been able to stop it, or at least to impede the attack."

While Ashcroft loved the idea, it did not meet with universal support even within Justice. "Kobach was very, very hawkish," said one former Justice official. "We didn't want every cop in Texas asking for papers." There was also sharp disagreement over the scale of the program. What Kobach and Ashcroft wanted, former Justice officials say, was a comprehensive scheme that would have involved registering every foreigner in the United States, much like the Smith Act of World War II. Indeed, when Ashcroft first announced the scheme at a June 2002 press conference with a mute Jim Ziglar beside him, he indicated that the goal was to track all foreign visitors. The INS and Ziglar were strongly opposed to anything of that scale, and it quickly became obvious that the government could not get something that large up and running quickly. "It was clear early on that you couldn't do everyone," agreed Brian Peterman, who shepherded the negotiations on the scheme through the White House.

So officials settled on a program that, like the Condor visa scheme, was targeted at travelers from Arab and Muslim countries. It required them to give more detailed personal information than was ordinarily required for visa applicants, and to give fingerprints as part of the visa process. They were required to re-register after thirty days in the United States, and to leave the country only through certain airports, where the INS would set up exit kiosks to verify that they had left before their visa expired.

As with Condor, the State Department raised many of the strongest objections to the new program. While the outlines of the plan were in place by November 2001, it wouldn't be implemented for nearly another year. "As soon as we were directed to have inter-agency meetings with the State Department, things ground almost to a halt," said Kobach. "We had meeting after meeting at the State Department over the program, and you had a lot of people raising objections. Some were just generally of the view that if we ever fingerprint anyone from a country, that country's leadership is going to hate the United States because their people are being treated like criminals."

State officials, and some in the White House, were also worried that any discriminatory scheme would make it difficult to gain cooperation from those countries in the war on terrorism. "We were very concerned about having a list at all, because it could be perceived as lining up your enemies when many of these countries also had to be our allies in the war on terrorism," said Peterman. Nonetheless, they settled on a list of twenty-five Muslim and Arab countries, plus North Korea, roughly the same list as the Condor countries, giving discretion to INS agents to "enroll" travelers from other countries if they raised any suspicions.

The initiative was finally launched on the one-year anniversary of the attacks, and became a public relations nightmare from the outset. Ejaz Haider, an editor at Pakistan's English-language *Friday*

*Times*, was arrested on January 28, 2003, by two armed INS agents outside the offices of the Brookings Institution, a prestigious Washington think tank where he was a visiting scholar. Haider is an influential opponent of religious extremism in Pakistan, exactly the sort of liberal, pro-democracy voice the United States has tried to encourage in Pakistan and other Muslim countries. He had arrived in the United States on October 22, 2002, and was told at Dulles Airport in Washington that he needed to re-register by December 2. But there was vast public confusion—and even confusion within the INS—about which countries fell under NSEERS. Haider said that when he had followed up with the INS he was told that Pakistanis did not need to re-register. State Department friends had similarly told him he was not covered by the program. They were wrong. The two INS agents who arrested him forced him to leave his wallet behind, and took him to an INS detention facility in Alexandria, Virginia. He was photographed and fingerprinted in ink and electronically, and told that his bail was set at $5,000.

Haider got out five hours later, but only because his boss at Brookings—Strobe Talbott, former deputy secretary of state—called up the State Department's top official dealing with U.S.-Pakistan relations to demand that he be released. But he left infuriated by his treatment. "It was not like I was in hiding," he said. "They could have contacted me at my office. Instead they decided to drag me off the road."

"For more than a century, people from all over the world have come to the United States to escape repression and enjoy its freedoms," he wrote in the *Washington Post* following his ordeal. "Perhaps for the first time in American history, we are witnessing the spectacle of families migrating from the United States in search of safety. It is argued that this policy is meant to increase security for the United States. A worse way of doing so could hardly be imagined. The policy is an attempt to draw a Maginot Line around America. Not only is it likely to fail in securing the homeland, it is creating more resentment against the United States. Does America need a policy that fails to differentiate between friend and foe?"

Arab and Muslim governments fumed about the new policy. Adel al-Jubeir, a senior Saudi official who later became Saudi Arabia's ambassador in the United States, demanded a meeting with Justice officials and threatened to impose fingerprinting requirements on Americans traveling to Saudi Arabia. The U.S. ambassador to Pakistan wrote a cable back to the State Department in Washington in early January 2003 that concluded: "To a large extent, the U.S. cannot win here on NSEERS, regardless of the facts (35 percent of Pakistanis in the U.S. are out of status). There are few things that Benazir Bhutto and President Musharaff agree on, but NSEERS is one of them."

The program caused similar outrage among other Muslim allies of the United States. In Indonesia, the U.S. ambassador sent a cable back to the State Department in February 2003 warning that NSEERS "has created an enormously negative backlash here" that "has undercut our efforts with key policymakers and elites that had done the heavy lifting for us on our most difficult issues. . . . Moderate Muslim leaders feel unable to speak out in support of the U.S. and have cancelled trips to the United States in protest. Our allies warn we are raising Muslim hackles when we can least afford to do so." In Bangladesh, the ambassador wrote that "many Bangladeshis were shocked and hurt by the country's inclusion in NSEERS" despite the country's clear support for the U.S. fight against terror.

But it was the final component of the scheme, targeting foreigners already in the United States, that proved to be the most controversial. Kobach was not content just to put his plan in place for future travelers to the United States "We recognized the very real risk that there were probably already people in the country we should be concerned about," he later said. Therefore, in late 2002 the INS launched the domestic portion of NSEERS. It required citizens of those countries already living in the United States to come forward and register with the INS. It was the most confusing of all the post-9/11 initiatives launched by the Justice Department, and it snared thousands of people who simply failed to understand what was required of them.

While Ziglar and his INS team had largely acquiesced in the creation of NSEERS, they were strongly opposed to the domestic registration scheme, and even some of the more hawkish Justice Department officials were wary of the plan. They feared it could be an even worse public relations debacle, with crowds stampeding the local INS offices around the country, and that the resources required to register those already living in the country would detract from more urgent priorities.

In an effort to avoid a flood of registrants, the INS set different deadlines for different nationalities. The first tranche required registration by all men over the age of sixteen who were citizens of Iran, Iraq, Libya, Sudan, and Syria and temporary residents in the United States (that is, they were not permanent residents or naturalized Americans). They were ordered to appear at a local INS office between November 15 and December 16, 2002. The penalties for failing to register were severe—a fine of up to $1,000 or six months in prison. In addition, anyone who failed to register would automatically be considered out of status and subject to deportation. But compliance with the registration requirements was not any guarantee of immunity; anyone found to have overstayed a visa or violated some other immigration law also faced immediate detention and deportation.

In Los Angeles, which has one of the largest Iranian communities in the world outside of Tehran, the turnout for registration overwhelmed the capacity of the local INS office. The registration process took about eighteen minutes for each individual, and the INS had failed to deploy anything close to the number of officials needed to keep the lines moving smoothly. As a result, anyone whose status was the least bit ambiguous was arrested and detained while the INS tried to sort out their case. Many of those who showed up to register had green card applications pending under a process known as 245i that allows some would-be immigrants to seek permanent residence in the United States without returning home first. These and hundreds of others were arrested, causing panic among those still waiting to register. One INS official who opposed the program from the outset recalled turning on the television on December 16, the final day for Iranians to register, and seeing the news reports of the chaos outside the INS office in Los Angeles. "I told you so," he thought to himself.

Lawyers who tried to advise clients on whether they were required to register were unable to do so. Faith Nouri, an immigration lawyer who chaired the NSEERS Committee for the Los Angeles County Bar Association, said she went to a local meeting of INS and Customs officials that was meant to clarify the new law. She asked about whether one of her clients, who was in the United States on political asylum, would have to register, and was told by the officials that they had no idea and would have to check with senior officials in Washington.

The nationality requirements were particularly confusing. If someone had been born in Syria but had taken out Canadian citizenship, he or she was still considered Syrian for the purposes of registration. One Palestinian computer engineer in Florida went to the immigration office in Tampa to see whether Palestinians were required to register. There was no category for Palestinians, but since he was born in a Lebanese refugee camp, INS officials decided he was Lebanese and had missed the deadline for registration. He was arrested and detained, though charges against him were later dropped.

Zaif Safdar had been living in the United States for eleven years when his troubles began in March 2003. A native of Pakistan, he had come to the United States for undergraduate studies in engineering at the University of Rochester and then went on to do graduate work at the University of Pennsylvania and at the University of Chicago. When he graduated, he was hired by AT&T to work in its Bell Laboratories division. In 2002, he decided to return to graduate school at Johns Hopkins University; when he was accepted into the program, he quit his job at Lucent and applied for a student visa. As a result of the huge processing backlogs, the INS ordinarily allowed foreign students already in the United States to begin their program of study while their visa applications were still pending. Therefore, when Safdar showed up in March to register under NSEERS (Pakistan and Saudi Arabia were part of the program's third tranche, which had a March 21 registration deadline), he technically had no visa that allowed him to be living in the United States.

He was handcuffed and taken to jail, but released a day later when friends came to post his bail. He was immediately put into deportation proceedings. It was not until two weeks after his release that the INS informed him of the reason for his detention. He had quit his job at Lucent, begun his graduate program, and then applied for his visa, a decision he says was made in consultation with officials at Johns Hopkins. But according to the INS, he should have applied for the student visa before quitting his job; because he had not, he had violated the terms of his previous visa and was therefore in the country illegally. In the past, the INS would likely have ignored such a small error, "but now there's this zero tolerance policy, with no room for error," his lawyer said.

He decided to fight the deportation order, and a hearing was set for March 24, 2004. It was a risky decision. If he had given up and agreed to return to Pakistan voluntarily, he would have been free to reapply for a visa to return to the United States, though he would have lost at least a year of his program. If he was deported, however, he would be barred from returning to the United States for a decade. Fate—or perhaps his persistent lobbying of members of Congress—intervened. The night before his deportation hearing, he finally received his student visa. Because he had a valid visa in hand, the judge dismissed the case.

Unlike many, Safdar has little resentment over his treatment. "I've always felt a lot of gratitude and appreciation for the United States and what I was able to get from this country," he said. His ordeal came from what he called "the erratic implementation of a questionable policy." But, he said, "eventually it was my American friends who corrected the wrongs of the process."

# Chapter 4

------

# THE TECHNOCRATS

BY THE TIME TOM RIDGE left the Bush administration at the end of 2004, he had become a figure of national ridicule. The impossible scale of the task of constructing a new Department of Homeland Security, his own malleable leadership style, and what to his allies looked like a determined attempt by his administration adversaries to cut him down to size had left him the butt of jokes on late-night talk shows. In a free association test, most Americans shown a picture of Ridge would have come up with duct tape, cellophane, or color-coded charts. To his many supporters that still rankles as an injustice, and less as an indictment of Ridge than of the man he worked for. "Name me one person whose reputation has been enhanced by serving this president," fumed one of his closest aides. "Nobody."

But when Ridge arrived in Washington in October 2001, he had a different stature altogether. The nation's capital was still in shock from the 9/11 attacks when two packages filled with a fine whitish powder arrived at the offices of Senate Democratic leader Tom Daschle and his colleague Pat Leahy, with notes warning: "You cannot stop us. We have this anthrax. Death to America. Death to Israel. Allah is great." It followed similar packages sent in September to five different news organizations. Newspapers were

filled with authoritative-sounding stories quoting government officials claiming the anthrax was weapons-grade material that could
only have come from terrorists working in close collaboration with
a government bioweapons program. Two of the city's postal workers died simply from inhaling the spores as the letters had passed
through distribution facilities. While the anthrax attacks turned
out not to be the work of Al Qaeda—to this day no one has yet
been identified as responsible—for many weeks it seemed that the
follow-on attack that Ashcroft and others had feared had already
arrived. Worse, it appeared that the nightmare scenario of terrorists armed with weapons of mass destruction (WMD) was already
a reality.

Ridge emerged as the commanding, reassuring figure that
Washington, and the country, desperately needed. A tall, rugged-
looking ex-Marine with a deep, resonant voice, a square jaw, and
slicked-back jet black hair, he filled up the cameras at a time when
the nation was on the verge of panic. Even his title—White House
director of Homeland Security—was reassuring for a country feel-
ing a level of insecurity it had not experienced since the Cuban
missile crisis forty years earlier. For a brief period in the fall of
2001, the nation was looking to Ridge to define and create an entirely new function for the U.S. government: protecting its citizens
from terrorist attacks on its own soil.

Like President Bush, Ridge was a border-state politician, and
he had been governor of Pennsylvania since 1994. Pennsylvania is
not truly a border state in the way that, say, Texas is; it doesn't even
share an international land boundary. But Ridge had grown up in
Erie, a bleak railroad and steel town that lies across the lake from
Ontario and less than an hour's drive from the Canadian border.
His father—a traveling salesman and U.S. Navy veteran—often
worked two jobs to support the family, even though they lived in
publicly subsidized veterans' housing. The young Ridge earned a
scholarship to Harvard, from which he graduated with honors in
1967, and then went on to enroll at the Dickinson School of Law
in Carlisle, Pennsylvania.

After his first year at law school, his number came up in the lottery draft for Vietnam. His father encouraged him to leave for Canada, but Ridge stayed, even passing on a chance to enroll in officer's training and instead enlisting in the infantry. When he arrived for basic training in Louisiana in 1969 at the age of twenty-four, he was the only man in his unit with a college degree. He served in Vietnam for seven months, losing part of his hearing from artillery fire and earning the Bronze Star for Valor for his role in a March 1970 firefight with a small Viet Cong force. Like so many who served there, he came back a skeptic about the war and how it had been fought. "I never doubted the courage of the warrior but will always doubt the way the war was conducted," he would say later. And he returned with a particular notion of what leadership meant, even in a crisis. "Leadership involves communication, trust in others. My brand of leadership, even though it was a small group of people, wasn't necessarily, 'This is what we're going to do, that's it.' It was, 'This is what we're going to do, this is why we're going to do it.'"

In 1982 Ridge was elected to the U.S. House of Representatives from Erie, a traditionally Democratic district, and went on to win reelection six times on wide margins. Though the Republican Party was moving steadily to the right during his tenure in Congress, Ridge's voting record was notably moderate, which probably kept him from becoming Bush's running mate in 2000, or his secretary of defense. Among the votes that raised conservative eyebrows were his support for a 1994 measure banning assault weapons, his vote to cut back on Reagan's Strategic Defense Initiative, and his backing for a higher minimum wage. He was also, despite his Catholic faith, moderately prochoice in a party where opposition to abortion had become a litmus test for a Republican base that was increasingly dominated by evangelical Christians.

After his election as governor of Pennsylvania, Ridge had put much of his energy into guiding the economic transition of a state whose core industries, particularly steel and other manufacturing businesses, were in decline. He went on trade missions to Canada,

South America, Asia, Israel, and Ireland, drumming up exporting opportunities for big companies like Westinghouse and Heinz and dozens of smaller ones as well. Following the passage of NAFTA, he launched a new export strategy to pair small local companies with bigger companies from Pennsylvania that had operations in Mexico in order to help them compete and grow. The goal of the strategy was one hundred thousand new jobs in the state; by the end of the decade Pennsylvania's exports to Canada and Mexico had reached all-time highs, totaling $9 billion in 1999 and helping to bring the state's unemployment rate down to 4.5 percent, a drop of two percentage points in five years.

Like Bush, Ridge had carved out a long record in favor of open borders, on both trade and immigration. He was a vigorous opponent of congressional legislation passed in 1996 that required the creation of an entry-exit system at the U.S. borders, a law that was aimed at giving the government a fuller picture of who had come to the country and whether they had left. Ridge joined other border-state governors in arguing that it was impractical to expect Canadians and Mexicans who visited the country to report to U.S. border control officials on their way back home. They warned that implementing the provision would create costly traffic jams and delays at the border, damaging trade and imperiling U.S. prosperity. Such pressure had succeeded in pushing back the congressional deadlines for the scheme to be implemented, so it was little more than a pilot project at a handful of airports when the 9/11 hijackers struck.

WHILE TERRORISM WAS NOT HIGH on the new Bush administration's foreign policy priorities, the question of whether a terrorist group might acquire a nuclear, chemical, or biological weapon was one that did worry Bush's new team, particularly Vice President Dick Cheney. The CIA had learned as early as 1996 from an Al Qaeda defector that Osama bin Laden was seeking to acquire uranium in Sudan that could be used in a nuclear device. That spring, Cheney tasked his top foreign policy aide, Lewis "Scooter"

Libby, with evaluating the risk that terrorist groups could acquire weapons of mass destruction, an issue that had been raised by the Hart-Rudman Commission and several other high-level studies. Libby had asked Steve Abbot, a retired navy admiral, to carry out the review. By early September, Abbot had assembled a team of about a dozen people. His first day on the job was September 10, and he was waiting outside Libby's office the next day when the planes struck in New York.

The group had barely formed and had only begun reviewing the different studies over the summer, but Abbot said that one conclusion was already clear before 9/11: that responsibility for securing the United States against a terrorist attack was so widely dispersed within the government that the only way to forge a coherent response was to have the White House coordinate the effort. Libby, along with Cheney and the vice president's top political adviser, Mary Matalin, quickly settled on who should be the coordinator: Tom Ridge. Ridge was a friend of the president's, a decorated war veteran, and was already, like New York City Mayor Rudy Giuliani, connected in the public mind with the recovery from 9/11. He had been elevated by the heroism of the passengers who stormed the cockpit of United Flight 93, crashing the plane into an empty farmer's field in Shanksville, Pennsylvania, rather than allowing the hijackers to fly to their intended target in Washington, the White House or the Capitol. On September 19, Bush's chief of staff, Andrew Card, called Ridge and asked him to come immediately to Washington to talk about a new position as the country's first White House director of homeland security. Reflecting the urgency of the time, within twenty-four hours Ridge had accepted and within two weeks he had resigned the governor's job and brought his family to Washington.

FROM THE BEGINNING OF HIS tenure at the White House, Ridge looked at the homeland security problem through the eyes of a border-state governor. While horrified by the terrorist attacks, he was also shaken by the immediate impact of the U.S.

response, in particular by the virtual shutdown of commerce at the land borders following the attacks. "We did what we had to do," he said, "but it really imperiled our economic interaction with our friends, north and south." The dramatic effects of the border measures "basically created a mind-set within which we operated from within the White House [and] throughout my tenure as secretary [of Homeland Security]. It was a mind-set that said, 'Look, we've got to make ourselves safer, but what's the economic impact?' You've got to make damn sure that you try to manage this in a way that's sensitive to the both of these national needs: security and the economy." While he never had long conversations with Bush on how to manage the borders after 9/11, the president seemed to share the same philosophy, without concerning himself much over the details. "It's not like we sat around and smoked cigars and drank coffee and said, 'Well, what are you going to do about this?' I remember it very vividly. He just said 'Go fix it.'"

Before he left Pennsylvania for Washington, Ridge took a crash course in the still rather scant academic and professional literature on homeland security. The first piece he read was coauthored by Admiral James Loy, the Coast Guard commandant since 1998, and was entitled "Meeting the Homeland Security Challenge." Written just before the attacks, it was heavily influenced by the Hart-Rudman Commission report and reflected a very different philosophy than the one that was inspiring the aggressive immigration enforcement campaign being waged by the Justice Department.

The first requirement of any response to a terrorist attack, Loy wrote, must be adherence to constitutional principles and to the rule of law. "Security measures, if carried too far, pose risks that may equal or even exceed those of terrorists and ill-intentioned foreign governments. . . . In fact, such overreactions have sometimes been the result desired by terrorists. Similarly, badly designed border controls could endanger international trade and the American economy."

But how could the United States avoid such an overreaction? Terrorism is a particularly insidious form of warfare because nothing is beyond the battlefield—office buildings, shopping malls, subways, even schools could all be targets, and protecting them all would require radical changes in the everyday lives of Americans. If it made sense to have scanners and explosives detectors at the country's airports, why not at subway stations or sports arenas or bus terminals and mall entrances? Loy looked at the problem though Coast Guard eyes, seeing in the country's lightly guarded seaports and its thousands of miles of unguarded coastline the same unlimited vulnerabilities. Trying to protect it all would be self-defeating. "The challenge facing the Coast Guard, the Customs Service, and other border control agencies is to develop ways to better protect the nation without sacrificing economic vitality in the process, and without breaking the federal budget," he wrote.

Homeland security, in other words, faced a fundamental dilemma. Completely protecting the country from another terrorist attack would require security measures that were so vast and so expensive that they would destroy the very things they were designed to protect. Lives would be saved, but at huge costs to liberty and the pursuit of happiness. President Dwight Eisenhower had faced a similar dilemma after the Soviet Union's explosion of a hydrogen bomb in 1953 forced the country to face the possibility of a devastating nuclear attack. Eisenhower's advisers had urged him to issue a national call to arms, and to begin construction of a massive network of blast and fallout shelters to prepare the country to survive a nuclear war. But Eisenhower rejected that recommendation, believing that putting the United States on such a permanent war footing would destroy the economy and imperil American democracy.

Loy drew similar conclusions, though he couched them in the less elegant language of modern management theory. The U.S. government, he argued, needed to develop a risk management mentality, which called for making sophisticated judgments about where to deploy scarce resources in combating the terrorist threat. Absolute prevention of terrorist attacks was impossible at any reasonable price, he argued. The government therefore needed to make difficult choices about which things to protect and how much they should be protected.

There were no easy formulas. If someone had tried to write one, it would have been something like (Consequences × probability) ÷ costs of prevention = priority. For example, the so-called nuke-in-a-box scenario, in which terrorists smuggled a nuclear weapon in a seagoing cargo container and detonated it in a port city like Los Angeles or New York, was highly improbable. There were enormous technical and political obstacles to terrorist groups developing or acquiring the bomb, and if they had, they would have been unlikely to send their prized weapon to the United States via a commercial container ship. But if it happened, it would kill hundreds of thousands of people, a devastating blow. Just as important, the costs of prevention were modest, involving closer tracking of containers and fairly inexpensive security devices. Therefore it had a high priority in homeland security planning. In contrast, a suicide or conventional bomb attack on the New York subway or the Washington metro had to be considered highly likely. But even effective attacks, such as the synchronized Madrid train bombings in 2004, had a death toll in the low hundreds—awful, but not catastrophic. And the costs of prevention—which would require forcing every passenger to walk through metal and explosives detectors—would be enormous in terms of inconvenience and delays. Thus there has never been more than a token effort, such as the deployment of a few bomb-sniffing dogs, to protect some of the most obvious targets in the country.

It was harder to make such judgments at the border, because the United States lacked much of the information it needed to make intelligent decisions about which people and things posed the greatest risks. "Information is the key," Loy wrote. "Databases from agencies and services, each with a partial view, must be fused so that the total picture emerges and effective intelligence is produced. With sufficient advanced information about inbound ships, cargoes, and crews, the border control agencies will have a significantly enhanced ability to separate the good from the bad."

Ridge invited Loy up to the governor's mansion in Pennsylvania for an hour-long briefing that turned into four. The technocrats' approach—that the clever use of information, intelligence,
and technology could largely avoid the trade-off between security
and the free flow of goods and people—was exactly what Ridge
was looking for. First, like Bush, he believed strongly in economic
openness, and he wanted to avoid making any choices that would
diminish that commitment. "Risk management is a pretty difficult
concept for people to buy into, but I think an absolutely critical
concept if you believe that your future prosperity is tied to the
prosperity of the rest of the world and that you need to build security measures that obviously make the country safer, but do not
close the front door," he said. While he and Ashcroft rarely clashed,
he said he had "a slightly different, I won't measure it, but a difference of opinion with regard to how one manages risk." Second, as
a White House coordinator he had no real power in his new post
beyond the power to persuade other agencies to adopt a common
approach. He certainly had nothing like the law enforcement arsenal that the Justice Department could deploy.

But the technocrats had the kind of coherent vision of what
could be done that Ridge needed to persuade Congress and other
parts of the executive branch to move in a new direction. Finally,
he had a very American faith in the ability of technology to solve
problems. He was particularly enthusiastic about biometrics—the
use of fingerprints, facial recognition technology, and iris scans as a
way of accurately identifying people in a quick and efficient manner. "Biometrics is the only conceivable way you can build a security protocol that substantially reduces the risk," he said, "but also
protects privacy and helps facilitate commerce, because it's the only
way to know that people are who they say they are."

THE TECHNOCRATS DOMINATED TWO GOVERNMENT agen-
cies in the post-9/11 Bush administration. The first was Ridge's
new White House Office of Homeland Security, which by the end
of 2001 had grown to a staff of nearly eighty people. Ridge brought

with him a number of trusted aides from his Pennsylvania governor's staff, including Mark Holman, who had been his chief of staff. Steve Abbot, the navy admiral who had been brought in by Cheney for the weapons of mass destruction task force, was asked to stay on as Ridge's deputy director and would chair many of the key meetings on the developing policy. And he sought out Richard Falkenrath, a brash young academic from Harvard's Kennedy School of Government who had written one of the few books on homeland security, a 1998 tome called *America's Achilles' Heel* that warned of the dangers of terrorists acquiring WMDs. Falkenrath would get a key post as Ridge's new policy planning director, responsible for churning out new ideas at a time when innovation counted for much more than established wisdom. But it was hard to build an effective support staff. Many were detailed from other government agencies, particularly from the military, and most had little or no White House experience to prepare them for the interagency battles that would follow. And the office remained seriously understaffed. By April 2002 it had filled only half of the 180 personnel slots that been allocated. In comparison, even the White House drug czar's office had more than a hundred people.

The real power base for the technocrats was Robert Bonner's Customs Service. If not for 9/11, Bonner might not have even won Senate confirmation for months. In a small foreshadowing of the fights that would come over the use of technology in homeland security, Bonner's nomination was being blocked because Customs had refused to spend money that Congress had earmarked for a highly experimental imaging system known as pulsed fast-neutron analysis that was supposed to improve security at ports by allowing for rapid, nonintrusive inspection of the contents of cargo containers. Customs officials were persuaded that the technology was useless and had balked at spending the $10 million that Congress had appropriated for a pilot project, an earmark inserted by an Oklahoma congressman on behalf of a state company that was marketing the technology. As a result, James Inhofe, an Oklahoma senator, had used one of the many peculiar prerogatives of the Senate to place a hold on Bonner's nomination until he committed to launch the pilot project. Following the attacks, Inhofe immediately lifted his hold, and Bonner was confirmed by the Senate the next week. Customs did agree to try out the technology on the southern border with Mexico but, as one Customs veteran put it, "It failed as anticipated and it cost several million dollars to disassemble and remove."

Bonner's aggressive actions after 9/11 won him admirers and detractors in equal measure. He was seen as smart, tough, and effective but also as enormously arrogant and a bit of a bully who would simply roll over opponents within the government to advance his own interests and those of the Customs Service. One of Bonner's first initiatives was to begin pressing foreign airlines for the same advanced information on passengers that was given to the government by the domestic airlines, and had first been used by Customs to identify the nineteen hijackers on the morning of the attack. By mid-November 2001, Congress had passed a new aviation security act that required federal screening agents at all airports, the deployment of armed air marshals on flights, and the securing of cockpit doors against forced entry. As part of that legislation, Customs got a provision slipped in that required all airlines flying into the United States, domestic and foreign, to provide Customs and the INS with the name and identification of each passenger, and with reservation data showing when, where, and how the tickets had been purchased. The hope was that such advanced information would help the government to identify potential terrorists before they could carry out an attack, not after the fact, as had been done on 9/11.

The legislation set a January 1, 2002, deadline for all airlines to begin providing passenger data or face big fines, but with the urgency that was shared across the government after 9/11, Bonner was not willing to wait. In November 2001, as soon as it become clear the legislation would pass, Customs warned some sixty foreign airlines that any airline that failed to share such data immediately would face searches of every one of its passengers when their planes landed in the United States. Several balked. In an effort to send the strongest message possible, Bonner started with Saudi Airlines and other carriers from the Middle East, which initially refused, ordering that every passenger on incoming Saudi flights be diverted to secondary inspection and questioned thoroughly before being allowed into the country. The delays were staggering. George Heavey, who was Customs executive director of field operations, said that scrutiny was particularly heavy for arriving foreign students, who could face waits of four, five, even eight hours before being allowed into the country. Within two days of these full searches, Bonner said, Saudi Airlines was on the phone to Customs eager to comply with the new requirements.

To Customs, such advance information was the only feasible way to identify dangerous individuals without disrupting the normal flow of travelers across the border. If the information was in hand well before someone arrived in the United States, it would give Customs and other agencies time to check against lists of known terrorists, but more importantly, to try to identify any links that unknown passengers might have to known terrorists. That was obvious if they were on the same flight, but could even be true for people trying to enter days or even months later. The watch lists, which contained names of terrorists known to the intelligence agencies so that State Department, INS, and Customs officials could keep them out of the country, were critically important, but they were of no help for "clean" operatives who had no history of terrorist activity. The passenger data was a critical tool for linking the known and the unknown.

One former Customs official contrasted this targeted approach with what he called the "grossly unexclusive" methods used by the screeners at U.S. airports, which involved subjecting every passenger to the same level of basic scrutiny, with more in-depth searches done on a largely random basis. "The approach we took at the border was very different," he said. But it was also far more difficult to implement. Searching everyone, however disruptive, had the virtue of simplicity and was easy to sell to a Congress and a public demanding tough action.

CANADA BECAME THE FIRST TEST of the technocrats' border approach. In some ways, it was an odd place to start building the new homeland security architecture. The nineteen hijackers had all come directly on planes from overseas; none had transited through Canada, despite some early rumors that one or more had entered the United States on boats from Nova Scotia. And there were more obvious threats exposed by the plot. Zacarias Moussaoui, who was arrested in Minneapolis just days before the attacks when he aroused suspicion by seeking out flight schools where he could learn to fly a Boeing 747, was a French citizen, underscoring the vulnerabilities of the visa waiver program, which allowed most European citizens—including radicalized Muslims—to travel to the United States with no prior checks.

But while it was not a factor in the 9/11 attacks, there was a real terrorist threat from Canada. The Ressam arrest in 1999 had showed the possibility that a terrorist could use Canada as a transit point to the United States. The long northern border was lightly defended in most places, and virtually every known terrorist organization in the world had some presence in Canada. Canada has served as an organizational and financial hub for a number of terrorist attacks around the world; further, Canada's extremely liberal policy on refugees meant that almost anyone could show up, claim political persecution, and be released to live freely in the country for months until a hearing could be held. Ressam had demonstrated that terrorists could exploit such generosity. More importantly for the technocrats, Canada was the perfect place to showcase their argument that security and openness would have to go together. The two-way trading relationship with Canada is the largest in the world, and while it matters much more to Canada than to the United States, nearly a quarter of American exports go north. Any significant disruption in cross-border trade would do serious damage to the U.S. economy, and even a modest slowdown would upset the powerful American car industry, which was fully integrated across the forty-ninth parallel.

Most importantly, unlike the Arab states or even the Europeans, the Canadians were willing partners. The near shutdown of the border after 9/11 had been an alarm bell for a country whose three major cities are within an hour's drive of the United States and where 85 percent of its exports are sent south. The Canadian Council of Chief Executives, a powerful lobbying group of CEOs that is the Canadian equivalent of the U.S. Business Roundtable, had immediately seized on the economic threat posed by tougher border measures. It was pushing for a "perimeter" strategy that would involve bolstering external borders in both Canada and Mexico to keep terrorists out of North America, while reducing scrutiny and easing congestion at the land borders with the United States. That would require Canada to move closer to U.S. policy on issues such as visas and refugees in order to assuage American fears that Canada could be used as a back door by terrorists. "I think we're going to have to conform in some cases more to U.S. standards if we're going to create a North American security system," said David O'Brien, chief executive of Canadian Pacific, a big rail, shipping, and hotels conglomerate.

Paul Cellucci, the former governor of Massachusetts who was appointed ambassador to Canada by Bush, had been urging a similar strategy, fearing that the alternative was to continue the tight border screening that had been implemented after 9/11. "Canada's national interest depends on easy access to the U.S. market," said Stephen Kelly, a career State Department official who was Cellucci's deputy chief at the U.S. embassy in Ottawa after 9/11. There was also a long history of cooperation between the two countries on trade, border management, intelligence sharing, and other issues, which made it a logical place to start.

Still, the United States initially met with strong resistance. Jean Chrétien, the Canadian prime minister, had been a popular leader for nearly a decade in good measure because, unlike his predecessor, Brian Mulroney, he kept a wary distance from the Americans. While a slim majority of Canadians had accepted the benefits of freer trade with the United States, they were overwhelmingly suspicious of any moves that smacked of importing American policies into Canada. Chrétien carefully tried to respond to demands from Washington to tighten border controls without being seen publicly as kowtowing to the United States. For instance, in an internal memo Canadian border officials were ordered to give special scrutiny to travelers who had spent time in Pakistan, Afghanistan, or fourteen other countries described as "zones of conflict or terrorist training centers." The directive further called for close checks of anyone with aviation experience or a university background in engineering, computers, chemistry, or physics, and scientists working in the nuclear, defense, and communications fields. Yet just three days after the attacks, Chrétien announced publicly that Canada would make no changes to its immigration or border control measures. "I don't think Canadians are prepared to say that Washington can dictate our policies for who comes into Canada," his foreign minister, John Manley, said just before Chrétien left for Washington to show his support for the United States.

But the pressure for action was growing quickly in Washington. As part of the USA Patriot Act proposed by Ashcroft's Justice Department, Congress authorized a tripling of the number of Customs inspectors on the Canadian border, to more than 5,000, and a similar tripling in Border Patrol agents to 900. The U.S. Congress was showing it was prepared to harden the border on its own, with or without Canadian cooperation. Polls in the wake of the attacks also indicated that a vast majority of Canadians were willing to support closer cooperation with the United States on border issues. "The Canadian public . . . seems to sense something Mr Chrétien doesn't," wrote Drew Fagan, a columnist for the Toronto *Globe and Mail.* "The old concepts of Canadian sovereignty seem outdated at a time when citizens on both sides of the border feel under unprecedented threat and when Canada's economic interests are completely tied to the U.S."

Canadian resistance quickly crumbled. In late October, Manley traveled to Washington for his first meeting with Ridge in the White House, and the two began to talk about ways to improve border security while addressing the long border delays that had continued after 9/11. The next day, the Canadian government acknowledged that it was in negotiations with the United States on more closely harmonizing the two countries' policies on visas and refugees.

Once the Canadian government had made the decision to open negotiations with the United States on the border, progress came quickly. In November, Treasury secretary Paul O'Neill traveled to Ottawa to a meeting of the so-called G-20 countries dealing with development issues, a favorite topic of Canada's finance minister, Paul Martin. In a meeting room at the historic Chateau Laurier, part of the grand chain of turn-of-the-century Canadian Pacific hotels across the country, the two men convened their top border officials, including Bonner on the U.S. side, to discuss what could be done to strengthen the mutual border without disrupting commerce or the free movement of people. Martin and O'Neill had much in common: both had successful careers in business and found themselves repeatedly frustrated in government by the lumbering ways of their bureaucracies. They hit it off superbly, and O'Neill proposed an ambitious six-week deadline for coming up with a package of measures.

Kelly, the deputy chief of the U.S. mission in Ottawa at the time, says there was enormous skepticism from the teams on both sides about the deadline. "Maybe when he was in the private sector that was a reasonable expectation," he said. But 9/11 had changed the art of the possible in government, and within several weeks bureaucrats on both sides had come up with the outlines of what would be known as the Smart Border Action Plan.

Their idea was to use intelligence sharing, cooperation with the private sector, and new technologies to bolster security, rather than simply relying on agents spread out along the border to keep out terrorists. The goal was not to cause disruption that would deter terrorist plots, but to deter such plots without causing disruption. As Kelly said later: "The 'smart border' would be one that called for using technology and better intelligence and information sharing between the two countries so that they could stop people or discover plots or threats long before they got to the borders. That's the basic underpinning of the whole smart border concept."

Intelligence sharing came first. In early December, Ashcroft traveled to Ottawa to sign an agreement committing both countries to exchange more information on terrorism investigations and to strengthen cross-border cooperation by police, immigration, and Customs officials. They also agreed to pass along information on visa denials, so that if one country refused to issue a visa to a foreigner suspected of terrorism or other crimes, that person would also be refused a visa by the other country. Canada also agreed to tighten up its own visa system and its screening of those seeking refugee status. These were breakthroughs that would not have been possible without the fear and urgency created by 9/11. Prior to the attacks, the United States had several times gone to the Canadians to urge some harmonizing of visa policies between the two countries, only to be soundly rebuffed. "The answer would be, 'We're not going to let the United States decide who gets into Canada,'" Kelly recalled. The United States was particularly concerned over some of the Polynesian microstates, such as Vanuatu, Nauru, and Tuvalu, as well as several Caribbean countries, where passport fraud was rampant. Following the Ashcroft visit, the Canadians announced that they would end visa-free travel from those countries. Within a year, Canada would take the more controversial step of reimposing visa requirements on Saudi Arabia and Malaysia. "The spirit of the time very much was, 'No more screwing around, we've got to do this,'" said Kelly. "It's in both our interests."

With progress coming fast in the negotiations with Canada, Ridge moved to take control of the talks. Ridge knew Canada well and as governor had been acquainted with John Manley, the Canadian foreign minister who was taking the lead on many of Canada's post-9/11 initiatives. Canadian officials, who grow weary of reminding their American counterparts of the importance of trade with Canada, were impressed that at the first meeting between the two Ridge was already well aware that Canada was Pennsylvania's top foreign market. Ridge and Manley signed the Smart Border Declaration in Ottawa less than a month later, on December 12, 2001, with a thirty-point list of key initiatives. "We want to make it easier for the average Canadian or American to cross the border," Ridge said in announcing the deal. "Our goal is to do everything we can to eliminate the wait and hassle for no-risk travelers so we can focus on stopping high-risk individuals."

There was no single dramatic breakthrough in the accord, but instead a series of smaller measures that added up to something like a new vision of how to manage borders in an age of terrorism. The two countries agreed to share advance passenger information and reservation data for all flights between Canada and the United States, but more importantly, to share information on international flights coming into either country so that neither country could be exploited as a weak link by terrorists. Each committed to begin developing secure identification cards for their citizens and current residents, including some kind of biometric identifier so that the documents could not be forged. Following 9/11, the United States had shut down the so-called NEXUS program, which allowed frequent border crossers who had registered with the government and undergone background checks to move quickly through special lanes. The agreement called for restarting and reinvigorating that program. Few of the new measures came easily, however. The Canadians had greater concerns over privacy than the United States, and the negotiations on the terms for sharing passenger information would take nearly two years to be resolved. The disputes over details have continued. As late as early 2008, Canada was pushing back against U.S. demands that it share passenger information on all Canadian flights that were crossing U.S. airspace but not landing in the country, such as flights from Toronto to the Caribbean or directly to Mexico.

Most of the other innovations concerned the movement of commercial goods across the border. The enormous volume of container traffic coming into both countries from overseas, and across the border by rail and truck, could not possibly be inspected adequately to ensure that neither terrorists nor their weapons were being smuggled across. For instance, a trucker would normally arrive at the border with a sheaf of papers containing information about the cargo he was carrying, forcing the Customs inspector to either accept the declaration or take the laborious step of opening the truck to verify the contents. For the technocrats, the challenge after 9/11 was to identify which shipments demanded closer scrutiny and which could be confidently waved through. Canada had been pushing an idea it called "customs self-assessment," in which certain high-volume shippers that had been vetted by the government would be allowed to speed through "fast lanes" at the border, freeing up agents to inspect unknown shipments. Further, both governments began talking about new procedures that would permit companies that had been screened by the governments to pack their goods, electronically seal them in a container at the factory, and then transmit information on the cargo and the driver directly to Customs officials at the border. That information would then be used to "preclear" the shipment and the truck would simply be able to drive through a special lane at the border. By April 2002, Customs had set up a scheme known as the Customs-Trade Partnership Against Terrorism (C-TPAT), beginning with a pilot program in Detroit that involved sixty prescreened companies, including Ford, GM, Target, and Motorola.

The goal, Bonner said, was "removing from the vast haystack of trade the legitimate, secure commerce that we don't need to be as concerned about. Reducing the haystack will increase security against terrorist attack, but at the same time move us to a system that processes goods faster, more efficiently, and at less cost to business." The two countries also pioneered an initiative to share information on oceangoing container shipments arriving in either country, in order to prevent dangerous cargo from being off-loaded in one country and shipped by rail to the other without ever undergoing inspection. They agreed to allow Customs agents from each country to be posted in the other, to bring the intelligence of both to bear in identifying suspicious cargo. That agreement would mushroom into one of Bonner's signature programs—the Container Security Initiative—in which he persuaded almost all of the major shipping countries in the world to allow American Customs inspectors to be posted abroad to help vet U.S.-bound cargo long before it ever arrived in the United States.

The ideas were sometimes better in theory than in practice. The costs of gaining trusted-shipper status, for example, were high, discouraging many smaller companies from participating. Many of the border crossings were not equipped to funnel trucks into fast lanes, sometimes forcing truckers to wait in long lines with cars and other trucks to cross bridges or other barriers before they could veer off into the preferred lanes. And the two sides could not reach agreement on everything. The United States, for instance, wanted to move the inspection process away from the congested border line and do its clearance in Canada before trucks actually reached the border. But the issue was politically sensitive on both sides. Bonner wanted the Customs inspectors who would be stationed in the preclearance zones to carry guns and to have the authority to make arrests if they identified drug dealers or other criminals seeking entry into the United States. Those demands were unacceptable to Ottawa, which saw them as dangerously diminishing Canada's sovereignty on its own soil. No deal was reached.

Despite the problems, on the whole the initiative was a success, particularly in increasing the amount of information in the hands of border inspectors without significantly slowing processing time. The post-9/11 shutdown had demonstrated the enormous costs of requiring detailed inspections of every vehicle crossing the border; the Smart Border Initiative showed that a greater level of security could be reached at much lower cost—one of the primary tenets of the risk management approach to the border that Loy had tried to impress on Ridge during their first meeting in Pennsylvania. "We really did accomplish the purpose of reinventing the goods transfer process between the United States and Canada, so that not only was it excellent, but it was enormously better than what had existed before 9/11," former Treasury secretary Paul O'Neill said later.

But the negotiations with Canada also brought into the open the rivalry that was already building within the U.S. government over who would take charge of the new realm of homeland security. Ashcroft, who was trying to establish himself as a kind of domestic terrorism czar, had been furious that details of his agreement with Canada had leaked out before his trip to Ottawa, fearing it would downplay his role and give the spotlight to Ridge when he arrived a week later. Customs and the INS also tried to minimize Ridge's involvement in the negotiations with Canada. "Well before the Ridge-Manley accord we had started meeting with our Canadian counterparts to significantly improve security against the terrorist threat," Bonner told the *New York Times* in February 2002. "The truth is that most of the initiatives that came out of that trip in early December, these were points that were already brewing here," echoed Jim Ziglar of the INS. "Everything in the Ridge-Manley documents was already on the table and close to having something done on it." White House officials acknowledge that they seized on the negotiations with Canada in part because it was possible to show quick progress and demonstrate that Ridge's office was making positive contributions. "There were deliverables coming out. It was hard to point to something and say we made a difference, and you could do that here," said Lt. Col. Chris Hornbarger, who was recruited from the army by Falkenrath, Ridge's Harvard-trained policy chief, to come work on homeland security policy.

The defensiveness of the traditional border agencies was not surprising. In addition to what they saw as encroaching on their turf, Ridge was trying to do something far more threatening. He was trying to do away with them entirely.

BY JANUARY 2002, THE LESSONS learned in the negotiations with Canada and the initiatives being pursued by Bonner's Customs Service had begun to coalesce into a blueprint for what those in Ridge's Office of Homeland Security called "the border of the future." Falkenrath directed Pancho Kinney, a former aide to Clinton's drug czar, Barry McCaffrey, who had been brought into the

White House to try to emulate the Canadian success in negotiations with Mexico, to draw up a paper summarizing the approach. Its big idea was to use intelligence and information systems in a sophisticated manner to push the U.S. border outward. The goal was to build a layered defense that did not rely solely on the instincts of border officials to make correct decisions in an instant on individuals they knew nothing about.

The paper, which was circulated internally within the government but never made public, began:

> The border of the future will be radically different from today's linear border dominated by ports of entry and extensive sectors between them. The border of the future will instead be a continuum framed by land, sea and air dimensions, where a layered management system enables full visibility of vehicles, people and cargo coming to and departing from our country. The border of the future will provide greater security through better intelligence, coordinated national efforts, and unprecedented international cooperation against the threats posed by terrorists, the implements of terrorism, international organized crime, illegal drugs, illegal migrants, agricultural pests and diseases, and the destruction or theft of natural resources. At the same time, the border of the future will be increasingly transparent to the efficient flow of people, cargo, and vehicles engaged in legitimate economic and social activities.

In a phrase that would be echoed many times by President Bush, the paper said, "We are not attempting to build a 'Fortress America' with militarized borders creating barriers between our homeland, our neighbors, and our international partners." It was in essence a declaration of the technocrats' founding principles for border security.

The paper called for U.S. border policy to be driven by five principles, all of which had been part of the U.S.-Canada accord: first, the government should embrace the idea of "risk-based decision making" that would allow for the focused use of limited enforcement resources; second, high-risk and low-risk traffic should be separated as early as possible, to allow for the more effective use of intelligence; third, the United States should cooperate with other governments to develop agreed standards and procedures; fourth, intelligence information should be organized so that it could get to frontline inspectors in the timely fashion needed to block entry by suspect individuals; and fifth, border control needed to be reviewed constantly in the light of threat assessments.

What it added up to was a faith in the government's ability to use technology and intelligence to sort the bad from the good. On January 25, 2002, four days before Bush delivered his famous "axis of evil" speech, the White House released its Action Plan for Creating a Secure and Smart Border, giving official sanction to the technocrats' blueprint for the border of the future. It said that the United States "requires a border management system that keeps pace with expanding trade while protecting the United States and its territories from the threats of terrorist attack, illegal immigration, illegal drugs and other contraband." To do this, it said, "The use of advanced technology to track the movement of cargo and the entry and exit of individuals is essential to the task of managing the movement of hundreds of millions of individuals, conveyances and vehicles."

Setting out a vision of the border of the future was one thing, but implementing it was another altogether. Looking at the long history of dysfunction, particularly within the INS, Ridge believed that unless the government reorganized its border agencies, it would be impossible to implement the sort of futuristic system he envisioned. He had directed Falkenrath almost immediately to begin considering such reorganization, and by the middle of November 2001 rumors were starting to circulate in Washington that Ridge was preparing to propose something dramatic. At a conference hosted by the Fletcher School of Government, Ridge was asked about whether he was considering a consolidation of the different government agencies that dealt with border security. Chris

Hornbarger, Falkenrath's new aide, had stayed up late the night before working on Ridge's speech and said there was a robust debate
among the staff over whether to include an outline of the proposal
in the speech. They decided it was premature. Ridge's answer, however, effectively confirmed the rumor, because he acknowledged
that the White House was looking at "whether we want to have
multiple organizations tasked with the same responsibilities."

Ridge had his staff assemble a history of the various efforts to
consolidate U.S. border functions. The record stretched back to
1929, when President Herbert Hoover in his State of the Union
address had called for bringing together the Immigration Bureau,
Customs, and the Coast Guard into a single agency housed within
the U.S. Treasury. That plan had passed the House of Representatives, but lobbying from the different agencies—which hated the
idea of merging—helped to kill the scheme in the Senate. That was
as close as the reformers would ever get. In the 1970s the Carter
administration floated the concept of "total border management"
as an alternative to what it saw as the duplication, inefficiency, and
lack of coordination at the border. It laid out a variety of options,
including the merging of the principal border agencies and the
transfer of visa policy functions from the State Department to the
INS. None of the schemes got off the ground. After that, a variety of commissions had recommended streamlining or consol-
idating the functions of the different border agencies, but those
recommendations were never embraced by the administration or
Congress.

Ridge and his staff believed that 9/11 represented a historic
opportunity to carry out the long overdue consolidation of the border agencies. Card, the White House chief of staff who brought
Ridge in, had urged them to be ambitious, counseling that pushing
through a small change would be almost as hard as pushing through
a big one. In the West Wing of the White House, Falkenrath quietly began putting together options for border reorganization, and
at the beginning of December, Ridge was briefed by his staff on
several alternatives. Ridge favored one that would create a National

Border Administration, to be housed in an existing cabinet department, out of the merger of the Coast Guard, the Customs Service, the enforcement wing of the INS (which included both the border inspectors and the Border Patrol), and the Agriculture Department's inspection arm. It was left undecided which department would take the new agency. Falkenrath's staff drafted a white paper detailing the proposal, which called for creating a "single accountable agency" to replace the nearly dozen agencies that had some piece of border security. "The record of coordination and cooperation among the separate agencies with border security responsibilities has been problematic for years and remains mixed," the paper said. On December 20, Ridge and his deputy, Steve Abbot, took the proposal to the Oval Office, briefing the president, Card, Bush's national security adviser, Condoleezza Rice, and other top White House officials. A rare photograph of the small Oval Office meeting was taken, only because the White House had laid down a new presidential rug and this was the first meeting to take place on it. Bush was supportive and urged Ridge to take it to the heads of the various departments and agencies that would be affected.

Even with the president's encouragement, however, the proposal ran into a buzz saw of opposition. Bonner had gotten wind of the scheme and began lobbying the White House for his own alternative, which was quickly dubbed the "Customs on steroids proposal" by its opponents, including Jim Ziglar at the INS. Ziglar at the time was pushing his own internal reorganization proposal, which would have clearly separated the service side of the INS—which handled citizenship, green card, student visa, and other similar applications—from the enforcement side, which included the Border Patrol and INS agents responsible for upholding immigration laws inside the country. Bonner's proposal, however, would have taken the enforcement arm of the INS, including the Border Patrol, out of the INS and given it to Customs, making the Customs Service the largest law enforcement agency in the country, dwarfing even the FBI. Ziglar was also annoyed because he and Bonner and Loy, then the Coast Guard commandant, had been

informally discussing how to cooperate more closely after 9/11, but
Bonner had taken his scheme to the White House without telling
them first. Bonner, however, saw his plan as a less dramatic alternative to the Falkenrath scheme and believed it would achieve the
same results. "You're using a howitzer when a rifle shot will do," he
told one of Ridge's officials involved in the plan. But the proposal
was quickly rejected by Ridge's staff as being overly "Customs-
centric."

Instead, Ridge began briefing several of the key agencies on the
Falkenrath plan, calling Ashcroft and Deputy Defense Secretary
Paul Wolfowitz on December 21 and later that day convening an
informal meeting with Paul O'Neill, Secretary of Agriculture Ann
Veneman, Secretary of Transportation Norm Mineta, and Larry
Thompson, Ashcroft's deputy, to give them the heads-up that he
would make a formal proposal to the cabinet.

As is the normal process in the U.S. government, before any
decision is made by the full cabinet, it is chewed over by what
is known as a deputies committee, a group usually composed of
the number two official in each agency, but sometimes including
slightly lower-level officials. On January 3, 2002, the deputies met
to consider the proposal. It turned into an extraordinarily bitter
meeting. Deputy Secretary of Transportation Michael Jackson,
who would later become deputy secretary of Homeland Security
in Bush's second term, dubbed the scheme "the Christmas massacre." Ziglar warned of the unintended consequences of reorganization, cautioning that it would be a huge administrative burden and
could force them to change the immigration court system. No one
at the meeting thought it was the right way to go. Bonner was not
wholly opposed, but even he favored his own, different approach.

The cabinet officers who met the next day, with the president
in attendance and Card chairing, were no more enthusiastic. Norm
Mineta, the transportation secretary who stood to lose the Coast
Guard from his agency, said that whoever wrote the proposal had
not served the president well. Though he had no love for Ziglar's
INS, Ashcroft did not want to lose the exclusive powers it gave

him to hold suspects in terrorism investigations. He said he did not want to be forced to negotiate with some other agency when he needed the INS to detain someone in a terrorism case. Colin Powell, the secretary of state, warned of the enormous legislative obstacles that would face any big reorganization plan. The congressional committees, he said, considered the executive branch agencies their "wholly owned subsidiaries" and would not react well to any plans to change the existing structure. It was better, he argued, to use the existing organizations and assign clear responsibilities to those agencies. Donald Rumsfeld, the defense secretary, showed his disdain for the entire process by sending Peter Verga to represent him—a deputy undersecretary of defense who was three rungs below the secretary. Only O'Neill was mildly enthusiastic, but he criticized Ridge for not being ambitious enough. He favored something on the scale of the German interior ministry, which would have pulled together all of the domestic law enforcement agencies in the country, even though it would have meant a significant cannibalizing of the Treasury Department. He wanted to merge not only Customs, but also the Secret Service and the Alcohol, Tobacco and Firearms Bureau, both part of Treasury. Justice would have been the other big loser, because O'Neill wanted to pull out the FBI as well as the INS. He even suggested that it be called the Department of Homeland Security.

In the face of such opposition, Bush pulled back and told Ridge to reconsider. Ari Fleischer, the chief White House spokesman, urged that the dispute not be made public, since it was the most serious disagreement in Bush's cabinet since the 9/11 attacks and would damage the unified face the administration had shown in public. The next week, however, the proposal was leaked to the *New York Times*, which noted that it had "set off a storm inside the Bush administration." While the plan was probably dead already, the leak killed it for good.

Ridge's staff was dismayed by the opposition. "If we can't get this done, what can we do?" Falkenrath wondered. "I was thinking it may be badly written, but it's not that bad," Chris Hornbarger said later.

But he acknowledged that the whole process was poorly handled. "We were amateurs, not in the sense of being dumb, but in how we tackled the idea. We didn't build allies beforehand to get results out of the interagency process. We moved quickly and it hit a wall."

Ridge made a second effort, in March 2002, persuading Bush to allow him to float another alternative plan, one that would take Customs out of the Treasury and merge it with the INS as part of the Justice Department. O'Neill, who was the least turf-conscious of all the cabinet secretaries, was willing to let Customs go, and Ashcroft was happy to take it. "I suppose cabinet secretaries are supposed to be territorial and fight off all comers and try to keep things as they were when Alexander Hamilton created them, but that wasn't my idea of how the government ought to function," O'Neill said. But when Ridge took the proposal to Congress, he was immediately shot down, most forcefully by the powerful House Ways and Means Committee, which had jurisdiction over Customs and would lose that control if it went to Justice.

Rebuffed yet again, Card directed Ridge to take a stealthier approach. Almost from the moment Ridge's position in the White House was created, pressure had been growing in Congress to elevate Ridge's role into a formal cabinet position. Advocates such as Joe Lieberman, the moderate Connecticut Democrat who had been Al Gore's running mate in 2000 and thus a potential political rival to Bush, had argued forcefully that Ridge should have both budget and direct authority over homeland security. Gary Hart and Warren Rudman had both recommended a formal department, arguing that as a homeland security czar he could not hope to coordinate all the agencies with a piece of the task. "Mr. Ridge should have authority and resources for the nation's domestic security just as the defense secretary has the resources to defend the nation overseas," they asserted. Even members of Congress who cared less about the issue were frustrated by their inability to call Ridge to testify before Congress, because of his place on the White House staff rather than in a cabinet agency over which Congress had direct authority.

The combination of congressional pressure and the White House's inability to force through even a more modest reorganization of the border agencies led Card to abandon the effort to win consent from the cabinet and instead to draw up a new plan in secret. Otherwise he risked putting his boss, President Bush, in the untenable position of objecting to legislation creating a new homeland security department that looked certain to pass Congress. He formed a small group—two people from his staff, one from the White House budget office, and Falkenrath and General Bruce Lawlor from Ridge's staff—and directed them to work in complete secrecy to devise a new plan. The president, he told Ridge, wanted the group to start from scratch and decide how to create the ideal homeland security agency. "Nothing is off the table," Card told Ridge.

Two months later, on the evening of June 5, Card called the same cabinet secretaries who had nixed Ridge's border plan and broke the news. The president, he told them, had decided to support a new Department of Homeland Security that not only would merge the INS, Customs, and the Coast Guard, but would add all or part of nineteen other agencies—170,000 staff in all. Card told them that the plan was final, and that no special pleading by any of the cabinet agencies would be considered.

Given Ridge's inability to persuade the cabinet on the merits of a single border agency, the White House probably had no choice but to go ahead on its own. Bush had not wanted a new cabinet department for homeland security, but Congress was moving ahead, and without a plan in hand the White House would have had little influence over the design of the new agency. Ridge had tried to get the support of the cabinet colleagues and failed; a plan they didn't support was better than no plan at all. But it was an inauspicious start.

The single border agency favored by Ridge would have been much more manageable than the sprawling Department of Homeland Security that resulted, which had all the border responsibilities but was also in charge of disaster planning and response, protecting the president through the Secret Service, and a host of other unrelated missions. And it would have been housed in an existing department like Treasury or Justice, giving it far more clout in the interagency battles to come than the orphan that was created. "It would have been a tight, cohesive agency with a reasonably focused mission," said Chris Hornbarger, one of Ridge's aides. "It's odd that there could be all those experienced people saying this was bad policy. But it was the right way to go."

Even worse, the way the department was created left a trail of bitter feelings. One of Ridge's senior aides would later brag that he had "slam-dunked" the whole cabinet by drawing up the DHS plan in secret and shoving it down their throats. But in government, victories and defeats are rarely final; the losers would have plenty of chances to fight back, leaving the new department far weaker than any of its architects in the White House and Congress had envisioned.

# Chapter 5

# THE SCAPEGOAT

It took more than a month after September 11—an eternity in the hyperpoliticized world of modern Washington—for the blame game to begin. Ironically, it was Mary Ryan, a devout Catholic, who cast the first stone. Just eight months later, she would become the only administration official ever to be fired as a result of the terrorist attacks.

As assistant secretary of state for consular affairs for the previous nine years, Ryan was the person in charge of the consular corps, the nearly two thousand State Department employees who issue passports to Americans and visas to foreigners and take care of U.S. citizens when they run into trouble overseas. At the 230 visa-granting U.S. embassies and consulates around the world, their primary job is to scrutinize the millions of people who want to come each year to live, visit, work, study, or do business in the United States. It is the traditional first posting for graduates of the U.S. Foreign Service exam, an elite group whose reward for being among the just two hundred chosen annually for the service is a mind-numbing and occasionally career-destroying job. With the abolition of visa requirements for most visitors from western Europe in the late 1980s, consular postings are normally in Africa, Latin America, and Asia, where the clamor to visit the United States produces long lineups outside many embassies hours before their opening. After the obligatory two- to four-year stint, most consular officers get out as quickly as possible to the more glamorous worlds of the State Department's political or economic sections, where they can observe foreign countries from the comfort of a cubicle or enjoy polite lunches with their government officials, rather than confront the teeming masses each day at the visa window. One internal State Department assessment said that most Foreign Service officers considered consular work "a period to be endured and kept as short as possible." The black humor in the department jokes that if you love a country, don't go there and stamp visas because pretty soon you won't love it anymore. "It's a colossal drag on morale," said Larry Wilkerson, who was chief of staff to Secretary of State Colin Powell. "We lose a lot of Foreign Service officers in those first two or three years because they can't stand it."

Throughout the 1990s, staffing failed to keep up with the growing number of visa applicants; by 2001 just six hundred consular officials were processing more than 10 million visa applications each year. A consular officer in one of the busiest posts might consider nearly five hundred applicants each day. That left perhaps a minute for a junior officer, often with little knowledge of the country and only a developing grasp of the local language, to judge whether the person on the other side of the wicket should be allowed to come to the United States. An employee who managed only fifty visa applications an hour "would be considered slow," said one career consular officer. Mistakes were inevitable, frequent, and tolerated.

But nobody had ever made such a big mistake before. On October 11, the Justice Department went public with the fact—based on information supplied by the State Department—that at least thirteen of the nineteen hijackers had entered the United States on valid visas issued by U.S. consular officers. Ryan was scheduled to testify the next day before a Senate judiciary subcommittee with responsibility over "technology, terrorism, and government information." The committee was chaired by Dianne Feinstein, a California Democrat who had become one of her party's leading hawks on border security after the attacks. She had called for a moratorium on issuing visas to foreign students wishing to study in the United States and had urged an end to the visa waiver program that allowed millions of Europeans to get on a plane to the United States each year with no prior vetting by the U.S. government. When her committee convened at 10:04 a.m. on October 12, she was looking for contrition, for an admission of mistakes made and a promise of corrections. She did not get it from Mary Ryan.

With Ziglar beside her, and her staff sitting in the row behind, Ryan launched into a vigorous defense of her consular officers. In her opening remarks, she detailed the many steps taken by her department during the 1990s to build the nation's first computerized terrorist watch list so that consular officers would automatically be alerted if someone on the list applied for a U.S. visa. Using information provided by the State Department's own intelligence arm, as well as the FBI, the CIA, and the National Security Agency, the system was designed to put all the government's information on known terrorists at the fingertips of every consular officer around the world. It was fully automated, and in practice it was impossible to approve a visa without first running the name of the applicant against the terrorist watch list. In addition, she said, the visas themselves contained a digitized photograph and other security features designed to prevent fraud. "I can say with confidence that we are using today a state-of-the-art visa name-check system, and we continue to seek and exploit new technologies to strengthen our capabilities," she said. The system was already one of the best in the world and would get even better, she promised. So how had the 9/11 hijackers so easily foiled such a sophisticated system? She gave no specific answer in her opening statement, but underscored a single point: "We are only as good as the information that goes into the system. If we have no information on the aliens from other agencies, then the name-check system is not as good as it could be."

That was not good enough for Feinstein. Her first question was disarmingly blunt. "What, in your view, went wrong in the issuance of valid visas that permitted these thirteen terrorists to legally enter the United States, or do you view their entry as acceptable risk?"

It was the sort of question that few administration officials—and certainly not a career official whose life had been inside the government for more than three decades—would answer directly under the spotlight of a Senate hearing. It called for a delicate and evasive response of the "mistakes were made and we'll get to the bottom of it, Senator" variety. But evasiveness was not in Ryan's character.

"What went wrong is that we had no information on them whatsoever from law enforcement or from intelligence," she said, taking direct aim at the FBI and the CIA, the two most powerful agencies in the U.S. government outside of the Pentagon. "And so they [the hijackers] came in, they applied for visas. They were interviewed and their stories were believed." She continued: "We have had a struggle with the law enforcement and intelligence communities in getting information . . . and were constantly told we were not a law enforcement agency and so they couldn't give it to us. Other agencies fear compromise of sources and methods."

Former colleagues of Ryan say she was enraged when she learned after the attacks that the CIA had information that two of the hijackers had met with Al Qaeda operatives in Malaysia in January 2000. That information was never shared with the State Department, which granted visas to both men when their names did not appear as hits on the watch list. Again showing none of the caution that those at her level in government usually brought to Capitol Hill, she shared her rage with Feinstein's committee. "My question is, when did we have this information as a nation, as a government? When did we know that [they] had met with Osama bin Laden operatives? And if it was known before we issued a visa, why didn't we know?"

Feinstein quietly played out the rope. "How do you answer that yourself?"

"I don't know, Madame Chairwoman," Ryan continued. "Either it is a colossal intelligence failure, in which case we had no information about them . . . or there was information that was not shared with us who are the outer ring of border security." George Lannon, Ryan's principal deputy who was sitting behind her that morning, slumped in his chair and felt the blood drain from his cheeks. He would later recall: "I knew we were doomed after that—that the intelligence and the FBI guys were going to come after us. I saw the handwriting on the wall." Indeed Ryan was later ordered to a meeting at CIA headquarters in Langley, Virginia, by the director, George Tenet, demanding that she explain herself.

If the hearing had ended there, however, it might still have blown over quietly. According to Lannon, who was at the CIA meeting with Tenet, the director was surprisingly conciliatory, and his staff backed up her charge that the agency's information on the two hijackers should have been passed to State so that they could have been placed on the terrorist watch list. And Feinstein was impressed with Ryan's insistence that the FBI and the CIA would have to reconsider their hoarding of intelligence about terrorists on the grounds of protecting sources and methods. Congress, which would later set up two commissions to investigate what went wrong before the attacks, was already zeroing in on the lack of information sharing within the administration as a critical problem. "I think Ambassador Ryan has hit the nail on the head," the senator said.

But Feinstein was not quite finished with her questioning. In a second round, she began with a lengthy statement summarizing the hearing. "Let me just say that from my perspective, one overwhelming thing comes through: thirteen out of the nineteen terrorists obtained valid visas. Clearly our system is not able to prevent a terrorist from getting a visa legally to come into this country. That ought to be a sobering fact for all of us." The solution, she said, was to create a single terrorist-oriented database accessible throughout the government, an idea that would not come to fruition for another five years. "I'm really concerned about continuing to appropriate money for systems that don't talk to each other. This is a colossal failure of our visa system. It doesn't keep people out who would come in and destroy us. So what else would you have a visa system for if not to do just that? We might as well do away with it all and let everybody just come and go as they want to."

Ryan had heard enough. In yet another gross breach of the normal Washington protocol that requires administration witnesses, particularly midlevel officials, to show obsequious deference to senators on their home turf, Ryan interrupted Feinstein. "I have to say it is a failure of intelligence rather than a failure of the visa system. If we had the information, we would not have issued visas to these people. We did not have the information."

Feinstein shot back: "Then that information on individuals has to go into that centralized system."

Ryan cut her off again: "Absolutely, but please don't say it is a failure of the visa system. I have visa officers all over the world who are devastated by the fact that they issued to these people. One of them told me, 'You can tell me that it's not my fault because we didn't have the information, but it is just as if a child ran in front of my car and I killed the child and everybody said it wasn't my fault. I have to live with that for the rest of my life.'" Her voice rose, pleading with the senator. "So it isn't a failure of the visa system. It is a lack of information sharing, a lack of intelligence. We have to fix that, Madame Chairwoman. We have to fix it."

Feinstein was not persuaded. "It is a failure of the system," she came back in an icy tone. "You know, I hear one agency blame another and it is very upsetting to me. We don't have a system that works."

From that day on, the Honorable Senator Dianne Feinstein would only refer to Ambassador Mary Ryan as "that woman."

MARY RYAN DEVOTED HER LIFE to two things—God and the State Department. Friends describe her as perhaps the most devout person they had ever met. She had studied theology at Trinity University and attended church every day of her working life in Washington. On the morning of the 9/11 attacks, she was in Charleston, South Carolina, with Frank Moss, her deputy in charge of passports, for a conference on passport management. When they learned of the attacks, they were forced to rent a car for the 450-mile drive back to Washington because U.S. airspace had been closed to all commercial traffic. Ryan was especially worried about a nephew who worked in Jersey City and regularly rode the PATH trains that ran under the World Trade Center. "I swear she reduced a set of rosary beads to dust," said Moss.

Johnny Young, a former U.S. ambassador to Bahrain and Sierra Leone and her closest friend in the State Department, described her as "deeply steeped in the Catholic Church." In many ways her life was a model of Christian simplicity. She dressed in austere clothing in subdued colors, wore sensible shoes, lived most of her Washington life in a rental apartment, and wrote out her working notes and even personal letters on sheets of yellow foolscap. The church also inspired her with what her friends and colleagues say was a passionate commitment to justice, a determination to do the right thing in all parts of her life. She would chronicle that internal struggle in letters to Young, whose career she had nurtured for three decades.

But if God was her touchstone, the State Department was her life. At the time of the terrorist attacks, she was the longest-serving official in the department, and only the second woman in its history to be named a career ambassador, a title awarded to the most outstanding Foreign Service officers. Former colleagues describe her as the smartest, hardest-working, and straightest-talking person they knew in the government. By the time she was dragged in front of Feinstein's committee, Ryan had acquired something more than simple respect in the department; it was closer to adoration. For many young consular affairs officers, she was a role model, and she put enormous energy into nurturing the careers of those below her.

Her political masters in the Bush administration would say, in retrospect, that her immense loyalty to her consular officials, which was reciprocated, should have been a red flag that she would defend her staff rather than carry out their wishes. "Mary Ryan had been there the longest of any of the assistant secretaries, but she was totally beloved," said a former top aide to Colin Powell, the secretary of state. "It was one of the few times the secretary and I let our hearts overrule our heads. We made an error; we should have moved Mary originally."

Instead, when Powell finally fired her in July 2002 amid a cacophony of criticism from Congress and the conservative media over State's role in letting the hijackers into the country, there was a vitriolic outpouring from consular officers around the world, accusing him of succumbing to modern-day McCarthyism. "Powell had gained the respect and admiration of the Foreign Service by being a man of the people and standing by his troops, and we felt like he let us down," Young would say later. Lisa Bobbie Schreiber Hughes, a career consular officer who worked in the White House after 9/11 and is now ambassador to Suriname, said that Powell, who had come from the military and was deeply steeped in its ethos, "never fully understood that ours is also a very proud service, with our own icons and our own traditions. To have one of our own treated that way was inexcusable. And he just never got that."

To understand that anger, it is necessary to appreciate the sense of disrespect that most consular officers felt long before September 11. They were second-class citizens in an institution—the professional Foreign Service—that itself felt increasingly second class because of the growing influence of political appointees in the department's upper ranks. Within the career corps, the State Department has a star system, and the stars do not come out of consular affairs. The glamour postings are the political and economic jobs, and ambitious Foreign Service officers quickly gravitate to those posts. And they are rewarded for those decisions. While about 30 percent of U.S. ambassadors are political appointees who land in Paris, London, or Tokyo as patronage for their loyalty to a president, the remaining 70 percent are career State Department officials. Of those, the vast majority are political officers, followed by economic officers, and then a smattering who are specialists in public diplomacy. In 2001, the two other State Department career tracks—consular and management—were barely represented in the prestigious ambassadorial ranks. Dianne Andruch, who worked for Ryan in the 1990s as her special assistant and later became her deputy in charge of services for U.S. citizens abroad, said the consular and administrative branches of State were the "stepchildren" of the service. "They don't consider us real diplomats. If you wanted to really be seen as somebody, you'd better be doing political or economic work. You certainly didn't want to be a consular officer." Powell had made it one of his missions to correct this imbalance, but that had only just begun to influence the department's promotion policies when 9/11 hit.

But long before Powell came to the department, Ryan had begun to change that culture, carving a path for others who wanted to find another road to advancement. As a woman, Ryan had faced additional hurdles and her choices in life only emphasized how difficult it was to overcome those obstacles and rise within the department. She never married or had children, and so she could devote all her waking hours to the department and to her church. She attended the 6:30 mass at St. Stephen Martyr Roman Catholic Church in Washington, D.C., every morning before heading straight to Foggy Bottom. In a crisis where consular officers would have to work around the clock in three eight-hour shifts, Ryan would show up during each shift, and then later write notes to those involved thanking them for their work.

She also put tremendous energy into supporting the careers of other consular officers. "She was known for developing junior officers, and especially women," said Maura Harty, her successor in the job. "If you were in the service a minute less time than Mary, she was your mentor." As a career counselor in the department, she oversaw the careers of hundreds of Foreign Service officers. Johnny Young, who first met her when he was on assignment in Doha, Qatar, said she took a particular interest in the careers of promising young African Americans. In addition to Young, she helped oversee

the promotion to the ambassadorial ranks of three other black Foreign Service officers. He called her his *padrina*, saying, "I wouldn't
make a move without her."

It was not always a pleasant experience for those under her.
Andruch called her "probably the best boss I ever had" but then
quickly added, "She scared me. She intimidated me. She was very,
very smart. I was scared to death because I was always on the verge
of screwing up. I was always afraid I wouldn't live up to her ex-
pectations." In her first employment evaluation as Ryan's special
assistant, Ryan had given Andruch a mediocre review, indicating
that she was not yet ready for a promotion. But Andruch said it
only encouraged her to work harder and smarter.

Ryan joined the Foreign Service with a posting in Naples in
1966, after graduating from St. John's University in New York in
1965 with a master's degree. From there she rotated assignments
overseas with a gradual climb up the ladder in Washington, D.C.
After stints in Honduras and Mexico, she returned to Washington
in 1975 as a management officer with responsibility for Africa. In
1980, she was sent to Africa for the first time, working as an administrative counselor responsible for the management of U.S. embassies in the Ivory Coast and Sudan. In 1988, more than two decades
after joining the service, she was rewarded with an appointment as
ambassador to Swaziland.

In her career with the State Department up to that point,
Ryan had steered clear of politics, working with equal success under Democratic and Republican presidents. But in 1990, she suddenly got tangled in the worst of Washington's political schem-
ing. In 1988, President George H. W. Bush had named Elizabeth
Tamposi as assistant secretary of state for consular affairs, the top
consular position. While all presidents are free to fill such jobs with
ill-qualified political appointees, Tamposi, known as Betty, was a
particularly egregious choice. Just thirty-four years of age at the
time of her nomination in 1989, she was distinguished only by
her ties to John Sununu, the former New Hampshire Republican
governor who was Bush's chief of staff. She came from a powerful

political family in New Hampshire, which for its size carries inordinate clout because it is the second state to vote during the long primary season that determines the presidential candidates for each party. Betty's father, Sam Tamposi, was the son of an immigrant from Avdhela, Macedonia, a Romanian village settled by Greeks, and rose from being a vacuum cleaner salesman to become one of New Hampshire's biggest land developers, and a part owner of the fabled Boston Red Sox baseball franchise. He was a major contributor to Sununu's successful run for governor and helped finance Bush Sr.'s 1988 primary victory in the state that would carry him to the presidency. Betty herself had leveraged the family name into a seat in the New Hampshire legislature, but then lost in a bid for a congressional seat in Washington in the 1988 elections. The State Department was her consolation prize.

To the career staff in consular affairs, Tamposi was almost intolerable. She knew little about the subject but was extremely well connected in the White House and attuned to the slightest criticisms of her performance percolating up from below. "The Tamposi days were very difficult, very trying times in virtually every respect," said Barry Kefauver, who was then the executive director for consular affairs and in charge of its day-to-day management. "I would come home late at night and think that I couldn't go back in the next day. It was agony." But Kefauver was determined to survive her regime, and the best way, he thought, was to surround Tamposi with high-quality career people "who could carry the ball." He picked up the phone to Ryan in Swaziland, and pleaded with her to return to Washington; surprisingly, he says, she agreed. She came back as the principal deputy assistant secretary for consular affairs. "It was a huge mistake, in retrospect," Kefauver admits.

The working relationship between Tamposi and Ryan unraveled almost immediately, and Tamposi fired her along with thirteen other senior officials in a complete housecleaning of the upper ranks of the consular service. After her dismissal by Tamposi, Ryan was appointed by Secretary of State James Baker to direct the Kuwait task force following the invasion of Kuwait by Saddam

Hussein's army. The assignment put her in charge of a group of consular officers who were working in three shifts, twenty-four hours a
day, seven days a week, to try to gather information on the roughly
3,000 Americans who were trapped in either Kuwait or Iraq following the August 2 invasion. On the first day after the attack, the department received more than 4,600 calls from frantic relatives, and
in the next several days the volume would rise to as many as 600
calls an hour. John Hotchner, who now works on counterterrorism
at the State Department, handled the midnight to 8:00 a.m. shift,
and said Ryan was frequently on the job during the early-morning
hours. It was the first assignment that demonstrated to her political
masters that she was capable of handling the department's most delicate missions; her codirector on the task force was Ryan Crocker,
who would go on to a legendary State Department career culminat-
ing in his appointment as ambassador to Iraq in 2007 when the
second Bush administration was trying to dig itself out from the
botched aftermath of the overthrow of Saddam.

Two years after Iraq invaded Kuwait, Ryan would become the
beneficiary of Tamposi's downfall. In October 1992, less than a
month before the national election in which Bush appeared headed
for defeat at the hands of Bill Clinton, *Newsweek* reported that Bush
administration officials had ordered a search of Clinton's passport
records. Following Bush's defeat in the November 3 vote, reporters
for the *Washington Post* and the *New York Times* revealed that Tamposi had personally searched the passport records of Clinton, his
mother, and the independent third candidate for president, Ross
Perot.

Throughout that fall, rumors had circulated that Clinton, who
as a student was opposed to the Vietnam War, had written a letter
seeking to abandon his American citizenship in order to avoid the
military draft. If true, it would have been an extraordinary revelation, perhaps fatally damaging Clinton's campaign on the eve of the
vote. Several news organizations, as well as a Republican member
of Congress, Gerald Solomon, had filed Freedom of Information
Act requests seeking the passport records. Normally such FOIA

requests can take months, even years. But Baker, who had left the job he loved as secretary of state to return to the White House as chief of staff to rescue Bush's reelection bid, had wondered out loud to several of his aides if the requests could be expedited.

Following conversations with Janet Mullins, a top White House political adviser, and Steven Berry, a political appointee who handled congressional affairs for the State Department, Tamposi ordered a search of the passport records, sending three consular officials to remove the file from the Washington National Records Center. The file was brought back to Tamposi's home. It contained Clinton's entire passport history but no evidence that Clinton had ever sought to renounce his citizenship. There were, however, staple holes and a tear in the corner of Clinton's passport application, suggesting that a page may have been removed. Tamposi forwarded the papers to the FBI, which quickly concluded there had been no tampering. But that did not prevent President Bush, in a desperate attempt to close the gap with Clinton, from suggesting on national television a month before the vote that someone might have tampered with Clinton's passport records to hide some wrongdoing. The Clinton campaign called the investigation into the passport files "an outrageous abuse of power [and] a blatant use of the State Department for political purposes."

When full details of the search began to emerge after Bush lost the election, Tamposi was quickly fingered as White House officials sought to insulate the president from the scandal, which by then had been crudely dubbed "Passportgate." Tamposi was fired. The next year, President Clinton nominated Ryan for the job as assistant secretary of consular affairs. "Having suffered the slings and arrows of Betty Tamposi had the institutional effect of enhancing her career," said Kefauver.

RYAN INHERITED THE BUREAU OF consular affairs at one of the most challenging junctures in its history. Issuing visas—which is the critical first step in determining who will be allowed into the country and who will be barred—is now considered a basic function of government. The State Department first began requiring visas for certain foreigners in 1884, and then expanded the system at the end of World War I. The motivation was largely security—what one historian called "a form of self-defense against foreigners considered dangerous or inferior." The Passport Control Act of 1918 for the first time required anyone seeking to travel to the United States to obtain permission from a U.S. embassy or consulate abroad. It was considered a temporary wartime measure, but it was kept in place due to fears of a massive emigration from Europe following the war. In 1924, Congress mandated a permanent visa process for all European immigrants or travelers, one part of the larger series of restrictive laws that brought an end to the prewar immigration wave. Almost immediately, the new visa rules became a subject of controversy. Critics accused the State Department of prejudice against Jewish immigrants, and complaints were rife about the arbitrary and opaque decision process. As one journalist wrote at the time: "The powers of the chief of the Visa Office are almost unlimited, and appeal against his decision is practically impossible." But while the rules would be tinkered with many times, the system set up after World War I remains in place today.

By the end of the twentieth century, administering that system had become a gigantic undertaking. From 1993 to 2001, during Ryan's tenure, the number of non-immigrant visa applications adjudicated by consular officers grew from 7 million a year to more than 10 million. The demand for U.S. passports doubled to more than 7 million a year. Yet throughout this period, consular service staffing declined as budgetary constraints cut the recruiting of junior officers from more than 200 a year to less than 100. "The motto in the department in the 1990s was 'Do more with less' to the extent that it seemed to me we were expected to do everything with nothing," Ryan would later tell the 9/11 Commission. At the same time, some in the department were becoming increasingly concerned over the threat posed by Islamic extremism. On February 26, 1993, just three months before Ryan formally took up her duties as assistant secretary for consular affairs, a huge truck bomb was detonated in the underground garage beneath the World Trade Center towers in New York City. It ripped a massive hole seven stories into the buildings, killing six people and injuring more than a thousand. While the bombing, carried out by Sunni Muslim extremists, failed to destroy the towers, it was the first clear indication that the United States faced a new enemy determined to murder thousands of innocent civilians on U.S. soil.

For the State Department, the failed 1993 attack was a severe indictment of its visa-granting procedures. The spiritual leader of the bombers, Sheikh Omar Abdel-Rahman, better known as the "blind sheikh," had been granted a visa at the U.S. embassy in Khartoum, Sudan, a country that at the time was harboring Al Qaeda leader Osama bin Laden. Sheikh Rahman was well known to U.S. intelligence for his radical activities in Egypt, and his name had been placed on an internal State Department watch list in 1987. Further, in early May 1990 the U.S. embassy in Cairo had warned the embassy in Khartoum that Egypt's "leading radical" had left for Sudan and could be seeking to travel to the United States. But when Rahman applied for a visa on May 10, 1990, a local Sudanese employee in Khartoum failed to check the microfiche on which the watch list was kept, believing that the fifty-five-year-old cleric posed no threat, and then lied to the U.S. consular officer who issued Rahman's visa by telling him that the check had been run. The consular officer in Sudan, further, was unaware of the warning that had just been issued by the U.S. embassy in Egypt concerning Rahman's intentions. It was an appalling failure. In 1995 Rahman was convicted of conspiracy and sentenced to life in prison in connection with the World Trade Center bombings and a separate plot to blow up the Lincoln and Holland tunnels, the George Washington Bridge, and the United Nations building in New York City.

Chastened by those mistakes, Ryan made it one of her primary tasks to build a computerized name-check system whose integrity would not be subject to the whims of local officials, and to make that system more robust by adding the names of those suspected by the CIA or the FBI of involvement in terrorist or other serious criminal activities. In doing so, she and her officials were far ahead of their time. The Clinton White House was only just beginning to awaken to the threat posed by Islamic extremists. While State would later be pilloried as soft on terrorism, the department was far ahead of any other agency in the U.S. government in responding to what was still a poorly understood threat. In 1987, it had already set up the first terrorist watch list established by any of the border security agencies, known as TIPOFF. It was designed by a career employee at the department's Bureau of Intelligence and Research, John Arriza, who then became a passionate advocate for the system within the government. But it was set up only after difficult negotiations with the intelligence community that allowed the names, nationalities, birth dates, and passport numbers of suspected terrorists to be declassified and made available to consular officials. In 1991, State agreed to share the list with the INS and the Customs Service, which had no similar capability.

In 1993, following the attack in New York, Ryan built on the initial TIPOFF system by initiating the Visas Viper program, in which State officials would meet regularly with representatives of the intelligence agencies to encourage them to share the latest information on suspected terrorists. By 2001, the TIPOFF list of suspected terrorists or supporters contained about 60,000 names, though the list remained incomplete because the FBI in particular refused to share much of what it knew with State. According to the 9/11 Commission, in 2001 State's own intelligence arm provided 2,013 source documents for the TIPOFF list and the CIA added 1,527; the FBI provided just 63, fewer than what was gleaned from newspapers and other public media. At the same time, State had built a larger system, known as CLASS, for Consular Lookout and Support System, which contained the records of every visa denied by any consular officer. By the end of 2000 that system had 8.5 million names, with 2.5 million of those added in 2000 alone.

Ryan's efforts were critical to that success. In 1994, after considerable personal lobbying by Ryan, Congress had passed legislation that allowed the department to charge a fee to foreign visa applicants and to retain that fee. The department would use that money to implement congressional legislation that required the deployment of tamperproof machine-readable visas worldwide by 1996, and to automate the terrorist name-check system. The legislation provided an annual windfall that grew to $300 million by 1999 and allowed Ryan to put in place a global, computerized system within eighteen months.

The staff report of the 9/11 Commission called the results "impressive." In February 1993, nearly half of the State Department's visa-issuing posts—111 in total—were forced to do laborious microfiche checks on visa applicants; by September 1995, the system was fully automated. It was not the only improvement. Foreign names, and particularly Arabic names, posed a huge problem because of the many possible variants in the English spellings of the same name. The State Department developed, and in 1998 deployed, sophisticated software that would automatically check all the variant spellings of Arabic names; the program was later extended to other languages as well. By the spring of 1997, the department had also built secure broadband computer links among every one of its embassies and consulates and the headquarters in Washington. Within minutes, any consular officer anywhere in the world could check any visa application and call up a digital photograph of the applicant. At a time when the FBI had no internal e-mail and used paper case management files, and the INS couldn't even hold a murderer whose details were entered into its border watch system, Ryan's accomplishments were extraordinary. Despite the many failings prior to 9/11, the TIPOFF system had worked as it was supposed to. For instance, Ramzi bin al-Shibh, who was the roommate of the plot's ringleader, Mohammed Atta, and himself one of the key planners, tried four times in 2000 to get a visa to come to the United States. Each time he was rejected because his name was in TIPOFF.

IT WAS THAT RECORD THAT Mary Ryan had in mind when she told Senator Feinstein that the department's visa system was "state-of-the-art." But she was wrong. In spite of the impressive progress of the 1990s in adding new hurdles for known terrorists wanting to enter the United States, Feinstein's off-the-cuff judgment was more accurate. For all the technological advances that came under her watch—and they far exceeded those of any government agency outside of the Customs Service—the visa system was indeed badly broken.

The weaknesses were not technological; they came, in a phrase that would be used many times during the investigations into the attacks, from "a failure of imagination." Organizations, governmental or otherwise, have a hard time doing more than one or two big things well. For the consular service in the 1990s, the big thing was managing the enormous growth in travel to the United States. The cold war had ended and the iron curtain had been lifted in Europe, while in Asia, explosive economic growth had created a huge new middle class with global aspirations. The result: travel to the United States boomed. And except for the growing concerns over illegal immigration from Mexico, there was no question that the United States should encourage the trend. Democrats wanted an open door for refugees and a generous policy of family reunification. Republicans wanted a steady supply of foreign workers to keep the chamber of commerce happy. Both favored more foreign students for the universities, more skilled workers for Silicon Valley, more tourists to fill the hotels, and more wealthy Arabs paying full fare for treatments at U.S. hospitals.

The State Department, quite reasonably, reflected those priorities. The *Foreign Affairs Manual*, which contains the various policies and regulations that are supposed to guide the behavior of consular officers, said that the U.S. government's policy was "to facilitate and promote travel and the free movement of people of all nationalities to the United States, both for the cultural and social value to the world and for economic purposes." That policy was reinforced by constant pressure from Congress to speed up the visa process and avoid any delays or disruption. Congressional staff had been given a special hotline in the State Department, and frequently would call directly to overseas consular officers to demand that visas be issued for some relative, friend, or business partner of a constituent. Not that Ryan or most State Department officials needed strong prodding to carry out the open-door policy. "I think if you asked Mary whether she favored open borders or closed borders, she would have been on the open borders side," said Grant Green, the undersecretary of management in President George W. Bush's first term, and Ryan's direct boss.

But in the 1990s, that was hardly a controversial stance. Consular officers were far more likely to be reprimanded for denying visas than for issuing them. "Prior to 9/11, we were under a lot of pressure to have people processed for visas in an expeditious manner," said Andruch, Ryan's aide. "The basic attitude was that these countries were our friends and the United States should do everything possible to facilitate travel. Make it easier on them. Let them come and be students and businesspeople and boost the economy. That was what Mary Ryan was trying to do and that's what she was under pressure to do—until something happened and then everybody ran away from that position."

In addition to managing the huge influx of travelers, the second big thing to hit the State Department in the 1990s was efficiency in government, or what became known as "best practices." The concept of best practices in business, while it dates back to the 1950s, really caught on at the end of the twentieth century because of efforts by the U.S. government. Worried about what was seen as the rising competitive threat posed by Japanese manufacturing companies, the Reagan administration in 1987 launched a national award for quality management and named it after Reagan's first Commerce secretary, Malcolm Baldridge, who was killed in a tragic horse accident. The Baldridge Awards were aimed at restoring the competitiveness of U.S. companies by identifying and rewarding cutting-edge management practices. The idea was not just to single out specific companies but also to highlight behaviors that could be emulated by other companies, thus boosting overall U.S. economic performance. The key was measurement: companies that could demonstrate they were making better products with fewer and less expensive inputs were the ideal candidates for the award.

While the Baldridge Awards had the good fortune to coincide with the emergence of modern computing technologies, there is no question that the goal was achieved in an impressive fashion. Productivity—doing more with the same inputs—soared, from an average gain of 1 to 1.5 percent annually between 1973 and 1995 to an average of 2.5 percent in the last half of the 1990s. Governments, too, quickly began to embrace the concept. Al Gore, Clinton's vice president, championed a National Partnership for Reinventing Government, with the goal of "making the entire federal government less expensive and more efficient." It explicitly endorsed modern business management concepts of how to streamline organizations: giving more power to employees to respond to customer wants; removing rigid procedural requirements, which were ridiculed as unnecessary red tape; and cutting expenses by focusing the organization on its "core mission."

One of the techniques used by Gore to carry out his initiative was to direct all government departments to designate one or more "reinvention laboratories" within their agency. In the State Department, Consular Affairs was the first to receive that designation, in April 1993. The results were apparent in the instructions that began flowing to consular officials in U.S. embassies around the world. In language that could have come directly from McKinsey or any other management consultant, the State Department's *Consular Best Practices Handbook* from 1997 to 2000 laid out "three key goals that every consular manager should try to achieve: high quality decision making, more efficient processes, and improved customer service." It was a mind-set in which foreign visa applicants were seen as "customers" who were to be served by U.S. government officials. The department's official history of the period says that the goal was to "reinvent consular functions" by getting them to "work better, cost less, and get meaningful results by putting customers first, cutting red tape, empowering employees, and cutting back to basics."

COMPARED TO THESE TWO PRIORITIES—ENCOURAGING greater travel to the United States and doing it with fewer resources—the department's counterterrorism effort, for all its technological proficiency, was a distant third. Nowhere was that more evident than in Saudi Arabia, where fifteen of the nineteen hijackers would receive their visas.

For half a century, Saudi Arabia had been the most important U.S. ally in the most volatile region of the world. It was a marriage of convenience in which the United States provided military security for the Saudi ruling family in exchange for a Saudi commitment to maintain the free flow of oil and keep prices stable. After the first Gulf War in 1991, the Saudi kingdom's importance had only been elevated, becoming the key base for the United States to pre-position military material in the region and direct its airpower to enforce the containment of Saddam Hussein's Iraq. According to one consular official interviewed by the 9/11 Commission staff, "our mission in Saudi Arabia [was] to be as accommodating as we possibly could." It was an inauspicious place for an experiment in government efficiency.

Wyche Fowler, a former Democratic senator from Georgia who was appointed by President Clinton as ambassador to Saudi Arabia in 1996, was particularly aggressive in insisting that the demands of the fifteen thousand members of the Saudi royal family be accommodated, even if they violated normal consular procedures. In one case he ordered a consular officer to grant a visa to the servant of a Saudi diplomat despite the diplomat's refusal to provide any evidence that the servant was being paid at least minimum wage, as required by U.S. law. In a far more serious case, Fowler fired the U.S. consul general in Riyadh, ordering him to leave the country within twenty-four hours, because he insisted that all servants of the royal family come in for interviews before being granted visas to the United States. Fowler then accused him in a performance review of failing to follow embassy policies.

While the high politics of the U.S.-Saudi relationship made intense scrutiny of many Saudi visa applicants almost impossible, there was a more banal reason why Saudis almost always got their visas: they were rich. The biggest hurdle for visitors wanting to come to the United States is the presumption, written into U.S. immigration law since 1952, that anyone arriving in the country intends to immigrate and stay. To overcome that presumption, individuals must demonstrate strong ties to their home countries— family, work, a history of traveling and returning—that make it highly unlikely they will remain in the United States. after their visas expire. Further, a visa applicant must show that he or she has enough money to travel to the United States, spend time there, and return. For most Saudis, this was not a problem. As one consular official who issued a visa to a hijacker told the 9/11 Commission: "It was factual, as far as our statistics showed, that they just weren't economic immigrants. . . . They spent a lot of money, they went on their vacations, they loved to go to Florida, and then they came back." Or as George Lannon, Ryan's former deputy, later put it: "Saudis didn't come and dig ditches; they didn't go to work in McDonald's. They partied and they left." Indeed, official State Department policy in the 1990s was to treat all Saudi visa applicants as having overcome the "intending immigrant" presumption. That meant that, unlike most visa applicants around the world, Saudis were not required to fill out visa application forms completely, did not need to show proof of home address or financial means, and in many cases were not required to appear for a personal interview.

The practice was not uniformly lax, according to the 9/11 Commission investigation. At the U.S. consulate in Jeddah, unlike in the capital of Riyadh, more than half of all visa applicants were interviewed during the 1990s, especially male Saudis between the ages of sixteen and forty. Jeddah is a gateway for Muslim pilgrims visiting the holy sites of Mecca and Medina, and U.S. consular officials there were conscious of the danger that Muslim extremists might seek visas to the United States from there. Apart from the required check of the TIPOFF watch list of known terrorists, consular officers would give extra scrutiny to those with long beards or short robes, and applicants from certain provinces known to harbor extremists. But even in the tougher environment of Jeddah, there was no consistency. One of the consular officers there had a high refusal rate and was at one point reprimanded for denying too many visas; another was less persuaded that Saudis posed any security risk, and he had a higher approval rate. That one consular officer in Jeddah would issue eleven of the nineteen visas received by the hijackers.

The best-practices model also had a significant impact on the consular service in Saudi Arabia prior to 9/11. On September 11, 2000, Thomas Furey was posted as the new consul general in Riyadh. He seemed a natural choice for such a difficult assignment. Furey had just spent three years supervising the largest consular operation in the world, in Mexico City, where he oversaw a staff of 150 Foreign Service officers and 350 local hires who processed 2 million visa applications in 2000. When he got to Riyadh, he would later tell the 9/11 Commission, his impression was that the office was "chaotic and dysfunctional." Visa applications had been growing by 5 percent a year, but Washington had refused to authorize funds for more consular officers, insisting that the problem was lack of efficiency. There were also huge security concerns, though they were based not on the anticipation of future terrorist attacks inside the United States but rather on the reality of previous ones against U.S. targets abroad. In 1998, Al Qaeda terrorists had set off nearly simultaneous truck bomb explosions outside the U.S. embassies in Nairobi, Kenya, and Dar es Salaam, Tanzania, killing more than 220 people and wounding 4,000 more. The Riyadh embassy seemed acutely vulnerable to a similar attack. Every day huge crowds of Saudis and nationals of other countries working in Saudi Arabia would descend on the embassy, milling around outside waiting for their turn at the visa wicket. On the busiest days as many as 800 people would come into the embassy, a number that the State Department's security officer in the region considered a grave security risk.

So Furey set about finding a solution. In the quest for greater efficiency, the State Department's consular handbook had recommended that consular officers reduce the number of personal interviews to save time and resources, and to "spare applicants the inconvenience of appearing in person." The United States had sought similar shortcuts before. After the fall of the Berlin Wall, the demand for visas from eastern Europe became so large that there were literally riots outside the U.S. embassy in Poland. In response, the United States started to accept visa applications through the mail or packaged up by travel agents. Furey looked at several options. He considered setting up a new appointments process, relying on either a fee-for-service 900 telephone number or the postal system. But the former was illegal in Saudi Arabia and the latter too unreliable to handle passports. He then set up a drop box on the outside wall of the embassy in Riyadh, but that did little to speed up the system. Then he hit on another idea. Most Saudis traveling to the United States made their reservations through travel agencies. Since the early 1970s, a number of U.S. embassies had set up procedures that allowed travel agents to handle the initial stages of the visa application; by 2000, nearly forty embassies and consulates were using such procedures. Emulating what was seen as a "best practice," Furey set up a system to authorize ten selected travel agencies to handle the initial stage of the visa application, eliminating the need for Saudis to line up outside the embassy. Instead, as they were making their travel reservations, Saudis would fill out a U.S. visa application, pay the visa fee, and leave their passports with the travel agent. On a daily basis, the agents would deliver those applications to the embassy in Riyadh for processing. If the application was approved, it would be sent back through the travel agent; if consular officials wanted to interview an applicant, he or she would be notified by the travel agent to appear at the embassy for an interview. A visa applicant would only be rejected after an interview.

Furey was so happy with the innovation that he gave it a catchy name—Visa Express—and ordered it to be used throughout Saudi Arabia by June 1, 2001. In a cable to Mary Ryan three weeks later, he gushed: "The number of people on the street and coming through the gates should be only 15 percent of what it was last summer. The RSO [regional security officer] is happy, the guard force is happy, the public loves the service (no more long lines and they can go to the travel agencies in the evening and not take time off from work), we love it (no more crowd control stress and reduced work for the FSNs) and now this afternoon [we] discovered the most amazing thing—the Saudi government loves it." In the three months before 9/11, three of the nineteen hijackers would get their visas through the Visa Express program.

Both Furey and Ryan believed that such efficiencies could be introduced without increasing the risk of a terrorist slipping through. Furey later told the 9/11 Commission that he had simply been unaware that Saudi citizens posed any security threat to the United States. Ryan was less naïve but believed that her technological innovations had set up a web that would catch any known terrorists as long as the intelligence agencies reliably provided the names. The problem—her failure of imagination—was the unknown terrorists. While two of the nineteen should have been on the TIPOFF watch list, the other seventeen were largely invisible to U.S. intelligence agencies. The 9/11 Commission would argue that, had consular officers been better trained in the techniques of terrorist travel, there were indicators in the passports of several of the hijackers that might have raised red flags. But consular officers were given no training that would help them to spot the travel tactics used by terrorists.

That left the interview process—the gut check by an experienced consular officer—as the only real line of defense. But only two of the nineteen were interviewed; the rest received their visas sight unseen.

JOEL MOWBRAY WAS ONE OF the new breed of journalist cum political operative whose influence had begun to grow with the spread of the Internet and blogging, the proliferation of cable news outlets, and the revival of talk radio. He had graduated with a law degree and worked for a Republican member of Congress, but he quickly found that the megaphone of modern media was a much surer road to gaining attention in conservative circles. And he was tenacious—as one of his colleagues wrote approvingly, he sunk his teeth into a story "as if he were a pit bull that caught up with a jogger." When he got his teeth into the State Department in the spring of 2002, his goal wasn't simply to hold on but rather to shake it into pieces. As he would later write, he wanted to expose "a corrosive culture that puts the interests of other nations ahead of America's."

There is a firm belief, in a certain wing of the Republican Party, dating back to the Joe McCarthy era and the hearings of the House Committee on Un-American Activities in the late 1940s, that the State Department is filled with officials who, if not outright traitors, are less than fully loyal to the United States. That strain went dormant for much of the 1980s but then resurfaced with the rise of a more aggressive brand of conservatism in the mid-1990s. The best example is Ann Coulter, the controversial conservative columnist, who wrote a revisionist history of the McCarthy era that insisted that, if anything, McCarthy had been too sympathetic to the State Department. In the Bush administration, she had many avid followers. As one former official in the Bush White House put it: "State Department officials were viewed by many in the White House as treacherous pigs. They really were. They weren't viewed as loyal. A lot of people believed that." In that environment, Mowbray found an eager audience.

On June 14, 2002, the website of the conservative *National Review* published a piece by Mowbray entitled "Catching the Visa Express," which shone a spotlight on the program that Furey had set up to streamline the visa process in Saudi Arabia. It didn't demand a lot of shoe leather. Nine months after the attacks, the U.S. embassy in Riyadh was still touting the program on its website, bragging that "applicants will no longer have to take time off work [and] no longer have to wait in long lines under the hot sun."

In the post-9/11 environment, it was a good story that seemed to the Coulter strain of conservatives to epitomize everything that was wrong with the State Department. The lead almost wrote itself. "Three Saudis who were among the last of the Sept. 11 homicide hijackers to enter this country didn't visit a U.S. embassy or consulate to get their visas; they went to a *travel agent* [emphasis in original], where they submitted a short, two-page form and a photo. The program that made this possible, Visa Express, is still using travel agents in Saudi Arabia to fill this vital role in United States border security." Mowbray threw in few damning anonymous quotes. One senior consular affairs official described the program as "an open-door policy for terrorists." There was particular outrage that the program had not been shut down after 9/11. Visa Express, he wrote encouragingly, "was an obvious target for congressional hearings and public outcry."

There was enough truth to what Mowbray wrote to give the story credence. While the rest of the government was scrambling to remake its operations after 9/11, Consular Affairs under Ryan was largely trying to build on what had been done before the attacks—and to fend off Justice Department demands for much harsher measures. A report by the State Department Inspector General's Office in December 2002 would conclude: "The post September 11 era should have witnessed immediate and dramatic changes in CA's direction of the visa process. This has not happened. A fundamental readjustment by Department leadership regarding visa issuance and denial has not taken place."

The continuation of the Visa Express program after 9/11 was a good symbol of that failure. The 9/11 Commission investigation would conclude that, while Visa Express did not substantially increase the security risk, it removed an important tool from the consular officer: the ability to size up a visa applicant and request an interview on the spot. Based on the evidence, there were plenty of good reasons to eliminate the program after 9/11, yet State had not moved to do so.

But Mowbray, like so many of the new generation of bloggers, made it personal. The problem, he wrote, was Mary Ryan. Ryan, he charged, had intentionally nurtured a "courtesy culture" that was anathema to America's ability to weed out would-be terrorists. That culture "is inherently inimical to the types of reforms necessary to keep out terrorists," he wrote. "It—and she—must go." Mowbray's crusade was immediately picked up in conservative media circles. The program was dubbed "Travelocity for Terrorists" and the story got heavy coverage on the conservative Fox News and on talk radio.

The sudden attack caught the department off-guard. George Lannon, Ryan's deputy, said later, "We thought we'd put out that fire." In December 2001, *U.S. News & World Report* had published a nearly identical story about the Visa Express program, but it had received little attention and the story had blown over. But this time the department badly fumbled the response. Andruch, testifying before Congress, mistakenly claimed on June 12 to the House Committee on Government Reform that the Visa Express program "has been shut down." It had not, and the misstatement further fueled the controversy. Then, rather than moving immediately to end the program, State quietly tried to bury it. After Mowbray's story, the embassy in Saudi Arabia attempted to conceal the program on the embassy website, taking out the promotional language that had encouraged Saudis to use the Visa Express system and replacing it with dry bureaucratese. Mowbray also caught the department out in what looked like a deliberate attempt to mislead, securing documents that showed that the refusal rate for Saudis and third-country nationals in Saudi Arabia was nearly 25 percent. State had insisted that the refusal rate for Saudis alone, which the department claimed was just 3 percent, justified the program, but later issued a statement that the refusal rate "has nothing to do" with the program. The changing claims all smacked of a cover-up, which only made it a better story.

THERE WAS ANOTHER REASON MOWBRAY'S story had such an impact. In early June 2002, just before Mowbray's *National Review* piece appeared, Lannon and Catherine Brown, a State Department attorney, were escorted into a secure room in the New Executive Office Building across from the White House. They were ordered not to bring any paper, pens, or recording devices. There they were allowed to sit and look at the draft of the White House's proposal for the new Department of Homeland Security written by the team under Andy Card, a summary of which was made public on June 6.

Up until that time, Colin Powell had largely stayed out of the battles that Mary Ryan was fighting. Handling the complicated diplomacy surrounding the war in Afghanistan and the buildup to the coming war in Iraq was more than a full-time job. Powell had spoken out in the White House against the creation of single border agency back in January, but as he would say later, when news about the White House proposal for a new DHS first began dribbling out, "I was sitting back fat and happy saying, 'I don't see what this is going to have to do with me.'" But what Lannon and Brown discovered, buried in the forty pages of dense type in the still-secret text of the proposal, was that the White House wanted to transfer complete authority over visa policy to the new department. When Lannon reported back with his findings, Powell immediately got on the phone to Card. "I said to Andy, 'We want to be team players but you cannot believe that it makes any sense to move the consular function out of the State Department and to move it into Homeland Security.' It's Homeland Security, not running 290 facilities around the world with their own personnel system, and it's a personnel system that's integrated into the FSO [Foreign Service officer] system. You can't just shred it out and give it to Homeland

Security." But Card, who was dealing with a flood of calls from angry cabinet members set to lose one agency or another, was unsympathetic. "He said, 'Nope, there's nothing I can do about it.' They were insistent that since they were going to wrap up everybody else, they had to wrap up the State Department too," Powell said.

The White House proposal did not actually call for transferring the consular service to the new DHS, but instead, giving DHS authority over visa policy, which would give it the power to determine which foreigners would need visas to come to the United States and what kind of visas they would need. DHS would also have the final operational authority to decide whether to reject a particular visa application. It did not propose making consular officers wear DHS uniforms, however, and in many ways was not a radical change from the status quo; State already shared authority over the visa process with the Department of Justice, though prior to 9/11 Justice had largely abdicated that role. But the threat that State could lose the consular function entirely was a real one. Congress, not the White House, would write the law, and there were many in the Republican-controlled House of Representatives who were eager to see State emasculated, including James Sensenbrenner, the powerful Republican chairman of the House Judiciary Committee. Congressman Dave Weldon, who chaired one of the relevant subcommittees in the House, called a hearing June 26 and urged that the entire Bureau of Consular Affairs be moved to DHS. "The State Department views the issuance of visas as a diplomatic tool," he said. "The day is past when it should be viewed that way. It is now clearly a national homeland security function." To support his argument, he invited testimony from Mowbray and from two former consular officials who had offered critical quotes in Mowbray's articles.

Rebuffed by Card, Powell went instead to Tom Ridge in an effort to present a united position to Congress. Ridge and Powell had not known each other long, but they shared a common bond as soldiers who had served in Vietnam, and they had worked together on some youth programs when Ridge was governor of Pennsylvania and Powell was running America's Promise, his national charity aimed at lifting up underprivileged children and teenagers. He picked up the phone to Ridge, suggesting a face-to-face meeting at the White House to resolve the issue. In Powell's telling, that meeting saved the State Department. "We talked it through for the better part of an hour and a half, and I said, 'Tom, here's what I think you ought to do. I'll give you the policy—you determine who you want to come in the country and not come in the country. It's homeland security policy, not foreign policy. But I have a complete system that works, it is up and running with its own personnel. I'm telling you, the last thing you need on top of everything else you're getting is an international organization with 290 places that are integral part of the embassies that belong to the State Department." Ridge readily agreed and would later say that he had no interest in running the consular service because the new department simply didn't have the capacity to take on that function. "It was easy for me," he said.

Lannon, Ryan's deputy who would be sent up to Capitol Hill to defend publicly the Ridge-Powell compromise, was privately scornful of the outcome. The White House proposal did not call for stripping State entirely of the consular function, he pointed out, and argued there was little danger Congress would do so either. While in theory DHS could have put its uniforms on consular officers around the world, there was little chance of that happening. "They [DHS] were never really intending to take over the visa process anyway," said Lannon. "They didn't want it; it was always policy they wanted."

The meeting between Powell and Ridge was meaningless, he said. "It was one old soldier to another old soldier saying, 'You're not going to shoot me in the ankle here, are you, Tommy boy?'" he later said dismissively. "He [Powell] got nothing."

With Powell now fully engaged in trying to keep his department intact, the clock was running out on Ryan. As the lightning rod for congressional and conservative critics, Powell was under growing pressure to cut her loose. "We all loved Mary, she was really beloved by the consular officers, but she was starting to cause

me difficulties with the Hill," he admitted later. "She really was
not flexible enough and responding flexibly enough to the political
and bureaucratic demands of the post-9/11 period. Changes were
necessary and we had to be a little more contrite about what we
were doing in order to save it." At the meeting with Ridge and his
staff to discuss whether State could retain its visa responsibilities,
Powell had already signaled his growing displeasure by ordering her
not to speak up, saying later that "she was about to have a nervous
breakdown over the issue." It got to the point, said one of Powell's
closest aides, that they even stopped inviting her to some of the
higher-level interagency meetings. "She didn't get the message," he
said, "that it was no longer business as usual."

On July 8, a Monday, Grant Green called Ryan into his office.
She had offered to resign before, telling Green that she was willing
to step down if her continued presence was hurting the department, but he had refused. That day, however, he said it was time for
her to retire. The meeting, he recalls, was short. "I think she knew
because she had already said if it was not working she was ready to
resign. I don't think it was a great surprise." Ryan didn't argue, he
said, and didn't point any fingers.

Green said Powell was left with little choice but to let her go.
"There were times that Mary just wouldn't accept that she had
to go to the Hill with a little bit of mea culpa," he said. "Mary
was very good. It's just that at this time when everyone in town
was trying to point a finger and level blame, that Consular Affairs was very susceptible to taking that blame." He added: "In the
eyes of some of the senior leadership of the department, she just
couldn't change course."

That same week, three committees on the House of Representatives approved legislation that retained the State Department's
role in issuing visas but handed policy over to the new DHS. An
amendment later offered by Weldon to move the entire consular
function to DHS was defeated on the House floor. The Senate
adopted similar language that was included in the final DHS legislation, preserving State's administrative role.

Later that month, the new U.S. ambassador to Saudi Arabia, Robert Jordan, shut down the Visa Express program. In an internal cable that was promptly leaked to Mowbray and to the *Washington Post*, Jordan wrote: "I am deeply troubled about the prevailing perception in the media and within Congress and possibly the American public at large that our current practices represent a shameful and inadequate effort on our part."

The following August, Consular Affairs halted the practice, in all its embassies and consulates around the world, of waiving interviews for visa applicants who appeared to pose little risk. From that point on, any foreign national who required a visa to come to the United States, with only a handful of exceptions, would be required to appear for an interview.

POWELL'S DECISION TO LET RYAN go provoked jubilation from her critics. The *Wall Street Journal* editorial page chortled that it was "Secretary Powell's admission that his department isn't all it ought to be," while one of Mowbray's colleagues at the *National Review* called her "a vanquished villain."

Inside the department, however, the reaction was one of anger and anguish. The U.S. consul general in Rome, who was on the verge of retirement, fired off an e-mail to senior State officials and to his consular colleagues that was promptly leaked to the *Washington Times*. "All of this smacks of the days of Senator Joe McCarthy, when a witch hunt conducted in the name of protecting Americans from the Communist menace ruined the careers of Foreign Service Officers," he wrote. Another consular official, hitting the Reply All button, wrote: "We assume Mary's replacement will not be a career officer with a balanced approach but a neo-Nazi who views us as incompetent or criminal." Grant Green promptly called Lannon, who had been named the acting assistant secretary, into his office, angrily ordering him to "get your people in line." But if Lannon was more diplomatic than his consular charges, he was seething nonetheless. Powell held a small, private ceremony for Ryan, at which he presented her with the Distinguished Service Award for her career accomplishments. "Powell never acknowledged Mary at all," Lannon complained. "His presentation was, basically, 'Well, old Mary's decided to hang it up,' as opposed to 'We've thrown her off the sled to get the wolves off us,' which is what it was. He would never acknowledge that she took the hit. I was livid. I was appalled."

Ryan's friend Johnny Young, despite his admiration for Powell as a fellow African American, is no more forgiving. "From the day he walked into the department, he talked about his troops and standing by his troops. He had earned our love and respect, and when we needed him most he abandoned us and sacrificed Mary."

Powell, too, has carried a grudge. Rather than throwing up some "neo-Nazi" to replace Mary, as his critics had feared, he picked Maura Harty, Ryan's deputy and close friend and another highly respected career officer. The choice was despised by Ryan's conservative critics; Mowbray called her "a protégé and clone of Mary Ryan [who] will likely maintain the very policies for which her predecessor was fired." The White House refused to push for Harty's confirmation, but Powell insisted he could drive the nomination through the Senate by himself. "I had to fight like a dog, but I got her confirmed and she's been there ever since," he said.

The criticisms from Ryan's supporters still rankle. Powell said he tried to engineer a quiet and dignified retirement for Ryan, but that her backers went public to complain that she had been forced out. "Whether they liked it or not, it was necessary to do in order to save the consular corps. And I always have a little bitterness that I had to get that kind of abuse when in fact I kept the consular corps from going to the DHS."

AFTER LEAVING THE STATE DEPARTMENT, Ryan went back to school, graduating from a two-year program in parish administration from Trinity University. Although her mother had been a banker, she had no interest in earning money for its own sake. She asked Andruch, her former assistant, for a letter of recommendation to allow her to volunteer at George Washington University in Washington, administering the Eucharist to bedridden patients.

She tutored students in the D.C. public schools and taught as a visiting diplomat at Georgetown University.

In January 2006 Ryan attended a funeral for a former secretary of Johnny Young's. After the service, Young and his wife had both hugged her, and on the way home in the car shared their observation that she was "skin and bones." Young sent her an e-mail, and she wrote back to tell him that she was suffering from myelofibrosis, a cancer of the bone marrow that usually afflicts those over sixty. He was the first friend she had told about her illness. She said that she had three treatment options: a bone marrow transplant, which would be extremely painful and risky; extended chemotherapy; or treatment with interferon. She chose the latter, but it made her very tired and weak.

In the third week of April 2006, she had lunch with Lannon, who noticed she had grown frighteningly thin. She told him it was a cold and not to worry. The following week, she was scheduled to have lunch with a friend, but she failed to show up. He grew worried, and asked the superintendent of her building to let him in to her apartment. He found her lying dead in her bed on April 25, 2006.

Her funeral at St. Stephen Martyr Roman Catholic Church was overflowing. Johnny Young said the Prayer to the Faithful, and Maura Harty delivered the eulogy. "It was an incredible funeral," Young would later recall. "If the terrorists had come they could have wiped out half the diplomatic corps."

# Chapter 6

# THE CONSEQUENCES

ON THE MORNING OF MARCH 13, 2002, President Bush did something he admitted was quite rare for him. He picked up the newspaper and read a front-page article. It concerned two of the 9/11 hijackers, Mohammed Atta and Marwan al-Shehhi. More than six months after the two had died when they piloted the planes that crashed into the World Trade Center, the article said, the INS had approved their applications for student visas to take flying lessons. The forms had been mailed to the Huffman Aviation flight-training school in Venice, Florida, two weeks previously, with no one at the INS facility apparently noticing the names of the two most notorious of the nineteen hijackers. "I could barely get my coffee down," a visibly angry Bush sputtered at a press conference that morning. "I was stunned and not happy. Let me put it another way—I was plenty hot." He said that major changes were needed at the INS and that his attorney general, John Ashcroft, "got the message, and so should the INS."

After the president's public dressing-down, Ashcroft immediately issued a blistering statement that promised a full investigation of the "disturbing failures," adding, "It is inexcusable when document mismanagement leads to a breakdown of this magnitude. Individuals will be held responsible for any professional incompetence that led to this failure." Jim Ziglar was livid too, but at his boss rather than at his staff. Angered over what he saw as Ashcroft's gratuitous slap at the INS and his refusal to defend the agency, he stormed into the attorney general's office and was, he admitted later, "pretty nasty actually," handing in his resignation on the spot. It would have been a serious embarrassment to the Bush administration, which was still projecting to the public the image of a united team fighting the new war on terrorism. Ashcroft asked him to reconsider. The White House also did not want the issue to escalate into a full-blown crisis. Josh Bolten, Andy Card's quiet, efficient deputy and a Senate staff veteran like Ziglar, stepped in to calm down the INS chief and persuaded him to remain. "It's the only reason I stayed," said Ziglar. "I had a very high regard for Josh Bolten."

After his anger cooled, the incident persuaded Ziglar that his patient efforts to nudge the INS bureaucracy into reforming itself were not paying off. As Michael Cronin, who was promoted to assistant INS commissioner for inspections after the visa debacle, put it: "That was when he finally came in and did away with the niceties of the consultant strategic planning processes and the organizational planning processes and just did it." He reassigned four of his senior officials and accepted responsibility for what he called "an inexcusable blunder." He pledged to put in place by the end of the year a new electronic system to keep track of all foreign students in the United States and said that the INS would meet a goal of processing all visa applications within thirty days. But he continued to be defensive about his agency's performance. "Changes in INS operations were already being proposed, but last week's incident prompted us to move more swiftly and more publicly," he said at the National Press Club. "I take responsibility for not doing a good job letting the public know how much the agency is doing to improve operations."

Ziglar would stay in the job for another eight months, but he announced his resignation in August 2002 in the face of what he feared was a plan by Ashcroft and his chief of staff, David Ayres,

to oust and embarrass him. Instead, Ziglar penned his own letter of resignation, sent it to the president, and in a decision that
showed how poisonous his relationship with Ashcroft had become,
released it to the press before sending it to the attorney general. "I
wasn't going to take any chances," he said. Anti-immigration activists welcomed his departure. Mr. Ziglar was "never a good fit even
before September 11," said Mark Krikorian, executive director of
the Center for Immigration Studies, which advocates a crackdown
on illegal immigration and lower levels of legal migration. "He was
ambivalent about the law enforcement part of the job," Krikorian
said, "and that was especially inappropriate after the attacks."

A week before Ziglar's departure in November 2002, Bush
signed the legislation passed by Congress to create a new Department of Homeland Security. It split off the INS's citizenship and
immigration processing arms into one part of DHS and merged the
Border Patrol and INS inspectors with Customs into a single new
entity responsible for border security. When DHS was launched in
2003, Customs chief Rob Bonner took charge of the new agency,
which was renamed Customs and Border Protection. Bonner made
no secret of his contempt for the INS, which he called "a paranoid
schizophrenic organization." The traditional white uniforms of the
INS border inspectors were exchanged for Customs blue, and Bonner picked his own officials to take charge of seventeen out of the
agency's twenty regional field offices. "There were probably a few
legacy INS people who thought it was a Customs takeover," Bonner acknowledged. But Bonner was savvy enough to leave the powerful Border Patrol unchanged, allowing them to continue wearing
their traditional green uniforms. "They would have walked off skyscrapers for me after that."

The Atta and al-Shehhi scandal was, as Michael Cronin put it,
"the final nail in the coffin" for the INS, even though he and others
at the agency continued to fight for its survival "right to the brink
of the precipice." Mike Becraft, Ziglar's deputy, agrees. He said that
after that, "instead of asking questions they just decided to deep-six
the INS. We knew at that time that it was over." While many in

the administration had already wanted to get rid of the INS, the mishandling of the visas was proof of the urgency of the task.

THE VISA DEBACLE BROUGHT TO public attention something that was well known inside the government long before 9/11: of all the things that were broken about the INS, nothing was quite as broken as the system for granting student visas. While the State Department handled student visa applications from abroad, it was often the case that young foreigners would come to the United States on tourist or other temporary visas and then decide they wanted to stay to study, and those cases were handled by the INS. "The INS's foreign student program historically has been dysfunctional, and the INS has acknowledged for several years that it does not know how many foreign students are in the United States," said the Justice Department Inspector General's report ordered by Ashcroft after the visa scandal.

For a student visa system to work, the INS needed to be able to do something that it had never been able to do—process applications in a timely fashion. The typical foreign student would not normally learn until the spring of a given year whether he or she had been accepted for a program of study that was to begin in the fall. That meant that the INS needed to be able to consider and respond to a flood of visa applications each year in a two- to three-month window. It was rarely capable of doing so. As a result many foreign students would find themselves in illegal status for months at a time attending school without a student visa while they awaited INS adjudication, but prosecution was rare because INS agents understood that the processing delays left most people with no other alternative.

In the case of both Atta and al-Shehhi, they had arrived in the United States with lawful tourist visas in the spring of 2000, and then scrupulously followed procedure by submitting to the INS a change-of-status application in September 2000 to be allowed to remain in the country as flight-training students. As was often the case, they began the program while the visa was still being adjudicated and finished their flight training in December 2000. On January 4, 2001, Atta left the United States for Spain, returning six days later to Miami. When he arrived at the airport, INS inspectors had grounds for turning him around. For one, his tourist visa had expired a month before, and because his student visa had not yet been approved he had no legal grounds for reentering the United States. Also, by leaving the country, he had effectively abandoned his change-of-status application, under which individuals must remain in the United States unless they get special permission to leave. But the INS inspectors at the airport overlooked both violations. Atta had told one inspector that he was enrolled in flight school and was still awaiting an INS response to his application; that did not surprise the inspector, who later conceded that the system for tracking students was "garbage." So instead of blocking his entry over the visa violations, the inspector readmitted Atta on another tourist visa. Such a decision was far from unusual. As Cronin put it: "The inspector doing the work would have been perfectly aware that on the benefits side there were these incredible backlogs, making it virtually impossible for people to comply with the letter of the law. You have to look at the inspector's actions in that context." Technically, inspectors were supposed to issue such waivers of the student visa requirement only in emergency circumstances, but in practice they were nearly automatic. As the internal Justice report on the incident stated: "The INS's prevailing philosophy in dealing with foreign students at the ports of entry before September 11 was that students were not a concern or a significant risk worthy of special scrutiny."

Al-Shehhi's case was different, though the outcome was identical. He too had left the United States after completing his flight training and then reentered the country, so technically he had also abandoned his student visa application and had no legal grounds for returning. Like Atta, he told the INS inspector that he had been at flight school and said he was returning to do further training. But instead of insisting that he wait outside the country for his student visa to be approved—which is what the letter of the law required—the inspector allowed him into the country on a business visa, which is normally granted only to commercial pilots seeking further training, not to students wishing to become pilots.

Atta and al-Shehhi were not the only two of the hijackers to exploit the weaknesses in the system for approving and tracking foreign students. Ziad Jarrah, who flew United Flight 93, which crashed in Pennsylvania, was admitted as a tourist but then immediately enrolled in flight school in Florida without applying for a student visa, a violation of immigration law. But the school did not alert the INS, and Jarrah left and reentered the United States six times before the attacks without INS inspectors being aware that he had violated the terms of his tourist visa by going to flight school. Hani Hanjour, who flew the plane that crashed into the Pentagon, got a student visa in September 2000 from the U.S. consulate in Jeddah to attend an English as a Second Language school in Oakland, California, but he never showed up at the school. Yet the INS was never alerted of his failure to comply with the terms of his student visa.

Though appalling on many levels, what happened with the Atta and al-Shehhi visas—and with those of the other hijackers— was business as usual for the INS. The internal investigation later showed that the INS had actually approved Atta's and al-Shehhi's student visa applications in the summer of 2001, before the attacks. That was not exactly timely processing—it was nearly ten months after they had submitted their applications and six months after they had already completed their flight training at Huffman. The approvals were mailed to the two hijackers in July and August 2001, and separate copies were sent to a processing facility for eventual mailing to the flight school. There was normally a bit of a delay built in, on the theory that, had the initial visa application actually been processed on time, the INS wanted to be sure that the student had arrived at the school before the visa approval was mailed to the institution. In the case of Atta and al-Shehhi, however, it would take another seven months for the letters to finally reach the Huffman School in Florida. After 9/11, the INS had ordered a sweep of its computer systems to find anything connected to the hijackers, but the approval letters, known as I-20s, were in paper form only, sitting in the vault of a Kentucky contractor hired by the INS. Nobody in the facility noticed the names and nobody in the INS thought to track down the hard copies. Those were the letters that caused the president to choke on his coffee that morning.

WHILE THE PROBLEMS IN THE student visa system were well-known, prior to 9/11 there had never been the sense of urgency, or the necessary political muscle, to do anything about it. Foreign students, by almost every measure imaginable, had been an enormous boon to the United States.

No other country has anything close to the number of world-class universities as the United States. Britain has Oxford and Cambridge, Germany has Heidelberg, France has the Sorbonne, Japan has Tokyo University, but the United States has dozens of top-ranked schools. Depending on the survey used, somewhere between half and three-quarters of the world's top universities are in the United States. Throughout the postwar period, the best students from around the world have flocked to American universities. Since the mid-1950s, there had been a virtually uninterrupted rise in the number of foreign students enrolled in the United States, with the exception of a slight dip following the deep recession of the early 1980s. The numbers grew from fewer than 50,000 to a peak of nearly 600,000 by the year 2000.

The payoffs could be measured in multiple ways. In science and engineering in particular, foreign students and researchers had become increasingly important as American students showed less interest in those fields. By 2000, nearly 40 percent of the doctorates in science and engineering and 30 percent of the master's degrees awarded by U.S. universities were held by foreign-born students. The proportion was even higher in mathematics, computer science, and the physical and life sciences. Among postdoctoral students doing research at the highest levels, nearly 60 percent were foreign-born. The economic value of those graduates was extraordinary. The universities served as a pipeline into American business, channeling talented students into positions at the best U.S. companies or connecting them with financial backers if they wanted to strike out on their own. Once here to study, a surprisingly high percentage of the top foreign students remained. A 2001 study found that nearly two-thirds of those who received doctoral degrees in science or engineering were still in the United States two years later. At U.S. multinational companies surveyed by the National Academies, between 30 and 50 percent of researchers were foreign-born. "The research and development divisions of U.S. corporations continue to develop new technologies and remain internationally competitive in part because immigration provides them with the best talent in the world," said a major 2004 study on foreign students.

Bruce Alberts, president of the National Academy of Sciences, said that one of the "defining strengths" of the United States is that it is at the center of an international science and technology network built by people who are working in the country or who were educated here. "We benefit," he said, "from an extraordinary set of personal, professional, and cultural relationships due to the many people from other countries who are working in the U.S. science and technology enterprise, and due to the large number of science and technology leaders in other countries who have been trained in the United States."

Foreign students and researchers have long been successful at the highest levels of U.S. science and business. Historically, more than one-third of American Nobel Prize winners have been foreign-born; between 1990 and 2001 half were foreign-born. Many of the country's most successful immigrant scientists are household names, like Albert Einstein, Edward Teller, and Enrico Fermi, who were responsible for helping the United States beat Nazi Germany in developing an atomic bomb and later to stay ahead of the Soviet Union in the cold war arms race. More recently, the United States' lead in information technologies has been driven by immigrant engineers and entrepreneurs, including Andy Grove of Intel, Sergey Brin of Google, Pierre Omidyar of eBay, and Jerry Yang of Yahoo. But the real contribution is much broader than just a few stars. There are thousands of immigrants working throughout the ranks of U.S. companies, doing cutting-edge research at universities, or establishing and building their own companies. On one of the most important measures of innovation—the number of patents issued each year—the United States ranks far ahead of any other country in the world. Half those American patents are issued to foreign-owned companies and foreign-born inventors.

There are two big reasons the United States has been so successful in attracting and retaining foreign talent: openness and opportunity. The United States has long been the world's best place for the ambitious to thrive, particularly if they lack family or political connections in their home countries. In the older economies of Europe, for instance, advancement into business or the senior ranks of the government has normally depended on rising up through the right schools, a path that until quite recently has been closed to most immigrants. The same is true in Japan, though again it has started to change in the past few years. The United States, in contrast, has long had a more open university system that recruits primarily on talent rather than on nationality, accent, or pedigree. While money certainly helps, for both American and foreign students, the best graduate students have many options for financing their education through scholarships, teaching and research assistantships, and student loans. Once they graduate, many foreign students who remain in the United States have been able to take advantage of the world's best system for encouraging innovation and entrepreneurship. No other country has been able to match U.S. capabilities in venture capital and start-up financing, and immigrant entrepreneurs have made the most of this system. In Silicon Valley, for instance, immigrant entrepreneurs founded or cofounded over half of all start-up companies. Overall, some 40 percent of U.S. high-tech companies launched by venture capital were started by immigrants, and as of late 2006 these companies accounted for more than $500 billion in market value. Nearly half of those immigrant founders first arrived in the United States as students.

The contributions of foreign talent have become increasingly crucial as the U.S. economy has shifted from a fairly stable manufacturing base to dynamic sectors like information technology, financial services, and pharmaceuticals, which require constant innovation to succeed. Craig Barrett, the chairman of Intel, the world's largest maker of high-performance computer chips, has said that 80 to 90 percent of the revenue his company generates at the end of any given year comes from products that did not even exist at the beginning of the year. The regions where such capabilities are concentrated—San Francisco; Seattle; Boston; Washington, D.C.—have become what Bill Gates, the founder of Microsoft, calls "IQ magnets," attracting the most talented people from around the world. They have found here opportunities for tremendous success that, until quite recently, have not existed on the same scale anywhere else, and that success in turn has encouraged more to follow in their footsteps. Nothing has been more important to American competitiveness than its ability to attract such talented immigrants and to put their talents to the fullest use. As Richard Florida, the author of *The Rise of the Creative Class*, argues: "In today's global economy, the places that attract and retain this talent will win, and those that don't will lose. . . . Today, the terms of competition revolve around a central axis: a nation's ability to mobilize, attract and retain human creative talent. Every key dimension of international economic leadership, from manufacturing excellence to scientific and technological advancement, will depend on this ability." ↝

There have been diplomatic as well as economic benefits from the openness to foreign students. The State Department's website lists current and former foreign leaders who were educated at U.S. universities, and the list runs into the hundreds. It includes Jacques Chirac of France and Romano Prodi of Italy (both at Harvard), former UN secretaries-general Kofi Annan and Boutros Boutros-Ghali (MIT and Columbia), Gloria Macapagal-Arroyo, president of the Philippines (Georgetown), former Mexican presidents Vicente Fox, Miguel de la Madrid, and Carlos Salinas de Gortari (all at Harvard), former Israeli prime ministers Ehud Barak, Benjamin Netanyahu, and Shimon Peres (Stanford, MIT, and New York University/Harvard), and Prince Saud al-Faisal, Saudi Arabia's minister of foreign affairs (Princeton). The close ties that such former students have to the United States are hugely valuable to American diplomacy.

When he was secretary of state, Colin Powell said that foreign students "return home with an increased understanding and often a lasting affection for the United States. I can think of no more valuable asset to our country than the friendship of future world leaders who have been educated here." Robert Gates, the former CIA director who was president of Texas A&M University before being brought back to replace Donald Rumsfeld as defense secretary in the second Bush term, put it in even stronger terms: "In the last half century allowing students from other countries to study here has been the most positive thing America has done to win friends from around the world." There are counterexamples, of course. Sayyid Qutb, the intellectual founder of modern Islamic radicalism, spent a semester in 1949 at the Colorado State College of Education in Greeley, Colorado, and left angered about what he saw as the lax moral culture and spiritual breakdown of American society. But on the whole, exposure to American life seems to have had an overwhelmingly positive impact on foreign attitudes toward the United States. A 2006 opinion survey by the U.S. travel industry found that foreigners who had visited the country were almost twice as likely to have a favorable opinion of the United States as those who had not and relied on television or news reports for their image of America.

In addition to their benefits to the larger economy, foreign students have also been lucrative for the universities themselves, a big reason why they want to maintain high levels of foreign enrollment. In 2006–2007, foreign students paid nearly $10 billion in tuition and fees to American colleges and universities. At the undergraduate level in particular, foreign students usually pay the full cost of their education, not relying as heavily on university scholarships or the other forms of financial aid that many American students receive. For state universities, foreign students are charged out-of-state tuition rates, which can be five or six times as high as the rates charged to state residents. And the fees are even more important for an array of smaller technical and community colleges that try to recruit abroad.

THAT COMBINATION—THE PUBLIC INTEREST IN attracting foreign students coupled with the private financial interests of the universities themselves—had proved a formidable hurdle to efforts to tighten the student visa system before 9/11, even as the system had grown increasingly chaotic and unmanageable. By 2001, there were over 74,000 institutions in the country that accepted applications from foreign students. Harvard and Yale were on the list, but so were the Fayetteville Beauty College, the Academy of Animal Arts (a dog-grooming school), and the Acupuncture Academy. The list of approved institutions included golf and tennis schools, hotel management, English language schools, and every other manner of what could loosely be termed higher education or training. The INS rarely even visited the facilities to see if they were legitimate and could not begin to keep track of all the schools on its approved list. The Pacific Travel Trade School in Los Angeles, for instance, closed in December 2000. But fifty-one foreign students received visas to attend the school in 2001, and another twenty-two in 2002.

The lax system for monitoring student visas had arisen as a terrorism concern before 9/11. The Iranian hostage crisis in 1979, in which students stormed the U.S. embassy in Tehran and held fifty-two Americans captive, had raised fears about Iranian students in the United States. But there was no easy way for Washington to identify those students. That led President Jimmy Carter to order special registration for Iranian students and the deportation of any who had violated their visas, a scheme that was partially the model for the post-9/11 NSEERS program. In 1983 the INS had directed that colleges report the arrival and departure of foreign students, in an effort to keep track of whether they were actually showing up to study, but by 1988 the paper records flooding into the INS had piled so high that the agency told the institutions to stop sending them. "We had no place to store all that paper and, in any case, no one who could actually read it," said one INS official.

Then in 1993, Eyad Ismoil, a Jordanian citizen who had entered the United States on a student visa to attend Wichita State University before disappearing and remaining in the country illegally, drove a truck packed with explosives that was detonated under the World Trade Center towers—the first successful attack by Islamic extremists inside the United States. Following the attack, which killed six people and injured more than a thousand, the INS had prepared an internal report, completed in December 1995, which exposed many of the flaws in the visa system. Foreign students, it said, are "not subject to continuing scrutiny, tracking or monitoring when they depart, drop out, transfer, interrupt their education, violate status or otherwise violate the law." The report, which was developed in close consultation with university admissions officers, called for creating a sophisticated, computer-based tracking system that would give the INS immediate, updated information on the names and addresses of foreign students, their travel in and out of the country, and their current academic status. In the case of a student like Ismoil or the 9/11 hijacker Hani Hanjour, who failed even to show for school, red flags would go up immediately. It would also, importantly, contain information about their programs of study so that the INS would be alerted if a foreign student suddenly switched to a field like nuclear physics, raising security concerns.

It was a modest response to what had clearly emerged as a legitimate national security issue; in essence, it would simply put onto a computer system what the INS had been incapable of doing with paper records. In 1996, as part of a broader law aimed at cracking down on illegal immigration, Congress had ordered the creation of the computerized student tracking system and set January 1, 2003, as the deadline for it to be in place across the country. The next year, the INS launched a pilot project with universities in the North Carolina Research Triangle and other technical colleges in the South, involving about ten thousand students in total; the system worked well and was praised by Duke University and others involved. Like the best of the technocratic solutions, it increased security and efficiency at the same time, providing reliable tracking of foreign students while reducing paperwork and errors for over-burdened university administrators. It also had the potential for speeding up processing times for student visa applications, reducing or even eliminating the backlogs that had plagued the INS.

But the effort provoked extraordinary resistance from some parts of the higher education fraternity. In particular, there was a perception that the universities were being deputized to help crack down on international terrorism, a role that some schools feared would jeopardize their academic independence and their reputation. Gary Althen, who was then the president of NAFSA, the Association of International Educators, which was one of the Washington lobbying associations for the universities, said: "International education practitioners who want to be educators rather than deputies, who view foreign students and scholars as contributors to the education of us all rather than as potential terrorists, have no choice, it seems to me, but to pursue the repeal" of the new scheme. Althen expressed the concern that any mechanism that linked foreign students with international terrorism would somehow stigmatize the entire group and discourage those students from coming to the United States.

The universities have long been a powerful lobbying force in Washington. Members of Congress tend to look out for the interests of large local employers and institutions that are influential voices in their communities. The universities are both, and they are spread widely enough in the country that nearly every member of Congress has some stake in their success. The tracking scheme, however, was hard to object to on principle, and not much easier to block on practical grounds, since the pilot tests had been a success. Instead, the university lobbyists seized on a narrower, economic argument— that the universities should not have to collect the $95 fee charged to each foreign student to pay for the new system because that would require them to act as a tax collector for the government.

The opposition was only partially successful. The issue split the universities, pitting those who had cooperated with the INS and saw virtue in the system against the schools that opposed the tracking scheme and wanted it killed. Neither was quite powerful enough to prevail, but the opposition resulted in a scaling back and slower rollout of the Student and Exchange Visitor System, or SEVIS, as it was called by then. In July 2001, the INS was set to start the second phase at twelve Boston-area universities later that year, with further expansion in 2002, and claimed it could make the 2003 deadline. NAFSA was still pushing to dismantle the effort.

Within a week of the attacks, however, the higher education lobby had done a complete about-face, with NAFSA announcing that it would no longer oppose implementation of the tracking system. Congress had immediately focused on the loopholes in the student visa system, in part because it was Congress that had mandated electronic student tracking in 1996 and was eager to shift the blame to the INS for its failure to implement the scheme. That was the case even though opposition from some members of Congress, who were swayed by university lobbyists, had delayed its implementation. Within weeks, some members were threatening to impose far more draconian measures than a tracking system. Senator Dianne Feinstein of California said she would push for a six-month moratorium on the issuing of all visas to foreign students, calling the student visa program "one of the most unregulated and exploited visa categories."

With the support of the Bush administration, the universities succeeded in beating back the demand for a visa moratorium. In exchange, the schools promised immediately to begin informing the INS if any foreign student failed to show up for classes. The USA Patriot Act, passed in October 2001, reaffirmed the 1996 goal of having the computerized tracking system up and running across the country by January 1, 2003, and offered up $36 million in new funding to make it happen. The penalties for universities that failed to comply were severe—the potential loss of their ability to offer programs to foreign students. The United States' long love affair with foreign students was about to be tested as never before.

AS STUDENTS BEGAN TO RETURN for the 2002 academic year, the first full school year since the attacks, the universities began to see problems cropping up. More than 30 of Purdue's 4,000 foreign students could not get visas to return from abroad, and 48 of Penn State's 3,000 students were stranded. Temple University lost half its foreign graduate students in physics due to visa delays. The effects were concentrated, however. Students from Muslim countries were seeing long delays in the processing of their visa applications, but so was a narrower group of students and scholars from other countries, particularly China and Russia, who were studying science and engineering.

Uvais Qidwai, an assistant professor of electrical engineering at Tulane University in New Orleans, went home to Pakistan in the summer of 2002 to get married. He was in the United States on a valid visa, but when he went to the U.S. embassy in Islamabad to get his passport stamped for return, he was told that the embassy would have to get a security review from Washington. It took five months to get the clearance. He had been researching image processing, in particular seeking ways to improve the images captured by the infrared surveillance cameras used in security systems, research that could be extremely valuable in U.S. homeland security programs. Because of the security check, his research was delayed and he missed a National Science Foundation grant deadline, resulting in a sharp cut in his funding. For Qidwai and other Pakistani students and researchers, delays and hassles entering the United States became a regular part of their lives. Even after the security checks had been completed, he was subject to lengthy questioning, often for three hours or more, whenever he would travel abroad and return to the United States. In May 2005, he left the United States for a job in Qatar.

Qidwai was one of thousands of students and scholars who first felt the effects of the post-9/11 border measures. Tarek Aboul-Fadl, an Egyptian postdoctoral researcher who had also worked in Germany, Austria, and Japan, was invited in January 2001 to join the laboratory of Dr. Arthur Broom at the University of Utah working on a project supported by the National Institutes of Health to search for new anti-HIV drugs. He applied for a visa at the U.S. consulate in Cairo in February 2001 and received it in a week. He moved to Salt Lake City in May 2001 and his wife and children followed in August. "They enjoyed the school so much and their English language improved significantly," he said. "They have many American friends and still remember the nice days they spent there." The research went well and his grant was extended for a second year. But in May 2002 he returned to Egypt with his children, who needed to write exams in the Egyptian schools. On May 9, 2002, he applied to reenter the United States but was told that a security check had to be completed first. His visa was not renewed for another eighteen months. His HIV research was halted entirely, leaving several promising lines of investigation incomplete, and before he could return Dr. Broom closed the laboratory completely. "I was mad as hell and I still am," Broom said later. "It's impossible to know what would have been discovered and wasn't."

A physics project at Rice University was delayed while visas were pending for two researchers, one Chinese and one German. Vladimir Yamshchikov, a professor of molecular bioscience at the University of Kansas, lost two Russian student research assistants for his project on West Nile virus when they took trips to Russia and were unable to return. He advertised for replacements, but all the applications he received were from foreign researchers who were likely to face visa problems. "It's a ridiculous situation," he said. Jane Zhang, a graduate student studying leukemia at the University of Alabama at Birmingham, went home to visit her parents and faced months of waiting before she could return.

Sandia National Laboratory, a facility run by the U.S. Department of Energy, runs government-sponsored programs that invite Russian scientists to learn better ways to secure nuclear weapons materials. Between 2002 and 2004, 89 of the 305 scientists invited to attend the conferences ran into visa problems, which resulted in delays, cancellations, and in some cases, decisions to move the conferences to Europe.

Apart from countries with significant Muslim populations, including Egypt, Pakistan, and Indonesia, two other countries that were in no way associated with the terrorist attacks were hit particularly hard by the new visa restrictions. The visa problems for students from China and Russia were perplexing because neither was home to a terrorist movement aimed at the United States. Yet from Stanford to Harvard, stories started to spill out about Chinese students who had gone home for the summer and could not get visas to return to school. Most were science or engineering students, and many were graduate students. Nan Jiang was one of two graduate students in biochemistry at Louisiana State University who was stuck for months in China in 2003 waiting for visa renewals. Only one of nine top Chinese mathematicians who sought visas to attend an international cryptology conference in California in 2004 received visas in time.

Zhong Min Wang, a Chinese physics student studying at the State University of New York at Stony Brook, was one of some 300 foreign scientists working on the DZero experiment at Fermilab near Chicago, a Department of Energy–supported project that houses the largest accelerator for subatomic particles in the world and does cutting-edge research into the nature of matter. In the summer of 2002, he went home to China and was stuck there for nearly a year waiting for his visa to be renewed. Another Chinese colleague waited nearly two months for her visa to be renewed after a brief visit home. Dmitri Denisov, the Russian-born leader of the DZero experiment, said that for scientists from China and Russia, the visa applications would fall into "a black hole." He would follow up repeatedly with the State Department, which would only say that the applications were being processed but could offer no further information. The process, he said, became "completely unpredictable. Some people could get in quickly while others waited for a year. And you had no explanation why." The worst case involved a Russian scientist who had been working on the project since 1995. When he went back to Russia in 2002 and applied for a new visa to return to the United States, the application was delayed for nearly two years. "I still don't know why," said Denisov. But Denisov had no doubt about the consequences of those types of delays for large-scale scientific research: the likelihood of a similarly large facility being located in the United States in the future is, he said, "close to zero."

THE NEW STUDENT TRACKING SCHEME was part of the problem, but only a very small part. Under pressure from Congress, the INS had rushed to put SEVIS in place as quickly as possible, causing some serious technical problems. It was an enormous undertaking—the INS was required to check the more than 70,000 U.S. schools that enrolled foreign students to determine whether they were eligible to participate in the new scheme; only about 7,000 were finally recertified. The schools had to train administrators to operate a new computer system that would link their databases with other schools around the country, and with U.S. consulates abroad and INS inspectors at every airport in the country. One senior university official called it "a technological moonshot."

Not surprisingly, there were problems initially, even though it was rolled out in the spring of 2003 rather than during the much busier fall semester. Many schools found that data entered on students was lost in the system, or that they could not print the documents that foreign students needed to prove their enrollment and get student visas. In some cases, university administrators would hit the print button only to find that the documents appeared on the printers of another school thousands of miles away. A Belgian psychologist who was enrolled in a postgraduate program at Michigan State had his passport taken by U.S. officials and his visa application delayed for a month when the U.S. consulate in Brussels could not find his data on the SEVIS records. Issues also arose with students already in the country. In one case, the FBI arrested a student from Thailand who was attending Southeastern University in Washington, D.C., because the university mistakenly entered into the SEVIS database that she had dropped out and then could not correct the error.

Despite the problems, given the scale and speed of the rollout, SEVIS worked surprisingly well, and reinforced the technocrats' conviction that improving the security of the border and visa system—even something as broken as the student visa process—could be done without significantly disrupting the flow of foreigners coming into the United States. For an agency as maligned as the INS, it was an impressive accomplishment. After the agency was folded into DHS in March, the new department launched a huge effort to try to iron out the technical flaws in the system. DHS established a special "SEVIS response team" that worked closely with the universities to resolve problem cases. While the universities continued to grumble about SEVIS, they acknowledged that the department had put a herculean effort into making the new system work as well as possible as quickly as possible. Only a handful of foreign students were actually prevented from enrolling in their programs on time by problems with SEVIS. The Government Accountability Office, which monitors the performance of federal government agencies, found that while there were difficulties with the implementation of SEVIS, most schools "do not believe that SEVIS is the reason for the declining number of international students and exchange visitors coming to the United States."

Instead, the bigger problem that foreign students and researchers faced was with the new security screening systems set up by the State Department and the FBI, such as those aimed at students from predominantly Muslim countries. Much as with the background checks on immigration violators who were seized as terrorist suspects after 9/11, the FBI never deployed enough agents to carry out the task and did not have the technological capability to do the checks without a large number of agents. "They had to have a whole bunch of people manually going through each record and seeing where people had been or where they might have had contact, and then reached out to those specific areas to find out if there was any record of them potentially being terrorist-related," said Brian Peterman, who was the point man in the White House on visa policy issues. "It took a long time. It was very manually intensive." With consular officers terrified of making another mistake, the number of such security requests had doubled to nearly a thousand a day, even though the volume of travelers to the United States was falling sharply. Almost overnight, a visa application process that had taken days, or at most weeks, to complete turned into months as consular officers were required to wait for the FBI to finish its background checks.

The FBI wasn't the only problem. In August 2003 the State Department had ordered its consular officers to interview all visa applicants, ending the long-standing practice of waiving interviews for applicants who were considered routine and low risk. In some countries, that would force visa applicants to travel hundreds of miles from home for the interview and then return to a U.S. embassy again to get their visa if it was approved. In 2004, as part of a larger intelligence reform bill, Congress turned that into a statutory requirement, passing legislation that required personal interviews of every visa applicant between the ages of fourteen and seventy-nine, with only a handful of exceptions. In addition to the security delays that plagued some applicants, in many countries there were also long waits—in the worst cases up to three months—just to schedule the visa interview.

FOR STUDENTS AND RESEARCHERS, MUCH of the disruption came from another screening program, whose impact was felt far beyond the Islamic countries that were the primary source of concern over terrorism. In the immediate aftermath of 9/11, preventing Al Qaeda or an affiliated terrorist group from acquiring a nuclear or biological weapon had quickly shot to the top of the administration's list of security concerns. Richard Falkenrath, Ridge's policy chief, had written the definitive study of U.S. vulnerability to such an attack in 1998. Unlike a roadside explosive device or a suicide bomb—Al Qaeda's weapons of choice—developing a biological or nuclear weapon required sophisticated scientific training. And unlike the pilot training that some of the 9/11 hijackers had received, the sort of knowledge needed to build such weapons was not ubiquitous. While Falkenrath had pointed out that this knowledge was far more widely disseminated than ever before, much of it was still available only at the world's best universities and within a small number of companies working in the most advanced technologies in biological engineering and nuclear physics. And most of those universities and companies were in the United States. As a result, the administration believed that such knowledge could, at least to some extent, be controlled.

It was already known publicly that a key scientist in Saddam Hussein's nuclear weapons program had earned a doctorate in nuclear engineering from Michigan State University, and that three scientists involved in neighboring Iran's nuclear program were also U.S.-educated. The issue was even more acute in biological research. Iraq's top bioweapons scientist, Huda Salih Mahdi Ammash, dubbed "Mrs. Anthrax" by the United States, earned a doctorate in microbiology from the University of Missouri in 1983, a time when the United States was backing Saddam in Iraq's war with Iran. Those in the administration knew there were many other examples. "We were in effect populating the world's biological warfare labs," said Bruce Lawlor, Ridge's director of protection and prevention at the White House. "You had people coming to the United States, particularly in the biological sciences, who were coming to study advanced biology for the purpose of making vaccines. But when we examined it, we discovered that many of these individuals had in fact ended up working in biological weapons programs in unfriendly nations." He said that in a few cases there was even evidence to suggest that laboratories had been set up in the United States specifically to train foreign bioweapons researchers.

Ridge's White House Office of Homeland Security quickly seized on the issue. Homeland Security Presidential Directive-2 was the first substantive policy document prepared by Ridge's staff and signed by the president. The topic, "Abuse of International Student Status," was the largest single entry in that directive. The paper said that while the United States "benefits greatly" from international students coming to study in the country, the government would "implement measures to end the abuse of student visas and prohibit certain international students from receiving education and training in sensitive areas, including areas of study with direct application to the development and use of weapons of mass destruction." It further added that the government would "prohibit the education and training of foreign nationals who would use such training to harm the United States or its Allies."

In principle, such an approach represented an example of the kind of targeted risk management that Ridge favored. An attack by terrorist groups using weapons of mass destruction was the worst conceivable threat. In theory it might be possible to lessen the risk by controlling the dissemination of the knowledge needed to produce such weapons. And the number of people likely to be affected by such a screening process was fairly small. From 1995 to 1998, for instance, the number of students coming to the United States from the five Middle East countries that were considered state sponsors of terrorism—Iran, Iraq, Libya, Sudan, and Syria— had fallen from just under 4,000 to fewer than 3,000. While most of those were in engineering, science, or math, somewhere between 15 and 40 percent were in programs of study that raised no security concerns at all.

While the White House flirted for months with the idea of setting up a special group of technical experts to vet certain visa applicants, it was the traditional State Department visa system that became the tool for trying to keep such people out. Even prior to 9/11, the U.S. government had attempted to use visa screening to prevent the transfer of sensitive knowledge to what were known euphemistically as "countries of concern." In 1999 and then again in early 2001, the State Department sent a cable to each of its embassies and consulates spelling out new, more rigorous procedures for the visa applications of any students or scholars who were coming to the United States to study or work in any scientific field with potential military applications.

Many different types of science and engineering were caught up by those controls. Over the previous two decades, U.S. military strength had come to rely less on old-fashioned conventional weapons such as guns, tanks, fighters, and bombers and more on advanced information systems, guidance technologies, and sophisticated alloy materials. Where it was once possible to draw a fairly bright line between military and civilian technologies, by the turn of the twenty-first century the U.S. military edge was based primarily on technologies that also had widespread commercial applications. So the list of sensitive specialties included not only obvious concerns such as nuclear or missile technology but also a compendium of the country's leading technology sectors, including aerospace, biotechnology, remote imaging, advanced computing, robotics, ceramics, sensors, and high-performance metals and alloys.

In some cases the procedures were clear. For students from the "axis of evil" countries—Iran, Iraq, and North Korea—the State Department would automatically send any visa application back to Washington for what was known as a security advisory opinion. The SAO involved a more in-depth check by the State Department and the FBI to determine if granting the visa would raise security concerns. If the applicant was planning to study or do research in any of the listed technologies, a rejection was almost automatic. The harder cases involved countries like China, Russia, and Vietnam, which were friendly to the United States but still seen as potential military rivals. Consular officers were required to seek SAOs for any visa applicant who was working with any of the listed technologies, but in most cases the applications were approved. Under the normal procedure, the consular officer had to send the visa application to Washington, but if no concerns were raised within ten days the visa could be granted.

Despite the fears over weapons proliferation that predated the 9/11 attacks, the visa security review program, known as Visas Mantis, had long been a midget. In 2000, there were only about a thousand visa applicants reviewed under the Mantis program; in 2001, on a slightly higher volume of referrals, there were only three outright rejections. Yet after 9/11, the growing fears—constantly reinforced by Vice President Cheney, National Security Advisor Rice, and others at the top of the administration—that terrorists were seeking the knowledge to build weapons of mass destruction took that midget of a program and made it into a monster.

In 2002, the number of Mantis cases jumped to over 14,000, and then to more than 20,000 in 2003. Some of the increase came from the administration's decision to expand the list of scientific fields deemed sensitive in light of the post-9/11 homeland security concerns, adding such disciplines as community development, geography, and urban planning to the alert list. But most of it was the result of newly cautious consular officials not wanting to be blamed for letting in a foreign spy or terrorist seeking WMDs. That fear became especially acute as the United States moved toward war with Iraq, which was believed to possess biological and chemical weapons. Under the old rules of a ten-day turnaround, the growth in applications alone would not have shut down the visa pipeline. But by the summer of 2002, when the decision was made that the FBI had to approve all the Visas Condor applications in order to prevent any security mistakes, the Mantis applications were caught as well. That resulted in a growing backlog of students and scientists from countries such as China, Russia, and India who could not get into the United States until the FBI had finished its background checks.

By early 2003, the State Department acknowledged that the system had broken down almost entirely. The Government Accountability Office reviewed some 5,000 Visas Mantis referrals that were made between April and June of 2003. Of those, nearly 3,000 were science students and scholars, 60 percent of them from China and 20 percent from Russia. On average, the GAO found, it took more than two months just to do the security background checks. Applications from some places, particularly China and India, were sometimes taking more than four months. A handful of the cases sampled had been pending for nearly six months, and one for almost a year.

THE VISA DIFFICULTIES QUICKLY BEGAN to be felt in places besides the universities. Boeing, the aerospace company that is the United States' single largest exporter, was set to deliver a plane to China Southern Airlines in August 2002. China Southern, the biggest domestic airline in China, had been a Boeing customer since the mid-1980s and had long been sending its pilots to Boeing headquarters in Seattle to train on simulators and then fly the planes back to China. In June 2002, China Southern had applied for visas for eight of its captains and four first officers to receive pilot training on the new aircraft at Boeing's training facility in Seattle. By mid-August, when the plane was scheduled for delivery, the visas still had not been approved, and the U.S. consulate in Guangzhou was advising Boeing that it had no idea when they might be issued. China Southern was refusing to take delivery of the aircraft, because without training for its pilots it would be unable to fly the new plane. Boeing was forced to scramble, using one of its own pilots to fly the plane across the Pacific and then setting up special training for the China Southern pilots at a facility in China. It was the first of many difficulties that Boeing would face in getting visas for pilots, and it came at a critical time when the company was looking at its most serious competitive challenge from Airbus, the European consortium, which had got a much later start in China but was determined to catch up. David Wang, who was recruited from General Electric in 2002 to head up Boeing's China operation, said later that the problems faced by Chinese customers in getting to the United States "seriously affected our competitiveness." In 2004, for the first time, Airbus sold more planes in China than Boeing.

The story was similar in Saudi Arabia. By 2003, the number of

U.S. visas granted each year to Saudi citizens had fallen from more than 45,000 before the attacks to fewer than 10,000. In meetings with State Department officials in January 2003, the Saudis charged that the United States was "not living up to its end of the bargain" because it continued to subject Saudi flight crews and passengers to exhaustive screening when they arrived in the United States, even though Saudi Arabia was by then providing the advanced passenger information the Americans sought. Visa difficulties had similarly forced Saudi airlines to end flight training in the United States. According to a cable from the U.S. consulate in Jeddah, "the [Saudi] officials described in considerable detail their impressions that onerous entry and exit procedures in the U.S. have hurt commercial aviation ties and unfairly burden Saudi flight crews. They made clear that, without prompt resolution of this problem, U.S. aviation business with the kingdom would suffer." Over the next several years, Boeing lost significant market share to Airbus across the Middle East—a region it had previously dominated—and in 2007 Saudi Arabian Airlines placed a $1.7 billion order with Airbus, its first since 1981 with the European aircraft maker.

Boeing was not alone in its visa problems. Lucent, the telecommunications equipment maker that was later bought by Alcatel of France, faced similar troubles. More than twenty officials from Chinese companies that were buyers or potential buyers of Lucent's products had their visa applications rejected, damaging Lucent's relationship with buyers in the fastest-growing telecom market in the world. The State Department was also rejecting nearly 15 percent of the visa applications from Lucent workers who wanted to transfer to the United States from the company's overseas operations. Motorola, the largest U.S. maker of cellular telephones, experienced the same kind of problems in Vietnam. The State Department took more than six months to issue a visa to the head of a Vietnamese government delegation that wanted to come to the United States to examine two-way radios that Motorola was set to sell in a $10 million contract. As a result, the Vietnamese government reopened the competition to two of

Motorola's foreign rivals, Nokia of Finland and the British company Marconi.

It was not just large multinationals that were affected by the delays. In April 2002, Moore Nanotechnology, a New Hampshire company that is part of the 225-employee Moore Tool group, had inked a deal to sell a $500,000 precision lathe for making optical components to China's Harbin Institute of Technology. In August, one of the institute's engineers had sought a visa to come to the United States to inspect the lathe. Some delay was not surprising: the Harbin Institute, which has some 60,000 students, has ties to the China Aerospace Corporation, which is China's principal maker of rockets and missiles. Even before 9/11, any visa application would have faced scrutiny under U.S. laws designed to prevent the transfer of technology that could contribute to weapons proliferation. But after six months with no answer from the State Department, Harbin nixed the deal and bought the equipment from a British company instead, costing Moore about one-tenth of its 2002 revenues. In another case, Moore could not get a visa for an Indian engineer for training on equipment his company had already purchased, forcing Moore to bear the cost of sending its technicians to India to do the training.

While the delays and denials were costly for the companies, what was more troubling was that they could not get any clear explanation for the problems. Corporations, particularly big corporations with global reach, are adept at dealing with new government regulations, even onerous ones; what they cannot adapt well to is regulatory uncertainty, because uncertainty makes it impossible to plan. Now they were facing lengthy delays for critical personnel, and for buyers on lucrative contracts, but with no explanation as to why or when things might return to normal. Many in business complained that the decision process on visa applications seemed almost random.

In mid-August 2002 the president of the U.S.-China Business Council, which represents hundreds of American companies doing business in China, wrote to Colin Powell seeking some answers.

"We have attempted to determine the facts and the rationales surrounding this apparent change in U.S. visa procedure. Regrettably, we have not been able to gain a dependable understanding of what is transpiring," he wrote. While the delays seemed to arise from national security concerns, he surmised, "the reasons for China's inclusion are not self-evident."

Two weeks later, a broader coalition of business groups representing U.S. manufacturers, high-tech companies, and other multinational businesses weighed in with Powell as well. "American companies are already experiencing the negative fallout of these new procedures. Long-standing business relationships are being disrupted because visas cannot be obtained. Opportunities for new business relationships are being blocked. Personnel transfers within some U.S. corporations are being delayed."

The impacts were felt well beyond those few companies that had the courage to complain. Many simply adjusted their operations to work around the visa delays. Indian information technology companies, for instance, had relied on the easy flow of software engineers and others between the United States and India to handle contracts to provide back-office services for big U.S. companies. But as the wait times for visas grew to six months or more for many employees, big outsourcing companies like Infosys and Tata began to move more and more of the work to India rather than wait on visas for their U.S. operations. Before 9/11 one smaller Indian firm that provided information technology support for clinical drug trials had relied on more than one hundred Indian employees working in the United States on temporary visas. By the end of 2003, it had relocated virtually all of its employees to India to avoid the visa problems.

Amway, one of the largest direct-sale firms in the world, was planning to hold its 2004 convention for some 8,000 South Korean distributors in either Los Angeles or Hawaii, but changed its mind and opted for Japan due to the growing delays for visas created by the mandatory interview requirement and other restrictions. The International Consumer Electronics show in Las Vegas, which attracts nearly 20,000 foreign visitors each year, lost 20 percent of those in 2004 due to visa delays or denials. At the China Textile and Apparel trade show in New York, nearly half of the Chinese executives who wanted to attend could not get visas.

Many U.S. hospitals had long done a lucrative business in curing the ills of rich foreigners, a $2 billion-a-year industry involving some 70,000 patients. The most famous of those, the Mayo Clinic, lost hundreds of patients after 9/11 as foreigners in need of medical care, especially those from the Middle East, opted for Britain instead. "Previously patients were able to get visas for medical treatment in a matter of days. Now it's weeks and sometimes months, and some of the patients are quite ill," said a hospital official. By 2003 the clinic's numbers for patients from the Middle East were down by more than half, and other U.S. hospitals had seen similar declines.

Even traveling performers were affected by the visa problems. In 2006, Britain's leading symphony orchestra, Manchester-based Hallé, was forced to cancel a planned U.S. tour because the cost of sending more than one hundred musicians and staff to London for personal interviews at the U.S. embassy was prohibitive and the embassy refused to make special arrangements. "It seems a crying shame that the chance for this wonderful British orchestra to appear on the U.S. East Coast should be in part blighted by a too fanatical approach at the embassy," said Mark Elder, the symphony's music director. Smaller arts organizations are even less capable of dealing with the hassle and expense of obtaining visas for international performers. Isabel Soffer, associate director of New York's World Music Institute, which brings in performers from across the world, said that fewer managers and promoters are willing to take chances on overseas artists because of the high costs of the visa process and the risks of cancellation.

BY THE MIDDLE OF 2003, universities and American companies were starting to see numbers that demonstrated the severe impacts of the post-9/11 restrictions. From October 1, 2002, to

August 1, 2003, the State Department received just over 270,000 student visa applications and approved 175,000. That was 65,000 fewer visas than the United States had approved the previous year. By 2004, applications from Chinese students to American graduate schools had fallen 45 percent from pre-9/11 levels, and those from the Middle East had dropped by half.

What was equally striking was that foreign student enrollment in universities in other countries—particularly in Britain, France, Germany, and Australia—began to rise sharply at the same time. For American universities, the timing of the new security measures could hardly have been worse. Even prior to 9/11, other countries had begun to wake up to the competitive advantages that the United States was gaining from its unmatched ability to attract foreign students. The UK had launched a new initiative in 1999 aimed at attracting 75,000 additional international students to the country; Australia's universities had set up a cooperative organization to attract foreign students, and had seen the numbers nearly double in a decade. France, Germany, and even Japan—which was suffering from a drop in college-age students owing to its low birth rate—had begun similar recruiting efforts. In 2000, Canada issued four times as many visas to Chinese students as it had in 1998, and more than three times as many to South Korean students.

Before 9/11, however, the United States had been able to keep pace with that competition. In the 2000–2001 academic year, foreign student enrollment grew at its fastest rate since 1979, mostly due to growing demand from China and India. After 9/11, the number of foreign students enrolled in American higher education dropped for three years in a row, before recovering considerably in 2006–2007 to just below the pre-9/11 levels. The decline was even steeper among graduate schools, which attract most of the top foreign students. For the 2004 academic year, graduate applications from China and India, the two biggest sources of overseas students, fell by 45 percent and 30 percent, respectively. Based on past trends, the United States lost something like 150,000 foreign students—a quarter of the total number in the country—as a result of the decline in enrollment after 9/11.

The United States' loss has been the rest of the world's gain. In the five years after 9/11, the number of international students at British universities more than doubled. "International education is big business for all of the Anglophone countries; the United States traditionally has dominated the market without having to try very hard," a British university official told the *New York Times*. "Now Australia, the UK, Ireland, New Zealand, and Canada are competing for that dollar, and our lives have been made easier because of the difficulties that students are having getting into the U.S."

Thomas Gouttierre, the dean of international studies at the University of Nebraska, spent the fall of 2004 fighting with the State Department to get visas for forty-one graduate students who had been admitted but could not get visas in time. He said the United States was rapidly losing such students to other countries. "The word is out: it's easier and less demeaning to apply in Canada or the UK."

The declining numbers provoked a near-panic in the universities and in the scientific community over what they called a "visa-processing quagmire." Albert Teich, director of science and public policy at the American Association for the Advancement of Science warned that the visa delays "will do irreparable harm to scientific progress as well as U.S. competitiveness."

For the companies, the impacts were harder to measure. While some big companies and their Washington lobbying arms were quietly raising concerns with the State and Justice departments, and later with the Department of Homeland Security, there was a reluctance to be seen publicly questioning screening measures that were intended to prevent another terrorist attack. Bill Reinsch, the president of the National Foreign Trade Council, a lobbying group for big American multinational companies, said that in 2002 and 2003 there was no issue on which he got more complaints than the difficulties U.S. companies were facing with the visa process.

But only a handful were willing to go public with criticisms. "They can't challenge the policy head-on," he said, "because they're worried they will be accused publicly of being soft on terrorism."

Instead, he said, the companies quietly began to work around the problems. Boeing moved much of its pilot training outside the United States; Lockheed Martin, the aerospace and defense giant, began holding its board meetings in Paris; engineering companies like Fluor and Bechtel began moving more work offshore to London or other places in Europe that were easier for their foreign experts to reach and did not demand running the gauntlet of U.S. screening and other security measures "A lot of the clients we have were educated in the West, speak English fluently, and just have a real resentment that they get that sort of treatment," said David Marventano, a senior vice president for government affairs in Fluor's Washington office.

In an effort to highlight the issue, Reinsch's NFTC commissioned a survey in early 2004 based on confidential interviews with U.S. companies. It found that 60 percent of companies had run into visa problems, resulting in estimated costs over two years of more than $30 billion in lost sales, postponement of projects, forced relocation of contracts outside the United States, inability to bring employees to the United States, and damage to corporate reputations.

Despite such costs, administration officials—and particularly those in the State Department who had seen the dangers of appearing too soft in the war on terrorism—were unapologetic. "In the post–9/11 environment," Janice Jacobs, the deputy assistant secretary for visa services, told a House hearing in 2003, "we do not believe that the issues at stake allow us the luxury of erring on the side of expeditious processing."

# Chapter 7

# THE TRIAGE

COLONEL LARRY WILKERSON WAS ONE of Colin Powell's closest and longest-serving aides. An army pilot who had taught at the Naval and Marine Corps War Colleges, he joined Powell in 1989 as his top assistant shortly before Powell was named chairman of the Joint Chiefs of Staff. At the end of the first Bush administration, he had accompanied Powell back into civilian life and then returned to government as his chief of staff when President George W. Bush named Powell secretary of state. According to Wilkerson, Colin Powell was something extremely rare in the upper ranks of government. He was a kind man who treated his subordinates with the same respect that he treated his fellow cabinet secretaries and foreign dignitaries. That quality was one of the reasons he was so beloved by much of his staff after he came to the State Department.

But in late 2002, he began to pick on Maura Harty, the assistant secretary for consular affairs he had chosen for the job after he fired Mary Ryan. Powell liked and respected Harty, describing her admiringly as "a street-smart kid from Staten Island, a city kid like me, and she's tough as nails." Yet at the meetings that were held each morning, at which the top fifty or so officials of the department would gather, Powell began to berate her over the growing number of problems with the issuing of visas. At each meeting, said Wilkerson, Powell would start on his left—where Al Larson, his poker-faced undersecretary in charge of economic and business affairs, sat—and move around the room with questions about the most pressing issues in each domain. The exchanges were normally subdued and respectful, but when he got to Harty and consular affairs, "everyone would think, 'Batten down the hatches.'" Only Pierre Prosper, the department's ambassador for war crimes, who was dealing with the explosive issues of Guantánamo Bay and the treatment of prisoners in the war on terrorism, faced anything like the same scrutiny, Wilkerson recalls. Powell would pepper Harty with difficult questions about the lack of progress in overhauling the visa process, and she "consistently would come back with things that were not satisfying to the secretary. He thought she was not moving fast enough, that she was not grasping the depth of the problem and the urgency of the problem."

Their exchanges began to degenerate further. "He got really snappy and argumentative and even demeaning of her," said Wilkerson, who sat right behind Powell during the meetings. "It got so bad that I felt really sorry for her—she was being asked to do so much so fast." On several occasions, he said, he would lean forward and say, "God, boss, give her a break." The pressure took a toll on Harty. Wilkerson, who kept his door open at most times and was seen in the department as the surest route to getting a message to Powell, said, "People were coming to me who loved her and were saying she was almost blind from stress and the tension that had built up." A couple of times Deputy Secretary of State Richard Armitage met privately with Powell and urged him to take it easier on Harty, after which the meetings would be calmer for a week or two. But then something would trigger Powell's anger and it would start all over again.

To many officials at State who had seen tyrannical bosses in their government careers, Powell's treatment of Harty probably did not seem out of the ordinary. But Wilkerson knew it was. "It was so unlike Powell," he said. "It was not the way he operated. In sixteen years of working with Powell, I had never seen him upbraid a subordinate in front of his or her peers. Never."

FOR A SECRETARY OF STATE who was grappling with the prospect of an impending war in Iraq that was opposed by virtually all of the United States' traditional allies, it was amazing that something as mundane as visa processing would be the issue that made his blood boil. But as the post-9/11 efforts to tighten the U.S. borders began to take hold, Powell found himself pressed from all sides. "This was totally a stressful area," said Wilkerson. "It was rather extraordinary how much emphasis he brought to bear on this."

Powell needed to demonstrate that he had plugged the holes so no future terrorists would ever get visas to come to the United States. "We were under a lot of pressure to fix the visa system and make sure there were no shortcomings," Powell said. "Nobody wanted to have to be the next one to go before Congress after a terrorist attack and be ripped apart for letting someone into the country who shouldn't have been let into the country. So a zero-defects mentality crept into the system."

The task of creating a zero-defects visa system without unduly disrupting visitors from abroad fell on Maura Harty. Throughout the 1990s, the State Department had been asked by Congress and the White House to issue more visas with fewer staff, and now suddenly the demands had shifted entirely. "It was such a hellacious change and such a difficult and complex thing to do after you'd been doing the opposite for so long," said Wilkerson. "You didn't have the institutional fabric, you didn't have the philosophy, you didn't have the young people, you didn't have anybody who was operating off this sheet of music, and you didn't have the machinery or technology to support it."

Wilkerson understood the problems better than most. Immediately after Powell was confirmed as secretary, he had been tasked with evaluating the quality of the State Department's workforce and had concluded that much of the bureaucracy was underperforming. On top of that, a long failure to replenish by hiring new Foreign Service officers had left State anywhere from 1,000 to 1,500 employees short. After 9/11, the staffing problems were further exacerbated because many foreign nationals who had been doing routine visa processing work in the American embassies abroad were barred from doing so on security grounds.

Harty's consular affairs office tried to do its best with such limited resources, but there were enormous technical and institutional obstacles that repeatedly frustrated her, and in turn Powell. The government had a dozen different databases that contained the names of terrorist suspects, and none of them could talk to each other, increasing the risk that terrorists could inadvertently be issued a visa. While things improved after 9/11, the CIA and the FBI remained reluctant to share much of their intelligence information with the State Department. Before 9/11, there had been "zero, my words, zero, cooperation with the FBI and the CIA to give other names, to share that information," said Grant Green, Powell's undersecretary for management with responsibility for consular affairs. "They all thought that they would divulge sources and methods and all sorts of secrets." Even after the tragedy, he said, "when you wrap yourselves in the security blanket, as the agency is able to do and as the FBI is able to do in some areas, you can really delay cooperation." Further, after 9/11 the State Department relied heavily on the FBI to vet visa applicants, but the FBI's inability to master modern computer systems meant that the security checks were often paper-based, slow, and inefficient.

Apart from the identifiable problems, it was simply an enormous task to reshape the massive consular affairs bureaucracy to carry out its new mission. "People just don't understand the complexity of turning around all this machinery and pointing it in a different direction," said Wilkerson. Even before 9/11, visa processing was "an impossible job, and now you're going to ask us to implement all these finely tuned, finely honed standards that are going to tell us whether this guy is going to fly an airplane into the towers. Give me a break.

"Maura took that challenge on, but I think in some respects the secretary was not grasping the complexity of the change that had been ordered. He knew it had to be done and he wanted it to go as fast as humanly possible. And sometimes he felt that Maura, even though she was working twenty-hour days and driving herself to physical destruction, was not operating fast enough."

Powell was not prepared to be patient. In addition to his fears over State being blamed for another mistake, he was deluged with complaints over the delays, rejections, and humiliations that some foreign travelers were facing as a consequence of the tightened visa system or the new scrutiny from border and airport security officials. "I was deeply involved in it, because a lot of foreign ministers and college presidents and heads of government and state were calling me about some of the things that their citizens were being exposed to," Powell said.

In late September 2002, the first lady of Taiwan, Wu Shu-chen, had returned to Dulles Airport in Washington, D.C., at the end of an eleven-day trip to the United States. The day before, she had given a speech in the Congress expressing Taiwan's continued "sorrow for the 9/11 attacks" and pledging that Taiwan "will stand with America forever." Wu had been confined to a wheelchair since 1985, when she was run over by a tractor in a mysterious incident that some believed was an assassination attempt on her husband, Chen Shui-bian, who later became Taiwan's president. The wheelchair prevented her from going through the airport metal detectors that all airline passengers must ordinarily go through. But Wu was obviously no ordinary passenger, accompanied as she was by a retinue of diplomats, including U.S. State Department officials, and carrying a waiver from the State Department. "As you know, we handle Taiwan delicately," Powell said. But transportation security officials, who had no obligation to answer to the State Department, ordered her aside into a special room, away from her entourage, to do a more thorough inspection. According to Powell, who received an angry report from the Taiwanese government the next day, the officials stood in front of her and said: "Please stand up so we can look at the chair." She replied: "If I could stand up I wouldn't need this chair. This is the result of an assassination attempt."

It was a diplomatic debacle. "It took me about three days to get them off the ceiling, and I had to talk directly to the president of Taiwan about it," said Powell. "They wanted all kinds of things I didn't give them." A month later the story was leaked to the Taiwanese press and became a serious embarrassment for the Taiwan government. The opposition demanded the resignation of the country's foreign minister and its representative to the United States, accusing them of "failing to defend the dignity of both Taiwan and the first lady."

The search of Madam Wu was not the only fire Powell had to put out as a result of post-9/11 zeal. "It was like that almost once a week," he said. "I would send letters to Tom Ridge, and I would raise it in meetings with the president, saying we can't afford this kind of mindless approach." In another case, a young woman who was part of the royal family of Thailand had been given a student visa to come and attend college in the United States. The visa rules say that anyone traveling on a student visa cannot come to the country more than thirty days before his or her course of study starts, on the theory that otherwise some visitors might abuse their student status by working in the United States. In this case, however, she arrived thirty-five days in advance. "Okay, that's not good, it's a violation of the visa," Powell acknowledged. "So what do they do? They lock her up, put her in handcuffs, put manacles on her legs, and put her into a seclusion cell. She's hysterical, her mother is with her, and the mother's hysterical. People are calling the embassy. And when they finally release her, they tear up her visa and tell her to get on a plane and go back to Thailand and start all over again." Unlike the search of the Taiwanese first lady, the incident did not leak to the press, but it did cause another big diplomatic row for Powell to resolve. Such incidents, said Wilkerson, "affected the secretary and his ability to do his job in terms of protecting America's reputation."

Foreign ministers who would take the air shuttles between New

York, where the United Nations is headquartered, and Washington would be subject to what they considered humiliating searches. Cresencio "Cris" Arcos, a former State Department ambassador who handled international relations for Ridge after he became secretary of Homeland Security, said that within a week of starting the job he got a call from the Bangladeshi ambassador complaining about the NSEERS program for registering visitors from Muslim countries. "'We're friends,' they said. 'We're allies. Why are you treating our students this way?'" The program also angered countries that were not specifically targeted, such as Britain, Australia, and Canada, because initially the Justice Department required registration based on place of birth rather than citizenship, so citizens of those and other close U.S. allies also got caught up in the scheme.

Powell, who often spoke publicly of the diplomatic benefits of open borders, pressured his administration colleagues to respond. He set up special State Department units at several of the country's airports, including Dulles Airport in Washington, D.C., and at the Orlando and Los Angeles airports, to try to help foreign dignitaries run the gauntlet of airport security officials—to try, as he put it, to "exercise some sensible control over this." But even then, State had no authority over the DHS personnel who controlled airport security. DHS officials argued that they were not always the ones responsible for such problems. The two departments set up a special mechanism so that State could alert transportation security and border inspectors when foreign dignitaries were arriving, but State sometimes failed to make those notifications in a timely fashion. As a result, Harty and senior DHS officials like Randy Beardsworth, the operations chief for border and transportation security, often got dragged in to sort out individual cases.

Powell quietly urged the college presidents who were complaining to him to write letters that he could share with others in the Bush cabinet to try to build pressure to deal with the visa problems facing many students and researchers. "I got letters from Harvard, I got letters from Yale, I sent them to the president, I sent them to Andy Card, I sent them to Tom Ridge, to Mineta [the secretary of Transportation], saying somehow we have got to do a better job here because we are hurting ourselves. This is what the terrorists want us to do, to act afraid, not let people in. We are hurting ourselves by having systems that are beyond what is needed or are operated in ways that are mindless." In one case, the State Department even got a letter from the president's father, former president George H. W. Bush, complaining about the visa delays on behalf of Texas A&M University, which housed his presidential library.

BY THE TIME THE DEPARTMENT of Homeland Security was up and running in March 2003, there was no question that the "cops" were largely in control. The new and expanded visa screening requirements had given the FBI an effective veto over many visa applications, and the bureau was unable to do its security background checks in any timely fashion, resulting in long delays for many other applicants. The NSEERS program was tracking the movements of most Muslim male travelers to the United States, and had led to more than 12,000 people being arrested for overstaying a visa or some other immigration violation. The Justice Department and the FBI had continued to use immigration laws aggressively as a tool for detaining suspects in the war on terrorism.

But when Ridge took charge of the new department, he was not happy with the impact of those measures, even though as White House coordinator on homeland security he had acquiesced in their creation. "The world was kind of surprised that we pulled in the welcoming mat so quickly," he said later. Cris Arcos, his top official dealing with relations with other governments, was given the green light to publish an academic article discussing "reasonable and proportional security measures" in a post-9/11 world, another phrase for the risk management approach that Ridge favored.

The decision on whether a particular security measure was warranted, Arcos wrote, rested on "the point at which security measures become more burdensome and the added security too

marginal weighted against the costs to administer the measures."
SEVIS, the program for keeping track of foreign students, clearly
passed that test, he wrote; it had not been particularly disruptive,
and the information collected was valuable in ensuring that the
U.S. government had a better grasp on who was studying in the
United States and what each student was learning. But his evaluation of NSEERS was almost wholly negative. The decision to target specific nationality groups "unsurprisingly led to criticisms of it
being racially and religiously biased," he wrote. Further, the implementation had been "chaotic, inefficient and confusing." Even with
improvements in administration, the program had angered many
U.S. allies in the Muslim world who felt their citizens were being
singled out for delays and humiliation. "There is little doubt that
the implementation of NSEERS has contributed to the decline in
foreign students and has created negative impressions among the
very people the United States needs to convert to ideals of Western
democracy, rule of law and social equality," Arcos wrote. It was a
powerful indictment, and particularly so coming from someone
with a senior position close to Ridge.

With the launch of the Department of Homeland Security,
Congress seemed to have created a single agency where more considered decisions on the deployment of security measures could
be made. Under the risk management theories being pushed by
James Loy, Ridge's deputy, and others, a major task of the new
department would be to weigh the costs and benefits of different
options for stopping or mitigating future terrorist attacks and to
make the tough decisions about how to deploy limited resources.
Ridge's new role as DHS secretary at least nominally gave him the
authority to roll back the post-9/11 measures he disliked and build
a new system that fit more closely with his vision of the border of
the future.

But the department that Ridge found himself leading was not
well built for the task, and was torn by long-standing agency rivalries that had only been papered over when the White House
had reluctantly endorsed the creation of DHS. A *Washington Post*

investigation in the aftermath of Hurricane Katrina in 2005 concluded that the short history of the department was one of "haphazard design, bureaucratic warfare and unfulfilled promises."

Internally, the merger of the Customs Service and the INS had created something very close to the "Customs on steroids" plan that Rob Bonner had been pushing back in 2001. The new Customs and Border Protection agency (CBP), which combined the Border Patrol with the inspection arms of the INS and Customs, was the second-largest law enforcement agency in the country after the FBI, and would soon overtake the bureau to become the largest. The only reason it wasn't the biggest in 2003 was that the administration had insisted on splitting off the investigations and interior enforcement agents from Customs and the INS into a separate entity known as Immigration and Customs Enforcement (ICE), largely to prevent CBP from becoming too powerful. But due to miscalculations by the White House in setting budgets for the agencies, CBP was given too much money in its first two years and ICE too little, further empowering the former and weakening the latter. ICE pleaded to have funds reallocated, and was forced to freeze hiring, cut back investigations, and even release some aliens convicted of crimes because of the lack of detention space. But CBP, despite running a huge budget surplus, refused to allow funds to be shifted, and the dispute took almost eighteen months to resolve.

Worse, Bonner, who became the new head of CBP, made it clear he did not recognize the authority of the department that had swallowed his agency. As several of his former aides put it, Bonner saw himself as having been confirmed by Congress to run the oldest law enforcement agency of the U.S. government—the Customs Service—with a mandate that came directly from the president, not from Tom Ridge. He was particularly loath to take any directions from Asa Hutchinson, a former congressman from Arkansas and, like Bonner, a former head of the Drug Enforcement Administration, who was appointed by Ridge as his undersecretary of border and transportation policy. In the organizational charts, Hutchinson had direct authority over Bonner, but Bonner disdained Hutchinson and considered him an intellectual lightweight. Hutchinson, who like Ridge was a politican who believed in negotiation and compromise, found himself unable to control the authoritarian Bonner. In addition, Bonner had operational control over thousands of agents and inspectors and refused to take direction on any matter that he considered part of "operations" rather than "policy." Many of the early days of DHS would be spent by staff refereeing battles between Bonner and Hutchinson—or trying to keep them apart entirely.

Bonner asserted his authority at every opportunity. The CBP headquarters, for instance, was physically separate from the rest of DHS, located in the modern International Trade Center building around the corner from the White House rather than at DHS headquarters several miles away in a rundown former navy compound in the northwest of the city. CBP had its own internal security clearance system and did not recognize the system set up by DHS. A DHS official who had a badge with three stars—the department's highest level of security clearance—could not use the badge to get into CBP headquarters downtown. "They created an insular culture, which made them strong. But that culture permeated their senior levels," said a former DHS official who clashed frequently with some senior CBP people. He and others in DHS took to calling CBP "The Borg," a reference to the imperialist fictional race in the Star Trek movies who are all connected into a single mind. Bonner, he said, "was one of the best leaders I have ever seen, and one of the worst team players."

Ridge had not helped himself by creating a department that never made it clear who had authority over policy. Unlike most government departments, there was no policy planning office responsible for thinking through the department's strategic direction and pushing ahead with the secretary's key initiatives. Instead, several de facto policy arms sprouted up. Stewart Verdery, Hutchinson's deputy, largely played that role on border issues, but while he won considerable respect, even from Bonner, he was "trying to exercise leadership working for a guy whose authority we considered illegitimate," said a former Bonner aide. Richard Clarke, the former White House counterterrorism chief who in 2003 was still in the administration as head of cybersecurity, had tried to warn Ridge about the design flaws and predicted that the lack of a policy office would leave the secretary powerless to control all the independent fiefdoms. "Creating a significant policy shop is like Bureaucracy 101," Clarke's deputy, Roger Cressey, later told the *Washington Post*.

It was an unfortunate conflict, because Ridge and Bonner in many ways shared a common approach to the border: they both believed fervently in the idea of a "smart border," in the need to improve security without disrupting the free flow of goods and people across boundaries. But instead of working together toward that end, they were pulled apart by the structure of the department and by personality conflicts.

EXTERNALLY, THE PROBLEMS WERE EVEN more severe. While DHS had been the joint creation of Congress and the White House, neither was willing to cede much control to their new offspring. The department ended up reporting to more than eighty different congressional committees and subcommittees, which together included every single member of the Senate and virtually every member of the House. The Pentagon, with a budget ten times the size, had fewer than half that number of committees to placate. The result was that a huge portion of the senior officials' time was spent testifying to Congress, preparing reports, and trying to respond to countless demands from the Hill. In the first six months of 2004, for example, DHS officials testified to Congress a mind-boggling 126 times.

Most of Ridge's staff had gone with him to the new department, but the White House Office of Homeland Security was left intact with the role of continuing to coordinate the government's homeland security efforts across different agencies. Richard Falkenrath, the brash academic who had been Ridge's policy director, was instrumental in the design of the new department. He remained behind temporarily as the acting homeland security adviser and assumed considerable powers to shape the priorities of DHS.

Those who went with Ridge to DHS thought they were going to lead a new agency that would be responsible for planning, coordinating, and to a considerable extent implementing the administration's entire homeland security effort. But the decision to leave a White House homeland security staff intact made such a role impossible. In the debates over which would be responsible for setting and coordinating policy—the White House or the new department—the White House invariably won out. Susan Neely, who was Ridge's communications chief at both the White House and at DHS, said that in many ways he had been more powerful before the department was established. "You had a platform at the White House. Whenever you called a meeting at the White House, the other agencies came. Now we're over at the department and the agencies didn't come; they came up with all sorts of excuses."

To those in the White House, who saw themselves trying to do for homeland security strategy what the National Security Council did for national security strategy, the need for a big White House role was obvious. They wanted to develop and leave behind a clear doctrine for homeland security, and were not willing to relinquish this role to DHS. "One of their early conclusions was that even though DHS was supposed to play a big coordinating role, and did so to some extent at the operational level, at the strategic level it could not do that," said a former White House aide. "It's hard for a department to try to coordinate interagency policy; that just doesn't work."

There were early successes in cooperation between the White House and DHS, in particular Operation Liberty Shield, a crash effort to identify and safeguard some of the most likely domestic targets for terrorism in advance of the U.S. invasion of Iraq at the end of March 2003. The initiative was the largest effort to that point by Washington to enlist local and state officials and the private sector in shoring up defenses against a terrorist attack.

But to those at DHS, much of the White House's strategic planning looked like simple interference, often with a political motivation. By 2003, the Bush White House was already in the planning stages for the president's reelection campaign, and the president's role as a leader in the war on terrorism was going to be the centerpiece of that campaign. That placed constant pressure on DHS to dramatize its efforts to fight terrorism. In May 2003, for instance, the department carried out a successful nationwide simulation of a terrorist attack with mass destruction weapons, known as Topoff. Shortly after the exercise, which got dramatic and mostly positive press coverage, the White House began pushing DHS to do such simulations regularly, as often as once every month, a demand that, department officials retorted, was utterly impossible. "You'd have to go through a process to try and make them understand that the logistics and the coordination and the amount of work to try to do one every three or four years was enormous," said a former senior DHS official. "But they just did not understand how operations work. They wanted to be operations guys."

Even where the motives were substantive rather than political, DHS staff felt they were forced to answer a constant stream of queries, demands, and directives from the White House. Verdery recalls one memo from Falkenrath concerning the controversial CAPPS-II system to improve airport security by gathering more information on passengers; the memo posed fifty-five questions that needed to be resolved before the system could be launched. The program, which had envisioned using commercially available databases to glean evidence of suspicious behavior by passengers on domestic as well as international flights, aroused the fears of privacy advocates and was eventually killed in 2004 and replaced by an alternative program focused more on checking passengers against watch lists of suspected terrorists. The *Washington Post* reported on another memo in which the White House wanted regular updates on such obscure issues as uniforms for border guards, the curriculum for teaching border inspectors, and the choice of guns for DHS training academies. "The White House staff micromanaged the department in the worst of all ways," said Bruce Lawlor, who went over with Ridge to serve as his first chief of staff at DHS.

"What would constantly happen at DHS was that these impossible requirements were placed on you," said Lawlor. "You were kind of put between a dog and fire hydrant because the idea was often pretty good, but you couldn't get there from here in the amount of time that these people were demanding that you do it."

Finally, the interagency fights that had characterized the pre-9/11 era did not disappear, particularly with respect to the FBI and the Department of Justice, and the outcome was the same—DHS lost most of the battles. "We were to a large extent fighting Justice to make them behave consistently with our mandate not to disrupt the flow of commerce," said Asa Hutchinson. "The FBI's whole focus was law enforcement."

One of the first battles Hutchinson faced was to talk the FBI down from starting to make immigration arrests on its own authority. As his final act before the INS was pulled from the Justice Department and placed in the new DHS, Attorney General John Ashcroft had issued an executive order giving the FBI the authority to arrest foreigners on immigration violations, something that previously had been the exclusive prerogative of INS agents. For DHS, that order was an existential threat to its counterterrorism mission. Domestically, counterterrorism operations take place largely through what are known as the Joint Terrorism Task Forces, which bring together the FBI, DHS, and state and local police authorities to coordinate on investigations (a role that was augmented by the creation of "fusion centers" in the states in 2005). The task forces were created long before 9/11, but after the attacks they acquired a much bigger role, and their numbers mushroomed so that today more than a hundred are spread out across the country. For DHS, its power to enforce immigration laws was the main reason for its participation on the JTTFs. As Hutchinson put it later, the FBI "wanted to have that power so they didn't have to call DHS every time there was a JTTF investigation and they wanted to hold someone." But if the FBI assumed those powers, DHS would have had no role in the task forces, effectively cutting the new agency out of the information flow and making it irrelevant to the domestic counterterrorism mission. Ashcroft refused to rescind the memo despite strong complaints from DHS, and while the FBI did not use the authority frequently, there were several run-ins between FBI agents and DHS immigration agents.

Other losses were more consequential. Congress had envisioned that the new department would become an information clearinghouse for protecting the country against terrorist attack. On border issues, the most important databases were the various terrorist watch lists that were maintained by the State Department, the INS, and other agencies. The legislation that created the department said that DHS should take responsibility for integrating that information and fusing other intelligence on terrorist threats inside the United States. The FBI and the CIA had no interest in seeing that power land at DHS, however, and the White House agreed. In January 2003, Bush announced the creation of a Terrorist Threat Integration Center, under the control of FBI and the CIA, to handle the consolidation of watch lists and the flow of intelligence on homeland security. John Gannon, a former deputy director for intelligence at the CIA who was closely involved in setting up DHS, called the creation of TTIC "a body blow to the not-yet-functioning DHS."

"The president made it pretty clear where he wanted it," said Ridge. "He didn't want it in DHS. End of story." One of Ridge's aides called it "basically a White House effort to cut the legs out from underneath DHS intelligence."

Sometimes the fights were almost silly. Ridge had wanted to name the new enforcement office Investigations and Criminal Enforcement, to reflect the agency's big role in drug busts and other criminal investigations. But the FBI went to war to block that change, arguing that "investigations" were the purview of the FBI. "When I saw that one go by, I didn't have time," Ridge's transportation security chief and later deputy James Loy told the *Washington Post*. "I said, 'Oh . . . surely, for God's sake we're not going to waste time on that." But FBI director Robert Mueller took the fight to the White House, where he prevailed and forced DHS to change the name to Immigration and Customs Enforcement. "It got to the top, sadly," Loy said.

Ridge's effectiveness was also limited by his own leadership style, in which he tried to build consensus and lead by example rather than by knocking heads together. His closest aides recall him repeatedly returning from White House meetings to tell them he had been forced to stand down on one issue or another. "There was some frustration within some of my team that early on we didn't fight for more turf," Ridge acknowledged. Ridge never took to the internecine struggles that so characterize Washington's bureaucratic culture. From the outset, he was aware that DHS had far more on its plate than it could handle. "We hadn't built our turf enough to engage in turf battles," he said. "When we chose to be aggressive, we were aggressive in areas where I felt we could deliver."

"It's an acquisitive culture," Ridge added. "Some of [the agencies] have that Pac-Man approach, they like to just gobble up as much jurisdiction as they can. And it's pretty difficult to, in my mind, justify being aggressive, looking for more responsibility and jurisdiction when you haven't even poured the cement for the basement. So we limited our battles."

What was less clear at the time was that Ridge's own ties with the White House had deteriorated as well. Ridge acknowledged that his relations with Andy Card, the White House chief of staff, who acted as the gatekeeper for the president, "were never very strong," even though Card had made the original phone call asking him to come to Washington. Some Ridge aides believe that his performance when he was at the White House—where for a period of time he became the administration's public face in the war on terrorism—ultimately became threatening to President Bush and his staff. "If you look at some of the photographs, the visuals of Ridge even in the company of the president and the vice president, this guy had it," said a former Ridge aide. "His visibility, his likeability, his articulateness, his instincts were so damn good that he just exploded. And we didn't understand that, we didn't understand what that meant inside the White House. We created in effect hostility among the president's men." Shortly after he left the White House in 2006, Andy Card gave an interview to author Ron Kessler in which he offered a bruising assessment of Ridge's performance as secretary. He said that while Ridge was "a very good public relations leader, I don't think that he exercised internal leadership. I wish that he had had a deputy that he had given a little more license to organize the new agency."

Ridge says that, for whatever combination of reasons, the result was that the White House consistently favored the older agencies over the new DHS. "We occasionally got rhetorical support. That was about it. But it seemed like a lot of the public and private support was directed toward Justice and the FBI." John Gannon, who turned down Ridge's offer to head DHS's powerless intelligence arm and instead became the first staff director of the House Homeland Security Committee, said that the White House had been ambivalent about creating DHS in the first place: "They never overcame their mixed emotions about having a DHS," said Gannon, "so whenever the White House needed to stand behind the department, it didn't. And when DHS asserted its authority, they backed the legacy agencies. That hurt the department, and it hurt Ridge personally."

Finally, what made the battles particularly difficult on border issues is that DHS—which had been created for the purpose of preventing another terrorist attack—found itself in the odd position of arguing that some of the security measures had gone too far after 9/11. As one former White House official put it: "We cast our net very, very broadly without recognizing that by doing so it would be almost impossible to walk it back quickly and efficiently, because any attempt to walk back would appear to be dismantling security safeguards that had been put into place for what appeared to be legitimate reasons."

DESPITE RIDGE'S IMPRESSIVE NEW TITLE and his public stature, the reality of the Department of Homeland Security was that his authority for carrying out the kinds of changes he wanted to see in U.S. border security was extremely limited. The only part of the vast border bureaucracy over which he exercised firm control was the small directorate run by Hutchinson that was in charge of border and transportation security. And the rest of the government, particularly agencies like the Justice Department which jealously guarded their prerogatives in the war on terror, was not willing to follow his lead.

Shortly after the creation of the department, for example, Ridge directed Hutchinson and Stewart Verdery, the assistant secretary in charge of border and transportation security policy, to come up with a scheme for fixing the growing array of problems in visa policy. Verdery helped draft a multipart plan that addressed what universities, business groups, and others had identified as the most serious obstacles to more efficient processing of visas. It called for greater flexibility on the State Department's new mandatory interview requirement, permitting State to waive the interviews for people who had been vetted and granted visas in the past. It proposed taking some power out of the hands of the FBI on security background checks by returning to the previous practice that allowed State to grant a visa if it had not been flagged by the FBI within a reasonable period of time, normally thirty days. The plan called for narrowing the list of fields that would trigger a security review under the Visas Mantis scheme, to allow the government to focus on real risks, such as the nuclear and biological sciences, rather than landscape architecture or urban planning. And Ridge wanted to see an end to the NSEERS program, believing that it had not paid security benefits remotely proportional to its economic and diplomatic costs. Ridge hinted at his thinking in an April 2003 speech to the American Association of Universities, acknowledging that the administration might have moved precipitously in cracking down on students and other foreign travelers after 9/11. "To universities and to those students, these aren't merely glitches or inconveniences," he said. "Taken together, we understand they threaten your ability to conduct research and obtain funding and attract the best students you possibly can, and they put your students and researchers at risk of severe delays, even deportation."

Many elements of the proposal would ultimately be implemented—but only after Ridge had left. In 2006, after Condoleezza Rice had replaced Colin Powell at the State Department and Michael Chertoff had replaced Ridge at DHS, the two departments announced the "Rice-Chertoff vision" for "secure borders and open doors in the information age," which included several of the measures that Ridge pushed for in 2003. But in 2003 the argument was impossible to win. As Verdery put it: "The FBI always held the trump card that any change was dangerous and therefore it shouldn't be done."

The State Department, while it was working feverishly to try to reduce the backlog in visa applications, had little interest in taking any suggestions from the new department, which it saw as threatening its historic control over the entire visa process. DHS pushed for changes to a long-standing provision of the Immigration Act known as 214b, which requires consular officers to assume that everyone seeking to come to the United States is intending to immigrate and requires that applicants provide evidence of their intention to return home. Even with the new terrorism concerns, 214b remains by far the most common reason for visa denials, and DHS was eager to find ways to reduce the high rate of refusal, particularly for business travelers. It proposed, for instance, allowing companies to put up a cash bond that would guarantee that certain visa applicants would return home after their stay. But State rebuffed the suggestion. Ridge also unsuccessfully urged the State Department to relax its rigid reciprocity rules, which had, for example, required Chinese visitors to renew their visas every six months because China would not grant U.S. citizens visas of more than six months. In early 2005, State got an agreement from Beijing to extend that validity to one year, but it wouldn't end the reciprocity requirement. Nor was State particularly eager to experiment with videoconferencing, which would allow some applicants to be interviewed without traveling hundreds of miles to the nearest U.S. embassy.

The White House was leery of any measures that would appear to mark a weakening of security—or could be made to appear so to the public. For example, the United States had long allowed tourists without visas to transit through American airports if they were traveling to other countries but not stopping over in the United States. It was a lucrative business for U.S. airlines, allowing them to carry European passengers to the Caribbean or Latin America through Miami, and Asian passengers to those same destinations through Los Angeles. But the security in the scheme was extremely lax. In some cases, international passengers were allowed to fly into the United States in New York or Los Angeles, board a domestic flight to another city, and then fly from that city to their ultimate destination abroad. It was an invitation to bypass the visa requirement to enter the United States, and there was intelligence evidence that terrorist groups were aware of the loophole. In August 2003, DHS and the State Department shut down the program, saying the government had received "specific, credible intelligence that certain terrorist organizations including al-Qaida have identified the visa and passport exemptions of those programs as a means to gain access to aircraft en route to and from the United States." After the threat level subsided, DHS went back to the White House with a proposal to reinstate the scheme for certain countries, provided the airline passengers had been properly screened in advance and they were not allowed to leave the airport terminal in the United States. But DHS was shot down by a senior White House official, who retorted, " 'If this increases the risk at all we can't approve it.' And there was no way it could pass this test."

Even with those setbacks DHS began to make progress in checking off the list of initiatives that Ridge had first sketched out in the White House under the rubric of the "border of the future." Europe was a major focus. Zacarias Moussaoui, a French citizen who would eventually be tried and convicted on terrorism charges related to 9/11, had demonstrated how vulnerable the United States could be to Islamic terrorists carrying European passports. Since 1988 travelers from western European nations, as well as a handful of others such as Japan, had been able simply to get onto a plane and show up in the United States with no prior permission from the U.S. government. The scheme, known as the Visa Waiver Program, was intended to speed travel to the United States from richer countries whose citizens were considered likely to return home. That allowed consular officers to be deployed instead at countries that were more likely to send illegal migrants to the United States. The result was that by the time of the 9/11 attacks, the majority of foreign travelers came to the United States without ever having been vetted by the U.S. government.

Before 9/11, there had already been concerns over terrorists and criminals entering the United States on fraudulent passports from visa waiver countries. One of the conspirators in the 1993 World Trade Center bombing had tried to enter on a false Swedish passport but was stopped when an INS inspector suspected the photograph had been substituted. Stolen passports were an endemic problem in some European countries; in Italy, France, and Belgium, blank passports were handwritten and kept at lightly secured municipal offices. When U.S. military forces invaded Afghanistan, they discovered hundreds of these blank passport books. With Europe facing a problem of homegrown Islamic radicalism, which was demonstrated by the deadly attacks on the Madrid railroads in March 2004 and the London subway in July 2005, the program posed an acute security risk for the United States.

Other incidents made the threat to the United States even more apparent. In December 2001, a British citizen named Richard Reid, who had boarded a transatlantic flight from Paris to Miami, was spotted by an alert flight attendant as he was trying to use a match to light a long fuse protruding from one of his shoes. With the help of other passengers, Reid was wrestled to the ground and handcuffed, and the flight was diverted to Boston. Reid, who admitted his membership in Al Qaeda, was later convicted on terrorism charges. Then, during the busy Christmas season of 2003 more than a dozen flights to the United States, most originating in France and the UK, were halted or turned around after the United

States discovered names in the passenger manifests that matched up with those on the so-called no-fly list of terrorist suspects that the United States wanted to keep from boarding aircraft. The incidents led DHS to raise its terror alert to orange, the second-highest level, though officials subsequently admitted that the matched names were mistakes and none of the individuals was actually a suspected terrorist.

As with the student visa program, there were threats from Congress after 9/11 to shut down the Visa Waiver Program entirely. Both the administration and the travel industry pushed back, arguing that the United States had no capability even to process the number of visas that would be required. Instead, Congress voted in 2002 to tighten the program by requiring European countries to develop secure, machine-readable passports with biometric information digitally encoded, and to report any lost or stolen passports to the United States, on threat of their country's visa waiver status being revoked.

The technocrats in DHS believed that the other solution to the visa waiver vulnerability was to gather more and better information on travelers coming from Europe so that border officials would have a chance to vet the names and run security checks before the flights had landed in the United States and before any of the passengers were allowed into the country. The same information had been given voluntarily by many airlines before 9/11, and after the attacks Customs had demanded it from Middle Eastern airlines flying into the United States. It had also been part of the Smart Border Accord with Canada. Congress had legislated that such advanced passenger information should be collected on all airline passengers coming into the United States.

Unlike the Muslim countries, however, Europe could not simply be bullied into compliance. The U.S. legislation on passenger information ran afoul of Europe's strict privacy laws. It took nearly a year and a half of difficult negotiations for the United States and the European Union to strike a deal, but eventually the EU agreed to give U.S. authorities access to the same passenger records that were being provided by U.S. and other international airlines. A subsequent deal, worked out in 2007 after European courts nixed the first arrangement on privacy grounds, narrowed the list of data provided. Shortly after that deal was inked, the EU announced that it would follow the U.S. lead and put in place its own passenger name records requirement. And in 2008, DHS announced that it would implement a new system requiring all travelers from visa waiver countries to apply online with the U.S. government for prior authorization to visit the United States. Such authorization would have to be received at least three days in advance of any flight, but could then be used for the next two years for any trips to the United States.

Rob Bonner was also working along similar lines, extending the container security system he had negotiated with Canada to the rest of the world. He pressured Rotterdam, Hong Kong, Singapore, and the world's other big ports to agree to station U.S. Customs agents on their soil to help in identifying suspicious cargo shipments that should be inspected before they were loaded on ships bound for U.S. ports.

These initiatives also helped to build a pattern of international cooperation in fighting terrorism. In the Christmas 2003 airplane incidents, the United States had dealt with the European airlines, with little success; subsequent crises were handled directly with the European governments. In 2006, such close cooperation helped the United States and UK governments to foil a nascent plot in which homegrown terrorists in the UK had planned to detonate bombs on several transatlantic airliners.

Outside of DHS, other agencies in the government were making similar progress. At the State Department, despite Colin Powell's dissatisfaction, significant strides had been made in working out the problems in visa processing. "In a nutshell, we get it," Maura Harty, the assistant secretary for consular affairs, wrote in early 2005. "The United States is preeminent in business, academia, and scientific research because of the ability to attract talented people from the far reaches of the globe. In 2004 the U.S. ambassador to Pakistan relayed that her British colleague had experienced an incredible increase in student visa applications in one year, from 2,000 to 6,000. This instance shows that the United States will not have the opportunity to host and educate 4,000 Pakistani students—an unconscionable loss."

Harty had begun chipping away at the visa delays immediately after taking the job. She had ordered all consular posts to give priority to the processing of student visas so that foreign students would be able to receive visas in time to start their programs of study. That meant scheduling visa interviews with students as quickly as possible and moving their applications to the top of the processing pile. While this did not end the waits, it shortened them considerably. In June 2004 for instance, a peak time for student visa applications, students and scholars applying through the U.S. consulate in Shanghai were waiting just two weeks on average for an interview, compared with nearly two months for other visa applicants. Once approved by the consular officer, some 97 percent of student visa applicants were getting their visas in a day or two.

On the technology background checks that had become such an enormous obstacle to science and engineering students from China, Russia, and India, the State Department and the FBI both brought on additional staff to help speed up processing times, with State creating a special five-person team dedicated solely to speeding up those cases. The department launched extensive training for consular officers to improve their ability to decide when they could approve applications and when they had to send them back to Washington for a security review. The system was fully automated so that all information was relayed electronically, further speeding up processing. Most important, in July 2004 State and the FBI implemented one of the major changes that had been suggested by Ridge and Stewart Verdery in their visa policy proposal that had been greeted so coolly just a year before. The FBI agreed that it would no longer have to complete thorough, time-consuming security background checks on every applicant before the visa could be issued; instead, unless the FBI explicitly objected to a visa applicant, State would be free to issue the visa and simply keep the FBI informed on the details of the application. By November 2004 the average processing time had fallen to just over two weeks, with less than 10 percent of the cases being delayed for more than two months.

John Marburger, who as director of the White House Office of Science and Technology Policy had heard continual complaints from universities and scientific organizations, said that by late 2004 these had virtually stopped. He quietly ended discussions that had been under way to try to create an interagency group of scientific experts to vet visa applications from students and researchers. "What happened in my view," he said, "was that the State Department fixed the problem."

The difficulties for students did not disappear, but their severity clearly lessened. In 2007, a National Academies survey actually showed slightly more complaints about visa delays than in 2003— nearly 1,300, versus fewer than 900. But whereas in 2003 one-third of those cases had involved delays of more than six months, by 2007 that was true in only 5 percent of the cases, while most had been delayed only one or two months. In the 2006–2007 academic year, the overall number of international students grew by 3 percent—the first significant increase since 9/11—while the number of new international students jumped by 10 percent.

SIGNIFICANT PROGRESS WAS ALSO MADE on the security side. One of the most difficult problems in the post-9/11 era had been to integrate all the different government information databases that contained the names of suspected terrorists into a single list that would be available for those who needed it—consular officers, border agents, airport security inspectors, and state and local police. The big investigations by the congressional intelligence committees and by the 9/11 Commission had concluded that inadequate intelligence sharing was at the heart of the U.S. failure to prevent the attacks. The integration of terrorist watch lists, therefore, was probably the single most important step that the United States could take to keep known and suspected terrorists out of the country.

In his 2003 State of the Union address, Bush had announced the creation of the Terrorist Threat Integration Center, which directed the FBI, the CIA, the Pentagon, and the DHS to work together "to merge and analyze all threat information in a single location." It was later superseded by a new, CIA-led National Counterterrorism Center. By the end of 2003, the different agencies in charge of terrorist watch lists had agreed to consolidate their efforts through the NCTC and to distribute the information to frontline inspectors and local police through a new entity, the Terrorist Screening Center, run by the FBI.

Unlike many of the post-9/11 initiatives, whose claims to success rested on the supposition that they helped to deter or disrupt unidentified terrorist plots, the Terrorist Screening Center was quickly able to point to concrete successes. In its first month of operation in December 2003, the TSC reviewed some 54,000 individual cases referred by State Department consular officers for checks against the consolidated watch lists. Eighty of those visa applicants were found on the lists, and visas were denied to at least two individuals considered by the United States to be members of terrorist organizations.

There were problems. The process for vetting the names on the terrorist list was far too lax, such that almost any FBI agent could add a name to the list with little scrutiny. The FBI is virtually a franchise operation, with local agents running their own cases, and initially there was no oversight of how these agents added names to the watch lists. Stewart Baker, the assistant DHS secretary for policy, said this still remains a significant problem and the lists need to be pruned. Indeed, by 2008 the number of those suspected of some sort of terrorist connection had mushroomed from fewer than 160,000 in 2004 to more than 850,000, with 20,000 names being added every month. People wrongly placed on the list, or whose names are a close match to someone on the list, have struggled to get off. "Any agent could put information into the database, and it was terribly difficult to get out, and still is," said Randy Beardsworth, who held senior operations posts in DHS from 2003 to 2006. There was also strong disagreement over what the names on the watch list meant. "If so-and-so is on the watch list, that doesn't mean squat," Beardsworth said. "It means we have information on these people. It could be important or it could be innocuous." But "you had zealots who wanted everyone on the watch list kept out."

That zeal was partly responsible for the Christmas 2003 actions diverting or halting more than a dozen transatlantic flights, and for the bizarre decision in 2004 to force the landing of a London-to-Washington flight in Bangor, Maine, because the singer Cat Stevens, who had converted to Islam, was aboard the flight. Officials later acknowledged that, while Stevens might have been worth watching, he should not have been on the no-fly list, and indeed had been in the United States just a few months previously. Similar names were another huge problem. Senator Ted Kennedy was one of several prominent politicians who were repeatedly stopped at airports because their names matched that of someone on the list. He finally had to plead personally to Ridge to get the error corrected. In another case, a senior French official was added to the no-fly list even though the report on the individual entered by an ICE agent noted clearly that the information tying him to terrorism was only rumor and innuendo. The French were so furious that they held up cooperation on several important counterterrorism initiatives until his name was removed from the list. Current DHS officials say that the watch lists are still inadequate for determining who should be kept from boarding commercial flights.

FBI officials acknowledge the mistakes but say they are gradually fine-tuning the system. Leonard Boyle, the director of the Terrorist Screening Center, said that the 850,000 names on the list include multiple spellings and variations, and in fact there are probably fewer than 400,000 people. About 95 percent of those are foreign citizens, not Americans or legal residents in the United

States. In most cases, those on the list are not people the government wants to see arrested or even necessarily denied permission to enter the United States. In 2006, for instance, some 20,000 people were flagged by the watch list, but only a small fraction of those were arrested or barred from entering the United States; Customs and Border Protection officials, who dealt with about 10,000 of those "hits," arrested or turned back only 550 people. Instead, most are seen as having some link to terrorist groups that are deemed worthy of monitoring, and following their travel patterns is "an incredibly valuable intelligence tool," Boyle said. DHS has also worked closely with the airlines to try to clear up misidentifications so that individuals with names similar to one on the list are not stopped every time they travel.

While serious problems remain with false matches, the TSC has succeeded in making available to officials across the government data on terrorists and their associates that was previously scattered around the agencies. Following a model first created by the State Department in its TIPOFF terrorist watch list, the TSC protects the confidentiality of intelligence sources by making only names, and sometimes fingerprints or other limited biographical data, available to frontline agents. These include consular officers who issue visas, border inspectors who authorize entry into the United States, state and local police who want to run name checks, and transportation security officials responsible for airline safety. If a hit comes up, those officials make direct contact with TSC agents who have access to the full classified data so they can make quick decisions on how to handle the individual.

Additionally, the United States has been linking up its watch lists with those of European and other allies, as well as sharing fingerprints and other personal data, to build an international picture of the movement of suspected terrorists and their supporters. Over time, it may give the United States something close to a global capacity to monitor those individuals who are the most likely to attempt another terrorist attack.

The advance passenger information on incoming international

flights has also proved extremely valuable. In 2003, a CBP agent at Chicago's O'Hare Airport turned back Raed al-Banna, a young Jordanian who arrived on a flight from Amsterdam, even though al-Banna had previously lived in the United States on a legal visa and the visa was still valid. The passenger data, run through what is known as the Automated Targeting System, had flagged al-Banna for extra scrutiny. Under questioning, he admitted that he had supported himself through a variety of petty jobs in the United States—a violation of his tourist visa—and was put on a plane back to Jordan. Two years later, U.S. officials say that al-Banna's fingerprints were identified on a forearm handcuffed to the steering wheel of a car that was packed with explosives and detonated outside a health clinic in the Iraqi city of Hilla, killing more than 130 people in one of the worst suicide attacks of the Iraq War.

The technocrats ran into surprisingly few political obstacles outside the administration itself. In particular, although there were some objections that collecting information on students and travelers was a fundamental violation of privacy rights, these objections were far more muted than many in the government had anticipated. Partly, this reflected the changed calculations of a post-9/11 world—government intrusions that would have been deemed unacceptable before the terrorist attacks suddenly seemed like reasonable precautions. But the biggest reason that objections regarding privacy did not derail the technocrats' plans is that the schemes were aimed mostly at foreigners.

United States privacy rules restrict the sort of information the government can gather and store on citizens or permanent residents; the same protections do not apply to those traveling into the country. The SEVIS database is limited to foreign students, not American students; the passenger name record requirements are aimed almost exclusively at international flights into the United States, and virtually all the names on the terrorist watch list are foreigners. Traditional privacy concerns simply do not carry as much weight with foreign travelers to the United States, because there is a reasonable assumption that border inspectors have a right to know in detail why non–U.S. citizens are coming to the country and what they will do while they are here. Even American citizens traveling abroad do not enjoy the full range of normal privacy protections when they return to the border; they can be searched, for example, on the basis of mere suspicion rather than any probable cause. Most of the objections from U.S. privacy groups were aimed at what was essentially collateral damage from the data gathering efforts, such as Americans whose names inadvertently matched that of a foreigner on the terrorist watch list.

The contrast between the rules at home and those at the border is most apparent with regard to information about passengers. Despite difficult negotiations with the EU and Canada, passenger name records are now available to the U.S. government for all incoming international flights. Yet the efforts of transportation security officials to run essentially the same checks on domestic flights—through the CAPPS-II system and its successor known as Secure Flight—have been stalled repeatedly because of opposition from privacy and civil liberties groups.

Despite these successes, what had quickly become clear to Ridge and his staff was that they would not be able to roll back NSEERS or the other Justice Department schemes they disliked unless they had something big to put in its place that would satisfy the cops that they were tough enough on security. What Ridge settled on was an ambitious plan to fingerprint and track the arrival and departure of every single foreigner coming to the United States.

ON APRIL 29, 2003, RIDGE was set to deliver the most important speech he had given since becoming secretary of homeland security. The date marked the end of the first hundred days of DHS, which since Franklin Roosevelt's New Deal has been the measure for accomplishment in a crisis. He decided to use the speech to roll out what would become the new department's signature initiative on the borders—the creation of a comprehensive, automated system to record the entry and exit of every foreign traveler into the country. It was an ironic choice for the department's flagship program. As governor of Pennsylvania in the 1990s, Ridge had joined with border state governors in the South and the North in lobbying to kill the idea, arguing that the border delays it would create would shut down commerce.

The scheme was first approved by Congress in 1996, when concern over illegal immigration had reached a peak. Its champion was Lamar Smith, a Texas Republican whose main goal was to fortify the southern border against illegal immigrants from Mexico, but it passed the Congress largely because it was justified as a counterterrorism measure following the 1993 World Trade Center bombing. It required the INS to create within two years an automated scheme for tracking the entry and exit of every single foreigner who came to the United States; while that information could be useful for terrorism and drug investigations, its main purpose was to identify visa overstayers, who were thought to account for some 40 percent of those living in the country illegally.

After the 9/11 attacks, Smith had continued to argue forcefully that shutting down illegal immigration was a critical element of the war on terrorism. "Citizens understand that if you don't know who's coming into the country, like illegal immigrants, then you don't know what's coming into the country, like terrorist weapons," he wrote in the conservative *National Review* in 2003. He had been given a 100 percent approval rating by the Federation for American Immigration Reform, a lobbying group pressing for lower levels of legal and illegal migration to the United States.

Like the proposal for student tracking that was part of the same 1996 legislation, the scheme had hit a wall of opposition from those interests with a strong stake in openness. While it might be possible to construct such a system at the nation's airports, doing so at the land borders seemed impossible without creating enormous delays that would strangle the growing cross-border commerce that had been accelerated by NAFTA. The Border Trade Alliance, which represented Texas business interests, had teamed up with northern border governors like Ridge to oppose the plan. Much as with the student tracking system, this lobbying had prevented the entry-exit scheme from getting off the ground despite the congressional legislation, and the deadlines for implementation had been repeatedly pushed back: when 9/11 hit, the first implementation at airports was not scheduled until the end of 2003.

Like the student visa plan, after 9/11 Congress had resurrected and toughened up the 1996 law. The USA Patriot Act in 2001 mandated that the new system would need a biometric component to ensure that the United States could accurately identify visitors to the country, and the Enhanced Border Security Act in 2002 further dictated that the system would have to be compatible with other government databases. It also required the United States to begin including biometric identifiers, such as fingerprints, in visas that could be read at U.S. airports and directed that other countries would have to meet that standard in their passports for travel to the United States.

When Ridge took over at DHS, the end of 2003 deadline for implementing the new system at U.S. airports was one of the most daunting he faced. Almost immediately, his top officials began complaining publicly that it could not be met at any reasonable cost. Hutchinson told the *Financial Times* in mid-April that the plan was "not do-able in the time frame Congress has given us" and that the costs were likely to be far higher than Congress had estimated. He expressed further skepticism about including a biometric standard. "If you have a biometric standard that presupposes you're going to read that biometric standard," he said. "If it adds for each [person] 30 seconds, at some of the ports of entry you would increase the wait time by hours."

Just a week later, as Ridge was set to deliver his speech at the National Press Club, his officials were urging him to take any mention of the entry-exit scheme out of the speech, insisting, as Hutchinson had, that the end-of-year deadline was impossible. They were pressuring Bruce Lawlor, who had come over from the White House as Ridge's chief of staff, to pull it out of the speech. But when Lawlor called Ridge to convey the message, he had to take the phone away from his ear because Ridge was yelling so loudly. Ridge not only refused to take it out of the speech but took a further step that baffled many on his staff: he promised to implement the system with a full biometric component, which would require recording the fingerprints of every visitor to the country.

Ridge said later that he had come to see biometrics as the only way to marry security and commerce, because it would allow border officials to identify individuals accurately and to separate those who required more scrutiny from those who could be quickly and safely welcomed into the country. "To distinguish one John Smith from another John Smith you need biometrics and that's why I was so insistent upon it. It seemed to me to be foolhardy to build a system on anything other than technology," Ridge said.

Its introduction allowed him finally to do away with part of the NSEERS program that DHS so disliked. In December 2003, Ridge abolished the domestic registration scheme for Muslims already in the United States and eliminated the requirement that travelers re-register after they had been in the country for thirty days and one year. "There were not the significant leads that we had hoped for," said Hutchinson, Ridge's undersecretary in charge of border security. "It did not prove to be necessary for security purposes." DHS officials were even more critical in private. "The intention seemed at times almost to be to harass people who were somehow seen as being to blame for 9/11," said another senior DHS official. "It was in effect a huge indictment of the FBI, which had no sources or contacts in local Muslim communities, and therefore no alternative to just rounding people up."

But in endorsing the new scheme, Ridge helped to set into motion a dynamic that would become evident only after he left office at the end of the first Bush term. He had linked the tools of the technocrats—advanced information systems and biometrics—to the goals of the cops: sealing the U.S. borders against terrorists by halting illegal immigration.

THE NEW PLAN WAS GIVEN a catchy acronym—US-VISIT— that underscored how sensitive Ridge and others at DHS had become to the charge that the country was closing its doors to the world. They feared that the fingerprinting scheme would be perceived as a particularly hostile measure. The name was the work of Dennis Murphy, Bonner's former communications chief, who had crossed over to work for Hutchinson. "It was designed to get the message out that the United States was still a welcoming country," said Jim Williams, a career government official with experience in managing complex systems who was recruited by Beardsworth from the Internal Revenue Service. It was unpopular nonetheless; Williams said the Japanese lobbied particularly heavily against it, saying that the fingerprinting regime reminded them of the occupation under MacArthur. Brazil issued angry denunciations of the program and began fingerprinting Americans coming to Brazil in retaliation. But the initial reaction did not last long; by 2007, Japan had become one of the first countries to emulate the U.S. scheme and others were announcing plans to follow.

Even after committing publicly to meet the congressional deadline, Ridge had to fight several battles before he could launch US-VISIT. Shortly after he made his National Press Club announcement, a senior FBI official went to see Hutchinson, demanding that the bureau take control of the new system. By the FBI's logic, since the system was based on fingerprints, and since the FBI maintained by far the largest database of fingerprints in the government, it should be the one to run the program. This was one of the few times that Ridge managed to resist and win a major turf battle against the FBI. "You talk about a welcoming America, and the first person you see is an FBI agent to welcome you to the country? Please, give me a break!" said Ridge. "So Asa just pushed them back. I don't know whether [FBI director Robert] Mueller decided to call off the dogs or whether there was somebody else there who thought, well, maybe we'll probe and if we see an opening we'll get it. Well, Asa wouldn't let him have the opening and neither would I."

Even after it gave up any effort to control the new system, the FBI fought to make its fingerprint system the basis of the new scheme. There was a strong security argument in its favor. For criminal investigations, the best type of fingerprint record is referred to as a "full-rolled" print, which requires that each finger not only be pressed to a surface but also rolled in order to get as full a print as possible. That allowed agents to compare the prints in their databases with even tiny fragments of fingerprints that might be recovered in a criminal investigation. From a security perspective, such a full fingerprint, known as a ten-print, was the most useful. The U.S. military had recovered and was cataloging fingerprints taken from Al Qaeda safe houses in Afghanistan following the invasion, and was lifting fingerprints in Iraq as well. Requiring a full ten-print from all visitors would—assuming the Pentagon agreed to share its fingerprint records—allow border inspectors to compare prints with those obtained by the military, a potentially valuable tool in keeping would-be terrorists out of the United States. Further, a ten-print would allow for visitors to be checked immediately against the FBI's huge criminal database.

But the practical and public image problems of such a system were enormous. The government was already worried about the message that would be sent to the world when it started fingerprinting visitors, and a full-roll ten-print—even one using a digital scanner as opposed to the old ink-and-paper system—would look far too much like a criminal interrogation of every traveler. Worse, the best estimates the government had were that the process would take as long as five to six minutes for each traveler, an impossibly long time, and would require border agents to handle the fingers of travelers physically to get a full print. A less intrusive alternative favored by the FBI was known as a slap-ten, and would require a traveler simply to press eight fingers, and then the thumbs separately, straight down on a digital reader. But even this system had its problems. The White House commissioned several studies that showed that taking all ten prints could slow the entry process down significantly—as long as forty-five seconds per traveler—which would still lead to huge lineups at U.S. airports. Despite the resistance from the FBI, DHS and the White House agreed to start with a more modest plan—two digital fingerprints and a photograph, which was the standard used by the INS and inherited by DHS, at least until the system was up and running well. "It was a really big issue and it got down to what was doable at that point," said Brian Peterman, who handled the issue in the White House. Williams, the first director of US-VISIT, agreed: "If we'd used the FBI system, we would have shut down the economy of the United States."

Having fended off the FBI, Ridge then had almost as tough an obstacle in Bonner and the CBP. To get the new scheme launched, Ridge decided to cut out CBP and give operational control to a new group under Williams that reported directly to Hutchinson. As far as CBP was concerned, US-VISIT was an open threat to one of its core functions: managing the entry of people into the country. Not surprisingly, Bonner was not enthusiastic about the new system. Williams says it was a battle at every step. "I just always felt that CBP was both openly and underhandedly fighting us," he said. To help keep CBP at arm's length, Williams decided to use an outside private contractor to develop and integrate much of the technology for US-VISIT. The contract, which was worth a potential $10 billion over ten years, ultimately went to Accenture, a U.S. company that had courted controversy by relocating its head office in Bermuda for tax purposes. It was the first huge contract tendered by DHS, and it immediately set off a scramble among defense contractors and consulting firms to try to get a piece of the business.

The scheme envisioned that by the end of 2003 the government would deploy at all U.S. international airports terminals equipped to take photographs and display other data on travelers and digital readers that could capture their fingerprints. It would initially be used just for those who required visas to come to the United States. Visitors from the visa waiver countries would be exempt. Even such a modest effort had some immediate value. First, it would allow for another layer of checking against the government watch lists. The State Department's system, TIPOFF, was a name-based system, but the new scheme would build on the IDENT fingerprint-based system that had been developed by the INS. Most of those prints were from immigration violators, but there were also some prints of those suspected of links to terrorism in the system as well. Second, it would help to prevent visa fraud, since the State Department had begun requiring fingerprints for visas, which could then be checked at the airport to ensure that the visa holder was the same person who had applied abroad. Third, it would reduce passport fraud, which was considered one of the most likely ways that a terrorist known to U.S. intelligence might nonetheless be able to get into the country. Once a traveler was "enrolled" in the system, his fingerprints would be permanently linked to his passport, so if his passport was lost or stolen and someone else attempted to use it to enter the United States, it would immediately be detected. Similarly, if he tried to enter the country under another name or on a different passport, he would be stopped. Finally, if an exit system could be built, it would provide useful information for the FBI and other law enforcement agencies, which could use the data to determine if a terrorist or criminal suspect who had entered the United States had left or still remained in the country.

Though it was sold to the public and to other countries on counterterrorism grounds, the logic of the system was no different than it had been in 1996 when it was being pushed as a means of cracking down on illegal immigration. If a fully functioning entry and exit system could actually be constructed, the United States would be able for the first time in its history to identify—by name, photograph, and fingerprints—a significant percentage of those who were living in the country illegally. That number was thought to exceed 12 million, of which some 40 percent had first arrived in the United States on legal visas and thus could be targeted by US-VISIT. What would the government do with that information? Apart from a general pledge to chase down terrorists and criminals, no one at DHS answered that question.

Despite the fears voiced by Hutchinson and others of the huge delays that might result, the implementation of the new system was planned meticulously. Bearing in mind the chaos that had accompanied NSEERS, the technical problems with the initial rollout of the SEVIS student tracking system, and the huge visa backlogs that had been created by the security background checks for the Mantis and Condor schemes, Ridge was determined not to repeat those mistakes. A pilot project was set up in Atlanta to test out the scheme. One of the country's highest-powered public relations firms, Fleischmann-Hilliard, was hired to mount a PR offensive around the world to try to calm the expected negative reaction. "Up until that point, everyone's idea of fingerprinting was that it was part of being arrested," said P. T. Wright, who came over from CBP to serve as Williams's operations manager on the project. And the internal rivalry was probably a motivator as well. Wright, who became an enthusiast for the system despite the skepticism of his Customs colleagues, says that just a week before the launch he was warned by the CBP director of field operations, Jay Ahern, that the launch would probably fail. It was rolled out at 115 airports in January, the slowest travel month of the year. Williams had developed a contingency plan that called for shutting down the fingerprinting if the lines grew too long. It wasn't needed: on average it took just ten to fifteen seconds for an inspector to check a traveler's passport, take a photograph and the two fingerprints, and send him on his way. As Williams later put it, the entire experience was "underwhelming." "We didn't want to hurt tourism, and there was enough negativity over visa policy already," he said. "We tested, tested, and tested to make sure it worked."

As Hutchinson had predicted, the price tag was higher than Congress had anticipated, close to $1.5 billion over the first four years, and estimates running into the tens of billions for construction of the total system. But it did offer an added layer of security, particularly against criminals whose fingerprints were held by the United States or its allies. In one case, DHS was able to identify through his fingerprints a man arriving from Costa Rica who had been hunted unsuccessfully by Interpol for a decade for embezzlement. In another case a murder suspect from Russia was apprehending trying to cross from Canada. In 2005, the 9/11 Public Discourse Project, which was set by the ten commissioners to press for full implementation of the 9/11 Commission's recommendations, gave US-VISIT a strong passing grade: a B on a report card littered with Fs, Ds, and Cs. For Williams, the best compliment of all was one he got from Rob Bonner. "He came up to me at one point, and he said, 'You know, I didn't think this was a good idea. But you've done an excellent job.'"

THE CREATION OF US-VISIT WAS the signature accomplishment of Ridge's tenure at DHS. By September 2004, the system was working well enough that it was expanded to include all travelers coming from Europe, Japan, and other countries where visas were not required to visit the United States. Over its first four years, it would capture the fingerprints and other data from some 90 million travelers to the United States. Some 1,500 people would be denied entry into the United States because of some sort of adverse information, most of them visa overstayers, but some of them criminals. And it did so without disrupting the movement of people into the United States, which had been one of Ridge's top priorities. From a risk management perspective, it seemed to pass the test: it increased security with minimal disruption.

But as a tool for keeping terrorists out of the country, it raised as many questions as it answered. Unless the United States was lucky enough to have a fingerprint record, the system would not by itself keep even a known terrorist out of the country. And it was no use against a plotter who was unknown to U.S. intelligence. The system was universal, so it did not raise the same complaints over discrimination and racial targeting that had been made against the NSEERS system. But ultimately its rationale was the same. US-VISIT would identify those who had overstayed visas. Five of the hijackers had overstayed their visas. Therefore, if the United States had in place a system that enabled the government to identify and deport those who remained in the country illegally, then maybe a future act of terrorism would be prevented. But was the United States really prepared to arrest and deport every illegal immigrant because a handful might be terrorists?

# Chapter 8

# THE FENCE

*Fearful people build walls; confident people tear them down.*
—President George W. Bush, September 6, 2001

In June 2004, a dozen Border Patrol officials in southern California launched a sweep in search of illegal immigrants, rounding up and arresting some 450 people over several weeks in the suburbs of San Diego and Los Angeles. The raids were unusual—most arrests of illegal migrants outside the immediate border area had taken place at worksites, and even then the numbers were not particularly large. While several surveys had estimated that some 11 to 12 million illegal immigrants were living in the United States in 2004, just over 100,000 had been arrested that year in so-called interior raids, slightly fewer than was normal during the 1990s.

The approach by the Temecula Border Patrol was much more direct—suspects were questioned at bus stops and outside schools, churches, and hospitals or were pulled over in their cars. Those who could not prove lawful residence were arrested, and many were deported. The arrests were sensational and controversial. Opponents of illegal immigration hailed the sweeps as the first serious effort at immigration enforcement that the local region had seen since the 9/11 attacks, while local Spanish-language newspapers were filled with frightening stories that led even some legal Hispanic immigrants to stay away from churches or keep their kids home from school.

Since 1994, when Governor Pete Wilson backed Proposition 187 to deny education and social services to illegal immigrants, no place in the country had been more divided on the issue than California. Critics argued that educating the children of illegal migrants or caring for them in hospitals was bankrupting the state, while sympathizers said that the state's lucrative agriculture and tourism industries would collapse without the migrant labor force.

When the Temecula sweeps were launched, Asa Hutchinson at DHS immediately began getting complaints from some members of Congress. After a brief investigation, he ordered a halt to the arrests. The decision was couched in bureaucratic terms—such actions, he argued, should have been carried out by Immigration and Customs Enforcement agents responsible for interior arrests, not by the Border Patrol, whose primary responsibility was to police the immediate border area. That move provoked its own backlash among some people in the region, who believed that Washington was making no serious effort to crack down on the continued high level of illegal migration over the southern border, which if anything had accelerated since the 1990s. At the urging of Darell Issa, a local Republican member of Congress who was getting pressure from the communities over the halt, Hutchinson agreed to accompany him to Temecula to host a town hall meeting on the issue.

The meeting, held in a local auditorium, was expected to attract about two hundred people. Instead, nearly a thousand showed up, spilling outside the hall into the streets. Protestors stood outside waving placards that shouted "Deport Asa." In front of a hostile crowd, Hutchinson tried to make a constitutional and bureaucratic defense of his decision to shut down the sweeps. He argued that Border Patrol agents should be patrolling the border and did not have the right or the responsibility to do identification checks inside the country in search of illegal migrants. DHS, he said, wanted agents responding only to specific intelligence and not doing random searches. He was shouted down. His efforts to appeal to family values were no more successful. "The thing about the illegal population in the United States, most of them work hard, they love their family," he said to the jeering audience.

In the weeks leading up to the meeting, Hutchinson's office had been flooded with e-mails and letters protesting his decision, many of them encouraged by local radio broadcasters John Kobylt and Ken Champeau, who used their program, *The John and Ken Show*, to campaign for a broad crackdown on illegal immigrants. They were part of an increasingly vocal campaign on local and national talk radio programs, and on national television, led by Lou Dobbs of CNN, calling for a clampdown on illegal immigration. In an effort to defuse the opposition, Hutchinson agreed to appear on *The John and Ken Show*. "That was a mistake," he admitted later.

Kobylt quickly had Hutchinson tongue-tied, leaving him sounding defensive and evasive as he tried to duck any responsibility for ordering an end to the sweeps and refused to make a clear commitment to restart them. The Bush administration, the broadcaster charged, was "not doing its job in protecting southern California from the illegal alien invasion." Hutchinson tried to push back, citing raids on a handful of employers in the United States, including the giant retailer Wal-Mart, but could recall no specific arrests in California. He promised to continue enforcement actions but refused to make any pledges on when and where. He said he was committed to enforcing the law, but had no explanation for the millions of illegal migrants who had easily managed to avoid law enforcement.

Finally, the talk show host hit on an argument that Hutchinson could not duck. "How come after 9/11 we didn't seal off the border with Mexico? I've heard your boss Tom Ridge talking about the threat to America. With tens of thousands of people coming over the Mexican border each year, if not more, don't you think Al Qaeda could be among them?" Hutchinson was cornered. "That's a concern," he admitted. "If we cannot protect our border from economic migrants, we cannot protect our border from terrorists."

It had taken a relentless, badgering radio talk show host to expose the obvious contradiction at the heart of the Bush administration's post-9/11 effort to shore up the U.S. borders against terrorists. Bush believed in keeping the borders as open as possible, particularly with Mexico. He had no desire to see a crackdown along the country's southern border, or to see federal agents operating in his name engaged in sweeps of Hispanic immigrant communities in an effort to flush out those in the country illegally. Yet in the aftermath of the terrorist attacks, he had authorized a strategy in which tough enforcement of immigration laws was the primary weapon used to keep suspected terrorists out of the country, or to detain them if they were already inside the United States. If immigration enforcement was the weapon of choice, how could the administration simply ignore Hispanic immigrants, where the illegal population numbered in the millions? If porous borders were a danger to the country—as many in his administration had repeatedly asserted—how could he look the other way while thousands of Mexicans and other Latin Americans found ways to simply walk into the country unannounced every day? How could he guarantee that those same routes through the desert or across the river would not someday be used by terrorists? It was a question for which the technocratic proponents of smart borders had no convincing answers. But the cops did.

For most of Bush's first term, his administration had tried to avoid the issue of whether stopping terrorists at the border would require keeping out all illegal migrants—particularly the millions who had come from Mexico seeking better-paying jobs. At times the answer appeared to be yes. The White House's 2002 "National Strategy for Homeland Security" had included "illegal migrants" along with terrorists, the implements of terrorism, international organized crime, illegal drugs, cyber crime, and destruction or theft of natural resources on the list of bad things that would be halted by the smart border of the future. But it did not even hint at a strategy for how the thousands of miles of unsecured U.S. land borders might actually be sealed against such ills, or how many billions of dollars would be required for the task. Instead it merely asserted that "the federal government will allocate resources in a balanced way to manage risk in our border and transportation security systems while ensuring the expedient flows of goods, services and people."

Schemes such as advance passenger information and reservation data, the integration of terrorist watch lists, and SEVIS had been designed to help identify potential terrorist concerns with minimal disruption to travel into the United States. Even the heavier-handed programs like NSEERS and the Visas Mantis and Condor screening that had caused so much disruption had at least been targeted, however crudely, at particular groups deemed likely to pose a terrorist threat. But US-VISIT was the first program to contemplate a far more ambitious goal—that the United States might actually be able identify every foreign traveler who had come legally to the United States and know whether they had left the country when they were required to. That begged the obvious question: what about those who had come illegally in the first place? If security against terrorists required keeping track of millions of people who had come to the country legally, then surely it required stopping those who were coming illegally.

Shortly after 9/11, the United States and Mexico had begun their own negotiations to try to emulate the U.S.-Canada Smart Border Accord. The two countries signed a similar agreement to improve information sharing and intelligence cooperation in March 2002, but the United States never had any faith that the Mexican government could live up to its end of the deals. "The difference is we have close cooperation with the Canadian authorities," said Bruce Lawlor. "In Canada we have a great deal of confidence that if we know there's a problem we can call the Canadian authorities and they will act. That is not the case with Mexico. They view the border as our problem, not their problem. The Canadians view the border as our problem collectively." Mexican officials, in turn, told the United States that they were prepared to enter into comprehensive agreements to improve security against terrorism, but only as part of a package that also addressed the migration issue. In 2002, the United States was not prepared to even consider such a concession.

Under Ridge, the Department of Homeland Security had all but avoided the issue of unauthorized migrants crossing from Mexico. Since the 9/11 attacks, attention to securing the country's southern border had actually waned. In the 1990s, amid growing concern in California, Arizona, and Texas over illegal immigration, Congress had approved a threefold increase in the number of agents along the southern border, from 3,000 to slightly over 9,000. But since the 9/11 attacks, that growth had stopped. Instead, following the directions of Congress in the USA Patriot Act, the administration had rushed to recruit new agents for the northern border with Canada, which was the bigger concern from a terrorism perspective. In just three years, the number of agents there had grown from 350 to nearly 1,000, tripling the force but leaving it still just a fraction of the one deployed along the southern border. From a terrorism perspective, it was an obvious choice—Al Qaeda had already tried to use Canada as an overland route to the United States, and there were many reasons to fear it could do so in the future. The southern border was not immune from the threat. There were concerns in particular that established routes for drug smuggling from Mexico into the United States—which had become a growing problem since the Coast Guard had largely succeeded in shutting down the Caribbean sea routes from South America to the Gulf Coast—might be used to smuggle terrorists or their weapons across the border. But it was largely a hypothetical fear, and there were clearer and more present dangers from the Middle East, parts of Asia, Europe, and Canada.

Ridge said very little about illegal immigration during his time in office. His clearest statement was in December 2003, when in response to a question he told a town hall meeting in Florida that most illegal immigrants in the United States were not a threat to national security and should be given "some kind of legal status." He made no link to homeland security or to the war on terrorism, but his aides defended the position on terrorism grounds, saying that it would strengthen security to be able to identify illegal migrants living in the country rather than forcing them to continue to live and work in the shadows.

AFTER 9/11, THE NEGOTIATIONS WITH Mexico on a migration accord had come to an abrupt halt. Bush had hoped to bring along the Congress by starting with passage of the Development, Relief and Education for Alien Minors (DREAM) Act, which would have taken a small first step by granting legal residence to any illegal migrant who was brought to the United States as a child and then attended college or served in the military. It would also have guaranteed lower in-state tuition rates for those students at state colleges. After 9/11 there was "there was no, zero, zilch interest," said John Maisto, who handled Western Hemisphere affairs in the White House. Mexico's decision in 2003 to oppose the U.S. invasion of Iraq from its seat on the UN Security Council had further soured relations between the two countries and reduced prospects for cooperation on migration issues.

Bush had never abandoned the idea of resolving the illegal immigration issue, however. Even while his administration had been consumed with the wars in Afghanistan and Iraq, a small group of White House officials had continued to work quietly on immigration reform proposals. It was led by a team in the White House Domestic Policy Council and was focused heavily on the thorny problem of selling Congress on a scheme that would allow many of the illegal immigrants already in the United States to remain, much as had been done in the last big overhaul of immigration laws in 1986. There was particular concern over how to design a program that would not be perceived as "amnesty," because there was widespread agreement that the amnesty for illegal immigrants in the 1986 law had made the problem worse.

When President Bush walked into the East Room of the White House in January 2004, a president defined by 9/11 gave little sign that he recognized how much 9/11—and his administration's own reaction to the attacks—had changed the debate over immigration. Instead, he unveiled a generous plan that envisioned what amounted to a pardon for the millions of illegal immigrants already living in the United States.

At another time it could have been an inspirational speech. "Over the generations we have received energetic, ambitious, optimistic people from every part of the world," Bush said. "By tradition and conviction, our country is a welcoming society. America is a stronger and better nation because of the hard work and the faith and entrepreneurial spirit of immigrants. . . . One of the primary reasons America became a great power in the twentieth century is because we welcomed the talent and the character and the patriotism of immigrant families."

He sympathized with the plight of illegal migrants trying to enter the United States. "Many undocumented workers have walked mile after mile, through the heat of the day and the cold of the night," he said. "Some have risked their lives in dangerous desert border crossings, or entrusted their lives to the brutal rings of heartless human smugglers. Workers who seek only to earn a living end up in the shadows of American life—fearful, often abused and exploited."

His proposal called for the creation of a new temporary worker program that would allow Mexicans to work in the United States and to move freely back and forth across the border. This was intended to end the incentive for people to cross over and work illegally in the United States, and was to be accompanied by tougher sanctions against employers who hired illegal immigrants. For those already in the country unlawfully, they would be eligible for the new program, provided they paid a one-time penalty fee. The White House attempted to avoid the "amnesty" label by pointing out that illegal migrants would not automatically be eligible for permanent residence or citizenship, as had been the case in the 1986 immigration reform legislation.

While most of the speech concerned the economic benefits of immigration, Bush argued that immigration reform would also allow for a more targeted, focused approach in the war on terrorism.

"Our homeland will be more secure when we can better account for those who enter our country, instead of the current situation in which millions of people are unknown, unknown to the law," he said. "Law enforcement will face fewer problems with undocumented workers, and will be better able to focus on the true threats to our nation from criminals and terrorists."

In the middle of an election year, Congress was not prepared to take up the president's call to move on immigration reform, and Bush did not push for any immediate action. By the time legislation was introduced the following spring, Tom Ridge was no longer the man responsible for seeing it through.

WHEN MICHAEL CHERTOFF BECAME THE new secretary of Homeland Security in February 2005, he inherited a department that was deeply dysfunctional and poisoned by internal rivalries, but one that had nonetheless managed to make some significant progress in using border controls to stiffen the United States' defenses against terrorism. Chertoff was not Bush's first choice to replace Ridge; the White House had picked Bernard Kerik, the New York City police chief and a close associate of New York City mayor Rudy Giuliani. It looked like another effort by the administration to continue reminding the public of 9/11 by more closely associating itself with Giuliani and his heroic image after the attacks. But Kerik withdrew his name when it was revealed that he had hired illegal immigrants to work as his housekeeper and nanny, a convenient excuse for much deeper problems that would eventually see him indicted on tax evasion and corruption charges.

Chertoff's record was mostly outside the public eye. A rabbi's son who had graduated magna cum laude from Harvard Law School in 1978, Chertoff had begun his federal government career in the mid-1980s working for Giuliani, who was then the U.S. attorney for Manhattan, and he became lead prosecutor in a series of Mafia investigations. He quickly climbed up the ranks of the Justice Department, becoming the U.S. attorney for New Jersey in 1990. He was reappointed by Bill Clinton after the Democrats captured the White House in 1993, but stayed only a year before returning to private practice. In 1995 and 1996, he was brought in by Senate Republicans to serve as special counsel on the Whitewater investigation of alleged financial wrongdoings by the Clintons, a position that reassured skeptics in the Republican Party who were concerned about his political loyalties.

In many ways Chertoff was the anti-Ridge. Ridge was an ebullient politician, a back-slapper who made everyone around him feel important. Chertoff had no time for such pleasantries. Hawk-eyed and always intensely focused, he had the power to stare down rivals and possessed an intellect and a sharp tongue that, honed by years of courtroom practice, as one admiring reporter put it, "can make smart people look stupid." Ridge's leadership style was to try to build consensus before moving forward; Chertoff, in contrast, at times seemed almost too decisive. His decision while in the Justice Department to prosecute Arthur Andersen, the auditing firm, as part of the investigation into the financial fraud that led to the collapse of energy giant Enron, ended up destroying the venerable company, even though its conviction on obstruction of justice charges was later slapped down by the Supreme Court.

"There's nothing sloppy about Michael. He likes to win," a friend who worked with him in New York City told the *Washington Post*. "As my kids would say, you could classify him as a nerd. He lives and breathes and thinks this stuff, but I wouldn't want to get in his way at Homeland Security."

At his Senate confirmation hearing before Democrats in February 2005, however, it was not politics or his courtroom manner that was at issue, but his record in the Justice Department. Following Bush's election, he had rejoined the department as John Ashcroft's assistant attorney general in charge of the criminal division, one of the department's most powerful posts. In that position, he had been among the most forceful advocates for the aggressive use of immigration laws to detain terrorist suspects, a tactic that had led to hundreds of innocent people being imprisoned for many months, and in some cases beaten and abused while in detention.

At his confirmation hearing, however, he cleverly walked the line between justifying such abuses and repudiating his own actions. He insisted that the detention policy was sound but that he had not participated in the decisions on where and how those arrested would be jailed. "I was troubled to see that certainly the plan as conceived had not always been executed perfectly," he said. Senator Joe Lieberman, the Democrat who had been a leading advocate for the creation of DHS, pushed for a commitment by Chertoff to reconsider how immigration law was being used in the war on terrorism. "Immigration law is greatly lacking in some of the fundamental due process protections that we associate with what it means to be American or to be in America," Lieberman said. Chertoff promised to work on the issue.

But there was no indication that he had rethought the approach. Indeed in a December 2003 essay for the conservative *Weekly Standard*, after he had left the Justice Department and been appointed by President Bush as an appeals court judge, he insisted that: "In the wake of September 11, the government quite self-consciously avoided the kinds of harsh measures common in previous wars. During the nineteenth and well into the twentieth centuries, the government responded to domestic violence with a panoply of extraordinary measures, including suppression of criticism; separate treatment of noncitizens; arrests and searches without warrants; and preventive detention." He was confirmed as Homeland Security secretary by a vote of 98 to 0; even Senator Hillary Rodham Clinton, who had voted against his judicial nomination in 2003 over Chertoff's role in the Whitewater investigation, supported him this time.

AFTER TAKING CHARGE AT DHS, Chertoff launched a comprehensive review of the department and went into a shell with his closest advisers while he tried to figure out what to do with the massive structure he had inherited. In early July, he unveiled a reorganization dubbed DHS 2.0 that did away with the Border and Transportation Security arm, which had battled repeatedly with the

Customs and Border Protection agency, and created a new policy secretariat aimed at giving the department the strategic direction it had been lacking under Ridge.

While the reorganization was generally well-received, those left over from the Ridge regime quickly felt left out. The most significant casualty was US-VISIT, Ridge's signature program at the border. After the reorganization, the US-VISIT office was put under the direct authority of the new deputy secretary, Michael Jackson, who had been a protégé of Andrew Card's, serving as his chief of staff when Card was secretary of Transportation for the first President Bush. Jackson had been the chief operating officer at Lockheed Martin before returning to the Transportation Department as deputy secretary in 2001, where he played a key role in implementing new airline security measures. Jackson was an enthusiastic proponent of "outsourcing" government functions to big private contractors like his former employer Lockheed. After he came to DHS, US-VISIT was one of thirty-one direct reports to Jackson in the new organizational chart. Jim Williams, who ran the program, said he couldn't even schedule a meeting with Jackson, and that eventually Jackson stopped returning his phone calls. In early 2006, Williams quit in frustration and took another senior job in the government as chief of government procurement for the General Services Administration.

But the program was also in trouble for reasons that had nothing to do with bureaucratic infighting. Despite the impressive success in rolling out the entry portion at airports, the rest of the scheme was far more technically complicated. DHS met the congressional deadline for introducing the scheme at U.S. land borders at the end of 2005, but it was implemented in a minimal way that resulted in border agents taking fingerprints from less than 2 percent of those crossing by land. Only travelers who would otherwise have required a visa to come to the United States, which excluded almost all Canadians and most Mexicans, were required to enroll in the program.

The exit portion of the system was even more problematic.

Unlike many European countries, U.S. airports are not configured in a way that funnels international travelers through checkpoints that can be used by border officials to record an exit from the country. One possibility was to get Transportation Security Administration officials who were screening passengers for dangerous objects to do the checkout portion. But TSA had no interest in taking on the task, and it was not clear how international passengers could easily be segregated from domestic passengers in airport screening. A second possibility, the one DHS is now pursuing, was to get the airlines to take the fingerprints when foreign passengers checked in for international flights. But the airlines argued that, with the check-in process increasingly becoming automated, it would further slow down an already overburdened system by forcing international passengers to check in with agents on every flight.

Airports were easy compared with the land borders. Any scheme that envisioned forcing everyone to get out of their cars and give a fingerprint before leaving the country was obviously a nonstarter. U.S. cities along the Mexican and Canadian borders were already complaining that their economies would be devastated if such a plan were implemented. DHS began experimenting with radio-frequency technologies that in theory could allow travel documents such as passports to be read remotely from the vehicles as cars approached the border. Such a system would not have the certainty of a fingerprint, but some DHS officials saw it as a promising way to start. They argued that the exit system should be put into place gradually as the technology improved. Then a major GAO investigation released in December 2006 concluded that the systems could not read the documents accurately most of the time, and that any technical solution was still years away. Chertoff, who along with his deputy Jackson had little faith in the technology, shut down the land exit pilot program immediately after.

The decision was hailed as a victory by border communities worried about delays. Stewart Baker, a former general counsel at the National Security Agency who came out of private law practice to become Chertoff's policy chief, said that implementing the exit portion would cost "tens of billions of dollars" and was simply not feasible. "It is a pretty daunting set of costs, both for the U.S. government and the economy," he told the *New York Times*. "There are a lot of good ideas and things that would make the country safer. But when you have to sit down and compare all the good ideas people have developed against each other, with a limited budget, you have to make choices that are much harder."

Chertoff said the scheme could not be implemented without enormous disruptions along the border. "If we required all the people leaving the country by land going into Canada to stop to give a biometric print," he told reporters following the decision, "you would see lines that are ten or fifteen miles long, stretching from the border deeply into New York or into Detroit." Baker said that, while the entry screening helps to keep terrorists out of the country, an exit system would be "an immigration accounting system. It's less about safety and more about immigration record-keeping."

Chertoff was not entirely hostile to the program. In particular, he saw the value of a more comprehensive entry (as opposed to exit) system that would permit the fingerprints of foreign travelers to be checked against the full U.S. database of criminal and suspected terrorists. In late 2007, DHS began rolling out new fingerprint readers at U.S. airports to take all ten prints from incoming travelers. Improvements in the technology had allowed the development of readers that were nearly as fast as the two-print readers, and the growing number of prints in the system—reaching over 90 million by the end of 2008—had resulted in a growing number of false matches due to the sheer volume of prints. The ten-print readers promised greater accuracy that would reduce those errors, and greater security as well.

While Williams and other former DHS officials acknowledged the formidable technical problems that still faced US-VISIT, they believed that Chertoff and Jackson soured on the program largely because it was a Ridge creation on which they could not leave their own mark. "It just lost momentum. Things that we wanted to do just sat on the deputy secretary's desk," Williams said. "We became part of the old program."

WITH PRESIDENT BUSH'S DECISION TO push for immigration reform, the new priority was how to seal the southern border against illegal migration. In the Congress, supporters of the president's plan for immigration reform—led by Republican Senator John McCain and Democratic Senator Ted Kennedy—introduced legislation in May 2005 to create a new guestworker program and offer a path to citizenship for illegal immigrants already in the United States. The goal was to reintroduce the kind of circularity that had historically existed between the U.S. and Mexico, with Mexicans crossing the border freely to work in the United States, often for just part of the year, and returning home just as freely. The bill was even more explicit than Bush had wanted in offering an amnesty for illegal migrants already in the United States. In essence it would have given sanction to the kind of deal that Bush and Mexico's president, Vicente Fox, had been negotiating up to the eve of 9/11 and that Bush had laid out in his January 2004 speech.

But instead of building bipartisan consensus, it provoked a furious backlash, led by House Judiciary Committee chairman Jim Sensenbrenner and other Republican conservatives who had been important allies for the administration in its counterterrorism initiatives. Sensenbrenner had taken the lead on much of the legislation that built the post-9/11 border security architecture, often working closely with the administration. He was particularly useful in setting deadlines that had helped the administration press Europe to improve the security of its passports and to offer up advanced information on travelers coming to the United States. "Sensenbrenner was a great ally. We needed a bad cop and he played the role," said Asa Hutchinson. Sometimes he had gone a bit too far for the administration's liking. President Bush had been forced to make a personal plea to Sensenbrenner to extend the passport deadlines for two years when it became clear that several

European countries would miss the deadline; Sensenbrenner gave him one year.

But Sensenbrenner had long been a staunch opponent of illegal immigration, earning a 100 percent approval rating from the anti-immigration organization FAIR. And as the illegal immigrant population continued to grow in the United States, that stance had become increasingly popular in the Republican Party. The House Immigration Caucus, headed by Tom Tancredo, the virulently anti-immigrant Colorado Republican, had grown from a handful of members in 1999 to more than ninety by 2006. "I recognized right from the beginning that amnesty would never be accepted by the American people," said Sensenbrenner. "I don't think the president realized that it was beyond his capability to define amnesty in his own terms."

The terrorist attacks had also given traditional immigration opponents a club they had long been lacking. It was one thing to argue that immigrants were overpopulating the schools or draining social service budgets or that a new generation of immigrants would for some reason be more difficult to assimilate than the previous generations; it was another to argue that some of them might be plotting to kill thousands of Americans. Sensenbrenner said that as new security mechanisms had been created to make legal entry into the United States more difficult, "it became more and more evident that the next round of terrorists would not get their passports stamped at a port of entry when it was so easy to enter the country illegally."

Immediately after 9/11, groups like FAIR and the Center for Immigration Studies (CIS) seized on the terrorist threat as the most potent rationale for the crackdown on illegal immigrants they had long been advocating, and even for a reduction in the number of legal migrants. Mark Krikorian, the executive director of CIS, argued that while "defeating and discrediting radical Islam is the ultimate objective, our first goal has to be to keep the enemy from crossing our border and ferreting out those who have already made it in." Ultimately, he argued, "The security implications of large foreign-born populations cannot be avoided"—the only way to protect the country against terrorism was to make each step along the immigration trajectory as difficult as possible, in order to weed out potential terrorists.

After 9/11, Congress, and particularly the Republican House, had generally been deferential to the administration on terrorism initiatives, which were considered matters of national security. As long as the administration's agenda consisted of tightening the borders in the name of security, Sensenbrenner was a reliable ally. The same was not true, however, of immigration reform, which had long been considered a prerogative of Congress. Sensenbrenner and the House Republicans flatly rejected the McCain-Kennedy bill, insisting that the border must first be secured against illegal migration before any other initiatives could be implemented. They introduced legislation, which passed the House in December 2005, that promised one of the toughest crackdowns in American history on illegal immigration. It made illegal entry into the United States a felony, so that border crossers risked not just being turned back but potentially imprisoned for up to a year. It required mandatory detention of all non-Mexican illegal migrants until they could be deported. It made it a felony to offer any sort of assistance to an illegal immigrant living in the United States. Finally, and most notoriously, it called for the construction of 700 miles of double-layered fencing along the nearly 2,000-mile southern border.

For two years after the introduction of the McCain-Kennedy bill, the two sides were deadlocked. The Sensenbrenner bill could get through the House, but could not pass the more evenly divided Senate. Even a toughened-up version of McCain-Kennedy could not win assent in the House. But one thing was certain: whatever the legislative outcome, DHS would be asked to expand significantly what was already a vast effort to keep illegal immigrants out of the country. Under Chertoff, whose background was all in law enforcement, DHS embraced the task enthusiastically.

WHILE ROB BONNER WAS ONE of the first proponents of the smart border, which called for using information to identify possible terrorists without disrupting legal travel across the borders, he in no way saw this in conflict with the traditional Customs and INS missions of keeping out illegal immigrants. Instead it was Bush's White House that initially had no desire for a crackdown on the southern border, fearing it would hurt the president's effort to build support with Hispanic voters. But Bonner was eager. At one point he was even slapped down in private by Chertoff for speaking out too enthusiastically about the Minutemen, a self-styled citizen's militia group that was carrying out armed patrols of the border region in Arizona and California. Bonner told the *New York Times* that it was useful "having citizens that would be willing to volunteer to help the Border Patrol."

Since the middle of 2004, Bonner's Customs and Border Protection had been working on a program it dubbed America's Shield Initiative (ASI), which was aimed at using new surveillance methods such as remote sensors, spy drones, and other high-tech means to gain "operational control" over the southern border. It was couched in the broadest possible terms as an effort to "secure the borders against illegal aliens, potential terrorists, weapons of mass destruction, illegal drugs, and other contraband."

The initiative had been bedeviled from the outset. A precursor program to use remote surveillance along the Canadian and Mexican borders, launched in 1997, was shut down after an investigation by the inspector general of the General Services Administration discovered poorly installed defective equipment that had not been properly supervised by the government's contractor. While CBP officials insisted that they had learned from the mistakes, ASI ran into a similar set of problems. The plan called for using pilotless aircraft and motion sensors along the southern border—at a cost of $2.5 billion over five years—to help detect illegal migrants trying to walk across the desert into the United States. But in an eight-month test in Arizona, the technology only succeeded in helping Border Patrol agents capture about 1,300 illegal immigrants, less than half a percent of the total number captured in the region during that same eight months. Some agents denounced it as a publicity-grabbing waste of money, and in early 2006, after a critical GAO report, ASI was scrapped as well. DHS officials say that Chertoff's deputy Michael Jackson was particularly eager to halt the program, believing it should be taken away from CBP and given to a private contractor.

Much as with US-VISIT, the programs for the southern border envisioned a very different use for technology than in the original counterterrorism programs that had been embraced by the technocrats after 9/11. The technocrats' idea was to use technology to help sift out a small number of potential terrorist threats from the huge mass of ordinary travelers. US-VISIT had already changed that approach by insisting that security required the ability to monitor the legal entry and exit of every foreigner coming to the United States, not just those the government had some particular reason to worry about. ASI took the next logical step by premising security on the ability to stop every illegal migrant as well.

The twin failures of previous border control initiatives, coupled with technical problems that were plaguing efforts to complete US-VISIT, should have warned Chertoff on the difficulties of grand schemes aimed at controlling entry into the United States. Instead, in November 2005 he unveiled the biggest effort yet, known as the Secure Border Initiative (SBI). SBI was much like its predecessor initiatives, only bigger and with a greater role for the private sector. Technology was a key part: Boeing, which like many of the big government contractors had discovered that closing borders was almost as lucrative as opening them, was contracted to develop a network of "virtual fences" in which cameras and radar set atop towers along the border were supposed to detect people trying to sneak into the country. Additional unmanned aerial vehicles, including the Predator, first used by the CIA and the Air Force, would be deployed to monitor even more remote regions. But SBI also called for ramping up more traditional enforcement measures, such as vastly increasing the number of Border Patrol agents and adding new agents to do interior raids. The long-standing practice of "catch and release" in which many illegal migrants were freed until their immigration hearings would be ended by adding thousands of detention beds to hold them in custody and "re-engineering" the process to deport people more quickly. Through SBI and other measures, DHS promised that it could gain operational control over the borders by 2013, at a cost of some $8 billion.

Chertoff's embrace of the southern border strategy was supposed to be of a piece with Bush's immigration reform proposal. He frequently argued in public that efforts to stop illegal migration would fail unless there were new legal channels for immigrants or temporary workers to come to the United States. "When you try to fight economic reality, it is at best an extremely expensive and very, very difficult process and almost always doomed to failure," he said in early 2006. But from a terrorism perspective, his decision to pour resources into the southern border—which was also being pushed aggresively by Congress—was a perplexing one. Indeed, he admitted in a Fox Radio broadcast in June 2007 that he did not know of a single case where terrorists had used the southern border to cross into the United States.

Yet unlike his predecessor, Tom Ridge, who was constantly torn between tough enforcement and facilitation of commerce and travel, Chertoff had no such ambivalence about his own role. Immigration reform would make enforcement easier, but enforcement was his priority regardless. Over time, he became less and less tolerant of complaints that border security measures were damaging the country by keeping out those it wanted to let in.

WITH THE CONGRESS DIVIDED OVER immigration reform, the House and Senate forged ahead on the one measure on which they could agree—the construction of a fence along the border. Just a week before the November 2006 congressional elections, Bush signed the bill. "Unfortunately, the United States has not been in complete control of its border for decades and, therefore, illegal immigration has been on the rise," he said. "We have a responsibility to enforce our laws. We have a responsibility to secure our borders. We take this responsibility seriously." The bill directed that some 700 miles of pedestrian and vehicle fencing be built along the border with Mexico.

In 2007, the Senate made one more attempt to pass an immigration reform bill. But even with the Democrats gaining seats in the Senate and taking back control of the House, the divisions of the previous year over immigration had become even deeper. A final effort at compromise died in the Senate in June. The bitterness carried over into the primary campaign for the presidential nominations. John McCain, who had been expected to win the Republican nomination easily, suffered a near-death experience over opposition to his immigration proposals among many Republicans. Chastened, McCain shifted his stance and promised that if he became president, he would secure the border first before moving forward with other parts of his immigration plan. His campaign recovered.

Within weeks of the collapse, Chertoff was promising the toughest enforcement effort in the country's history. He pledged that by the end of 2008, DHS would field more than 18,000 Border Patrol agents, nearly double the number he had inherited when he came to office, and that 370 miles of the border fence would be built. He promised to quadruple the number of ICE teams charged with hunting down illegal immigrants and build enough detention beds so that everyone caught inside the country illegally could be held in jail until they were deported. "Until Congress chooses to act," he said, "we are going to be taking some energetic steps of our own."

WITH CHERTOFF'S DECISION TO MAKE tough immigration enforcement the priority of the Department of Homeland Security, the original goal of stopping terrorists faded further and further from the center of DHS activities. According to a study in mid-2007 by TRAC, a university group that does detailed research based on government documents uncovered through Freedom of Information Act requests, the growing enforcement effort has been almost wholly unrelated to terrorism. In the first three years of the department's existence, which is the latest data available, DHS filed immigration charges against more than 814,000 people; in only a dozen of those cases did DHS make a claim of terrorism or support for terrorism. That was a smaller number than before the 9/11 attacks. Nonetheless, by 2007 immigration had become the highest law enforcement priority of the U.S. government. That year, more than a quarter of all criminal cases investigated by the Justice Department were immigration-related cases, up from just 10 percent a decade before. But if the counterterrorism impact is unclear, there is no question that the U.S. government is identifying and deporting many more illegal immigrants than ever before; since 2001, the annual level of deportations has more than doubled to nearly 250,000 a year, by far the biggest number in U.S. history.

On any given day now, more than thirty thousand people—including not just illegal immigrants but also legal ones convicted of what are often minor crimes—are being held in jails across the country awaiting deportation. Refugees seeking political asylum are similarly jailed until their cases are resolved; if they arrive with families, their children, including small children, are imprisoned with them. As with those detained after 9/11, many languish in jail for months and occasionally even years while their cases grind through the immigration legal bureaucracy.

Indeed, the campaign is starting to resemble what Kris Kobach had wanted all along. Kobach was the ambitious young Justice Department official who, after 9/11, persuaded Attorney General John Ashcroft that immigration law was the most powerful weapon he had in the fight against terrorism. The NSEERS scheme he launched ensnared thousands of people for immigration violations in the name of fighting terrorism. After leaving the Justice Department and going back to his career as a law professor, he was retained by FAIR, the anti-immigration lobby group, to lead a lawsuit against Kansas's policy of allowing the children of illegal immigrants who had lived in the state and graduated from Kansas high schools to pay lower in-state tuition rates at state universities. He defended the town of Hazelton, Pennsylvania, which was one of the first places in the country to crack down on illegal immigrants by authorizing large fines against landlords who rented to them and denying business permits to companies that employed them. The ordinance was struck down by a federal district court in 2007 on the grounds that only the federal government could pass and enforce immigration laws.

Kobach had wanted to enlist every local and state police force in trying to identify illegal immigrants so that every time a driver was pulled over for speeding or a pedestrian ticketed for jaywalking, his immigration status would be checked. Since the collapse of the immigration reform bill, more than half the states in the United States have given their cops that power, with the blessing of DHS. Dozens of cities have pledged that local police will do the same and are handing over to DHS anyone who cannot prove his or her legal status in the United States, further distracting DHS from its core mission of keeping out terrorists.

DHS officials argue that the statistics on immigration enforcement tell a misleading story about the fight against terrorism. In some cases, they say, immigration charges are filed when investigators believe that more serious offenses have been committed, only because the goal is usually to deport the offender and simple immigration violations are easier to prove than more complex criminal or terrorism charges. They argue that the deterrent value of aggressive immigration enforcement is real but difficult to measure.

Critics who say that the United States will never be able to stop every illegal migrant are missing the point, they argue. The goal is to make it so difficult and expensive to get here illegally—by forcing migrants to hire smugglers or to pursue other elaborate strategies to get into the country—that most will decide it's not worth the cost and simply give up. Further, by raising the difficulty of entering, it increases the odds that the government will be able to identify and stop genuinely dangerous people like terrorists and criminals. "It's much harder to get into the United States, and that's progress," said a former senior DHS official. "Now you have to hire a smuggler, which gives us an opportunity to penetrate the smuggling networks, which helps us to identify the high-threat folks. The more planning it takes, the more opportunities we have."

The economic costs of the enforcement campaign are still being measured. Some farms, for instance, say they are no longer planting crops that require pickers because the Mexican workers who were once so readily available are no longer coming; others have watched crops rot because they could not hire enough pickers. And the diplomatic costs of building such barriers have already been high. John Maisto, who left the White House in 2003 and was appointed by Bush as U.S. ambassador to the Organization of American States, said the enforcement policy has been "poisonous" for U.S. relations with Latin America. "They fail to understand why we think it's necessary, why there's this reaction against people who are needed in the U.S. economy coming to work. They think it is racially motivated. They see it as a false U.S. focus on security."

Jorge Castañeda, the former Mexican foreign minister, put it more succinctly. For all his warmth to Mexico, and his liberal stance on immigration reform, President Bush will be remembered as "el presidente del muro," the president who tried to build the wall.

THE COLLAPSE OF IMMIGRATION REFORM also ended what had been the best opportunity for addressing the myriad problems that still remain for people who want to come to the United States legally. The effort by Ridge's DHS and the State Department to entice foreigners back to the United States was gradually replaced by a new series of measures that, while each could be justified on security grounds, keep making it incrementally more difficult to travel to the United States. "DHS has literally been additive, additive, additive without a discussion of what the added benefit of the new measures is," says Frank Moss, who until 2006 was the top State Department official in charge of passport security.

In 2004, as part of an intelligence reform bill, Congress implemented the recommendation of the 9/11 Commission that the United States close "the North American loophole" by requiring a passport or other secure identification documents for travel to and from Canada, Mexico, and the Caribbean. The requirement, known as the Western Hemisphere Travel Initiative (WHTI), will be fully rolled out by mid-2009. It made considerable sense from a security perspective but set off a scramble in both the United States and Canada when the governments were unable to keep up with new demand for passports.

In December 2007, the United States raised the cost of applying for a temporary visa to $131, double what it had been before 9/11; if the application is rejected, the money is forfeited. And that doesn't include the cost of traveling to the U.S. embassy or consulate for the personal interview and fingerprints, which in many cases involves an overnight trip to a capital city. The State Department says that, because of the higher costs of security reviews, it is still losing money on each visa application.

On visa wait times, while improvements continue to be made from the post-9/11 period, it is still very difficult for many foreigners to get a visa to come to the United States. In 2007, fifty-three of the State Department's foreign consulates and embassies were still reporting wait times of thirty days or more to get a visa interview, though the delays have continued to be reduced.

Nor, with resources being poured into shoring up the southern border, was DHS doing anything to deal with a growing array of new delays that has continued to plague many aspects of the immigration and visa process. By 2006, more than 1 million people were waiting on the department to process their applications for permanent residence in the United States, many of these delayed by lengthy FBI security background checks. A survey in 2007 suggested that about one-third of these were considering leaving the United States, and with strong economic growth in countries like China and India they have many more opportunities that might lure them home.

The result has been that, while the government has taken some significant steps to ease travel to the United States, the perception of much of the world is that it is getting harder. "The problems haven't gone away; they've got worse in some respects," says Liam Schwartz, one of the most prominent immigration lawyers in Israel. "It's like the United States is doing its best to team up with foreign countries to stem the brain drain to the U.S. I'm contacted just about every day by colleagues who say their clients felt humiliated in applying for visas. The hit the U.S. has taken in its prestige abroad is just phenomenal."

In January 2008, the *Sunday Times* of London published an article in its survey on travel to the United States that began with this withering lead: "We would like to apologise for a terrible omission in last Sunday's feature '10 Steps to a Stress-Free Summer.' We forgot to include 'Don't go to the U.S.A.' . . . Nowhere else can a visitor expect such a spirit-crushingly frosty reception."

Such publicity has kept travelers away from the United States despite the plummeting dollar. In 2007, China displaced the United States as the world's third most-visited country, after France and Spain. Overseas travel to the United States was still down nearly 10 percent from pre-9/11 levels, at 23 million people, some 10 million fewer than what would have been expected if the United States had simply retained its share of the global travel boom—an unprecedented plunge.

The foreign student numbers, despite rebounding from the post-9/11 lows, have also been discouraging. The most recent survey by the Council of Graduate Schools found that the total number of foreign graduate student applications grew just 3 percent in 2008, the lowest since 2005. The study concluded that one cause is fierce competition from other countries for foreign students, as well as better efforts by countries such as China, India, and South Korea to keep their best students at home. But the visa problems and the perception of American hostility to foreign students remain major hurdles, the report said. "[M]any prospective students," it said, "see the United States as a dangerous and unwelcoming country."

Government officials charged with promoting foreign investment in the United States also say that the problems remain
serious. In a survey carried out in early 2008 by the Council on
State Governments, three out of four said they had run into problems getting visas for potential foreign investors in the state. Some
states—including Florida, Georgia, Massachusetts, Mississippi,
and Nevada—said the problems were serious, particularly for companies from China, India, and Brazil. Southern states, which have
been the most aggressive in trying to attract foreign investment,
reported the most difficulties.

In late 2007, the U.S. Commerce Department quietly published a paper entitled *Visas and Foreign Direct Investment*, which
gently suggested that the difficulty that foreign business travelers
faced in coming to the United States had reduced their willingness
to invest in the country. Commerce officials say that when they
travel around the world to promote American exports or encourage investment, they are bombarded with complaints about the
hurdles to traveling to the United States. The paper put it more
delicately. "The presence or perception of delays in obtaining the
necessary visas can give an international investor the impression
that it may be difficult to finalize or oversee an investment in the
United States," it said. Jerry Levine, the president of Mentor International, a San Francisco–based consulting group that develops
international business opportunities for companies and governments, says that on visas "the perception is very bad, but the reality
isn't too good either."

For companies seeking skilled employees from abroad, or trying
to bring in business customers, the picture remains only marginally
improved. Bill Reinsch, whose National Foreign Trade Council led
the corporate effort to roll back some of the post-9/11 restrictions,
said companies had largely given up fighting over the issue "and
devised ways to get around the delays and refusals." ExxonMobil has increasingly taken to meeting with customers and business
partners in Europe and Singapore. Information technology companies unable to get visas for foreign employees have relocated them

in other countries. In July 2007, Microsoft threw a small bomb by announcing that its new software development facility would be built in Vancouver, Canada, rather than at the company's head-quarters a hundred miles south, in Redmond, Washington. One of the main reasons for the decision, the company said, was that it would be easier to "recruit and retain highly skilled people affected by immigration issues in the United States." Jack Krumholz, the company's director of government affairs, said: "We currently do 85 percent of our development work in the United States, and we'd like to continue doing that. But if we can't hire the developers we need . . . we're going to have to look at other options to get the work done."

The company, along with many other high-tech companies, has been particularly frustrated by the cap on H1-B visas for skilled workers, which is set at just 65,000 to 85,000 annually. There had been hopes that the number would be increased as part of the im-migration reform legislation, but that hope died along with the Senate bill. Last year Microsoft was unable to get visas for a third of the foreign job candidates it wanted to hire. As a result, the compa-ny's chairman, Bill Gates, testified to Congress, "many U.S. firms, including Microsoft, have been forced to locate staff in countries that welcomed skilled foreign workers to do work that could oth-erwise have been done in the United States, if it were not for our counterproductive immigration policies." Bill Watkins, the chief executive of Seagate Technology, the maker of computer storage devices, said: "Every person who gets a Ph.D. in the U.S. should get a green card. I've got to hire those people. If I can't hire them here, we'll start moving the infrastructure of R&D offshore. I have R&D in Singapore now. I can hire MIT graduates there—and get subsidies for it."

The problems are not limited to the high-tech industries. A 2007 report on New York City's financial industry warned that U.S. immigration and visa policies "are making it hard for non-U.S. citi-zens to move to the country for education and employment, which works directly against New York's competitive advantage. . . . By contrast, the free movement of people within the European Union is enabling the best people to concentrate in other financial centers—particularly London—where immigration practices are more accommodating."

By the summer of 2007, the land borders were also starting to see delays worse than anything since the immediate aftermath of 9/11. At the northern border "delays of up to three hours were not uncommon even at some border crossings not known for extensive wait times," said a study by the Canadian Chamber of Commerce. While cross-border traffic at the U.S.-Ontario land border fell 4 percent from 2006, average wait times in the tunnel that connects Windsor to Detroit doubled to twenty-four minutes. At the Blue Water Bridge, further north, wait times were more than an hour on thirty-eight days in July and August, prompting the bridge's private operator to dub it "the summer from hell."

At the southern border, U.S. agents at the border crossings began in the summer of 2007 gradually to increase their scrutiny of the documents of border crossers in preparation for the tighter rules that are to be put in place no later than 2009 under WHTI. The result was delays of two hours or more at many of the crossings into the United States. Ralph Basham, the commissioner of Customs and Border Protection, called the new document checks "a security imperative," and added: "A safer border is well worth the wait."

Kathleen Walker, an El Paso–based immigration lawyer who was the head of the American Immigration Lawyers Association, said that such delays are only a fraction of what will occur if the United States ever tries to implement the full procedures called for under US-VISIT or the document checks mandated under WHTI. "The truth," she said, "is that you do not have the physical facilities, or the technology, or the training, or the accountability to go to 100 percent on US-VISIT or WHTI."

IN FEBRUARY 2008, CHERTOFF WENT to Harvard University in an effort to tackle these criticisms head-on at the most important and prestigious center of higher learning in the world. It was a powerful speech, perhaps the most impassioned he had given during his time in office. He went back over the history of Washington's efforts prior to 9/11 to prevent terrorist attacks. The country had been warned, he said, by the failed 1993 World Trade Center bombing by Islamic terrorists, by the arrest of Ahmed Ressam at the U.S.-Canada border, and by the foiled plot to blow up the Lincoln and Holland tunnels in New York that had been devised by followers of the blind sheikh, Omar Abdel-Rahman, after he was mistakenly given a visa to enter the United States. He reminded the audience of the Hart-Rudman Commission report and of other experts who had warned that the United States faced serious threats of a terrorist attack.

In the 1990s, he said, the government had tried to take steps to reduce the likelihood of such an attack being carried out successfully. Congress had passed a system to track student visas, with a particular emphasis on students from states known to sponsor terrorism—the precursor of what became SEVIS. It had directed the administration to monitor the entry and exit of foreigners into the country, the forerunner of US-VISIT. But "each of these efforts was stopped in its tracks." The universities had helped block the student tracking scheme out of fears that it would drive away foreign students; the border states and communities had helped to kill the entry-exit system because they feared it would interfere with travel across the borders and hurt their economies. "In the absence of a high-consequence attack that dramatized the risk," he said, "there simply was not the public will to move forward on implementing these initiatives."

The terrorist attacks, however, had changed everything. "In the immediate aftermath, we took some very vigorous and dramatics steps, which I don't think would have been accepted prior to September 11th." The intelligence agencies were forced into real sharing of information; the terrorist watch lists were integrated; airline security was bolstered. The government built "a robust student-tracking system" and deployed a fingerprint system for identifying foreigners coming to the country. But as the years crept by without another attack, he said, opposition to these and further measures began to grow. "Although a couple of years after 9/11 it would not have seemed conceivable that a business-as-usual mentality could creep back into our public mindset," he said, "it has begun to return."

Since the announcement of the plan to build a fence along large stretches of the U.S. border with Mexico, many in Texas and other border communities had risen up to oppose the plan. Chertoff was dismissive of their concerns. "The fence may spoil the view; they may view the fence as an unfriendly signal to their trading partners on the other side of the border; maybe they're concerned that the fence is going to inhibit the ability of their cattle to get to the river." On the Canadian border, Chertoff called the new document requirements for border crossers "a no-brainer" for improving security. Yet that too had drawn opposition from "border businesses that are concerned that the people who have to carry documents may not want to cross the border on impulse to go to a football game, or to purchase something in the United States now that the dollar is a little bit cheaper." Such hostility from small groups with an interest in an open border "threatens to overwhelm the greater good," he argued, and block the implementation of security measures that would protect the whole country.

Nor, he continued, should public opinion be swayed by the individual stories of hardship. He warned of "what I would call a Gresham's law for government, where a single heart-wrenching story, that is perhaps atypical, tends to drive out a good policy that makes sense for the large majority of people." While he said that such complaints shouldn't always be ignored, making policy based on those experiences "doesn't tend to look at the greater good." Chertoff made it clear what he believed the greater good to be. Whatever the ultimate fate of immigration reform, he said, "almost everybody agrees you've got to secure the borders."

For Chertoff, said a senior DHS official who left the department recently, securing the borders is going to be his legacy. The goal is to stop all unlawful entry across the country's 6,000 miles of land borders, something that had never been achieved by the United States in its history, and something no large country that holds any attraction for immigrants has ever managed to do. For what had long been the most open country in the world, it was almost an unthinkably big task. "In the history of the world, nobody's ever secured borders," said the official. "The Great Wall of China didn't work. It's never worked, and we are trying to do it."

LESS THAN THREE WEEKS AFTER Chertoff's speech at Harvard, DHS revealed that the first big pilot project in the Secure Border Initiative had failed utterly. The project, led by Boeing, involved the installation of cameras and radar atop nine mobile 100-foot towers deployed near the border in the Arizona desert. The radar was supposed to detect the movement of people across the border, relaying that data back to a command center in Tucson sixty-five miles to the north. The command center would then lock the cameras in on the targets and funnel the information to Border Patrol agents in vehicles equipped with secure laptop computers to receive the data. The agents would use that information to move in quickly to make arrests. The goal of the pilot project was to secure 28 miles out of the nearly 2,000 miles of southern border with Mexico.

The technology malfunctioned from the start. The information systems chosen for the project could not transmit the data quickly enough to the command center to allow for agents to respond. The radar system would stop working in the rain or in other harsh weather. Brush, rocks, and other obstacles made it difficult to detect targets, making it impossible to envision how such a system might work on the heavily treed northern border. The cameras could not show clear images at distances of greater than 5 kilometers, half of what had been promised. And there were fears that the towers posed an easy and tempting target for heavily armed drug gangs and human smugglers who have proliferated along the border because new security measures have made it almost impossible to cross the border without their help.

The failures of the pilot project forced DHS to halt any further deployment of similar technology. At the end of February, the department announced that it could not meet its initial goal of completing one hundred miles of virtual fencing by the end of 2008, saying that even that modest target could not be achieved until at least the end of 2011.

In response to the debacle, the chairman of the House Homeland Security Committee hauled the top DHS officials on the project before his committee to deliver a blistering warning that the department was running out of time to make good on its pledge to secure the country's borders. "Gentlemen, I cannot be more clear," he said. "If you can't get it right, we will look elsewhere for people who can."

# Conclusion

—————————

ON NOVEMBER 14, 2007, A fire broke out in the Anchorage Inn, a historical landmark in the tiny town of Rouses Point, New York, near the U.S. border with Quebec. Under a mutual aid agreement that had been in place since the 1950s, the local county was able to call on firefighters from Quebec to help out if their volunteer fire department was overwhelmed. On average, Quebec would send firefighters across the border about thirty times each year, while Rouses Point in turn would send its firefighters to help out in Quebec.

But that weekend, the Canadian fire truck that arrived with lights flashing and sirens blaring was ordered to stop by the U.S. Customs and Border Protection officials at the small border crossing. The firefighters were each asked to produce identification. The agents ran the truck's license plate against their databases to be sure it was legitimate. One of the firefighters whose identification was checked apparently had a criminal record, raising doubts about whether he should be allowed to cross the border to fight the blaze in Rouses Point. By the time CBP officials had determined to their satisfaction that the firefighters should be permitted into the country, eight minutes had passed. When the truck finally made it to the Anchorage Inn, the historic structure had burned to the ground.

"It's embarrassing," said Chris Trombley, the chief of the local volunteer fire department. "We're calling for help from another country and the first roadblock they hit is at our border."

The CBP officials that day were only doing their job. Under new procedures, which will be fully implemented by 2009, everyone crossing the border—including firefighters—will be required to present some secure form of identification, such as a passport, a birth certificate, or a secure driver's license. The sharing of criminal and terrorist databases has allowed border officials to identify many with criminal records, from serious felons to minor violators, who would have entered the country unnoticed a decade ago. The decision to check the background of one of the firefighters was completely appropriate if his name showed on one of those databases. And tough enforcement policies allow for few exceptions; if one of the firefighters indeed had some record of a serious crime, the CBP official who allowed him into the country could have been reprimanded, or worse. Just six months earlier, an American with a rare, contagious, drug-resistant form of tuberculosis had been allowed to come from Canada back into the United States at another New York border crossing, causing a furor in Congress and embarrassment for DHS. The border inspector who missed the computer alert to stop the TB patient was suspended and then forced into retirement. An eight-minute delay to prevent any similar consequences was hardly unreasonable behavior by the border officers. According to the logic laid out by Secretary Chertoff in his Harvard speech, any anger over the destruction of the Anchorage Inn was misplaced. While the town could mourn the loss, it should acknowledge that it was a small price to pay for the larger national interest in securing the border.

Yet the actions of the border officials, while completely in accordance with the new policies and procedures adopted in the post-9/11 world, were obviously absurd. By refusing to let the fire truck through quickly, CBP officials undermined a half-century of cross-border working partnerships that had been developed to secure both sides of the border against the real and present threat of fires that were too big to be handled without outside help. The risk that the same border delays could happen again in the future has left that community and other American towns along the border less secure, not more.

The officials at the border saw their responsibility through a single lens, which has been reinforced repeatedly since 9/11—keeping bad people out of the United States. But that should not have been the only measure; it was equally important that they be able to let good people into the country quickly and efficiently. By failing to do so, it was the United States—not Canada, not the firefighters themselves—that paid the highest price.

SEVEN YEARS AFTER THE 9/11 attacks, it is much harder for a terrorist to enter the United States than it used to be. It is also much harder for everyone else. America's near-term security against terrorist attacks has been strengthened, but its longer-term security, which relies on a vibrant economy and on strong relations with the rest of the world, has been compromised. Openness, while it poses certain threats, has long been one of the vital components of American security. There is a serious risk that, in the name of protecting the country against another terrorist attack, we will continue to weaken the foundations of America's economic advantage, damage its diplomacy, and ultimately harm its national security.

The experience of Rouses Point has been played out across the country. Many of the steps taken to secure American borders against terrorism have had consequences that have made us less secure. The ability of the United States to attract the most ambitious immigrants from around the world has been a central reason for its economic and diplomatic success, yet we are now making it harder for them to come here at a time when other countries—many of them no less vulnerable than the United States to terrorist attacks—are making it easier. In the European Union, for instance, a single visa now works for twenty-four different EU member states, interviews are not required routinely, and wait time for a visa rarely exceeds three weeks; in addition, the EU admits citizens of more countries without requiring a visa. The EU remains in many ways a much less welcoming place for migrants than the United States, and it faces its own serious problems with border security on its eastern and southern frontiers. But the huge advantage that the United States has long enjoyed in attracting the world's best and brightest is narrowing. Unless the United States does a better job of easing entry into the country, it will continue to pay a heavy price: the loss of companies that are not established here, meetings and conferences that are not held here, technologies that are not developed here, and future world leaders who are not educated here.

The solution is not to dismantle the whole panoply of post-9/11 border controls. Many were long overdue and have demonstrated their value in helping the United States to use its borders as a way to intercept or turn back people who intend to do serious harm to the country. Terrorists are at their most vulnerable when they are trying to cross national borders, and intelligent border controls are one of the best means the United States has for preventing a repeat of 9/11. The kind of blissful ignorance about terrorist threats that characterized border policy in the 1990s was naïve at the time, and to go back to such a system in light of what we know now would be completely irresponsible.

On the other hand, the United States has experimented with the "get-tough approach" long enough to have learned some lessons and make adjustments that can reestablish this country's tradition of openness without weakening its security. Three conclusions in particular stand out from the post-9/11 story:

- First, immigration enforcement and counterterrorism are two different things, and for either to be effective they need to be separated.

- Second, managing the risk of terrorism means exactly what it says, which is accepting that there are risks and that the consequences of trying to eliminate all those risks are worse than learning how to live with them.

- Finally, the United States needs to become as serious about encouraging good people to come to this country as it has been about keeping bad people out.

The biggest mistake of the post-9/11 period is that immigration and terrorism have become intertwined to the point where it has become almost impossible to separate them, not only in the political debate but also in the actual policies being implemented. In the aftermath of the attacks, government officials seized on immigration law as their preferred weapon, because of the nearly unlimited powers it gave them to keep suspicious people out of the country and to arrest and detain without criminal charge those who were already living here.

For many reasons, immigration enforcement has been the default response of the U.S. government in trying to shore up the country against the danger of further terrorist attacks. It has the virtue of simplicity—it does not require new legislation or complex analyses of the nature of the threat. It simply requires that existing agencies aggressively enforce laws that in most cases are already on the books. That has also made it an easy sell politically for officials who, in the aftermath of 9/11, badly wanted to demonstrate to the public that they were responding to the tragedy. Immigration enforcement is easy to measure—you can count up the numbers of people screened, arrested, jailed, deported, or turned back at the border, and the figures sound impressive even if there is not a single terrorist among them. The U.S. government is obsessed with such "metrics," with finding easy ways to measure the results of its actions. Immigration enforcement provides plenty of metrics: illegal migrants arrested, detention beds filled, visas denied, and miles of fence constructed. The quiet work of counterterrorism does not easily lend itself to such numbers.

Kris Kobach, the Justice official who played a key role in several of the programs, and has remained a leading proponent of the argument that enforcement equals security, said that "September 11 awakened the country to the fact that weak immigration enforcement presents a huge vulnerability that terrorists can exploit."

That was simply the wrong conclusion, and one that has cost the United States dearly. Enforcing immigration laws does not catch terrorists; it catches immigration violators.

Take Kobach's favorite example, which was the hijacker Ziad Jarrah, who was in the country on an expired visa and was pulled over for speeding two days before the 9/11 attacks. Under the enforcement logic, if the traffic cop had been able to determine that Jarrah was here illegally, he would have been arrested, detained, and deported, and the plot might have been exposed. But in 99.99 percent of cases, the illegal immigrant pulled over for speeding is not going to be a terrorist; he's just going to be an illegal immigrant. Yet the cop would have to arrest him regardless. The result—as we are seeing now in states like Arizona, New Jersey, and parts of California—is that a huge amount of police time is being spent identifying and detaining illegal migrants. At best, that is a distraction from fighting serious crimes and cooperating on terrorism investigations; at worst it is a major diversion of law enforcement resources that makes the country more vulnerable to another attack. While there are some good reasons for better enforcement of immigration laws, their effectiveness in stopping terrorists is not one of them.

The report card on those efforts makes for pretty dismal reading. Of the main post-9/11 schemes to use immigration enforcement tools to catch or deter terrorists, none has proved particularly worthwhile for fighting terrorism.

The Justice Department's internal investigation into the lengthy and sometimes brutal detentions of more than 750 foreigners arrested in the months after 9/11 showed that nearly all of them had committed some sort of immigration violation. But not a single one was ever charged with a terrorism-related offense, and the FBI has never claimed that it gained any valuable leads for the investigation out of those detentions. Most of the men simply languished in jail for months, held on immigration violations until they were finally deported.

According to investigators for the 9/11 Commission, who had full access to classified internal government documents and interviewed many law enforcement officials, there is also little evidence that the profiling schemes aimed at Arab and Muslim travelers have succeeded in identifying or excluding terrorists. It concluded that the initial twenty-day hold on visas for men from Muslim countries that was put in place in November 2001 "yielded no useful antiterrorism information and led to no visa denials." That was replaced by the Condor scheme, which required detailed FBI and CIA background checks on the same class of visa applicants. By April 2004, 130,000 visa applications had been run through the security checks, but not a single one was denied on terrorist-related grounds, according to the 9/11 Commission, and there is no evidence that any terrorists have been trapped by the scheme since.

In the NSEERS program for registering those from predominantly Muslim countries, about 140,000 people registered, and the government told the 9/11 Commission that eleven of them had some connection to terrorism. But the commission was pointedly skeptical of the claim. Six of those, it said, were arrested under circumstances that may not have been connected to NSEERS; two came up as hits on terrorist watch lists when they arrived at U.S. airports, and thus were unrelated to NSEERS. The other three claims were even more ambiguous. Where the program was effective was in immigration enforcement. Nearly 84,000 foreigners living in the United States came forward to register under NSEERS; about 13,000 of those, some 16 percent, were found to be in violation of an immigration law and were put into deportation proceedings.

Even a more sophisticated border screening system, like the US-VISIT program, has shown its worth in catching criminals or previous immigration violators, not terrorists. In the first three years of its operations, through January 2007, some 76 million visitors to the United States had their fingerprints taken; this helped border officials to intercept 1,800 people who had either criminal records or previous immigration violations. But no terrorists have fallen into that net. Yet that does not stop the Democratic majority on the House Homeland Security Committee from warning that every day the U.S. delays in expanding the system, "the nation's vulnerability to terrorist attack grows."

The best that can be said for these programs is that they probably turned up some useful intelligence and law enforcement leads related to terrorism. In particular, the FBI was able to use the threat of deportation to recruit informers within Arab or Muslim communities in the United States; a number of those interviewed under NSEERS said they had been pressured by the FBI to become informants in order to avoid deportation. The 9/11 Commission concluded that Al Qaeda operatives "appear to have been aware of U.S. immigration laws and regulations, and to have structured their travel and entries to the United States with those constraints in mind. . . . The routine enforcement of laws, including those not specifically related to terrorism, can therefore raise obstacles for and in some cases have a deterrent effect on individuals intending to commit terrorist acts." But given the extent of the disruption caused by those programs, that is hardly a strong endorsement of their value in fighting terrorism.

Immigration and counterterrorism have also become hopelessly entangled on the southern border, which continues to be the main route to the United States for most illegal immigrants. After the collapse of the congressional effort to reform U.S. immigration laws in 2007, the conventional wisdom is now that Americans will agree to overhaul the nearly fifty-year-old system for admitting legal immigrants only after the borders are deemed "secure." The Department of Homeland Security has embraced this goal, hiring thousands of Border Patrol agents, detaining hundreds of thousands of illegal immigrant men, women, and children, and investing billions in unproven border surveillance technologies.

Department officials concede that most of the homeland security money is being funneled into one mission—controlling the border with Mexico—that has almost nothing to do with the its core mission of preventing another terrorist attack. They will admit that there is no verified case of terrorists using the southern border to cross into the United States. They will agree that Mexico has an enormous incentive to ensure that it does not become a conduit for terrorists. They will acknowledge that Mexico has cooperated closely on counterterrorism, sharing data readily with the U.S. government in an attempt to keep terrorists out of North America.

"The Mexicans are very aware that a terrorist infiltration of the southern border would have staggering consequences for the openness of that border," said Stewart Baker, the DHS assistant secretary for policy who has been the architect of some of the tough new border measures. And yet pressed to explain why the department is so focused on that border, they argue that as long as illegal migrants can cross into the United States without detection, terrorists might find some way to do the same.

Terrorism has badly skewed the discussion of immigration because it has mixed up the most extreme and threatening scenario—the infiltration into the United States of individuals determined to carry out another huge attack—with the complex reality of trying to control thousands of miles of borders in an age of easy travel. Listen to any speech by DHS secretary Michael Chertoff and you will inevitably hear the same kind of phrase—our border security measures are meant to keep out "dangerous people, criminals, drug dealers and illegal aliens." But the policies needed to address each of these problems are quite different.

Drug enforcement, which has never been particularly successful in the three decades of the war on drugs, requires greater efforts to reduce domestic demand, good intelligence and law enforcement work, close cooperation with allies, and targeted border enforcement measures. Illegal immigration is primarily a function of labor demand; the solution is to create new avenues for foreign workers to come to the United States legally along with tougher sanctions to discourage companies from hiring illegal immigrants. Counterterrorism enforcement is about identifying and stopping the extremely small numbers of people trying to enter to country to do it harm, for which intelligence, information sharing, and constant cooperation with other countries are the primary weapons. By lumping these three together under the rubric of border security, the realities of all three are distorted. Instead the debate tends to fall into the simplistic rhetoric of talk show radio and television: if only the United States could truly seal its borders, then all these bad things could be kept out.

Unfortunately, Congress, the Bush administration, and a

vocal segment of the public have twinned terrorism and immigration enforcement. As a result, the perfectly secure border has become the goal of government policy. But holding any progress on immigration reform hostage to border security will make both impossible, because a secure border—one that is impervious not only to terrorists but to illegal drugs and illegal migrants—will remain elusive. In early 2002, the Immigration and Naturalization Service under Jim Ziglar carried out a study of what staffing levels would be needed to halt illegal immigration through enforcement alone. It concluded that the department would need:

- 27,960 investigators and special agents (compared to the 2,000 employed at the time of the study)

- 31,700 Border Patrol agents (compared to 10,000 at the time of the study, and 18,000 by the end of 2008)

- 21,500 immigration inspectors (compared to 5,000)

- 15,600 deportation officers (compared to 650)

- 1,440 attorneys (compared to 770)

- 110,000 detention beds (compared to 21,107 in 2002 and about 33,000 in 2008)

It is certainly possible to take issue with these estimates. DHS has largely ended "catch and release," for instance, with two-thirds fewer jail beds than what the study predicted. But what is clear is that, despite the enormous expenditure on all the elements of border security and enforcement, the country is still far short of the investment it needs to gain what Chertoff optimistically calls "operational control" over its borders. According to a recent comprehensive study based on interviews over three years with more than 3,000 Mexican migrants and potential migrants, the tough new border measures have done nothing at all to deter illegal migrants. Instead, migrants have adapted to a fortified border by hiring smugglers in greater numbers and at greater cost, and by remaining in the United States once they succeed in running the border gauntlet.

Such conclusions lead to another lesson that should be evident seven years after 9/11. Even with the vastly expanded resources that the country is willing to put into homeland security, the only intelligent way to keep terrorists out of the country is to think carefully about the benefits and costs of different measures—to adopt the sort of risk management approach that James Loy advocated when he first sat down with Tom Ridge seven years ago.

While the terrorist threat is a real one, and September 11 showed the potential for Al Qaeda and other groups to produce horrific destruction, it has also become increasingly clear that the number of individuals who pose a serious danger is tiny. John Gannon, a former deputy director for intelligence at the CIA who has been heavily involved in homeland security issues, says that the terrorists the United States needs to be worried about are "an infinitesimally small number." From a terrorism perspective, he argues, the goal of border security should be to home in on that limited number of threats, which is primarily an intelligence challenge. Border measures should be considered largely by the degree to which they improve the ability to gather information and intelligence that will help to identify that extremely small number of very dangerous people.

In 2004 one of Tom Ridge's aides, Cris Arcos, laid out a test for border security that still makes sense. He argued that we should look for "the point at which security measures become more burdensome and the added security too marginal weighted against the costs to administer the measures."

Many of the post-9/11 measures make sense by that standard. The consolidation and sharing of terrorist watch lists, the gathering of advance information on airline passengers coming to the United States, intelligence sharing with allies, and improvements in passport security have all made significant contributions to security. There are still problems with the accuracy of lists and with similar names that sometimes result in innocent people being de-layed in air travel. But on the whole these schemes have added only small burdens for most travelers. Privacy issues have made it more difficult to use similar screening efforts on domestic flights, but for foreigners traveling to the United States—who must accept a high degree of scrutiny if they want to enter the country—this is one of the best opportunities the government has to identify potential terrorists.

Similarly, by those criteria, it makes sense to move to a full ten-print fingerprint reader for overseas visitors, as is currently be-ing done. The system is almost as fast as the two-print readers that were first deployed under US-VISIT, adding little burden to the traveler. And it promises to give the system a genuine counterter-rorism value that it has lacked. The ability to check the fingerprints of incoming travelers against a database of prints collected by the U.S. military in genuine terrorist hot zones like Afghanistan and Iraq is the sort of precise tool that could distinguish the small num-ber of real threats from the huge mass of innocent travelers.

In contrast, moving forward with the construction of a system to track the exit of every visitor to the United States—as is cur-rently required under congressional law as part of the US-VISIT program—would be enormously burdensome. Under the best sce-nario being considered, it would require the airlines or transpor-tation security officials to take the fingerprints of every foreigner leaving the country, and would either shut down traffic at the land borders while everyone gets out of their car to give fingerprints, or would require the deployment of sophisticated remote readers that are probably still at least a decade from working. And the best that can be said for the counterterrorism value of such a system is that it would help investigators to determine whether someone of interest had left the country or not, though to a considerable extent such data is already available through airline passenger records.

A similar analysis would cause a reassessment of some of the current programs, particularly those targeted only at travelers from Muslim countries. Currently, a young man coming from any of the world's major Muslim countries faces at least five levels of screening: the initial visa interview and fingerprinting at the embassy; a more in-depth Condor security background check by the FBI; a check against his passenger reservation data before he arrives in the country; a second fingerprinting at the U.S. airport through US-VISIT; and the NSEERS registration, which covers all the same ground but will subject him to a further search when he lands in the United States and force him to register at specific airports to leave the country. From a security perspective, the initial process plus the confirmation of his identity on arrival has 99 percent of the value. It allows for the applicant to be checked against terrorist watch lists, and for the consular officer to decide whether his reasons for coming to the United States are evident, legitimate, and documented. In some cases, it may make sense to do a detailed FBI background check as well, but given the poor track record of the Condor checks in identifying terrorists, automatically forcing thousands of visa applicants to run the FBI gauntlet appears to bring added security that is "too marginal weighted against the costs to administer the measures." Finally, the NSEERS scheme adds nothing at all, except to subject lawful travelers to an unnecessary and humiliating level of additional scrutiny after they arrive in the United States.

The objection can always be made that reducing any of the existing border security measures, or failing to construct new ones, will leave the country slightly more vulnerable to a terrorist attack. But by that logic, the only real security would come from keeping everyone out of the United States, because even the best border defenses in the world are not likely to identify and stop a clever terrorist. What dismays Gannon, and many of the others I have interviewed, is how the United States has allowed the terrorist attacks to skew the country's priorities so that the goal of perfect border security is seen as a reasonable and appropriate one for the government. "Why did we get to the point," he asked "where we had to start worrying about 95,000 miles of coastline?"

THE UNITED STATES ALSO NEEDS to start matching its commitment to keeping bad people out with a bigger effort to help good people get in. In essence, this would be striking a new bargain with future generations of would-be travelers or immigrants to the United States, one in which the United States tries to offset the delays caused by tighter security measures with new efforts to make it easier to travel here.

There has already been some significant progress on this front. The State Department has put extraordinary efforts into processing visas for students and business travelers more quickly, and has even been chipping away at the long wait times for visa interviews. The recovery of travel to the United States since its low point in 2003 can be attributed in part to those efforts, even if the falling U.S. dollar is surely the biggest lure. After years of understaffing, State has hired more than five hundred new consular officers since 2001—a 40 percent increase—though it still remains understaffed given the new security responsibilities and rapidly rising demand for visas from countries like India, China, and Brazil.

For the most part, however, investments in encouraging travel to the United States have lagged far behind the new expenditures on border enforcement. Border and interior enforcement spending by DHS is well over $10 billion a year, most of that for Border Patrol agents. Citizenship and Immigration Services, in contrast, which is responsible for processing applications by newcomers to the country, has a budget one-quarter of that size, which is entirely financed by hefty fees paid by the applicants. In other words, the government considers that keeping people out of the country is a national interest that should be supported generously by the taxpayers, whereas bringing people here only benefits the foreigners who come, and therefore they should pay the full cost.

While the Border Patrol is on pace to double its 2001 size to 20,000 agents by the end of the Bush administration, spending to improve the legal ports of entry at the land borders is negligible. CBP estimates that it needs about $4 billion to upgrade the land crossings with Mexico and Canada, and outside estimates run as high as $10 billion. Congress in 2008 approved just over $300 million. And while the Border Patrol is growing as rapidly as possible, CBP is still several thousand officers short of what it needs to staff the land entry ports. Staffing at airports is similarly deficient. Yet Congress has had no problem finding $1 billion a year to build fences and deploy detection technologies along the southern border. The Congressional Research Service predicts that the cost of building and maintaining seven hundred miles of border fence could reach nearly $50 billion over the next quarter century.

Initiatives designed to identify low-risk travelers also need more attention, in part because they make the security job easier by reducing the number of border crossers who require greater scrutiny. Enrollment in the NEXUS program, in which Canadians are vetted in advance by the U.S. government and are supposed to speed past the border lineups, grew rapidly after 9/11, but has recently started to slow, in part because the bridge lineups are often so long that NEXUS drivers can't get into their preferred lanes. A registered traveler program to speed frequent fliers through security checkpoints is only just recently up and running. The concept of the trusted traveler could be extended into the visa processing area as well. Many of the visa delays that remain are a result of long waits for interviews. While first-time visa applicants should certainly be interviewed, there is no obvious security reason for subjecting those with visas to the same interview process every time their current visa expires and they must apply for a new one. That creates needless hassle for known, frequent travelers and diverts resources away from giving greater scrutiny to new visa applicants.

Finally, even as the United States is trying to close the door to the people it does not want, there are fewer legal ways to bring and keep the people we do want. Visas for highly skilled foreign workers are capped at a level so low that the annual quota is now routinely filled within days. In addition, foreign workers in the United States on temporary work visas face such long backlogs in applications for permanent residence that many are forced to leave. Other countries, which have caught on to the economic advantages brought by immigrants, are only too happy to find a place for them.

Despite the many obstacles, reestablishing the United States as one of the world's most welcoming countries would not be that hard to achieve if these lessons were learned. For all the blunders of the post-9/11 period, the United States remains an incredibly attractive place that ambitious people from across the world still seek out to study, work, and live in. All we have to do is invite them back, and they will come. The world demonstrated tremendous support for the United States in the days and months after 9/11, and even those whose lives were disrupted often said they understood why the United States needed to tighten its borders against future terrorists. If it would treat such people with greater respect and dignity when they try to come here, the inevitable delays and inconveniences associated with security measures would be more readily tolerated. Most of the people I interviewed, even after the ordeals they had faced as a result of the post-9/11 measures, still very much wanted to live in this country.

I FINALLY MET DR. FAIZ Bhora, the Pakistani heart surgeon whose visa troubles in 2002 and 2003 had started my effort to understand the U.S. response to the terrorist attacks. Shortly after we were introduced in 2007, he was embraced in a bear hug by a Chinese man who did not speak a word of English. In an operation that had lasted nearly twelve hours, Bhora and his colleagues at St. Luke's Roosevelt Hospital Center on New York City's West Side had removed a grapefruit-size tumor from the right lung of the man's seventeen-year-old son. The tumor, detected as a result of an x-ray taken in China, had wrapped itself around portions of the boy's spinal cord, raising a significant risk that the operation could result in paralysis. The parents had traveled to New York to live with relatives already in the United States so their son could have the lifesaving operation he needed. The operation was carried out using advanced robotic surgical techniques that have only been developed in the past few years and are only being used at a small number of the country's best hospitals. Just short hours after the operation, the boy could wiggle his toes.

After a nine-month wait in Karachi, Bhora had finally got his visa in late February 2003 and returned to Los Angeles the next month to take up his position at UCLA. "It was hard not to be angry, but mostly it was frustrating," he said. He knew many other

Pakistanis who were going through the same thing or worse. Hospitals had become reluctant to sponsor Pakistanis for the initial training visas that many used to complete their medical training, for fear they could run into visa problems. It seemed to sour him on his dream of working at UCLA; he stayed at the hospital only a year. The ordeal had at least one silver lining, however. He married an immigration attorney, Naveen Rahman, a pretty Bangladeshi woman he had met when she was working in the Los Angeles law firm that handled his visa problems.

His anger over the whole experience remains very close to the surface, though, in part because the U.S. government reminds him of it whenever he travels. As a young man from Pakistan, he still falls under the NSEERS program. That requires him to leave the country only through certain airports where he can "check out" with U.S. officials or risk being unable to return. In January 2007, he and his wife took a week's vacation to Costa Rica. When he returned to the United States, Bhora said, the CBP inspector "went through every single scrap of paper in my wallet," writing down phone numbers, passwords to his bank accounts, even his calling card from Costa Rica. He was held up for two hours while the agents rifled through his wallet. "He knew I was a cardiothoracic surgeon who had left for a week on vacation," he said angrily, "but it was as though I was entering the country for the first time."

Bhora says he thinks often about returning home to Pakistan, where life would be easier for him in many ways. But for the moment he remains, saving the lives of Americans, and others who have come here seeking their own little piece of the American dream.

# Sources

## Introduction

1    It was no accidental appointment: The details on Laks are from an interview with Faiz Bhora, May 15, 2007, and follow-up e-mails; the Laks quotation is from David Zisser, "UCLA Surgeon Honored at American Heart Awards," *UCLA Daily Bruin*, July 29, 2002.

3    "I really buttered him up": Interview with Faiz Bhora, May 15, 2007.

3    "Since August, I've been waiting": Telephone interview with Faiz Bhora, February 2003.

5    Dia Elnaiem was born: Details for this section are from two interviews with Dia Elnaiem, June 7, 2007, and December 20, 2007, and follow-up e-mails.

9    "It's always a question": Interview with General Bruce Lawlor, March 1, 2007.

10   "We as a nation had always": Interview with Admiral James Loy, former deputy secretary of the Department of Homeland Security, October 3, 2007.

11   If you live in Brazil: The wait times at different U.S. embassies and consulates around the world are updated regularly by the State Department. They are available at http://travel.state .gov/visa/temp/wait/tempvisitors_wait.php.

11   Imad Daou, a Christian from Lebanon: Telephone interview with Imad Daou, December 12, 2007, and interview in Nuevo Laredo, March 5, 2008, plus follow-up e-mail. Daou also showed me with copies of couple's I-212 pardon applications, which must be approved for him to be allowed back into the country and which provided more details of his experience.

13   Regardless of where you are from: John Dillion, "Valeria Vinnikova Says Her Situation Was Not Unique," Vermont Public Radio, November 16, 2007.

14   "the summer of hell": Comments made at the conference "Homeland Security and Canada-U.S. Border Trade: Implication for Public Policy and Business Strategy," October 25–26, 2007, Windsor, Ontario.

14   Delays have grown even though: Border Policy Research Institute, Western Washington University, "Diversity of the Ports-of-Entry Along the 49th Parallel," *Border Policy Brief*, September 2007.

14   On both borders, new requirements: Julia Preston, "Tighter Borders Delay Re-Entry by U.S. Citizens," *New York Times*, October 21, 2007.

14   foreign travelers now consider: Discover America Partnership, "Discover America Partnership/RT Strategies Survey of International Travelers," November 20, 2006, at http://www. tia-dap.org/pdf/International_Travel_Survey_Summary.pdf.

15    Overall, 10 million fewer people traveled to the United States: U.S. Department of State,
      "Non-Immigrant Visas Issued by Nationality, FY 1997–2006," and Report of the Visa Of-
      fice 2007, at http://travel.state.gov/visa/frvi/statistics/statistics_1476.html.

15    After nearly forty years of rapid growth: Open Doors, "Report on International Educational
      Exchange," Institute of International Education, November 2007, at http://opendoors.org
      .iienetwork.org/?p=113119.

15    "When you go to Europe": The comments by Governor Sanford were made at a meeting in
      Washington, D.C., hosted by the Organization for International Investment, May 10, 2007.

16    "Everyone knew it was an imperfect response": Interview with former senior Justice Depart-
      ment official, May 3, 2007.

17    "They are looking at us as terrorists": The quotations are from Edward Alden, "Visa Deadline
      Leaves Immigrants out in the Cold," *Financial Times*, February 18, 2003.

18    In early 2003 the Justice Department's inspector general: U.S. Department of Justice, Of-
      fice of the Inspector General, "The September 11 Detainees: A Review of the Treatment of
      Aliens Held on Immigration Charges in Connection with the Investigation of the Septem-
      ber 11 Attacks," April 2003, at http://usdoj.gov/oig/special/0306/full.pdf; hereafter "Fine
      Report ."

19    a "charade" that "bordered on ridiculousness": Michael Powell, "A Prisoner of Panic After
      9/11," *Washington Post*, November 29, 2003; telephone interview with Benamar Benatta,
      January 23, 2008, and interview in Toronto, April 21, 2008.

20    "this export of fear and anger": Interview with Richard Armitage, former deputy secretary of
      state, January 7, 2008.

21    "What made America the world's greatest power": Richard Florida, *The Flight of the Creative
      Class: The New Global Competition for Talent* (New York: HarperCollins, 2007), 68.

21    "At any given historical moment": Amy Chua, *Day of Empire: How Hyperpowers Rise to Global
      Dominance and Why They Fall* (New York: Doubleday, 2007), xxiii.

21    "At no time in our nation's history": Testimony of Lance Kaplan, "Use of Point Systems
      for Selecting Immigrants," Hearing Before the United States House of Representatives
      Committee on the Judiciary, Subcommittee on Immigration, Citizenship, Refugees, Bor-
      der Security and International Law, May 1, 2007, at http://judiciary.house.gov/media/pdfs/
      Kaplan070501.pdf.

22    The number of temporary visas granted each year: U.S. Department of State, Office of Visa
      Statistics, Table XVIII, "Nonimmigrant Visas Issued by Nationality, FY 1998–2007," at
      http://www.travel.state.gov/visa/frvi/statistics/statistics_4179.html.

23    "We've built a huge 186,000-person bureaucracy": Interview with Norman Neureiter, former
      science and technology adviser to Secretary of State Colin Powell, September 20, 2007.

24    "One of our secret weapons": The quotation is from Edward Alden, "Washington's Tough
      New Visa Policy," *Financial Times*, January 29, 2003.

# 1. The Borders

26    Ninety-four pounds of cocaine . . . In another bust: Details of drug busts come from Cus-
      toms News Releases, August 2001, at http://www.cbp.gov/hot-new/pressrel/2001/0907-06.
      htm.

26    "remained low and stable": U.S. Drug Enforcement Administration (DEA) Briefs and Back-
      ground, "Cocaine," at http://www.dea.gov/concern/cocaine_factsheet.html.

27    he could see black smoke rising: the details are from Robert Bonner's testimony to the Na-
      tional Commission on Terrorist Attacks Upon the United States (hereafter 9/11 Commis-
      sion), January 26, 2004, at http://govinfo.library.unt.edu/911/hearings/hearing7/witness_
      bonner.htm; from "A Conversation with Commissioner Rob Bonner, Council on Foreign
      Relations, January 11, 2005," at http://www.cfr.org/publication.html?id=7601; and from an
      interview with Dennis Murphy, March 6, 2007.

28    "had failed miserably": House Committee on Government Reform and Oversight, *National*

*Drug Policy: A Review of the Status of the Drug War*, 104th Cong., 2d sess. March 19, 1996, H. Rpt. 104-486, at http://www.fas.org/irp/congress/1996_rpt/h104486.htm.

28    For almost fifteen years: Information on Customs and passenger information comes from the Congressional Research Service (CRS) Report for Congress, "Terrorist Watchlist Checks and Air Passenger Prescreening," September 6, 2006, p. 5, at http://www.fas.org/sgp/crs/homesec/RL33645.pdf.

28    The data were examined by: The methods are described in U.S. General Accounting Office (now the Government Accountability Office, GAO), "U.S. Customs Service: Better Targeting of Airline Passengers for Personal Searches Could Produce Better Results," March 2000, at http://www.gao.gov/archive/2000/gg00038.pdf.

28    The information included: Information from interviews with former senior Customs officials.

29    by 2000 the United States was getting APIS data from sixty-seven carriers: U.S. Department of Justice, "INS Mission and Strategies: High Impact Agency Goals," May 29, 2001, at. http://govinfo.library.unt.edu/npr/library/announc/goals.htm.

30    "You start to create a trail": Information in this section is from interviews with Chuck Winwood, former deputy Customs commissioner, May 10, 2007, and Brian C. Goebel, former counselor and senior policy advisor to Customs commissioner Robert Bonner, March 12, 2007, and follow-up e-mails.

30    the number of personal searches: "Testimony of Raymond Kelly, U.S. Senate Committee on the Judiciary, Subcommittee on the Constitution, Federalism and Property Rights," August 1, 2001, at http://judiciary.senate.gov/oldsite/te080101sc-kelly.htm.

31    in certain rare and urgent circumstances: Interviews with Chuck Winwood, May 10, 2007, and John Varrone, September 27, 2007. Varrone was former assistant Customs commissioner in the Office of Investigations and acting commissioner on September 11, 2001.

31    would also be examined "judiciously": Winwood interview, May 10, 2007.

31    On the morning of September 11: Information for this paragraph is from an interview with John Varrone. September 27, 2007.

31    the names of the two men were not put on watch lists until August 2001: The story of the CIA's failure to put al-Mihdhar and al-Hazmi on the terrorist watch list has been told in detail in the investigation into the 9/11 attacks by the congressional intelligence committees (U.S. Senate Select Committee on Intelligence and the U.S. House Permanent Select Committee on Intelligence, *Joint Inquiry into Intelligence Community Activities Before and After the Terrorist Attacks of September 11, 2001*, 107th Cong., 2d sess., December 2002, S. Rep. 107-351, H. Rep. 107-792), and in *The 9/11 Commission Report: Final Report of the National Commission on Terrorist Attacks Upon the United States* (New York: W. W. Norton, 2004). In his memoirs, former CIA director George Tenet admits there was a "communication breakdown," but says the blame also resided with the FBI and other government agencies, which were aware of the same information but made no moves to put the two men on watch lists that would have kept them out of the country. George Tenet, *At the Center of the Storm: My Years at the CIA* (New York: HarperCollins, 2007), 194–200.

31–32  But when Customs ran the names: Interview with Robert Bonner, April 23, 2007.

32    With those two names in hand: Ibid.

32    "the FBI hasn't given Customs a single bit of credit for this": Quote and preceding information from Robert Bonner's testimony to the 9/11 Commission, January 26, 2004, and interview with Bonner, April 23, 2007.

32    "You're not going to know all the terrorist operatives": Interview with Robert Bonner, April 23, 2007.

34    The Bush administration thought rogue states: The cool reception to the commission's recommendations may also have been partly because Warren Rudman had endorsed the president's rival, Senator John McCain, in the 2000 Republican primary prior to the crucial New Hampshire primary, which was won by McCain, though Bush went on to secure the nomination.

35   "a tide of economic, technological and intellectual forces that is integrating a global community." Commission on National Security/21st Century, "Seeking a National Strategy: A Concert for Preserving Security and Promoting Freedom," April 15, 2000, p. 5, at http://govinfo.library.unt.edu/nssg/PhaseII.pdf.

35   As the most powerful and open country in the world, the United States was both an attractive target and an easy one: Commission on National Security/21st Century, "Road Map for National Security: Imperative for Change," February 15, 2001, p. 10, at http://govinfo.library.unt.edu/nssg/PhaseIIIFR.pdf.

35   "Terrorists and criminals": Ibid., p. 12.

35   On December 14, 1999: Ressam's story, and the details of his arrest, are told in Hal Bernton, Mike Carter, David Heath, and James Neff, "The Terrorist Within: The Story Behind One Man's Holy War Against America," a special report in the *Seattle Times*, June 23–July 7, 2002.

36   At nearby Blaine, Washington: Bureau of Transportation Statistics, *North American Trade and Travel Trends*, Table 13, "Top 10 U.S.-Canada Border Crossings for Incoming Passengers and Personal Vehicles, 2000"; U.S. Department of Transportation, Federal Highway Administration, "Border Crossing Freight Delay Data Collection and Analysis FY 2001 Data Collection: Pacific Highway (Blaine Border) Crossing," at http://ops.fhwa.dot.gov/freight/border_crossing.htm.

36   Customs officials have conceded: Elaine Shannon, "Manning the Bridge: At a Busy Canadian Border Crossing, Customs Chief Ben Anderson Is the First Line of Defense," *Time*, September 1, 2002.

36   Some two dozen foreign terrorists: Steven A. Camarota, "The Open Door: How Militant Islamic Terrorists Entered and Remained in the United States, 1993–2001," Center for Immigration Studies Paper 21, 2002, at http://www.cis.org/articles/2002/paper21/terrorism.html.

37   "The global economy's movement": Stephen E. Flynn, "Beyond Border Control," *Foreign Affairs* 79, no. 6 (2000), p. 57.

37   Between 1993 and 2000, the INS had added more than 5,000 agents: U.S. Government Accountability Office (GAO), "INS Southwest Border Strategy: Resource and Impact Issues Remain After Seven Years," August 2001, at http://www.gao.gov/new.items/d01842.pdf.

38   But border officials had no training in detecting the sorts of fraudulent documents: Thomas R. Eldridge et al., *9/11 and Terrorist Travel: Staff Report of the National Commission on Terrorist Attacks Upon the United States*, August 21, 2004, p. 89, at http://govinfo.library.unt.edu/911/staff_statements/911_TerrTrav_Monograph.pdf.

41   While Customs officials were busy: Interview with first former senior Justice official, March 22, 2007.

41   But Ziglar, by his own admission: Interview with Jim Ziglar, former INS Commissioner, October 9, 2007.

42   But on the day of the attacks: Statement of James W. Ziglar to the 9/11 Commission, January 26, 2004, at http://govinfo.library.unt.edu/911/hearings/hearing7/witness_ziglar.htm.

43   clearing a truck through the border every twelve seconds: Flynn, "Beyond Border Control."

43   More than a year after the 9/11 attacks: Interview with Brian Goebel, March 12, 2007.

43   "I've been doing this for seventeen years and I've never seen anything like this": Donald McArthur, "Aftermath of Terror: Border Clampdown Snarls Traffic; U.S. Issues Code 1 Security Alert," *Windsor Star*, September 13, 2001.

44   By 2001 the system was so finely tuned: Flynn, "Beyond Border Control," p. 59.

44   "a rolling inventory, just another part of the assembly line": Mary-Liz Shaw, "U.S. and Canada: Holding the Line: Two Neighboring Nations Try to Raise Defenses While Staying Friends," *Milwaukee Journal-Sentinel*, March 10, 2002.

44   "Just-in-time is the lifeblood": John Arnone quote in Dave Hall, "High Toll of Border Security: Businesses Hurt by Long Delays," *Windsor Star*, September 29, 2001.

44   had been forced to shut down five of its assembly lines: Information on Ford operations

is from Joseph Martha and Sunil Subbakrishna, "Manager's Journal: When Just-in-Time Becomes Just-in-Case," *Wall Street Journal*, October 22, 2001.

45  unplanned production losses: Testimony of Mark Nantis, Canadian Vehicle Manufacturers Association, to the Canadian Parliament Standing Committee on Industry, Science and Technology, quoted in Peter Andreas and Thomas J. Biersteker, *The Rebordering of North America: Integration and Exclusion in a New Security Context* (New York: Routledge, 2003), 8.

45  Toyota canceled shifts at its Georgetown, Kentucky, plant: Gail Kachadourian, "Shutdown Likely to Continue," *Automotive News* 76, no. 5948 (September 17, 2001).

45  Overall, they lost nearly: Ibid.

45  the Big Three were already begging U.S. Customs officials in Washington: Jeffrey Ball, "How Chrysler Averted a Parts Crisis in the Logjam Following the Attack," *Wall Street Journal*, September 24, 2001; Steven Brill, *After: How America Confronted the September 12 Era* (New York: Simon & Schuster, 2003), 45.

45  "I said, 'Goddammit'": Interview with Chuck Winwood, May 10, 2007.

45  Despite the doubling in cross-border trade: Flynn, "Beyond Border Control," pp. 66–67.

45  At an October 3 Senate hearing: Senate Committee on Appropriations, Hearing on Northern Border Security, 107th Cong., 1st sess., October 3, 2001, S. Hrg 107-341.

46  the Detroit border station before 9/11 required 174 INS agents: Becky Yerak, "Border Backups Take Toll on Metro Business and Truckers: Firms Hit Financially Due to Long Delays at Tunnel, Bridge," *Detroit News*, September 23, 2001.

46  the new inspection requirements: Marisa Taylor and Anna Cearly, "Alerts Make Wait Longer for Border Crossers," *San Diego Union Tribune*, September 13, 2001.

46  the number of cars and trucks crossing Ambassador Bridge to Detroit had fallen by half: Remo Mancini, corporate vice president of the Ambassador Bridge, quoted in Bob Meyer, "Secure Border Urged by Panel; Businesses Warned of Harm to Trade," *Windsor Star*, October 5, 2001.

47  At the southern border: Diana Washington Valdez, "Bridge Delays May Strain Area Businesses," *El Paso Times*, September 19 2001; Janine Zuniga, "Suffering San Ysidro; Sales Plunge As Mexican Shoppers Vanish, Refusing Long Border Waits," *San Diego Union-Tribune*, September 27, 2001.

47  The decline was similar on the Bridge of the Americas: Jason Blevins, "Safety Checks at Mexican Border Take Toll on 2 Cities' Economies," *Denver Post*, October 12, 2001.

47  Vicente Fox, called the economic aftermath of 9/11 "cataclysmic" for Mexico: Vicente Fox and Rob Allyn, *Revolution of Hope: The Life, Faith and Dreams of a Mexican President* (New York: Viking, 2007), 234.

47  For three days after the attacks: For details of air cargo troubles, see Mark Landler and Richard A. Opel Jr., "Ban on Airliners' Freight Has Business Scrambling," *New York Times*, September 15, 2001.

48  It wouldn't see that number again: Bureau of Transportation Statistics, "Airline Travel Since 9/11," Issue Brief Number 13, November 2005, at http://www.bts.gov/publications/issue_briefs/number_13.

48  Between August and October: Inspection and arrival data from the U.S. Department of Commerce, Office of Travel and Tourism Industries, "World and U.S. International Visitor Arrivals and Receipts," at http://tinet.ita.doc.gov/outreachpages/inbound.world_us_intl_arrivals.htm.

49  "For generations, America has prospered": "Written Testimony of William H. Gates, Chairman, Microsoft Corporation, Before the Committee on Health, Education, Labor and Pensions, U.S. Senate," March 7, 2007, at http://help.senate.gov/Hearings/2007_03_07/Gates.pdf.

50  It was not just a few: AnnaLee Saxenian, *Silicon Valley's New Immigrant Entrepreneurs*, Public Policy Institute of California, 1999, at http://www.ccis-ucsd.org/publications/wrkg15.pdf.

50  By the turn of the century: Rob Paral and Benjamin Johnson, "Maintaining a Competitive

Edge: The Role of the Foreign-Born and U.S. Immigration Policies in Science and Engineering," *Immigration Policy in Focus* 3, no. 3 (2004), p. 1.

51     More new immigrants came to the United States in the 1990s: Michael E. Fix and Jeffrey S. Passel, "U.S. Immigration at the Beginning of the 21st Century." Testimony Before the Subcommittee on Immigration and Claims Hearing on "The U.S. Population and Immigration" Committee on the Judiciary U.S. House of Representatives, August 2, 2001, at http://www.urban.org/publications/900417.html.

52     "The president gave me": Robert Bonner interview, "Border Line," *Los Angeles Business Journal*, January 23, 2006.

## 2. The President

54     Federal cutbacks in defense had led to the loss of thousands of jobs: For information about California's recession in the 1990s, see Richard W. Stevenson, "The Sputtering California Miracle," *New York Times*, October 17, 1991.

54     Yet from 1980 to 1990, illegal immigration had added 1 to 2 million to the state's population: See Hans P. Johnson, *Undocumented Immigration to California, 1980–1993*, Public Policy Institute of California, September 1996, at http://www.ppic.org/main/publication.asp?i=114.

55     [Bush's] victory in the governor's race over Richards: Sam Howe Verhovek, "Texas Elects George W. While Florida Rejects Jeb," *New York Times*, November 9, 1994.

55     "I am not opposed to educating or providing social services": "Bush opposes California Proposition 187," United Press International, November 10, 1994.

55     he personally confronted the California governor: Peter Wallsten, "Immigrant Issues Are Personal for Bush," *Los Angeles Times*, April 2, 2006. The quotation was confirmed with Governor Engler by the author.

55     Bush's beliefs about borders: See Kevin Phillips, *American Dynasty: Aristocracy, Fortune and the Politics of Deceit in the House of Bush* (New York: Viking, 2004), 117–119.

56     the roughly 1.4 million illegal immigrants in the state paid out $500 million each year: Office of the Comptroller, Texas, "Undocumented Immigrants: A Financial Analysis of the Impact to the State Budget and Economy," December 2006, at http://window.state.tx.us/specialrpt/undocumented/undocumented.pdf.

56     But the issue was personal for Bush: Richard Wolffe, Holly Bailey, and Evan Thomas, "Bush's Spanish Lessons," *Newsweek*, May 29, 2006.

56–57   [Bush] penned a strongly worded *New York Times* op-ed: George W. Bush, "No Cheap Shots at Mexico, Please," *New York Times*, August 20, 1995.

57     Bush denounced him as an isolationist: "Bush Assails GOP Candidate for Isolationism," *Austin American-Statesman*, August 15, 1995.

57     "If people can't make a living at home . . . they are coming": Jason Gertzen, "Bush Seeks to Refocus Military; Too Many Missions Take Toll, He Says," *Omaha World Herald*, January 15, 2000.

57     In 1998, he was one of nine governors to sign a letter: Christi Harlan, "Bush Joins Call to Allow Hiring More Skilled Foreign Employees," *Austin American-Statesman*, September 17, 1998.

58     "As a Texan, I have known many immigrant families": Elizabeth Bumiller, "Behind Bush's Address Lies a Deep History," *New York Times*, May 16, 2006.

58     "our biggest challenge will be to separate my uncle from the rest of the Republican Party": Scott Lindlaw, "Bush Courts California Hispanics, Gays," *Associated Press*, April 7, 2000.

59     "profoundly ambivalent about the immigrant": Daniel J. Tichenor, *Dividing Lines: The Politics of Immigration Control in America* (Princeton, N.J.: Princeton University Press, 2002), 289.

62     expulsion of any foreigner: Ibid., 142.

63     The INS came to life in 1864: Ibid., 66.

63     Lacking any real authority over the states: Ibid., 165.

64    a goal of completing airport inspections in an average of thirty minutes: U.S. Department of Justice, "INS Mission and Strategies: High Impact Agency Goals," May 29, 2001, at http://www.ins.usdoj.gov/graphics/aboutins/insmission/goals.htm.

64    "You're caught between the exclusionists and the expansionists": Interview with Michael Cronin, former assistant commissioner for inspections, INS, September 11, 2007.

65    "We were expected to do everything right": Interview with Michael Becraft, former chief of staff, INS, October 4, 2007.

65    "Serious problems undermine present immigration policies": U.S. Commission on Immigration Reform, *Executive Summary* (Washington, D.C.: 1994), v, at http://www.utexas.edu/lbj/uscir/becoming/ex-summary.pdf.

65    But by the end of 1995 the average wait time instead grew to between ten and seventeen months: U.S. GAO, "INS Management: Follow-up on Selected Problems," GAO/GGD-97-132, July 1997, p. 72, at http://www.gao.gov/archive/1997/gg97132.pdf.

65    Between 1994 and 2000, the backlog of applications increased fourfold: Douglas S. Massey, "Beyond the Border Buildup: Towards a New Approach to Mexico-U.S. Migration," *Immigration Policy in Focus*, 4, no. 7 (2005): 1–11.

66    nearly three-quarters of a million citizen applications: U.S. GAO, "Immigration and Naturalization Service: Overview of Recurring Management Challenges," October 17, 2001, p. 5, at http://gao.gov/new.items/d02168t.pdf.

66    there was no enforcement: "Statement of Glenn A. Fine, Inspector General, Department of Justice, Before the Senate Judiciary Committee Subcommittee on Technology, Terrorism, and Government Information," October 12, 2001, at http://www.usdoj.gov/oig/testimony/0110a.htm .

66    "If you dropped off your I-94, if you filled it out correctly: Interview with Jim Williams, former director, US-VISIT, October 19, 2007.

67    between 40 and 90 percent of those released never showed up for their hearings: Testimony of Senator Carl Levin to Senate Treasury Appropriations Subcommittee, December 5, 2001, at http://levin.senate.gov/newsroom/release.cfm?id=210528.

67    A Palestinian terrorist: Steven A. Camarota, "The Open Door: How Militant Islamic Terrorists Entered and Remained in the United States, 1993–2001" (Washington, D.C.: Center for Immigration Studies, 2002), 30.

67    as many as half of those who agreed to leave voluntarily never did so: U.S. Department of Justice, Office of the Inspector General, "Voluntary Departure: Ineffective Enforcement and Lack of Sufficient Controls Hamper the Process," Evaluation and Inspections Report I-99-09, March 1999, at http://www.usdoj.gov/oig/reports/INS/e9909/index.htm.

67    When the INS apprehended an illegal immigrant: U.S. Department of Justice, Office of the Inspector General, "Status of IDENT/IAFIS Integration," Report No. I-2002-03, December 7, 2001, at http://www.usdoj.gov/oig/reports/plus/e0203/letter.htm.

68    Angel Maturino Reséndiz: A good synopsis of his arrest record is in Michelle Malkin, *Invasion: How America Still Welcomes Terrorists, Criminals and Other Foreign Menaces to Our Shores* (Washington, D.C.: Regnery, 2002).

68    If anyone should have been a red flag in the IDENT system: The review of the INS's actions is in the U.S. Department of Justice, Office of the Inspector General, Special Report, "The Rafael Reséndez-Ramirez Case: A Review of the INS's Actions and the Operation of Its IDENT Automated Fingerprint System," March 2000, http://www.justice.gov/oig/special/0003/index.htm.

68    the IDENT system was so full of holes: "Statement of Glenn A. Fine," October 12, 2001.

69    Mexicans began to enter the United States illegally in roughly the same numbers: Douglas S. Massey, Jorge Duran and Nolan J. Malone, *Beyond Smoke and Mirrors: Mexican Immigration in an Era of Economic Integration* (New York: Russell Sage Foundation, 2002).

69    "for whatever length of time they want to stay": Reagan quoted in Tichenor, *Dividing Lines*, 255.

70    employer sanction provision the "keystone" of the bill: President Ronald Reagan, "Statement

on Signing the Immigration Reform and Control Act of 1986," November 6, 1986, at http://
www.reagan.utexas.edu/archives/speeches/1986/110686b.htm.

70      but only $34 million was spent: Tichenor, *Dividing Lines*, 263.

70      The congressional commission that in 1981: Ibid., 251.

71      "Maybe we should just brand all the babies": This account is taken from Martin Anderson,
        *Revolution: The Reagan Legacy* (Stanford, Calif.: Hoover Institution Press, 1988), 272–277.

71      the chief of the Border Patrol in the El Paso sector: Sue Anne Pressley, "On the Streets of
        El Paso, They're Feeling the Pinch: Border Crackdown Has Impact on Economy, Crime,"
        *Washington Post*, November 14, 1993.

72      Wilson campaign had flashed the White House telephone number: Roberto Suro, "Califor-
        nia Border Crackdown Vowed: With the Administration Under Fire, Reno Promises a New
        Effort," *Washington Post*, September 18, 1994.

72      Apprehensions went up threefold: "Arrests Triple on First Day of Crackdown at Border," *Los
        Angeles Times*, October 3, 1994.

73      The INS judged the enforcement operations of the 1990s a success: "Testimony of Michael
        A. Pearson, Executive Associate Commissioner for Field Operations, INS, Subcommittee on
        Immigration of the Senate Judiciary Committee," February 10, 2000, at http://www.uscis.
        gov/files/pressrelease/pearson.pdf.

74      by 2002 that number had fallen to 25 percent: Douglas S. Massey, "Beyond the Border
        Buildup."

74      Over the decade, the number of Border Patrol agents grew: Transactional Records Access
        Clearinghouse, "Border Patrol Report on Staffing," April 4, 2006, at http://trac.syr.edu/
        immigration/reports/143.

74      But instead of reducing the number of illegal migrants coming across the border: Sebastian
        Rotella, "Border Patrol Push Diverts Flow; Immigration: Operation Gatekeeper in San Di-
        ego Forces Illegal Crossers into Easier-to-Police Areas. But Smuggling, Desperation Grow,"
        *Los Angeles Times*, October 17, 2004.

75      the rates that immigrant smugglers, or coyotes, were charging quickly shot up: Tony Perry,
        "INS Program to Add Agents, Equipment Along Border," *Los Angeles Times*, June 24, 1995;
        Massey, "Beyond the Border Buildup."

75      "a more complex system of illegal practices": Peter Andreas, "The Escalation of U.S. Im-
        migration Control in the Post-NAFTA Era," *Political Science Quarterly* 113, no. 4 (1998–
        1999), 599.

75      The death rate among illegal border crossers soared: Jorge G. Castañeda, *Ex Mex: From
        Migrants to Immigrants* (New York: New Press, 2007), 58.

75      "It is one of the most horrible deaths that can occur for a human being": James Sterngold, "Dev-
        astating Picture of Immigrants Dead in Arizona Desert," *New York Times*, May 25, 2001.

76      an internal task force study on the issue: Interview with John Maisto, former director of
        Western Hemisphere Affairs, National Security Council, November 19, 2007.

76      "quite simply the cockiest man I have ever met": Vicente Fox and Rob Allyn, *Revolution of
        Hope: The Life, Faith and Dreams of a Mexican President* (New York: Viking, 2007).

76      He was flattered by Bush's effort: Ibid., 146–150.

77      "an orderly framework for migration": Joint Statement by President George Bush and Presi-
        dent Vicente Fox Towards a Partnership for Prosperity. The Guanajuato Proposal, February
        16, 2001, at http://www.whitehouse.gov/news/releases/2001/02/20010220-2.html; Ruth
        Ellen Wasem and Geoffrey K. Collver, "Immigration of Agricultural Guest Workers," CRS
        Report for Congress, Updated January 24, 2003, at http://digital.library.unt.edu/govdocs/
        crs/permalink/meta-crs-3731:1.

77      the two governments: Castañeda, *Ex Mex*, 79–80.

78      "The idea was to do it piece by piece": Interview with John Maisto, November 19, 2007.

78      He insisted, somewhat disingenuously: Jeffrey Davidow, *The U.S. and Mexico: The Bear
        and the Porcupine* (Princeton, N.J.: Markus Weiner, 2004), 222. Davidow's interpretation
        is almost surely disingenuous. The meaning of the phrase "single undertaking" is well un-

derstood in diplomatic circles, particularly in trade negotiations, to refer to a negotiation in which nothing is agreed until everything is agreed. That allows negotiators to put forward what could be politically costly concessions, but pull them off the table if the other side fails to respond with similar concessions.

78    Powell's State Department: Interview with Steve Fischel, former chief of legislation and regulation, Visa Office, State Department, May 10, 2007.

78    But Ashcroft's Justice Department had a much narrower vision: Ibid.

78    Ashcroft and officials in the DPC made it clear that they opposed amnesty: Interview with George Lannon, former acting assistant secretary, Consular Affairs, State Department, October 9, 2007; Castañeda, who was well plugged into the administration's behind-the-scenes battles thanks to the impressive intelligence network built by Mexico in Washington during the NAFTA negotiations, offers the same interpretation of Ashcroft's position. Ashcroft and Diana Schacht, who had the lead on the issues for the DPC, both declined to be interviewed for this book.

78–79   President Fox would later write that Ashcroft had opposed the effort: Interviews with Steve Fischel, May 10, 2007, and George Lannon, October 9, 2007; Fox and Allyn, *Revolution of Hope*, p. 228.

79    Davidow describes a January 2001 meeting: Davidow, *The U.S. and Mexico*, 220.

79    "the deliberations reflected the most frank and productive dialogue": Quoted in Castañeda, *Ex Mex*, 83.

# 3. The Cops

80    the FBI had deployed more than 4,000: "Fine Report," 11; Ziglar testimony to 9/11 Commission, January 26, 2004.

80    "a real, not an imagined, threat": Interview with second former senior Justice official, May 3, 2007.

80    "far too little real awareness of . . . the terrorist presence": John Ashcroft, *Never Again: Securing America and Restoring Justice* (New York: Hachette Book Group, 2006), 125.

81    "noise in the system": Ibid., 124.

82    Ordinary due process rights . . . are not required for noncitizens: See Daniel Kanstroom, *Deportation Nation: Outsiders in American History* (Cambridge, Mass.: Harvard University Press, 2007), 1–20.

82    "you're guilty until proven innocent": Interview with Jim Williams, October 19, 2007.

82    within twenty-four hours of being detained: Letter from Eleanor Acer, Director, Asylum Program, Lawyers Committee for Human Rights, to Richard A. Sloan, Director, Policy Directives and Instructions Branch, INS, November 19, 2001, at http://www.humanrightsfirst.org/us_law/loss/comments.pdf.

82    officials there decided they had the power to authorize much longer detentions: In February 2003, the Justice Department's Office of Legal Counsel altered some of those presumptions, ruling that the department could hold anyone ordered deported for at least ninety days, with no obligation to act before the end of that period. In some cases, the OLC ruled, immigrants could be held even longer provided that the detention was "supported by purposes related to the proper implementation of immigration laws" ("Fine Report," 106). In 2006, a federal judge in Brooklyn upheld that interpretation in a case brought by some of the 9/11 detainees, ruling that the 9/11 emergency justified extraordinary measures to confine noncitizens who fell under suspicion. He also ruled that the government had broad discretion to enforce the law selectively against noncitizens of a particular religion, race, or national origin, and to detain them indefinitely. Nina Bernstein, "Judge Rules That U.S. Has Power to Detain Non-Citizens Indefinitely," *New York Times*, June 15, 2006.

82    U.S. Supreme Court had ruled: See Migration Policy Institute, *America's Challenge: Domestic Security, Civil Liberties and National Unity After September 11* (Washington, D.C.: MPI, 2003), 52; hereafter "MPI Report."

83     Critics of the high level of illegal immigration: See, for example, Michelle Malkin, *Invasion.*

83     implementing a "no bond" policy: David Cole, *Enemy Aliens: Double Standards and Constitutional Freedoms in the War on Terrorism* (New York: New Press, 2003), 32–33.

83     immigration powers were "vast and underused": Interview with Michael Becraft, October 4, 2007.

83     "you can do a lot more than you can with probable cause": Ibid.

84     "Delay was victory": Interview with second former senior Justice Department official, May 3, 2007.

84     "probably overreacted": Interview with Jim Ziglar, October 9, 2007.

84     "the best way to deal with John was one-on-one": Interview with third former senior Justice Department official, November 16, 2007.

84     His main priorities at the department: See Michael Hirsh and Michael Isikoff, "What Went Wrong," *Newsweek*, May 27, 2002.

85     "I don't want to hear about al-Qaeda anymore": Philip Shenon, *The Commission: The Uncensored History of the 9/11 Investigation* (New York: Hachette Book Group, 2008), 247.

85     "a moral imperative for toughness": Ashcroft, *Never Again*, 280.

85     "he sees this as a civilizational clash": Quoted in Jeffrey Rosen, "John Ashcroft's Permanent Campaign," *The Atlantic Monthly*, April 1, 2004.

86     "You're talking about doing something that's grossly unconstitutional": Interview with Ziglar, October 9, 2007.

87     "I was persona non grata": Ibid. Ziglar's account was confirmed by another senior Justice official at the meeting who asked not to be identified. There are similar accounts in Thomas Ginsberg, "Government's Efforts to Thwart Terrorism Go Too Far, Critics Say," *Philadephia Inquirer*, June 16, 2003, and in Eric Lichtblau, *Bush's Law: The Remaking of American Justice* (New York: Random House, 2008), 5–7.

89     suspending habeas corpus for any foreigner: Interview with James Sensenbrenner, former chairman, House Judiciary Committee, April 3, 2008.

89     "Aggressive detention . . . is vital": U.S. Justice Department transcript, "Ashcroft Briefs on New Anti-Terrorism Immigration Policies," October 31, 2001, at http://www.globalsecurity .org/military/library/news/2001/10/mil-011031-usia05.htm.

89     border powers of the Justice Department were virtually unlimited: CRS Report for Congress, "Authority to Enforce the Immigration and Nationality Act in the Wake of the Homeland Security Act: Legal Issues," July 16, 2003, at http://digital.library.unt.edu/govdocs/crs/ permalink/meta-crs-7713:1.

91     "improve national security . . . while also facilitating the movement of goods and people": Interview with Admiral Brian Peterman, former special assistant to the president for Border and Transportation Security, White House Homeland Security Council, November 27, 2007.

91     "a massive program for registering all aliens": Interview with second former senior Justice official, May 3, 2007.

91     it settled for a more limited program: Interview with George Lannon, October 9, 2007; interview with Ziglar, October 9, 2007; interview with second former senior Justice official, May 3, 2007. See also "MPI Report," p. 13

92     "waged largely through anti-immigrant measures": Cole, *Enemy Aliens*, 21.

92     arrested more than 1,200 individuals: "Fine Report," 1; PENTTBOM, the code name for the 9/11 investigation, was an acronym for Pentagon/Twin Towers Bombing Investigation.

92     "We will use every available statute." Quoted in "Fine Report," 12.

93     "whether or not the alien was the subject of the lead": Ibid., 14.

93     "No distinction generally was made": Ibid., 16.

93     Shakir Baloch was arrested on September 20: The details of Baloch's case are from testimony by Baloch to the Criminal Justice Group of the United Nations in Geneva, April 4, 2003, at http://www.aclu.org/safefree/general/16887res20030627.html, and from Doug Sanders et al., "Surviving History, A Globe and Mail team looks at 11 people's lives though the prism

of September 11," *Globe & Mail*, September 7, 2002, and Chisun Lee, "INS Detainee Hits, U.S. Strikes Back," *Village Voice*, January 30–February 5, 2002.

94    Tarek Mohamed Fayad: Details of his story can be found in "MPI Report: Appendix," 16–18.

95    Another detainee: "MPI Report: Appendix," p. 37.

95    nearly half had been in the United States for at least six years "MPI Report," p. 7.

95    no intention of devoting significant time or resources: "Fine Report," 78; interviews with former senior INS officials.

96    "an individual arrested . . . posed no ongoing threat": Ibid., 74.

96    "They knew they couldn't control me": Interview with Jim Ziglar, October 9, 2007.

96    "pretty bloody appalling": Ibid.

96    "Just watch me": Ibid.

97    "any objection I had to this would have been written off": Interview with Jim Ziglar, December 20, 2007.

97    "a very poisoned sort of atmosphere": Interview with Jim Ziglar, October 9, 2007.

97    "Jim had a different opinion, and it hurt him": Interview with Mike Becraft, October 4, 2007.

97    "He had the responsibility to act": Interview with second former senior Justice official, December 19, 2007.

98    "it was not going to be productive": Interview with Jim Ziglar, October 9, 2007.

98    "no one who did law enforcement . . . was paying any attention to the immigration system": Interview with second former senior Justice official, May 3, 2007.

98    Ashcroft ordered Ziglar: Ibid.

99    priority be given to the "several thousand": "Memorandum from the Deputy Attorney General, January 25, 2002, Re: Guidance for Absconder Apprehensive Initiative." The memo was first leaked to the *Washington Post*. See Dan Eggen, "Deportee Sweep Will Start with Mideast Focus," February 8, 2002.

99    Sharif Kesbeh: The details for this section are drawn from Michelle Goldberg, "Banished from the American Dream," *Salon.com*, April 26, 2004; Gregory Katz, "In Houston, They Built a Business and Family. Deportation Had Left Them Struggling in a Harsh Land," *Houston Chronicle*, February 28, 2007; and from a telephone interview with Noor Kesbeh, June 18, 2007.

101–102    "demonstrated their contempt for our immigration system": Michelle Malkin, "Lawmakers Who Love Lawbreakers," syndicated column, October 12, 2002.

103    no claims to have apprehended any terrorists: *9/11 and Terrorist Travel*; see p. 155 and notes p. 167.

103    70 were found to be in the country illegally: "Statement of Johnny N. Williams, Executive Associate Commissioner for Field Operations U.S. Immigration and Naturalization Service, before the Senate Committee on Finance," January 30, 2003.

103    huge security threat posed by the government's lack of knowledge: Interview with second former senior Justice official, December 19, 2007.

104    "no way that any . . . consular officer would have denied those visas": Interview with Steve Fischel, May 10, 2007.

104    the department's procedures had all been properly followed: Transcript, Seventh Public Hearing of the National Commission on Terrorist Attacks Upon the United States, "Borders, Transportation and Managing Risks," January 26, 2004, p. 38, at http://govinfo.library.unt.edu/911/archive/hearing7/9-11commission_hearing_2004-01-26.pdf.

105    "That was never a Justice Department position": Interview with second former senior Justice official, December 19, 2007.

105    State considered it the "minimum buy-in": Interview with Richard Armitage, January 7, 2008

106    the State Department and the FBI agreed to drop the thirty-day clock: Kathleen C. Walker, "The Tale of the CONDOR and Security-Related State Department Developments Post 9/11," *Bender's Immigration Bulletin* 116, January 15, 2003.

107     "his real interest was not in being on the city council": Quoted in Cam Simpson, "Aspiring Politician at Center of Policy," *Chicago Tribune*, November 16, 2003.

107     "like he was doing a science project": Interview with Michael Becraft, October 4, 2007.

108     a new program to register all foreigners: Interview with Kris Kobach, October 3, 2007.

108     the government had the power to enforce registration selectively: Joseph D. Whitaker and Mark Harris, "U.S. Appeals Court Approves Iranian Student Deportation," *Washington Post*, December 28, 1979.

109     Mohammed Atta: For more on Atta's complicated visa history, see the discussion in *9/11 and Terrorist Travel*, 9–31.

109     "missed opportunities of tragic and colossal dimension": Interview with Kris Kobach, October 3, 2007.

109     "abuse of U.S. immigration laws was instrumental in the deaths of nearly 3,000 people": Kris W. Kobach, "The Quintessential Force Multiplier: The Inherent Authority of Local Police to Make Immigration Arrests," *Albany Law Review* 69 (2005).

110     "we might have been able to stop it": Interview with Kris Kobach, October 3, 2007.

110     "We didn't want every cop in Texas asking for papers": Interview with second former senior Justice official, May 3, 2007.

110     when Ashcroft first announced: "Attorney General Prepared Remarks on the National Security Entry-Exit Registration System," at http://www.justice.gov/archive/ag/speeches/2002/060502agpreparedremarks.htm.

111     "you couldn't do everyone": Interview with Brian Peterman, November 27, 2007.

111     "that country's leadership is going to hate the United States": Interview with Kris Kobach, October 3, 2007.

112     he was told that Pakistanis did not need to re-register: Anwar Iqbal, "Interview: Pakistani Newsman Held by INS," *United Press International*, January 31, 2003.

112     "took him to an INS detention facility": George Lardner, "Brookings Scholar Is Detained by INS; Registration Rules Snags Pakistani Editor," *Washington Post*, January 30, 2003.

112     "they decided to drag me off the road:" "The INS Registration Policy Is Inherently Flawed," *India Abroad*, February 7, 2003.

112–113  "The policy is an attempt to draw a Maginot Line around America": Ejaz Haider, "Wrong Message to the Muslim World," *Washington Post*, February 3, 2003.

113     Arab and Muslim governments fumed: Interview with second former senior Justice official, May 3, 2007.

113     "the U.S. cannot win here on NSEERS": DOS Cable, "Sharp Pakistani Criticism of NSEERS," quoted in *9/11 and Terrorist Travel*, 169.

113     The program caused similar outrage: Cable from Ambassador Ralph L. Boyce, U.S. Embassy Jakarta to Secretary of State Colin Powell, "NSEERS: Improving Our Security by Showing Flexibility," February 3, 2003; and cable from Ambassador Mary Ann Peters, U.S. Embassy Dhaka, to Secretary of State Colin Powell, "Scenesetter for Secretary Powell's Visit to Dhaka," June 3, 2003. Both were redacted and released by the State Department June 4, 2008, under a FOIA request by the author.

114     These and hundreds of others were arrested: See Henry Weinstein and Greg Krikorian, "Caught Between Dueling Policies: Hundreds of Middle Eastern Immigrants Who Overstayed Visas Hoped to Pay a Fine and Have a Hearing. Instead They Were Detained," *Los Angeles Times*, December 21, 2002. Interview with former senior INS official, May 3, 2007.

115     "I told you so": Interview with former senior INS official, May 3, 2007.

115     they had no idea: Interview with Faith Nouri, March 2, 2007.

115     "He was arrested and detained": Rachel L. Swarns, "Fearful, Angry or Confused, Muslim Immigrants Register," *New York Times*, April 25, 2003.

115     Zaif Safdar: This section is based largely on an interview with Zaif Safdar, July 5, 2007.

116     in consultation with officials at Johns Hopkins: The general counsel at Johns Hopkins has

disputed part of that account, saying that the school realized his application was late and had sent it Federal Express at the university's expense to lessen the delay.

116 Safdar has little resentment: Carlyle Murphy and Nurith C. Aizenman, "Foreign Students Navigate Labyrinth of New Laws; Slip-ups Overlooked Before 9/11 Now Grounds for Deportation," *Washington Post*, June 9, 2003.

## 4. The Technocrats

117 "Name me one person": Interview with former senior DHS official, September 24, 2007.

119 "I never doubted the courage": Frank Reeves and James O'Toole, "Ridge Returning to 'Nam in Peace," *Pittsburgh Post-Gazette*, May 13, 1999.

120 The goal of the strategy: "Ridge Says NAFTA Helping State's Exports to Canada, Mexico," Associated Press, March 30, 2000.

120 They warned that implementing the provision: Laura Eggertson, "States Join Border Fight," *Toronto Star*, July 25, 1998.

120 The CIA had learned as early as 1996: See Michael Scheuer, *Marching Toward Hell: America and Islam After Iraq* (New York: Free Press, 2008), 17.

121 but Abbot said that one conclusion was already clear: Interview with Admiral Steve Abbot, former White House deputy homeland security adviser, May 8, 2007.

121 Libby, along with Cheney: Brill, *After*, 54–55.

122 "We did what we had to do": Interview with Tom Ridge, former secretary of Homeland Security, October 29, 2007.

122 The first piece he read: Brill, *After*, 117.

122 "Security measures, if carried too far": Admiral James Loy and Captain Robert G. Ross, "Meeting the Homeland Security Challenge: A Principled Strategy for a Balanced and Practical Response," *Journal of Homeland Security*, September 2001, at http://www.homelandsecurity.org/journal/articles/ross_loy_uscg.htm.

125 "Risk management is a pretty difficult concept": Interview with Tom Ridge, October 29, 2007; and Robert Pear, "U.S. Pressuring Foreign Airlines over Manifests," *New York Times*, November 27, 2001.

125 "Biometrics is the only conceivable way": Ibid.

126 By April 2002 it had filled only half of the 180 personnel slots: Congressional Research Service, *Homeland Security Office: Issues and Options*, May 20, 2002, at http://www.opencrs.cdt.org/document/rl31421.

126 Customs officials were persuaded that the technology was useless: Interviews with two former Customs officials, May 10, 2007, and September 27, 2007.

127 As part of that legislation, Customs got a provision: Interview with Robert Bonner, April 23, 2007.

128 scrutiny was particularly heavy for arriving foreign students: Interview with George D. Heavey, former executive director field operations, Customs, February 7, 2008.

128 Within two days of these full searches: Interview with Robert Bonner, April 23, 2007.

128 "The approach we took at the border was very different": Interview with former senior Customs official, March 2007.

129 virtually every known terrorist organization in the world: See Stewart Bell, *Cold Terror: How Canada Nurtures and Exports Terrorism Around the World* (Toronto: Wiley, 2004).

130 "I think we're going to have to conform in some cases more to U.S. standards," Murray Campbell and Lily Nguyen, "Align with U.S. on Security, Executive Says," *Globe and Mail*, September 15, 2001.

130 "Canada's national interest depends on easy access to the U.S. market": Interview with Stephen Kelly, former deputy chief of mission, U.S. embassy, Ottawa, Canada, September 19, 2007.

131 For instance, in an internal memo Canadian border officials were ordered: Estanislao Oziewicz, "Border Alert Targets Pilots," *Globe and Mail*, September 19, 2001.

131    "I don't think Canadians are prepared to say that Washington can dictate": Steven Chase, "Ottawa Firm on Making Its Own Rules; Won't Bend to U.S. Pressure to Harmonize Customs, Immigration Policies, Manley Says," *Globe and Mail*, September 24, 2001.

131    "The Canadian public . . . seems to sense something Mr Chrétien doesn't": Drew Fagan, "Has PM Misjudged Mood on Security?" *Globe and Mail*, October 1, 2001.

132    "Maybe when he was in the private sector that was a reasonable expectation": Interview with Stephen Kelly, September 19, 2007.

133    Canadian officials, who grow weary of reminding their American counterparts: Drew Fagan, "U.S. Learning Value of Open Border," *Globe and Mail*, April 23, 2002.

134    The Canadians had greater concerns over privacy than the United States: Interview with George Heavey, February 7, 2008.

135    "removing from the vast haystack of trade the legitimate, secure commerce": Robert Bonner, "Open Address to Customs Trade Symposium," Washington, D.C., November 27, 2001.

136    "We really did accomplish the purpose of reinventing the goods transfer process": Interview with Paul O'Neill, former Secretary of the Treasury, September 24, 2007.

137    "Well before the Ridge-Manley accord we had started meeting with our Canadian counterparts": Joel Brinkley and Philip Shenon, "Ridge Meeting Opposition from Agencies," *New York Times*, February 7, 2002.

137    "There were deliverables coming out": Telephone interview with Lt. Col. Chris Hornbarger, former director of policy and planning, White House Homeland Security Council, August 24, 2007.

139    United States "requires a border management system that keeps pace with expanding trade": "Securing America's Borders Fact Sheet: Border Security," White House Office of the Press Secretary, January 25, 2002, at http://www.whitehouse.gov/news/releases/2002/01/20020125.html.

139–140  Chris Hornbarger . . . had stayed up late: Interview with Chris Hornbarger, August 24, 2007.

140    Ridge had his staff assemble a history of the various efforts: White House White Paper, "Modern History of Border Reorganization Studies and Efforts," December 2001, provided to author.

140–141   Ridge favored one that would create a National Border Administration: Based on conversations with several former White House officials, August 24, 2007, and September 17, 2007.

141    Falkenrath's staff drafted a white paper detailing the proposal: Alison Mitchell, "Official Urges Combining Several Agencies to Create One That Protects Borders," *New York Times*, January 12, 2002.

141    A rare photograph of the small Oval Office meeting: The photograph can be found at http://www.whitehouse.gov/news/releases/2001/12/images/20011221-2-1.html.

141    Ziglar was also annoyed because he and Bonner: Interview with Jim Ziglar, October 9, 2007.

142    "You're using a howitzer when a rifle shot will do": Interview with former senior White House official, December 18, 2007.

142    It turned into an extraordinarily bitter meeting: This account is based on 2007 interviews with several officials present at the meeting.

142    "the Christmas massacre": Interview with Steve Abbot, May 8, 2007.

142    Though he had no love for Ziglar's INS: Brill, *After*, 286.

143    Colin Powell, the secretary of state, warned of the enormous legislative obstacles: Interview with Pancho Kinney, former director of strategy, White House Homeland Security Council, September 17, 2007, and telephone interview with Colin Powell, former secretary of state, September 21, 2007.

143    Only O'Neill was mildly enthusiastic: Interviews with former senior White House official, December 18, 2007 and with Paul O'Neill, September 24, 2007.

143 The next week, however, the proposal was leaked to the *New York Times*: Alison Mitchell, "Official Urges Combining Several Agencies to Create One That Protects Borders," *New York Times*, January 12, 2002.

143 "If we can't get this done, what can we do?": Brill, *After*, 287.

143 "I was thinking it may be badly written, but it's not that bad": Interview with Chris Hornbarger, August 24, 2007.

144 "I suppose cabinet secretaries are supposed to be territorial": Interview with Paul O'Neill, September 24, 2007.

144 But when Ridge took the proposal to Congress: Brill, *After*, 397.

144 "Mr. Ridge should have authority and resources": Elizabeth Becker, "Homeland Security: Debating Whether New Agency Can Command, or Just Link Commanders," *New York Times*, September 22, 2001.

145 "Nothing is off the table," Card told Ridge: Brill, *After*, 409.

146 "It would have been a tight, cohesive agency": Interview with Chris Hornbarger, August 24, 2007.

146 One of Ridge's senior aides would later brag that he had "slam-dunked": Brill, *After*, 485.

# 5. The Scapegoat

148 "a period to be endured": U.S. Department of State, Office of the Inspector General, "Review of Nonimmigrant Visa Issuance Policy and Procedures," p. 12, December 2002, at http://oig.state.gov/documents/organization/16215.pdf.

148 "don't go there and stamp visas": Interview with Frank Moss, former deputy assistant secretary of state for passport services, September 19, 2007.

148 "We lose a lot of Foreign Service officers": Interview with Larry Wilkerson, former chief of staff to Secretary of State Colin Powell, February 15, 2008.

148 "would be considered slow": David T. Jones, "The Under-Appreciated Consular Cone," *Foreign Service Journal*, March 2001.

148 the Justice Department went public: The State Department had provided all its visa information on the hijackers directly to the FBI, George Lannon told me. By this time State had in fact already determined that all nineteen hijackers had received valid visas: fifteen in Saudi Arabia, two in the UAE, and two in Germany.

149 Ryan launched into a vigorous defense: This section is based on the transcript of the October 12, 2001, hearing ("The Role of Technology in Preventing the Entry of Terrorist into the United States," U.S. Senate Committee on the Judiciary, Subcommittee on Technology, Terrorism and Government Information, October 12, 2001 [Washington, D.C.: US Government Printing Office, 2002]), and on interviews with several officials present during the hearing.

150 "she was enraged": Interviews with George Lannon, October 9, 2007, Steve Fischel, May 10, 2007, and Frank Moss, September 19, 2007.

151 "I saw the handwriting on the wall": Interview with George Lannon, October 9, 2007.

151 the director was surprisingly conciliatory: Ibid.; in her testimony to the 9/11 Commission on January 26, 2004, Ryan says, in response to a question from one of the commissioners, that she had initially learned about the CIA's failure to pass along the names of al-Mihdhar and al-Hazmi during the meeting with Tenet. But Lannon insists that she and others at State had heard some internal discussion of the mistake prior to that meeting, a recollection shared by another former State official who attended the Tenet meeting. That version would seem to fit more accurately with the tone of Ryan's testimony to Feinstein's subcommittee, in which she questioned whether or not there was any intelligence information on the two hijackers, and if so why it was not shared.

152 "that woman": Interview with Steve Fischel, May 10, 2007.

153 "she reduced a set of rosary beads to dust": Interview with Frank Moss, September 19, 2007.

153     "deeply steeped in the Catholic Church": Interview with Johnny Young, October 30, 2007.

154     "we should have moved Mary originally": Interview with former senior State Department official, January 2008.

154     "we felt like he let us down": Interview with Johnny Young, October 30, 2007.

154     "he just never got that": Telephone interview with Lisa Bobbie Schreiber Hughes, ambassador to Suriname, former director for consular affairs and international programs on the White House Homeland Security Council, October 10, 2007.

155     Powell had made it one of his missions: Interview with Grant Green, former undersecretary of state for management, September 6, 2007.

155     Ryan had begun to change that culture: Background information about Mary Ryan from a telephone interview with Dianne Andruch, former deputy assistant secretary for overseas citizen services, State Department, September 10, 2007.

155     "she was your mentor": Quoted in Joe Holly, "Obituary: Mary Ryan, 65; Embattled Consular Chief," *Washington Post*, April 29, 2006.

157     "It was agony": Telephone interview with Barry Kefauver, former deputy assistant secretary of state for passport services, November 7, 2007.

157     "It was a huge mistake": Ibid.

158     Ryan was frequently on the job during the early-morning hours: Telephone interview with John Hotchner, State Department official, September 27, 2007.

159     had wondered out loud: This account is drawn from Bob Woodward, *Shadow: Five Presidents and the Legacy of Watergate* (New York: Simon & Schuster, 2000) and from U.S. Court of Appeals for the District of Columbia Circuit in Re: Janet Mullins, filed July 9, 1996.

159     "an outrageous abuse of power": Timothy Clifford and Jack Sirica, "Clinton Team: Probe a Smear," *Newsday*, October 15, 1992.

159     "Having suffered": Interview with Barry Kefauver, November 7, 2007.

160     first began requiring visas . . . in 1884: *9/11 and Terrorist Travel*, 69.

160     "self-defense against foreigners": Tichenor, *Dividing Lines*, 152.

160     "The powers of the chief of the Visa Office": Quoted ibid., 155.

160     "we were expected to do everything with nothing": "Statement of Mary A. Ryan to the National Commission on Terrorist Attacks Upon the United States," January 26, 2004, at http://govinfo.library.unt.edu/911/archive/hearing7/9-11commission_hearing_2004-01-26.pdf.

161     a severe indictment of its visa-granting procedures: *9/11 and Terrorist Travel*, 79–80. The commission's staff investigation, which relied on hundreds of interviews as well as access to classified documents from throughout the administration, is by far the most thorough account of the pre-9/11 period, and I relied on it extensively for this section.

161     The consular officer . . . was unaware: *9/11 and Terrorist Travel*, 50–51.

162     State agreed to share the list: Ibid., 79.

162     The TIPOFF list . . . contained about 60,000 names: Ibid., 81.

162     The FBI provided just 63: Ibid.

163     put in place a global, computerized system: "Statement of Mary A. Ryan," January 26, 2004.

163     The system was fully automated: Office of the Historian, Bureau of Public Affairs, *History of the Department of State During the Clinton Presidency (1993–2001)*, at http://www.state.gov/r/pa/ho/pubs/8525.htm.

163     Ramzi bin al-Shibh: "MPI Report," 10.

164–165     "to facilitate and promote travel": U.S. GAO, *Border Security: Visa Process Should Be Strengthened as an Antiterrorism Tool*, October 2002, at http://www.nationalreview.com/document/document-gao102202.pdf.

165     "she would have been on the open borders side": Interview with Grant Green, September 6, 2007.

165     "everybody ran away from that position": Interview with Dianne Andruch, September 10, 2007.

166  Productivity: Numbers from Bureau of Labor Statistics, "Productivity Change in the Non-farm Business Sector, 1947–2006," at http://www.bls.gov/lpc/prodybar.htm.

166  National Partnership for Reinventing Government: From the official history of the National Partnership for Reinventing Government, at http://govinfo.library.unt.edu/npr/whoweare/historyofnpr.html.

166  "three key goals": *9/11 and Terrorist Travel*, 83.

167  the most important U.S. ally: See Rachel Bronson, *Thicker Than Oil: America's Uneasy Partnership with Saudi Arabia* (New York: Oxford University Press, 2006).

167  In one case he ordered a consular officer: *9/11 and Terrorist Travel*, p. 121.

168  "They partied and they left": Interview with George Lannon, October 9, 2007.

168  having overcome the "intending immigrant" presumption: *9/11 and Terrorist Travel*, 122.

169  consular officers would give extra scrutiny: Ibid., 124–126.

169  "chaotic and dysfunctional": Ibid., 127

170  Afer the fall of the Berlin Wall: Interview with Barry Kefauver, November 7, 2007.

170  nearly forty embassies: U.S. Department of State, Office of Inspector General, "Review of Nonimmigrant Visa Issuance Policy and Procedures," December 2002.

171  "reduced work for the FSNs": Foreign Service nationals, citizens of the country in which a U.S. embassy resides; before 9/11 they were responsible for much of preliminary work on visa applications.

171  unaware that Saudi citizens posed any security threat: *9/11 and Terrorist Travel*, 127.

171  received their visas sight unseen: Ibid., 34.

172  "a corrosive culture": Joel Mowbray, *Dangerous Diplomacy: How the State Department Threatens America's Security* (Washington, D.C.: Regnery, 2003).

172  McCarthy had been too sympathetic: See Ann Coulter, *Treason: Liberal Treachery from the Cold War to the War on Terrorism* (New York: Random House, 2003).

172  "treacherous pigs": Interview with Pancho Kinney, September 17, 2007.

173  "This has not happened": State Department, Office of Inspector General, "Review of Nonimmigrant Visa Issuance Policy and Procedures," p. 18. December 2002.

174  a nearly identical story: Edward T. Pound, "The Easy Path to the United States for Three of the 9/11 Hijackers," *US News & World Report*, December 12, 2001.

175  "sitting back fat and happy": Interview with Colin Powell, September 21, 2007.

176  "now clearly a homeland security function": House Committee on Government Reform Subcommittee on Civil Service, Census, and Agency Organization, *Homeland Security: Should Consular Affairs Be Transferred to the New Department of Homeland Security?* 107th Cong., 2d sess., June 26, 2002, H. Rpt. 107-205.

177  "It was easy for me": Interview with Tom Ridge, October 29, 2007.

177  "They didn't want it": Interview with George Lannon, October 9, 2007.

177  "[Powell] got nothing": Ibid.

177–178  "she was starting to cause me difficulties": Interview with Colin Powell, September 21, 2007.

178  "She didn't get the message": Interview with senior State Department official, January 2008.

178  "I don't think it was a great surprise": Interview with Grant Green, September 6, 2007.

178  legislation that retained the State Department's role: Summary of legislative action found in Ruth Ellen Wasem, "Visa Policy: Roles of the Departments of State and Homeland Security," CRS Report for Congress, March 4, 2004, at http://trac.syr.edu/immigration/library/p50.pdf.

179  "a shameful and inadequate effort": Susan Schmidt and Glenn Kessler, "Powell Seeks Top Consular Official's Resignation," *Washington Post*, July 11, 2002.

179  "a neo-Nazi": Ben Barber, "Consular Officials Liken Visa Critics to Neo-Nazis," *Washington Times*, July 18, 2002.

179  "get your people in line": Interview with George Lannon, October 9, 2007.

180  "I was appalled": Ibid.

180     "he abandoned us and sacrificed Mary": Interview with Johnny Young, October 30, 2007.

180     "protégé and clone of Mary Ryan": Joel Mowbray, "Mary Ryan Redux," *National Review*, August 7, 2002.

180     "necessary to do in order to save the consular corps": Interview with Colin Powell, September 21, 2007.

180     After leaving the State Department: Interview with Johnny Young, October 30, 2007.

181     suffering from myelofibrosis: Ibid.

181     "It was an incredible funeral": Ibid.

## 6. The Consequences

182     President Bush did something he admitted was quite rare: See Katherine Q. Seelye, "Flash! President Bush Says He Reads Papers," *New York Times*, December 25, 2006.

182     "I could barely get my coffee down": White House transcript of press conference by the President, March 13, 2002.

183     "It's the only reason I stayed": Interview with Jim Ziglar, October 9, 2007.

183     "did away with the niceties of the consultant strategic planning": Interview with Michael Cronin, September 11, 2007.

183     "I take responsibility for not doing a good job": Kellie Lunney, "INS Chief Pledges to Speed Up Management Reforms," *GovernmentExecutive.com*, March 19, 2002.

184     "never a good fit even before September 11": Audrey Hudson, "Ziglar to Quit INS After Year at Post," *Washington Times*, August 17, 2002.

184     "They would have walked off skyscrapers": Interview with Robert Bonner, December 21, 2007.

184     "they just decided to deep-six the INS": Interview with Michael Becraft, October 4, 2007, and interview with Michael Cronin, September 11, 2007.

185     "The INS's foreign student program historically has been dysfunctional": U.S. Department of Justice, Office of the Inspector General, "The Immigration and Naturalization Service's Contacts with Two September 11 Terrorists," May 20, 2002, p. 12, at http://usdoj.gov/oig/special/0205/fullreport.pdf.

186     the inspector readmitted Atta on another tourist visa: *9/11 and Terrorist Travel*, 17–18.

186     "virtually impossible for people to comply with the letter of the law": Interview with Michael Cronin, September 11, 2007.

187     not the only two of the hijackers to exploit the weaknesses: *9/11 and Terrorist Travel*, 13–14.

188     somewhere between half and three-quarters of the world's top universities: Fareed Zakaria, "Is America in Decline? Why the United States Will Survive the Rise of the Rest," *Foreign Affairs*, May/June 2008.

189     between 30 and 50 percent of researchers were not Americans: National Academies, *Policy Implications of International Graduate Students and Postdoctoral Scholars in the United States* (Washington, D.C.: National Academies Press, 2005).

189     "immigration provides them with the best talent in the world": Rob Paral and Benjamin Johnson, "Maintaining a Competitive Edge: The Role of the Foreign-Born and U.S. Immigration Policies in Science and Engineering" (Immigration Policy Center, August 2004).

189     "an extraordinary set of personal, professional, and cultural relationships": Quoted in Michele Wucker, *Lockout: Why America Keeps Getting Immigration Wrong When Our Prosperity Depends on Getting It Right* (New York: Public Affairs, 2006), 131.

190     Half those American patents are issued to foreign-owned companies: Richard Florida, *The Flight of the Creative Class*, p. 141.

190–191    these companies accounted for more than $500 billion in market value: Stuart Anderson and Michaela Platzer, *American-Made: The Impact of Immigrant Entrepreneurs and Professionals on U.S. Competitiveness* (Washington, D.C.: National Foundation for American Policy, 2006).

191   comes from products that did not even exist at the beginning of the year: "Statement of Norman R. Augustine, retired chairman and CEO of Lockheed Martin and chair of the Committee on Prospering in the Global Economy of the 21st Century, to the House Committee on Science," October 20, 2005, at http://www7.nationalacademies.org/ocga/testimony/gathering_storm_energizing_and_employing_america2.asp.

191   "the places that attract and retain this talent will win": Florida, *The Flight of the Creative Class*, xv, 3.

192   The close ties that such former students have to the United States: See John N. Paden and Peter W. Singer, "America Slams the Door (on Its Foot): Washington's Destructive New Visa Policies," *Foreign Affairs*, May/June 2003.

192   "the most positive thing America has done to win friends from the world": Quoted in Yasmine El-Rashidi, "Mideast Money Pinch: U.S. Service-Sector Firms Feel Loss of Arab Spending," *Wall Street Journal*, May 5, 2006.

192   Sayyid Qutb: See Lawrence Wright, *The Looming Tower: Al-Qaeda and the Road to 9/11* (New York: Random House, 2006).

193   The Pacific Travel Trade School in Los Angeles: Cheryl W. Thompson, Marcia Slacum Greene, and Sarah Cohen, "INS Moves to Plug Student Visa Leaks," *Washington Post*, January 30, 2003.

194   the paper records flooding into the INS had piled so high: Kate Zernike and Christopher Drew, "Efforts to Track Foreign Students Are Said to Lag," *New York Times*, January 28, 2002.

194   "We had no place to store all that paper": Quoted in Allan E. Goodman, president and CEO, Institute of International Education, "Open Doors and Secure Borders: U.S. Student Visa Policy in the Post–9/11 World," January 2006, at http://www.ciaonet.org/casestudy/case005/case005.html.

195   "no choice . . . but to pursue the repeal": Jon Elliston, "Foreign Students Under Scrutiny," *Independent Weekly*, September 20, 2000.

197   Uvais Qidwai, an assistant professor of electrical engineering: Telephone interview with Uvais Qidwai, August 8, 2007.

198   His HIV research was halted entirely: E-mail exchange with Dr. Tarek Aboul-Fadl, received September 12, 2007.

198   "I was mad as hell and I still am": Quoted in Michael Stroh, "Tougher Visa Rules to Stop Terrorism Hamper Research," *Baltimore Sun*, July 13, 2003.

198   Jane Zhang, a graduate student studying leukemia: Lila Guterman, "Stalled at the Border: Many Research Projects Have Been Delayed or Disabled by Strict U.S. Visa Policies," *Chronicle of Higher Education*, April 11, 2003.

199   89 of the 305 scientists invited to attend the conferences ran into visa problems: National Academies, *Policy Implication of International Graduate Students and Postdoctoral Scholars in the United States* (Washington, D.C.: National Academy of Sciences, 2002), 77.

199   Only one of nine top Chinese mathematicians who sought visas to attend: John Markoff, "Chinese Cryptologists Get Invitations to a U.S. Conference, but No Visas," *New York Times*, August 17, 2005.

199   Zhong Min Wang, a Chinese physics student: Pamela Zerbinos, "Severe Visa Problems Threaten Research Collaborations," *American Physics Society News*, March 2003.

200   "I still don't know why": Interviews with Dmitri Denisov, June 13, 2007, and January 29, 2008.

201   could not find his data on the SEVIS records: Robert Becker, "Glitches Riddle Database to Track Foreign Students," *Chicago Tribune*, March 17, 2003.

201   the FBI arrested a student from Thailand: Diana Jean Schmemo, "Problems Slow Tracking of Foreign Students from Abroad," *New York Times*, March 23, 2003.

201   The department had put a herculean effort into making: "NAFSA Response to Department of Homeland Security SEVIS Updates," at http://www.nafsa.org/public_policy.sec/interna-

tional_student_1/iss_archive/nafsa_response_to_department_2. See also "Statement of Victor X. Cerda, Counsel to the Assistant Secretary, U.S. Immigration and Customs Enforcement, Before the House Committee on Education and Workforce, Subcommittee on 21st Century Competitiveness," at http://www.ice.gov/doclib/pi/news/testimonies/cerda031705.pdf.

201    Only a handful of foreign students were actually prevented from enrolling: Alison Siskin, "Monitoring Foreign Students in the United States: The Student and Exchange Visitor Information System," CRS Report for Congress, updated January 14, 2005, at http://fpc.state.gov/documents/organization/44016.pdf.

201    "do not believe that SEVIS is the reason for the declining number": U.S. GAO, "Homeland Security: Performance of Foreign Student and Exchange Visitor Information System Continues to Improve, but Issues Remain," March 17, 2005, at http://gao.gov/new.items/d05440t.pdf.

202    "It took a long time. It was very manually intensive": Interview with Brian Peterman, November 27, 2007.

203    three scientists involved in the Iranian nuclear program: Hillary Mann, "Open Admissions: U.S. Policy Towards Students from Terrorism-Supporting Countries in the Middle East," Policy Focus no. 34, Washington Institute for Near East Policy, 1997.

203    "We were in effect populating the world's biological warfare labs": Interview with Bruce Lawlor, March 1, 2007.

204    "implement measures to end the abuse of student visas": "Homeland Security Presidential Directive 2: Combating Terrorism Through Immigration Policies," October 29, 2001, at http://whitehouse.gov/news/releases/2001/10/20011030-2.html.

204    most of those were in engineering, science, or math: Benjamin Orbach, "Tracking Students from Terrorism-Supporting Middle Eastern Countries: An Update," Washington Institute of Near East Politics, December 1999.

205    the State Department sent a cable: U.S. State Department, "Summary of Special Processing Requirements," unclassified telegram, June 23, 2001.

206    about a thousand visa applicants who were reviewed under the Mantis program: Speech by Dr. John Marburger, director, White House Office of Science and Technology Policy, to the American Association for the Advancement of Science, April 10, 2003.

206    there were only three outright rejections: "Testimony of Janice Jacobs. Deputy Assistant Secretary of State for Visa Services, Bureau of Consular Affairs, House Committee on Science," March 26, 2003, at http://commdocs.house.gov/committees/science/hsy85890.000/hsy85890_0f.htm.

206    the State Department acknowledged that the system had broken down almost entirely: Edward Alden, "No entry: Tougher Visa Controls Are Creating Barriers to American Business," *Financial Times*, July 2, 2004.

207    A handful of the cases sampled had been pending for nearly six months: U.S. GAO, "Border Security: Improvements Needed to Reduce Time Taken to adjudicate Visas for Science Students and Scholars," February 2004, at http://www.gao.gov/new.items/d04371.pdf.

207    "seriously affected our competitiveness." Drawn from internal Boeing e-mails and from Kristi Heim, "Boeing Stumbles in Race for China," *Seattle Times*, June 20, 2005.

208    the Saudis charged that the United States was "not living up to its end of the bargain": Cable from the American Consul General in Jeddah Gina Abercrombie-Winstanley, "Saudi Civair: Policy Changes and Complaints," January 2003. Redacted and released by the State Department June 4, 2008, under a FOIA request by the author.

208    the Vietnamese government reopened the competition: Edward Alden, "Visa Restrictions Hamper U.S. Businesses," *Financial Times*, January 29, 2003.

209    Moore Nanotechnology, a New Hampshire company: Murray Hiebert, "Travel Pains: New Visa Rules for Visitors to U.S. Hurt Businesses That Need to See Overseas Customers," *Far Eastern Economic Review*, June 19, 2003; Tim Johnson, "Post-9/11 Memorial, Borders Tight," Knight-Ridder Newspapers, September 15, 2004.

210    "the reasons for China's inclusion are not self-evident": Letter from Robert A. Kapp, presi-

dent, U.S.-China Business Council, to Secretary of State Colin Powell," August 16, 2002, provided to author.

210    By the end of 2003, it had relocated virtually all of its employees to India: Edward Luce, Khozem Merchant, and Amy Yee, "Visas and the West's 'Hidden Agenda,'" *Financial Times*, April 9, 2003.

210    Amway, one of the largest direct-sale firms in the world: Alden, "No Entry," July 24, 2004; Lee Hockstader, "Post-9/11 Visa Rules Keep Thousands from Coming to U.S.," *Washington Post*, November 11, 2003.

211    the clinic's numbers for patients from the Middle East were down by more than half: Jeff Gottlieb, "Tighter Borders Squeeze Hospitals," *Los Angeles Times*, March 23, 2003.

211    "It seems a crying shame": David Ward, "Trouble and Cost of Visas Halts Hallé's US Tour," *The Guardian*, March 30, 2006.

211    fewer managers and promoters: Anastasia Tsioulcas, "Musicians Finding Their Way Through Visa Maze," *Global Rhythm*, July 28, 2006, at http://www.globalrhythm.net/WorldMu-sicFeatures/MusiciansFindingTheirWaythroughVisaMaze.cfm.

212    65,000 fewer visas: Jennifer Jacobson, "In Visa Limbo," *Chronicle of Higher Education*, September 19, 2003.

212    Canada issued four times as many visas to Chinese students: Beth McMurtrie, "Foreign Enrollments Grow in the U.S., but So Does Competition from Other Nations," *Chronicle of Higher Education*, November 16, 2001.

212    The decline was even steeper among graduate schools: See Council of Graduate Schools, *Research Report: Findings from the 2007 CSG International Graduate Admissions Survey*, November 2007, at http://www.cgsnet.org/portals/0/pdf/r_intlapps07_i.pdf.

212    graduate applications from China and India: Paul Mooney and Shailaja Neelakantan, "No Longer Dreaming of America: In India and China, Far Fewer Students Consider the U.S. the Best Place to Go," *Chronicle of Higher Education*, October 8, 2004.

212–213    the United States lost something like 150,000 foreign students: Marlene Johnson, CEO, NAFSA, presentation to the Secure Borders, Open Doors Advisory Group, July 17, 2007, at http://www.nafsa.org/_/document/_/nafsa_executive_director_2.pdf.

213    "International education is big business for all of the Anglophone countries": Sam Dillon, "U.S. Slips in Attracting the World's Best Students," *New York Times*, December 21, 2004.

213    "The word is out": Ibid.

213    "will do irreparable harm to scientific progress": Burton Ollag, "Wanted: Foreign Students," *Chronicle of Higher Education*, October 8, 2004.

214    "They can't challenge the policy head-on:" Interview with Bill Reinsch, president, National Foreign Trade Council, January 22, 2007.

214    "A lot of the clients we have were educated in the West": Interview with David Marventano, senior vice president of government relations, Fluor Corporation, January 11, 2008.

214    more than $30 billion in lost sales: Santangelo Group, "Do Visa Delays Hurt U.S. Business?" June 2, 2004, at http://nftc.org/default/visasurveyresults%20final.pdf.

214    "the luxury of erring on the side of expeditious processing": "Testimony of Janice Jacobs. Deputy Assistant Secretary of State for Visa Services, Bureau of Consular Affairs, House Committee on Science," March 26, 2003.

## 7. The Triage

215    "a street-smart kid from Staten Island": Interview with Colin Powell, September 21, 2007.

216    "It was so unlike Powell": Interview with Larry Wilkerson, February 15, 2008.

217    "a zero-defects mentality crept into the system": Interview with Colin Powell, September 21, 2007.

218    "zero, my words zero, cooperation with the FBI and the CIA": Interview with Grant Green, September 6, 2007.

219    "I was deeply involved in it": Interview with Colin Powell, September 21, 2007.

219    "As you know, we handle Taiwan delicately": Ibid.

220    "If I could stand up I wouldn't need this chair": Ibid.

220    "failing to defend the dignity of both Taiwan and the first lady": Lin Chieh-Yu, "Apologies, Anger over Wu Search," *Taipei Times*, October 24, 2002.

220    another big diplomatic row for Powell to resolve: Interview with Colin Powell, September 21, 2007.

221    "Why are you treating our students this way?": Interview with Cresencio Arcos, former director, Office of International Affairs, DHS, February 27, 2007.

222    a letter from the president's father: Interview with George Lannon, October 9, 2007.

222    "kind of surprised we pulled in the welcoming mat": Interview with Tom Ridge, October 29, 2007.

222    an academic article: Cresencio Arcos, "Reasonable and Proportional Security Measures on International Academic Exchange Programs," in William A Rugh, ed., *Engaging the Arab and Islamic Worlds Through Public Diplomacy* (Washington, D.C.: Public Diplomacy Council, 2004).

224    the short history of the department: Susan B. Glasser and Michael Grunwald, "Department's Mission Was Undermined from Start," *Washington Post*, December 22, 2005.

224    CBP was given too much money: Interview with James Loy, October 3, 2007.

224    CBP . . . refused to allow funds to be shifted: Justin Rood, Chris Strohm, and Katherine McIntire Peters, "Wasted Year," *GovExec.com*, March 1, 2006, at http://govexec.com/features/0306-01/0306-01s2.htm.

224    a mandate that came directly from the president: Interview with former CBP official, February 29, 2008.

225    "The Borg": Interview with Jim Williams, October 19, 2007.

226    "a guy whose authority we considered illegitimate": Interview with former CBP official, February 29, 2008.

226    reporting to more than eighty different congressional committees: "Homeland Security Oversight," Editorial, *Washington Post*, December 28, 2004.

226    DHS officials testified to Congress . . . 126 times: James Jay Carafano and Paul Rosenzweig, "What the 9/11 Commission's Report Should Contain: Four Recommendations for Making America Safer," Heritage Foundation Backgrounder no. 1778, July 13, 2004.

227    "You had a platform at the White House": Quoted in Glasser and Grunwald, "Department's Mission."

227    "at the strategic level it could not do that": Interview with former Homeland Security Council official, October 3, 2007.

228    "They wanted to be operations guys": Interview with former senior DHS official, September 2007.

228    one memo from Falkenrath: Interview with Stewart Verdery, former assistant secretary for policy and planning, Border and Transportation Security, DHS, Novermber 5, 2007.

228–229    "The White House staff micromanaged the department": Quoted in Glasser and Grunwald, "Department's Mission."

229    "between a dog and fire hydrant": Interview with Bruce Lawlor, March 1, 2007.

229    "fighting Justice": Interview with Asa Hutchinson, former DHS undersecretary for border and transportation security, March 20, 2007.

229    the FBI "wanted to have that power": Ibid.

230    "a body blow": John Gannon, "An Intelligence Approach to Domestic Security," in *The Forgotten Homeland: A Century Foundation Task Force Report* (New York: Century Foundation Press, 2006), 153–154.

230    "He didn't want it in DHS.": Interview with Tom Ridge, October 29, 2007.

230–231    "surely . . . we're not going to waste time on that": Quoted in Glasser and Grunwald, "Department's Mission."

231    "frustration . . . we didn't fight for more turf": Interview with Tom Ridge, October 29, 2007.

231     relations with Andy Card . . . "were never very strong": Ibid.

231     "this guy had it": Interview with former senior White House official, July 10, 2007.

232     "don't think that he exercised internal leadership": Ronald Kessler, "Andy Card: New York Times, Media Have Harmed Security," *NewsMax.com*, August 1, 2006.

232     "We occasionally got rhetorical support": Interview with Tom Ridge, October 29, 2007.

232     "That hurt the department": Interview with John Gannon, former majority staff director, House Select Committee on Homeland Security, April 3, 2008.

232     "almost impossible to walk it back": Interview with former White House official, October 10, 2007.

233     had not paid security benefits that were remotely proportional: Interview with Stewart Verdery, November 5, 2007.

233     "these aren't merely glitches or inconveniences": "Remarks by Secretary Ridge to the Association of American Universities," April 14, 2003, at http://www.dhs.gov/xnews/speeches/speech_0104.shtm.

234     "The FBI always held the trump card": Interview with Stewart Verdery, November 5, 2007.

235     "no way it could pass this test": Ibid.

236     hundreds of these blank passport books: Interview with James Sensenbrenner, former chairman House Judiciary Committee, April 3, 2008.

238     And in 2008, DHS announced that it would implement: DHS Announces Pre-Travel Authorization Program for U.S.-Bound Travelers from Visa Waiver Countries, June 3, 2008, at http://www.dhs.gov/xnews/releases/pr_1212498186436.shtm.

239     "an unconscionable loss": Maura Harty, "U.S. Visa Policy: Securing Borders and Opening Doors," *Washington Quarterly*, Spring 2005.

239     "waiting for just two weeks": U.S. GAO, "Streamlined Visas Mantis Program Has Lowered Burden on Foreign Science Students and Scholars, but Further Refinements Needed," February 2005, at http://www.gao.gov/new.items/d05198.pdf.

239     FBI both brought on additional staff: Ibid.

240     "the State Department fixed the problem": Interview with John Marburger, director, White House Office of Science and Technology Policy, September 14, 2007.

240     more complaints about visa delays: The National Academies, "Visa Questionnaire Statistics," December 31, 2007, at http://www7.nationalacademies.org/visas/visa_statistics.html.

240     the overall number of international students: Institute of International Education, *Open Doors: Report in International Educational Exchange*, 2007, at http://opendoors.iienetwork.org.

241     Eighty of those visa applicants: "Written testimony of Donna Bucella, director of the Terrorist Screening Center, before the House Committee on Government Reform, Subcommittee on National Security, Emerging Threats and International Relations," July 13, 2004, at http://www.fbi.gov/congress/congress04/bucella071304.htm.

241     the lists need to be pruned: Interview with Stewart Baker, assistant secretary for policy, DHS, March 31, 2008.

242     "zealots who wanted everyone on the watch list kept out": Interview with Randy Beardsworth, former assistant secretary of strategic plans, DHS, September 20, 2007.

242     "watch lists are still inadequate": Interview with Stewart Baker, March 31, 2008.

243     some 20,000 people were flagged by the watch list: Electronic Privacy Information Center, Comments on Proposed Rulemaking regarding the Implementation of the Automated Targeting System, September 5, 2007, p. 13, at http://epic.org/privacy/travel/ats/epic_090507.pdf.

243     "incredibly valuable intelligence tool": Interview with Leonard Boyle, director, FBI Terrorist Screening Center, November 14, 2007.

244     Raed al-Banna: Charlotte Buchen, "The Man Turned Away," *Frontline*, October 10, 2006; Scott MacLeod, "A Jihadist's Tale," *Time*, March 28, 2005; and "Remarks of Stewart Baker, Assistant Secretary of Policy, DHS, at the Center for Strategic and International Studies,

Washington D.C.," December 19, 2006, at http://www.csis.org/media/csis/events/061219_baker.pdf. Bonner told PBS that there was no evidence that al-Banna had intended to carry out an attack inside the United States.

244     the same protections do not apply to foreigners: See Privacy International, "Regulatory Challenges for U.S. and EU Airlines and Passengers," Briefing for the European Parliament, at http://www.privacyinternational.org/issues/policylaundering/pireportep.pdf. Stewart Baker, the assistant secretary for policy at DHS, made the same point in an interview with the author, March 31, 2008.

246     "you don't know what's coming into the country": Lamar Smith, "The Illegal Immigration Threat: A Top Homeland Security Priority," *National Review*, April 30, 2003.

247     "increase the wait time by hours": Edward Alden, "Lack of Time and Cash Threaten U.S. Visa Plan," *Financial Times*, April 19–20, 2003.

248     promised to implement the system with a full biometric component: Interview with Dennis Murphy, former DHS spokesman, March 6, 2007.

248     "foolhardy to build a system on anything other": Interview with Tom Ridge, October 29, 2007.

248     "did not prove to be necessary for security": Edward Alden, "Tracking of Visitors to U.S. Failed to Help War on Terror," *Financial Times*, December 2, 2003.

248     "a huge indictment of the FBI": Interview with former senior DHS official, March 2007.

249     "designed to get the message out": Interview with Jim Williams, October 19, 2007.

249     "the first person you see is an FBI agent": Interview with Tom Ridge, October 29, 2007.

250     The White House commissioned several studies: Interview with Brian Peterman, November 27, 2007.

251     "got down to what was doable": Ibid.

251     "shut down the economy": Interview with Jim Williams, October 19, 2007.

253     "it was part of being arrested": Interview with P. T. Wright, former director of mission operation and acting deputy director, US-VISIT, March 13, 2008.

253     "underwhelming": Jim Williams, Foreign Press Center briefing, January 10, 2006.

253     "we tested, tested, and tested": Interview with Jim Williams, October 19, 2007.

253     estimates running into the tens of billions: Robert O'Harrow Jr. and Scott Higham, "U.S. Border Security at a Crossroads," *Washington Post*, May 23, 2005.

## 8. The Fence

255     Opponents of illegal immigration hailed the sweeps: John M. Broder, "Immigration Raids, Far from Border, Draw Criticism," *New York Times*, June 15, 2004.

257     "That was a mistake": Interview with Asa Hutchinson, March 20, 2007.

257     Kobylt quickly had Hutchinson tongue-tied: *The John and Ken Show*, Audio Archives, July 8, 2004.

258     the list of bad things that would be halted: White House Office of Homeland Security, *National Strategy for Homeland Security*, July 2002, p. 22, at http://www.whitehouse.gov/homeland/book.

259     "In Canada we have a great deal of confidence": Interview with Bruce Lawlor, March 1, 2007.

259     they were prepared to enter into comprehensive agreements: See Castañeda, *Ex-Mex*, 95.

260     Ridge said very little about illegal immigration: Philip Shenon, "Ridge Favors a Status Short of Citizenship for Illegal Immigrants," *New York Times*, December 11, 2003.

261     "there was no, zero, zilch interest": Interview with John Maisto, November 19, 2007.

261     There was particular concern: Interview with Brian Peterman, November 27, 2007.

262     At another time, it could have been an inspirational speech: "President Bush Proposes New Temporary Worker Program," The White House, January 7, 2004.

263     Chertoff's record was mostly outside the public eye: Michael Powell and Michelle Garcia, "Amid Praise, Doubts About Nominee's Post-9/11 Role," *Washington Post*, January 31, 2005.

264 "can make smart people look stupid": Matthew Rees, "Who Is Michael Chertoff?" *Weekly Standard*, January 29, 1996.

265 "I was troubled to see": "Nomination of Michael Chertoff, Hearing Before the Committee on Homeland Security and Governmental Affairs of the United States Senate," February 2, 2005, at http://www.access.gpo.gov/congress/senate/pdf/109hrg/20170.pdf; also Eric Lipton, "Nominee Says U.S. Agents Abused Power After 9/11," *New York Times*, February 3, 2005.

265 "the government quite self-consciously avoided the kinds of harsh measures": Quoted in Powell and Garcia, "Amid Praise."

266 The exit portion of the system was even more problematic: The Europeans have different problems with plans to implement a similar, European-wide entry-exit system, in particular the lack of capacity to match entry data with exit data.

267 a major GAO investigation released in December 2006: U.S. GAO, "Border Security: US-VISIT Program Faces Strategic, Operational, and Technological Challenges at Land Ports of Entry," December 2006, at http://www.gao.gov/new.items/d07248.pdf.

268 "you have to make choices that are much harder": Rachel L. Swarns and Eric Lipton, "Administration to Drop Effort to Track If Visitors Leave," *New York Times*, December 15, 2006.

268 "an immigration accounting system": Interview with Stewart Baker, March 31, 2008.

269 "we needed a bad cop": Interview with Asa Hutchinson, March 20, 2007.

269 "President Bush had been forced to make a personal plea": Interview with James Sensenbrenner, April 3, 2008

270 "the next round of terrorists would not get their passports stamped": Ibid.

270–271 "security implications of large foreign-born populations": Mark Krikorian, "Hasta la Vista, Ziglar," *National Review*, August 20, 2002; "Will Curbing Immigration Improve National Security," *Wichita Eagle*, April 23, 2002.

272 "volunteer to help the Border Patrol": "Border Patrol Considering Use of Volunteers, Official Says," *New York Times*, July 21, 2005.

273 "the technology only succeeded": Eric Lipton, "Despite New Efforts Along Arizona Border, 'Serious Problems' Remain," *New York Times*, March 14, 2005.

273 Jackson was particular eager: Interview with former senior DHS official, Februaby 29, 2008.

274 "adding thousands of detention beds": Department of Homeland Security, "Fact Sheet: Secure Border Initiative," November 2, 2005, at http://www.dhs.gov/xnews/releases/press_release_0794.shtm.

274 "When you try to fight economic reality": Edward Alden, "Chertoff Battered but Not Bowed by Year in Office," *Financial Times*, March 13, 2006.

274 did not know of a single case: Geraldo Rivera, *Hispanic: Why Americans Fear Hispanics in the U.S.* (New York: Celebra, 2008), 125.

275 "We have a responsibility to secure our borders." Michael A. Fletcher and Jonathan Weisman, "Bush Signs Bill Authorizing 700-Mile Fence for Border," *Washington Post*, October 27, 2006.

275 He pledged that by the end of 2008: The White House, "Fact Sheet: Improving Border Security and Immigration Within Existing Law," August 10, 2007.

275 "Until Congress chooses to act": Quoted in Rivera, *Hispanic*, 117–118.

276 growing enforcement . . . almost wholly unrelated to terrorism: TRAC, *Immigration Enforcement: The Rhetoric, The Reality*, May 28, 2007, at http://trac.syr.edu/immigration/reports/178.

276 deporting many more illegal immigrants than ever before: Miriam Jordan, "Visa Violators Swept Up in Widening Dragnet," *Wall Street Journal*, April 10, 2008.

276 more than thirty thousand people: Dana Priest and Amy Goldstein, "System of Neglect: As Tighter Immigration Policies Strain Federal Agencies, The Detainees in Their Car Often Pay a Heavy Cost," *Washington Post*, May 11, 2008; Margaret Talbot, "The Lost Children: What

Tougher Detention Policies mean for Illegal Immigrant Families," *The New Yorker*, March 3, 2008.

278    "It's much harder to get into the United States": Interview with former senior DHS official, February 29, 2008.

278    no longer planting crops: See Paul Vitello, "Immigration Issues End a Pennsylvania Growers Season," *New York Times*, April 2, 2008.

278    "a false U.S. focus on security": Interview with John Maisto, November 19, 2007.

278    "el presidente del muro": Casteñeda, *Ex-Mex*, 165.

278    "additive, additive, additive": Interview with Frank Moss, September 19, 2007.

279    still reporting wait times of thirty days or more: U.S. GAO, "Long-term Strategy Needed to Keep Pace with Increasing Demand for Visas," July 2007.

279    "one-third . . . were considering leaving the United States": Vivek Wadhwa et al., "Intellectual Property, the Immigration Backlog, and a Reverse Brain Drain," Kauffman Foundation, August 2007, at http://www.kaufmann.org/pdf/reverse_brain_drain_10187.pdf.

280    "The hit the U.S. has taken in its prestige": Interview with Liam Schwartz, March 15, 2007.

280    "Don't go to the U.S.A.": Matt Rudd, "Travel to America? No thanks," *Sunday Times of London*, January 20, 2008.

280    Overseas travel to the United States was still down: Travel Industry Association, "United States Welcomed Two Million Fewer Overseas Visitors in 2007 Than in 2000," March 10, 2008.

280    "[M]any prospective students": Council of Graduate Schools Research Report, "Findings from the 2008 CGS International Graduate Admissions Survey," April 2008, at http://www.cgsnet.org/portals/0/pdf/r_intlapps08_i.pdf.

281    the problems were serious: "Survey of State Investment Promotion Officials by Council on State Governments," March 2008, provided to author.

281    reduced their willingness to invest in the country: U.S. Department of Commerce, "Visas and Foreign Direct Investment: Supporting U.S. Competitiveness by Facilitating International Travel," November 2007, at http://trade.gov/media/publications/pdf/visas07.pdf.

281    "the perception is very bad": Interview with Jerry Levine, November 13, 2007.

281    companies had largely given up fighting over the issue: Interview with Bill Reinsch, January 22, 2007.

281    increasingly taken to meeting . . . in Europe and Singapore: Jeff Bliss and John Hughes, "World's 'Worst' Visa System Scares Business Away from the U.S.," *Bloomberg News*, December 26, 2006.

282    "look at other options to get the work done": Todd Bishop, "Microsoft Plans to Open Software Center in B.C.," *Seattle Post-Intelligencer*, July 5, 2007.

282    "forced to locate staff in countries that welcomed skilled foreign workers": "Written testimony of William H. Gates, Chairman, Microsoft Corporation, before the Committee on Science and Technology, United States House of Representatives," March 12, 2008, at http://www.microsoft.com/presspass/exec/billg/speeches/2008/congress.mspx.

282    "we'll start moving the infrastructure of R&D offshore": Vindu Goel, "Making Room for Storage," *San Jose Mercury News*, November 25, 2007.

282    "directly against New York's competitive advantage": McKinsey & Company, *Sustaining New York's and the U.S Global Financial Services Leadership*, New York, January 2007.

283    "delays of up to three hours": Canadian Chamber of Commerce, *Finding the Balance: Reducing Border Costs While Strengthening Security*, February 2008, at http://www.chamber.ca/cmslib/general/0802findingthebalance20083393251.pdf.

283    "A safer border is well worth the wait": Julia Preston, "Tighter Border Delays Re-entry By U.S. Citizens," *New York Times*, October, 21, 2007.

283    "you do not have the physical facilities": Interview with Kathleen Walker, March 14, 2008.

283    Chertoff went to Harvard: "Remarks by Homeland Security Secretary, Michael Cher-

off at Harvard University," February 6, 2008, at http://www.dhr.gov/xnews/speeches/sp_1203020606566.shtm.

286     "It's never worked, and we are trying to do it": Interview with former senior DHS official, February 29, 2008.

287     it could not meet its initial goal: Evan Perez and August Cole, "U.S. Curbs Big Plans for Border Tech Fence," *Wall Street Journal*, February 26, 2008; and Spencer Hsu, " 'Virtual Fence' Along Border to Be Delayed," *Washington Post*, February 28, 2008.

287     we will look for people elsewhere who can: Statement of chairman Bennie G. Thompson, "Project 28: Lessons Learned and the Future of SBInet," House Homeland Security Committee, February 27, 2008, at http://homeland.house.gov/sitedocuments/20080227105946-89171.pdf.

## Conclusion

287     "It's embarrassing": Jeanne Meserve and Mike M. Ahlers, "Canadian Firetruck Responding to U.S. Call Held Up at Border." *CNN.com*, November 14, 2007.

290     "In the European Union": Secure Borders and Open Doors Advisory Committee, "Secure Borders and Open Doors: Preserving Our Welcome to the World in an Age of Terrorism," January 2008, 41, at http://www.dhs.gov/xlibrary/assets/hsac_SBODACreport508-compliant_version2.pdf.

292     "September 11 awakened the country": Rachel L. Swarns, "Fearful, Angry or Confused, Muslim Immigrants Register," *New York Times*, April 25, 2003.

294     not a single one was denied on terrorist-related grounds: Secure Borders and Open Doors Advisory Committee, "Secure Borders and Open Doors," 28.

294     Where the program was effective was in immigration enforcement: *9/11 and Terrorist Travel*, 158–59.

294     no terrorists have fallen into that net: "Statement of Robert Mocny, Acting Director, US-VISIT Program Department of Homeland Security, Before the Senate Committee on the Judiciary Subcommittee on Terrorism, Technology and Homeland Security," January 31, 2007, at http://www.dhs.gov/xnews/testimony/testimony_1170348170488.shtm.

294     "the nation's vulnerability to terrorist attack grows": Majority Staff of the Committee on Homeland Security, "America's Unfinished Welcome Mat: US-VISIT a Decade Later," June 2007, at http://homeland.house.gov/sitedocuments/20070628115232-48709.pdf.

295     pressured by the FBI to become informants: "Targets of Suspicion: The Impact of Post-9/11 Policies on Muslims, Arabs and South Asians in the United States," Immigration Policy Center, May 2004, 3; Peter Waldman, "A Muslim's Choice: Turn U.S. Informant or Risk Losing Visa, *Wall Street Journal*, July 11, 2006.

295     "a deterrent effect": *9/11 and Terrorist Travel*, p. 160.

296     "The Mexicans are very aware": Interview with Stewart Baker, March 31, 2008.

296     "dangerous people": "Remarks by Homeland Security Secretary Michael Chertoff at a Press Conference Regarding President Bush's FY 2009 Budget for the Department of Homeland Security," February 4, 2008, at http://www.dhs.gov/xnews/speeches/sp_1202219631845.shtm.

297     the department would need: Ziglar testimony to 9/11 Commission.

297–298    the tough new border measures have done nothing at all to deter illegal migrants: Wayne A. Cornelius et al., *Controlling Unauthorized Immigration from Mexico: The Failure of "Prevention through Deterrence" and the Need for Comprehensive Reform,* Immigration Policy Center, June 10, 2006, at https://www.immigrationpolicy.org/images/File/misc/CCISbriefing061008.pdf.

298     "infinitesimally small": Interview with John Gannon, April 3, 2008.

301     still remains understaffed: U.S. Department of Homeland Security, "Secure Borders and Open Doors."

301     double its 2001 size: U.S. GAO, "Border Security: Despite Progress, Weakness in Traveler Inspections Exist at Our Nation's Ports of Entry," November 2007.

302     The cost of building and maintaining: Tyche Hendricks, "Study Says Fence Cost Could Reach $49 Billion: Lawmakers' Estimate Falls Far Short of Total, Research Service Says," *San Francisco Chronicle*, January 8, 2007.

302     fewer legal ways to bring . . . the people we do want: See Jacob Funk Kirkegaard, "The Accelerating Decline in America's High-Skilled Workforce: Implications for Immigration Policy," Peterson Institute for International Economics, December 2007.

# Index

Abbot, Steve, 121, 126, 141
Abdel-Rahman, Sheikh Omar, 161, 284
Absconder Apprehension Initiative, 99–103
Action Plan for Creating a Secure and Smart Border, 132, 139
Advanced Passenger Information System (APIS), 28–31, 134, 243–44, 298
aerial vehicles, unmanned, 272–73
African embassy bombings, 169
Agriculture Department, 141
Ahern, Jay, 253
AILA. See American Immigration Lawyers Association (AILA)
aircraft industry, 207–8
airlines
  APIS and, 28–29
  information from foreign, 127–28
al-Banna, Raed, 244
Alberts, Bruce, 189
Algeria, 18–20
al-Hazmi, Nawaf, 31, 109
Alien Registration Act of 1940, 63, 91, 108, 110
al-Jubeir, Adel, 113

al-Mihdhar, Khalid, 31
Al Qaeda
  African embassy bombings and, 169
  Ashcroft and, 85
  nuclear weapons and, 120–21
  See also September 11, 2001
al-Shehhi, Marwan, 182, 185–88
al-Shibh, Ramzi, 163–64
Althen, Gary, 195
Ambassador Bridge, 43
American Immigration Lawyers Association (AILA), 94–95, 283
America's Achilles' Heel (Falkenrath), 126
America's Shield Initiative (ASI), 272–73
Ammash, Huda Salih Mahdi, 203
amnesty, 69–70, 74, 78–79, 261–62, 269–70
Amway, 210–11
Anchorage Inn fire, 288–90
Anderson, Ben, 44
Andreas, Peter, 75
Andruch, Dianne, 155, 156, 165, 174
Annan, Kofi, 191

anthrax attacks, 117–18
APIS. *See* Advanced Passenger Information System (APIS)
Arabs
    NSEERS and, 112–13
    registration of, 113–16
    screening of, 11, 299–300
    targeting of, 86, 111
    visa changes for, 91–92
    *See also* Condor program
Arcos, Cresencio "Cris," 221–23, 298
Armitage, Richard, 20, 216
Arnone, John, 44
Arriza, John, 162
artists, visa problems and, 211
Ashcroft, John
    Bush/Fox declaration and, 77–79
    Canada negotiations and, 133, 137
    Condor and, 3
    on habeas corpus considerations, 89
    in Homeland Security negotiations, 142–43
    on post-9/11 intelligence, 80
    pre-9/11 tenure of, 84
    reaction to 9/11 of, 82–84
    as religious man, 85
    visa moratorium proposal and, 104
    visa scandal and, 182–85
    *See also* Justice Department
ASI. *See* America's Shield Initiative (ASI)
Atta, Mohammed, 109, 163, 182, 184–87
Automated Targeting System, 244
automobile trade, 44–45
Ayres, David, 81, 183–84

backlogs
    Condor and, 106, 253
    green cards and, 14, 279
    of INS, 65, 195
    Mantis and, 206–7
    temporary work visas and, 302

    visa scandal and, 185–86
Baker, James, 157
Baker, Stewart, 241, 267–68, 296
Baldridge, Malcolm, 165–66
Baldridge Awards, 165–66
Baloch, Shakir, 93–94
Bangladesh, 113, 221
Barak, Ehud, 192
Barbour, Haley, 53
Barrett, Craig, 191
Basham, Ralph, 283
Beardsworth, Randy, 221, 242, 249
Becraft, Mike, 64–65, 83, 97, 107
Benatta, Benamar, 18–20, 93
Benton, Claudia, 68
Berry, Steven, 159
"best practices" concept, 165–66, 169–71
Bhora, Faiz, 1–4, 106, 303–4
biological weapons, 203
biometrics, 125, 248, 252
Blackmun, Harry, 86
Blue Water Bridge, 14, 283
Boeing, 207–8, 214, 273, 286
Bojinka plot, 16
Bolten, Josh, 76, 183
bombings
    of African embassies, 169
    of World Trade Center (1993), 16, 36, 161, 194
    *See also* September 11, 2001; terrorism
Bonner, Robert
    Border Patrol and, 184
    border security and, 272
    Bush and, 52
    Canada negotiations and, 137
    Customs and Border Protection Agency and, 184, 224–26
    DHS planning and, 141–42
    Hutchinson and, 225
    September 11 and, 25–33
    technology use and, 126–28
    trade security and, 135–36, 238

US-VISIT and, 251, 254
borders
    Canadian, 14, 43–46, 129–33, 283
    consolidation of agencies and, 140–41
    enforcement of, 71–72
    fences and, 274–75, 285, 302
    of future, 137–40, 235
    historical attempts to revamp, 140
    Mexican, 46–48, 269–78
    policy principles and, 138–39
    San Diego and, 72–73
Border Trade Alliance, 246
Boutros-Ghali, Boutros, 191
Boyle, Leonard, 242
Brazil, visa interviews in, 11, 249, 301
Brin, Sergey, 49–50, 190
Broom, Arthur, 198
Brown, Catherine, 175
Brown, Kathleen, 55
Buchanan, Pat, 57
Bureau of Immigration, 63. *See also* Immigration and Naturalization Service (INS)
Bush, George H. W., 158–59, 222
Bush, George P., 58
Bush, George W.
    background of, 55–56
    Fox and, 76–77, 79, 269
    in gubernatorial election, 58
    Hispanic vote and, 57–58
    immigration goals of, 8–9, 51–52, 53, 56–57, 258
    immigration reform speech of 2004, 261–63
    nomination of, 75–76
    trade beliefs of, 51, 57
    visa scandal and, 182
    Wilson and, 55
Bush, Jeb, 56, 58

California, immigration in, 54
Camarena, Enrique, 27

Canada
    border with, 14, 43–46, 129–33, 283, 285, 288–90
    as homeland security testing ground, 129–36
    intelligence sharing with, 133
    as partner, 130
    Smart Border Action Plan and, 132–36
    threats from, 129
    trade with, 42, 132, 134–36
    visa policy and, 133
CAPPS-II, 228, 245
Card, Andrew, 121, 140, 144–45, 175–76, 183, 231–32, 266
cardiothoracic surgery, 1
Carter, Jimmy, 108, 140, 193
Castañeda, Jorge, 77, 278
"catch and release," 67, 274, 297
"Catching the Visa Express" (Mowbray), 172–75
CBP. *See* Customs and Border Protection Agency (CBP)
Cellucci, Paul, 130
Center for Constitutional Rights, 94
Center for Immigration Studies (CIS), 270–71
Central Intelligence Agency (CIA)
    in Condor program, 4
    Ryan and, 150–51
Champeau, Ken, 257
Cheney, Dick, 120–21
Chen Shui-ban, 219–20
Chertoff, Michael, 81, 234, 263–66, 283–86. *See also* Homeland Security
Chidez, Manuel, 73
China
    Boeing and, 207–8
    Moore Nanotechnology and, 209
    students delayed from, 197–99
    visa reciprocity and, 234
    visa wait times and, 11, 301
Chinese Exclusion Act, 60–61

Chirac, Jacques, 191
Chrétien, Jean, 130–31
Chua, Amy, 21
CIA. *See* Central Intelligence Agency
    (CIA)
CIS. *See* Center for Immigration
    Studies (CIS)
Clark, Wesley, 107
Clarke, Richard, 103, 226
CLASS system, 162–63
Clinton, Bill, 50–51, 72, 158–59
Clinton, Hillary Rodham, 265
Cole, David, 92
Commerce Department, 281
Condor program, 3–4, 103–6, 111,
    206, 259, 294, 300
Congress
    Aviation and Transportation Secu-
        rity Act (2001), 127
    creation of DHS and, 144–45
    Enhanced Border Security Act
        (2002), 247
    failure of immigration reform and,
        271, 274–75
    Intelligence Reform and Terrorism
        Prevention Act (2004), 279
    Patriot Act, 89, 131, 247
    pressure over visas by, 165
    university lobby and, 195–96
    visa policy control and, 178
consolidation of border agencies,
    140–41
consular corps, 147–48. *See also* State
    Department
containers, shipping, 134–36
Container Security Initiative, 136
"cops" approach, 89–90
Coulter, Ann, 172
Council of Graduate Schools, 281
Council on State Governments, 281
courts, immigrants in, 83
"coyotes" (immigrant smugglers), 75,
    277
Creel, Santiago, 77

Cressey, Roger, 226
Crocker, Ryan, 158
Cronin, Michael, 64, 183, 184, 186
C-TPAT. *See* Customs-Trade Partner-
    ship Against Terrorism (C-
    TPAT)
Customs and Border Protection
    Agency (CBP), 224–25,
    243, 251, 253, 272–73, 283,
    288–89, 301–2
Customs Service
    APIS and, 28–29
    Container Security Initiative, 136
    creation of, 25
    drug seizures by, 26
    foreign airlines and, 127–28
    INS merger, 224–26
    INS vs., 41–42
    in National Border Administration,
        141
    9/11 hijackers and, 31–32
    Ressam arrest and, 35–36, 129
    technology acquisition by, 126
Customs-Trade Partnership Against
    Terrorism (C-TPAT), 135

Dam, Kenneth, 27
Daou, Imad, 11–13
Dartmouth College, 13
Daschle, Tom, 117
database integration, 240–41
Davidow, Jeffrey, 78, 79
*Day of Empire* (Chua), 21
DEA. *See* Drug Enforcement Admin-
    istration (DEA)
Dean, Diana, 36, 39
defense, layered, 39
de la Madrid, Miguel, 192
Denisov, Dmitri, 199–200
departure, voluntary, 67
detentions
    as blunt instrument, 90
    Justice Dept. investigation of, 18
    numbers of, 98

push for, 84–87
randomness of, 93–95
Ziglar and, 96–98
Development, Relief and Education
    for Alien Minors (DREAM)
    Act, 261
DHS. *See* Homeland Security
diplomacy
    foreign students and, 191–92
    travel as, 22, 24
    *See also* State Department
Dobbs, Lou, 257
Dodd, Chris, 97
Domestic Policy Council, 78–79, 261
Dorgan, Byron, 46
drug couriers, 29–30
Drug Enforcement Administration
    (DEA), 26, 28
drug seizures, 26
Dubai, visas and, 11
due process, 82–83

Eastland, James O., 85
economy. *See* trade
Eilert, Ed, 107
Einstein, Albert, 189
Eisenhower, Dwight, 123
Elder, Mark, 211
elections
    Hispanic vote in, 57–58
    of 1992, 158–59
Elnaiem, Dia, 5–8, 14
embassy bombings, African, 169
Enhanced Border Security Act
    (2002), 247
Engler, John, 55
entertainment, 211
Europe, immigration from, 61
European Union, 290–91
ExxonMobil, 281

Fagan, Drew, 131
FAIR. *See* Federation for American
    Immigration Reform (FAIR)

Falkenrath, Richard, 126, 137, 139,
    140, 143, 145, 203, 226, 228
Fayad, Tarek Mohamed, 94–95
Federal Bureau of Investigation (FBI)
    Absconder Apprehension Initiative
        and, 99–103
    battles with DHS, 229–331,
        249–50
    broadening of powers, 81–87
    in Condor program, 4, 103–6,
        294, 300
    investigation of 9/11, 80–81, 92–98
    Joint Terrorism Task Forces,
        229–30
    security review delays and, 95–96,
        106, 202
    suspect identification, 81–82
    terrorist watch lists and, 241–42
Federation for American Immigration
    Reform (FAIR), 54, 246, 270,
    276–77
Feinstein, Dianne, 7–8, 148–52, 164,
    196
fence, border, 271, 274–75, 285
Fermi, Enrico, 49, 189
Fifth Amendment, 82–83
*Financial Times*, 247
fingerprinting schemes, 248–54,
    267–68, 299
Fischel, Steve, 104
Flake, Jeff, 73, 74
Fleischer, Ari, 143
Fleiss, Heidi, 28
Florida, Richard, 20, 191
Fluor Corporation, 214
Flynn, Stephen, 37–38, 39
foreign direct investment, 15, 281
Foreign Service officers, 148, 154–55
foreign talent, 49–50, 188–207,
    213–14, 281–82
Fourth Amendment, 81–82
Fowler, Wyche, 167–68
Fox, Vicente, 47, 76–77, 78–79, 192,
    269

Furey, Thomas, 169–71

Galleani, Luigi, 61
Gallo, Columba Garnica, 58
Galvan, Maria, 56
Gannon, John, 230, 232, 298, 300
Garcia, Maria Guadelupe, 12–13
Gates, Bill, 49, 191, 282
Gates, Robert, 192
Gingrich, Newt, 34
globalization, 35, 48–52
*Globe and Mail* (Toronto), 131
Goebel, Brian, 43
Goldberg, Michelle, 100
Gonzales, Alberto, 56
Gore, Al, 144, 166
Gouttierre, Thomas, 213
Gramm, Phil, 79
Gramm-Rudman-Hollings legisla-
    tion, 33
Green, Grant, 165, 178, 179, 218
green cards, 14, 279
Grove, Andy, 49, 190
gubernatorial election, Bush and, 58

habeas corpus, 81–82, 89, 94
Haider, Ejaz, 111–12
Hallé (U.K. orchestra), 211
Hanjour, Hani, 109, 187, 194
Hart, Gary, 33, 144
Hart-Rudman Commission, 25,
    33–40, 121–22, 284
Harty, Maura, 155, 180, 215–19,
    221, 238–39
Hazelton, Pennsylvania, 277
Heavey, George, 128
hijackers, 31–32, 104, 108–9,
    148–52, 182, 185–88
Hispanic vote, 57–58
Holman, Mark, 126
Homeland Security
    America's Shield Initiative (ASI),
        272–73
    authority ambiguity in, 225–26
    beginning of, 125–26
    Border Patrol in, 255–56, 275,
        295, 301
    Chertoff reforms, 265–69
    Citizenship and Immigration Ser-
        vices in, 301
    consolidation of border agencies
        and, 139–44
    consular services and, 175–77
    creation of DHS, 144–46, 184
    Customs and Border Protection
        Agency (CBP), 224–25,
        243, 251, 253, 272–73, 283,
        288–89, 301–2
    Customs Service in, 126–28
    DHS 2.0, 265–69
    dilemma of, 123–24
    Immigration and Customs En-
        forcement in, 224, 231, 256
    Operation Liberty Shield,
        227–28
    as overkill, 23, 278
    planning of, 141–45
    reporting structure of, 226
    Ridge's vision of, 139–41
    rivalries and, 137, 223–26
    Secure Border Initiative (SBI),
        273–74
    shifting focus of, 275–77
    "technocrats" and, 90–91, 124–25,
        134
    Transportation Security Adminis-
        tration (TSA), 219, 267
    Treasury Department and, 143
    understaffing at, 126
    US-VISIT program, 248–54,
        266–69, 273
    visa policy control and, 175–78
    White House and, 226–29
    White House Office of, 125–26,
        137, 204, 226
Hoover, Herbert, 140

Hornbarger, Chris, 137, 139–40, 143, 146
Hotchner, John, 158
House Homeland Security Committee, 232, 287, 294
House Immigration Caucus, 270
*Houston Chronicle*, 101
Hughes, Lisa Bobbie Schreiber, 154
human capital, 21
Hussein, Zahid, 18
Hutchinson, Asa, 224–25, 229–30, 233, 247–49, 251–53, 256–58, 269

IBIS. *See* Interagency Border Inspection System (IBIS)
IDENT system, 67–68, 251
imagination, failure of, 164
immigration
    absconders and, 98–99
    amnesty and, 69–70, 79, 269
    Bush's goals surrounding, 8–9, 51–52, 53, 56–57, 261–63
    California and, 54
    Chinese, 60–61
    "cops" approach to, 89–90
    dangers of, 74–75
    in early twentieth century, 61
    entrepreneurship and, 49–50, 189–91
    failure of immigration reform, 271, 274–75
    globalization and, 48–52
    great wave of, 20
    history of, 59–64
    illegal, 69–73, 246, 252, 255–58, 260–62
    innovation and, 21
    Mexican, 73–75, 269
    mythologization of, 59
    1920 immigration law and, 62
    origin quotas in, 20, 62
    Ridge's stance on, 120, 260–61
    of talent, 49–50, 188–93
    "technocratic" approach to, 90–91
    terrorism vs., 275–77, 292–98
    *See also* visas
Immigration Act of 1891, 63
Immigration and Customs Enforcement (ICE), 224, 231, 256
Immigration and Nationality Act of 1952, 63, 89–90
Immigration and Naturalization Service (INS)
    Absconder Apprehension Initiative and, 99–103
    Benton murder scandal and, 68
    birth of, 63
    broadening of powers, 81–87
    Customs merger, 224–26
    Customs vs., 41–42
    dysfunction of, 64–65
    enforcement side, 66
    in Homeland Security planning, 142–43
    in National Border Administration, 141
    in 9/11 investigation, 92–98
    Operation Gatekeeper, 72–73, 75
    pressures on, 63–64
    service side of, 65–66
    visa scandal and, 182–88
Immigration Reform and Control Act (IRCA), 69
India, 11, 206–12, 279–81, 301
Indonesia, NSEERS and, 21, 113
Inhofe, James, 126–27
Intel, 49, 190–91
I-94 form, 66
INS. *See* Immigration and Naturalization Service (INS)
intelligence
    difficulties in, 80–81
    emasculation of DHS, 230
    Hart-Rudman Commission on, 39–40

intelligence (*cont.*)
    integration, 240–41
    sharing with Canada, 133
Interagency Border Inspection System
    (IBIS), 29, 32, 47
International Consumer Electronics
    Show, 210–11
internment, of Japanese-Americans,
    20
interviews, visa, 10–11, 171, 202, 301
investment, decline in, 15, 281
Iranian hostage crisis, 193–94
IRCA. *See* Immigration Reform and
    Control Act (IRCA)
Ismoil, Eyad, 194
Issa, Darell, 256

Jackson, Michael, 142, 266–68, 273
Jackson, Sheila, 101
Jacobs, Janice, 214
Japanese-Americans, in World War
    II, 20
Jarrah, Ziad, 108–9, 110, 187, 293
Jeddah, 168–69
Jiang, Nan, 199
*John and Ken Show*, 257
Joint Terrorism Task Forces, 229–30
Jordan, Robert, 179
Justice Department
    "cops approach" in, 89–90
    detention push by, 82–84
    investigation of detentions (Fine
        report), 18, 92–93, 96, 293
    special immigration courts, 83
    "spit on sidewalk" strategy, 81, 89
    turf war with State Department,
        104–6
    *See also* Ashcroft, John; Federal
        Bureau of Investigation (FBI);
        Immigration and Naturaliza-
        tion Service (INS)

Kefauver, Barry, 157, 159
Kelly, Ray, 30

Kelly, Stephen, 130, 132–33
Kennedy, Ted, 97, 101, 242, 269
Kerik, Bernard, 263
Kesbeh family, 99–102
Khosla, Vinod, 50
Kinney, Pancho, 137–38
Knisely, Bobbi, 26
Kobach, Kris, 106–10, 276–77, 292
Kobylt, John, 257
Korosec, Stan, 14
Krikorian, Mark, 184, 270–71
Kuwait, Iraqi invasion of, 157–58

Lagnos, Mike, 43
Laks, Hillel, 1–2
Lannon, George, 78, 104, 151, 168,
    174–75, 177, 179–81
Lanzaro, Gregory, 6
Lawlor, Bruce, 9, 16, 145, 203,
    228–29, 247, 259
layered defense, 39
Leahy, Pat, 97, 117
Leibovitz, Annie, 2
leishmaniasis, 6
Levine, Jerry, 281
Libby, Lewis "Scooter," 120–21
Lieberman, Joe, 144, 265
Lincoln, Abraham, 63
Lindsey, Larry, 45
Locke, Gary, 47
Lockheed Martin, 214, 266
Los Angeles, NSEERS registration in,
    114–15
Los Angeles Airport attack, failed,
    35–36
Loy, James, 10, 122–25, 136, 141,
    223, 230–31, 298
Lucent (telecommunications com-
    pany), 208

Macapagal-Arroyo, Gloria, 191
Maisto, John, 77–78, 261, 278
Malkin, Michelle, 101–2
Manley, John, 131–32, 133–34

Mantis program, 204–7, 233, 239–40, 259

maquiladoras, 46

Marburger, John, 240

Martin, Paul, 132

Marventano, David, 214

Matalin, Mary, 121

Mayo Clinic, 211

McCain, John, 76, 269, 275

McCain-Kennedy bill, 270–71

Metropolitan Detention Center, 19, 93–94

Mexico
    border with, 46–48, 259–87
    immigration and, 73–75
    intelligence sharing with U.S., 259
    migration accord negotiations, 76–79, 261, 269
    threats from, 260, 295–96

Microsoft, 49, 191, 282

Migration Policy Institute, 95

Mineta, Norman, 142, 222

mistreatment, at Metropolitan Detention Center, 19, 93–94

Mitchell, John, 86

Mohammed, Khalid Shaikh, 16

Moore Nanotechnology, 209

moratorium, proposed on visas, 104

Moss, Frank, 153, 278

Motorola, 135, 208–9

Moussaoui, Zacarias, 129, 235–36

Mowbray, Joel, 172–76, 179–80

Mueller, Robert, 81, 99, 231, 249

Mullins, Janet, 159

Mulroney, Brian, 130

Murphy, Dennis, 25, 26–27, 249

Muslims
    registration of, 113–16
    screening of, 11, 299–300
    targeting of, 111
    visa changes for, 91–92
    *See also* Condor program; National Security Entry-Exit Registration System (NSEERS)

myelofibrosis, 181

NAILS. *See* National Automated Immigration Lookout System (NAILS)

Nasir (Pakistani student), 17

National Automated Immigration Lookout System (NAILS), 29

National Border Administration, 140–41

National Commission on Terrorist Attacks in the United States (9/11 Commission)
    Customs Service and, 28
    hijackers' visas and, 167–71
    immigration laws and, 295
    intelligence sharing and, 240
    NSEERS and, 293–94
    Ryan testimony, 160
    State Department and, 163
    WHTI and, 279

National Counterterrorism Center, 241

National Crime Information Center (NCIC), 99, 110

National Foreign Trade Council, 213–14, 281

national ID card, 71

nationality requirements, for registration, 115

national origin quotas, 20, 62

National Partnership for Reinventing Government, 166

*National Review*, 172–75, 246

National Security Entry-Exit Registration System (NSEERS), 17, 110, 112–16, 221–23, 233, 248, 253–54, 259, 294–95, 300

National Strategy for Homeland Security (2002), 258

NCIC. *See* National Crime Information Center (NCIC)

Neely, Susan, 227

Netanyahu, Benjamin, 192
Neureiter, Norman, 23
*New York Times*, 55, 137, 143, 158,
    213, 268, 272
NEXUS program, 134, 302
1920 immigration law, 62
Nobel Prize winners, 189
"no fly" list, 237–42
North American Free Trade Agree-
    ment (NAFTA), 37, 44, 46,
    50–51, 76–77
"North American loophole," 279
Northrop Grumman, 18
Nouri, Faith, 115
NSEERS. *See* National Security
    Entry-Exit Registration System
    (NSEERS)
nuclear weapons
    Al Qaeda and, 120–21
    in risk management approach, 124

O'Brien, David, 130
Omidyar, Pierre, 50, 190
O'Neill, Paul, 132, 136, 142–44
Operation Blockade, 71–72
Operation Game Day, 103
Operation Gatekeeper, 72–73, 75
Operation Hold the Line, 71–72
Operation Liberty Shield, 227–28
Operation Tarmac, 103
outsourcing, 210, 266
O visa, 3

Pakistan, 1–5, 17, 21–22, 106,
    111–16, 197–99, 239
Palmer, A. Mitchell, 61–62
passenger data, 29–31
Passenger Name Records (PNR), 30,
    237–38
Passport Control Act of 1918, 160
"Passportgate," 158–59
Patriot Act
    biometrics in, 247
    Canadian border in, 131

habeas corpus in, 89
Peace Bridge, 43
PENTTBOM, 92–93
Peres, Shimon, 192
Peterman, Brian, 90–91, 111, 202, 251
Pickard, Thomas, 84–85
PNR. *See* Passenger Name Records
    (PNR)
police, hijacker encounters with,
    108–9
Polynesian microstates, 133
posthumous visas, 182–85
Powell, Colin
    DHS planning and, 143, 175
    foreign students, views on, 192
    Harty and, 215–17
    in Mexican migration talks, 77
    Ridge and, 176–77
    Ryan and, 175–80
    as White House fellowship recipi-
        ent, 107
privacy rules, 40, 244–45
Prodi, Romano, 191
productivity, increase in, 166
Proposition 13, 54
Proposition 187, 54–55, 256
public diplomacy, 22

Qidwai, Uvais, 197–98
quotas, national origin, 20, 62
Qutb, Sayyid, 192

Reagan, Ronald, 57–58, 69–71
refugees, 276
registration
    of Arabs and Muslims, 113–16
    in Los Angeles, 114–15
Reid, Richard, 236–37
Reinsch, Bill, 24, 213–14, 281
Reno, Janet, 72
Republican Party
    courting of Hispanics by, 57–58, 78
    rise of, 53
Reséndiz, Angel Maturino, 68

Ressam, Ahmed, 35–36, 129, 284
Reyes, Silvestre, 71
Rice, Donna, 33
Richards, Ann, 53–58
Ridge, Tom
    appointment to White House of,
        121
    background of, 118–20
    biometrics and, 125, 247–48
    border agencies and, 139–44
    Bush and, 122
    Chertoff vs., 264, 274
    creation of DHS and, 144–46,
        225–27
    immigration views of, 120, 260–61
    inter-agency battles, 228–32, 249
    leadership style of, 119, 231
    Loy and, 122–25
    Smart Border Declaration and,
        133–34
    Powell and, 176–77, 220
    "technocratic" beliefs of, 122, 125
    US-VISIT and, 245–49
    Vietnam and, 119
    visa reform proposal of, 233–35
    White House and, 231–32
    See also Homeland Security
Rise of the Creative Class, The (Flori-
    da), 20, 191
risk
    conceptions of, 9–10
    management approach, 10,
        123–25
Riyadh embassy, 169–71
Rosen, Jeffrey, 85
Rouses Point fire, 286–90
Rove, Karl, 57–58
Rudman, Warren, 33, 144
Rumsfeld, Donald, 143, 192
Ryan, Mary
    award for, 179–80
    background of, 152
    career of, 156
    CIA and, 151

    Clinton passport scandal and, 159
    consular corps and, 147–48
    culture change and, 155
    death of, 180–81
    dedication of, 155–56
    Feinstein questions, 148–52
    firing of, 178–80
    later years, 180–81
    National Review article and, 174
    1993 WTC bombing and, 161–62
    Powell and, 153–54, 175–80
    reactions to affair, 179–80
    in State Department, 153
    Tamposi and, 156–58
    Viper program and, 162–63

Safdar, Zaif, 115–16
Salinas de Gortari, Carlos, 192
San Diego border, 46, 47, 72–73
Sanford, Mark, 15
Saud al-Faisal, Prince, 192
Saudi Airlines, 16, 128
Saudi Arabia, 22, 167–71, 99, 133,
    167–79, 208
SBI. See Secure Border Initiative
    (SBI)
Schwartz, Liam, 280
screening, of Muslims, 11, 299–300.
    See also Condor program;
    National Security Entry-Exit
    Registration System (NSEERS)
secondary passenger screening, 11
Secure Border Initiative (SBI),
    273–74, 286
Sensenbrenner, James, 101, 176,
    269–70
September 11, 2001
    border shutdown following, 41–48
    detentions following, 18, 84–87,
        90, 93–98
    disagreements on implications of,
        87–91
    FBI and INS changes after, 81–87
    FBI investigation of, 80–81

September 11, 2001 (*cont.*)
    hijackers, 31–32, 104, 108–9,
        148–52, 182, 185–88
    United Flight 93, 109, 121
SEVIS. *See* Student and Exchange
    Visitor System (SEVIS)
shipping, 39, 134–36
SIOC. *See* Strategic Information
    Operations Center (SIOC)
Smart Border Action Plan, 132–36,
    139
Smith, Lamar, 246
Smith Act, 63, 91, 107, 110
smugglers, immigrant, 75, 277
Social Security cards, 70
Soffer, Isabel, 211
Solomon, Gerald, 158
South Carolina, 15
"spit on sidewalk" strategy, 81, 89
Stallone, Sylvester, 1
State Department
    as ahead of its time, 162
    antipathy toward, 172–73, 176
    "best practices" concept and,
        165–66, 169–71
    CLASS system and, 162–63
    Clinton passport scandal and,
        158–59
    culture change, 155–56
    disrespect within, 154–55
    efforts to reduce visa wait times,
        238–39, 301
    *National Review* article, 172–75
    NSEERS and, 111, 113
    9/11 Commission and, 163
    priorities of, 164–65
    Ryan in, 153
    Saudi Arabia and, 167–71
    turf war with Homeland Security,
        175–78
    turf war with Justice Department,
        104–6
    Visa Express program, 171–75,
        179

    *See also* visas
Stevens, Cat, 242
Strategic Information Operations
    Center (SIOC), 81
Student and Exchange Visitor System
    (SEVIS), 196, 200–202, 223,
    244, 284
students, foreign, 15, 188–93,
    211–13
student visas, 185–90, 193–207, 240,
    284
Sudan, 5–6, 161
*Sunday Times* (London), 280
Sununu, John, 156
Super Bowl (2003), 103
surgery, cardiothoracic, 1
Surret, Roy, 31
swallowers (drug couriers), 29–30
Syed, Qaiser, 17

Talbott, Strobe, 112
talent, foreign, 21, 49–50, 188–207,
    213–14, 239
Tamposi, Elizabeth, 156–59
Tamposi, Sam, 157
Tancredo, Tom, 270
"technocrat" approach, 90–91,
    124–25, 134
Teich, Albert, 213
telecommunications industry, 208–9
Teller, Edward, 49, 189
Temecula border sweeps, 255–56
temporary worker program, 56, 78,
    262
Tenet, George, 151
terrorism
    Ashcroft as uninterested in, 84–85
    characterization of threat, 8–9
    disagreements on implications of,
        87–91
    early, 61–62
    Homeland Security focus off,
        275–77
    risk-based assessment and, 9–10

risk management approach, 10,
123–25
suspects, 81–82
as unique form of warfare, 122–23
*See also* bombings; September 11,
2001
Terrorist Screening Center, 23, 241–43
Terrorist Threat Integration Center,
230, 241
Thompson, Larry, 81, 96, 99, 142
Tichenor, Daniel, 59
Tijuana, 46, 72–73
TIPOFF watch list, 162–64, 169,
171, 243, 251
tourist visas, 4
trade
in automobiles, 44–45
Bush and, 51–52, 57
Clinton and, 50–51
globalization and, 48–52
missions of Ridge, 119–20
U.S.-Canada, 42, 132, 134–36
Transactional Records Access Clearinghouse, 276
travel
as diplomacy, 22, 24
drop in, 15, 48, 280
by Saudis, 168–69
Treasury Department, 143–44
Trombley, Chris, 289
trucks, at Canadian border, 134–36
tuberculosis, 289

UCLA Medical Center, 1–3
United Flight 93, 121
universities
foreign competition and, 212–13
foreign students and, 188–93, 280
opposition to SEVIS of, 194–97
visa delays and, 197–200, 211–12,
240
unmanned aerial vehicles, 273
Uruguay Round, 50–51
U.S.-Canada Auto Pact, 44

U.S.-Canada Free Trade Agreement,
42, 44
U.S.-China Business Council, 209
USA Patriot Act. *See* Patriot Act
US-VISIT program, 248–54, 259,
266–69, 273, 283–84, 294,
299–300

Varrone, John, 31
Veneman, Ann, 142
Verdery, Stewart, 225, 228, 233–34,
239
Verga, Peter, 143
Vietnam, 119
Vinnikova, Valeria, 13
Viper program, 162–63
virtual fences, 273, 287
Visa Express, 171–75, 179
visas
as advance screening, 37
application fees, 279
for Arabs/Muslims, 91–92
business and, 207–11
Canadian issued, 133
Condor and, 3–4, 103–6, 259,
294, 300
Congressional pressure and, 165
consular corps and, 147–48
countries for special review, 105–6
cursory screening for, 4–5
defense of system by Ryan, 149–52
drop in issuances of, 15
in European Union, 290–91
foreign investment and, 15, 281
hijackers and, 104, 148–52,
182–88
history of, 159–60
H1-B, 51, 282, 302
increased demand for, 160
as insufficient, 37–38
interviews for, 10–11, 171, 202,
301
Mantis program, 204–7, 239–40,
259

visas (*cont.*)
    moratorium considered on, 104
    1993 WTC bombing and, 161
    O visas, 3
    policy responsibility, 103–4
    reform and, 104–6
    Riyadh embassy and, 169–71
    Saudi Arabia and, 22, 167–71
    for Sheikh Rahman, 161
    student, 185–90, 193–207,
        211–13
    tourist, 4
    understaffing and, 148, 160
    Viper program, 162–63
    wait times and, 11, 279
    weapons of mass destruction and,
        203–7
    *See also* immigration; State Depart-
        ment
Visa Waiver Program, 129, 149,
    236–38
voluntary departure, 67

Walker, Kathleen, 283
*Wall Street Journal*, 179
Wang, David, 207
Wang, Zhong Min, 199
Wanted Persons list, 98–99
war on drugs, 28
war on terror
    as lacking nuance, 8–9
    strategic disagreements on, 87–91
*Washington Post*, 112, 158, 179, 223,
    226, 228, 230, 264
*Washington Times*, 179
watch list integration, 240–41
Watkins, Bill, 282
weapons of mass destruction
    Al Qaeda interest in, 120–21
    Mantis program and, 206–7
    student status and, 203–7

    *See also* terrorism
*Weekly Standard*, 265
Weldon, Dave, 176, 178
Western Hemisphere Travel Initiative
    (WHTI), 279, 283
Wiens, Hansi, 13
Wilkerson, Larry, 148, 215–20
Williams, Jim, 66, 249, 251, 253,
    266, 268–69
Williams, Johnny, 75
Wilson, Pete, 53–55, 69, 72
Winwood, Chuck, 30, 31, 41, 42,
    45
Wolfowitz, Paul, 142
World Music Institute, 211
World Trade Center bombing (1993),
    16, 36, 161, 194
World War I, 20, 61, 160
Wright, P. T., 253
Wu Shuchen, 219–20

Yamshchikov, Vladimir, 198
Yang, Jerry, 190
Young, Brigham, 73
Young, Johnny, 153–56, 180–81
Yousef, Ramzi, 16

Zhang, Jane, 198
Ziglar, Jim
    Absconder Apprehension Initiative
        and, 98–99, 101
    background of, 41, 85–86
    Canada negotiations and, 137
    detentions and, 96–99
    in Homeland Security planning,
        142–43
    NSEERS and, 114
    resignation of, 183–84
    September 11 and, 41, 81–87
    study of INS staffing needs, 297
    visa scandal and, 182–85